The Thatcherite Offensive

Historical Materialism Book Series

The Historical Materialism Book Series is a major publishing initiative of the radical left. The capitalist crisis of the twenty-first century has been met by a resurgence of interest in critical Marxist theory. At the same time, the publishing institutions committed to Marxism have contracted markedly since the high point of the 1970s. The Historical Materialism Book Series is dedicated to addressing this situation by making available important works of Marxist theory. The aim of the series is to publish important theoretical contributions as the basis for vigorous intellectual debate and exchange on the left.

The peer-reviewed series publishes original monographs, translated texts, and reprints of classics across the bounds of academic disciplinary agendas and across the divisions of the left. The series is particularly concerned to encourage the internationalization of Marxist debate and aims to translate significant studies from beyond the English-speaking world.

For a full list of titles in the Historical Materialism Book Series available in paperback from Haymarket Books, visit:
www.haymarketbooks.org/category/hm-series

The Thatcherite Offensive

A Neo-Poulantzasian Analysis

Alexander Gallas

Haymarket Books
Chicago, IL

First published in 2015 by Brill Academic Publishers, The Netherlands
© 2016 Koninklijke Brill NV, Leiden, The Netherlands

Published in paperback in 2016 by
Haymarket Books
P.O. Box 180165
Chicago, IL 60618
773-583-7884
www.haymarketbooks.org

ISBN: 978-1-60846-697-9

Trade distribution:
In the US, Consortium Book Sales, www.cbsd.com
In Canada, Publishers Group Canada, www.pgcbooks.ca
In the UK, Turnaround Publisher Services, www.turnaround-uk.com
In all other countries, Publishers Group Worldwide, www.pgw.com

Cover design by Jamie Kerry of Belle Étoile Studios and Ragina Johnson.

This book was published with the generous support of Lannan Foundation and the Wallace Action Fund.

Printed in Canada by union labor.

10 9 8 7 6 5 4 3 2 1

Library of Congress Cataloging-in-Publication data is available.

In Erinnerung an Olivia

Contents

Preface and Acknowledgements   IX
List of Acronyms   XI
List of Tables and Figures   XIII

Introduction   1

PART 1
Thatcherism and the Neo-Poulantzasian Approach

1   The Hall-Jessop Debate   11

2   Neo-Poulantzasian Political Analysis   26

PART 2
Class and Politics in Britain, 1977–99

3   Method of Presentation   73

4   Pre-History: Britain in Crisis (–1977)   75

5   Emergence: A New Agenda for the Conservative Party (1977–9)   96
    Case Study: Preparing for Government – Conservative Policy Papers from 1977   99

6   Material Gains: Conducting Class Politics by Stealth (1979–84)   124

7   Instability and Confrontation (1984–8)   164
    Case Study: Attacking the Union Movement – The Miners' Strike   166
    Case Study: Dividing the Nation – The 'Big Bang' and the Liberalisation of Financial Markets   200

8   Stabilisation: Entrenching the Advance (1988–92)   235

9   Erosion: Losing Control (1992–9)   262

PART 3
The Aftermath

10   The Consequences of Thatcherism   275

11   New Labour and the Thatcherite Legacy   280

   Conclusion   289

   References   291
   Index   310

Preface and Acknowledgements

I have a somewhat ambiguous relationship to the object of my studies. As someone born in the mid-1970s, my memories of 1980s politics are vague; as a Continental European, my political socialisation was largely shaped by events that were only indirectly related to developments in Britain. Consequently, my knowledge of the Thatcher era is mainly second hand. But I believe that this does not necessarily weaken my analysis. As anthropologists know, observers unfamiliar with a social setting operate at a critical distance to it almost by default; they tend to see connections that 'insiders' overlook because these seem all too commonplace. Correspondingly, I hope my account of Thatcherism profits at least in some ways from my initial ignorance of many aspects of it. I can certainly confirm that studying the socio-economic physiognomy of Britain has fundamentally shifted my perspective on my former country of residence. Initial astonishment at some aspects of British social and political life has turned into a deeper understanding of why people do things differently from how I know it.

If working on my book was a journey into the heart of Britain, I travelled mostly by reading. Consequently, the first part critically assesses some of the key analyses of the Thatcher era and determines the entry point of my analysis. My area of focus is the debate between Stuart Hall, Bob Jessop and their respective associates on the nature of Thatcherism. I develop a conceptual framework and discuss my method of analysis, drawing upon both the contributions to the debate and the work of the Greek state theorist Nicos Poulantzas. In the next part, I apply my concepts to the politics of Thatcherism. My approach is process-oriented insofar as I describe my object as an ensemble of articulated developments in historical time. The final part is somewhat different in this respect because it is centred on outcomes. I summarise my findings, reflect on their political implications, discuss their limitations, and sketch a future research agenda.

The fact that I can contemplate future projects means that I have reached the end of an at times arduous road. It started with the idea of doing a PhD in sociology at Lancaster University; it ended, a decade later, with submitting this book manuscript, which is based on my PhD thesis. Looking back at my journey, the words of a well-known musician are crossing my mind. 'Without people, you're nothing', the late John Graham Mellor once remarked. And without people, I would not have been able to complete my thesis nor to turn it into a published book. There are a number of people whom I would like to thank sincerely for their support: Tim Hunt, Tom Wise and Luke Yates for seriously rocking out with me and making me feel at home in Manchester; Lars Bretthauer, Norman Fairclough, Steve Fleetwood, John Kannankulam, Julian Müller, Jörg Nowak and Andrew Sayer, all of whom read draft chapters and made valuable comments; Ian Bruff, who gave competent advice concerning the literature; Moritz Ege and my wife Verena Gallas, who proofread the draft manuscript; Norma Tiedemann, who supported me when I put together the bibliography; Myfanwy Williams, who was always prepared to help when I was struggling with the vagaries of the English language; Peter Thomas and Danny Hayward, my patient and supportive editors at the Historical Materialism Book Series; Simon Mussell, who copy-edited the manuscript with great care and skill; my anonymous referees, whose comments were constructive and valuable; my father, Andreas Gallas, who helped me out on several occasions when my finances were at a low ebb; my sister, Elisabeth Gallas, and my brother, Maximilian Gallas, on whom I was able to rely when my family hit hard times; Stefan Krupp, for being a true friend; and, last but not least, my PhD supervisor Bob Jessop, who invested a lot of time and energy in fostering my growth as a scholar and guided me on the rocky path to submission.

It goes without saying that I would have never succeeded in finishing this project without the love, support and patience of my wife Verena and our two sons, Milo and Ben. Verena deserves special credit for acting as the breadwinner of the family when I was writing up my PhD. I am saddened by the fact that my mother, Olivia Gallas, did not live to see the publication of my book. It was she who taught me that there is such a thing as society, and that solidarity beats egotism and greed. I dedicate this book to her.

Alexander Gallas
Berlin, March 2014

List of Acronyms

ACAS	Advisory Conciliation and Arbitration Service
ACPO	Association of Chief Police Officers
APEX	Association of Professional, Executive, Clerical, and Computer Staffs
ASLEF	Associated Society of Locomotive Engineers and Firemen
BNOC	British National Oil Company
BSC	British Steel Corporation
BR	British Rail
BT	British Telecom
CBI	Confederation of British Industry
CMP	Capitalist mode of production
CPS	Centre for Policy Studies
DM	Deutsche Mark
DTI	Department of Trade and Industry
EC	European Community
ECU	European Currency Unit
EEC	European Economic Community
EETPU	Electronic, Electrical, Telecommunications and Plumbing Union
ERM	European Exchange Rate Mechanism
GLC	Greater London Council
IMF	International Monetary Fund
ISTC	Iron and Steel Trades Confederation
LSE	London Stock Exchange
MTFS	Medium-Term Financial Strategy
NACODS	National Association of Colliery Overmen, Deputies and Shotfirers
NAFF	National Association for Freedom
NASDAQ	National Association of Securities Dealers Automated Quotations
NCB	National Coal Board
NGA	National Graphical Association
NHS	National Health Service
NIRC	National Industrial Relations Court
NRC	National Reporting Centre
NUM	National Union of Mineworkers
NUPE	National Union Public Employees
NUS	National Union of Seamen
NYSE	New York Stock Exchange
OFT	Office of Fair Trading
OPEC	Organization of Petrol Exporting Countries

PFI	Private Finance Initiative
PSBR	Public Sector Borrowing Requirement
RPI	Retail Price Index
SDP	Social Democratic Party
SIB	Securities and Investment Board
SOGAT	Society of Graphical and Allied Trade
SPG	Special Patrol Group
SRO	Self-Regulating Organisation
TGWU	Transport and General Workers' Union
TUC	Trades Union Congress
UDM	Union of Democratic Mineworkers

List of Tables and Figures

Tables

1. Retail Price Index (RPI), UK 127
2. Jobs in manufacturing, UK 134
3. Real GDP growth rate, Germany and UK 136
4. The continuities and discontinuities of neoliberalism in Britain 290

Figures

1. Fields and levels of neo-Poulantzasian political analysis 50
2. Government strategies in the Thatcherite era 64

Introduction

'I think in a way, we're all Thatcherites now', remarked David Cameron a few days after Margaret Thatcher's death in April 2013. He added that she had created 'a new consensus'.[1] Obviously, Cameron's intervention was not just a tribute to Thatcher, but also a reflection of a specific politics of history: by maintaining that there was a new political consensus in Britain, Cameron claimed victory for his worldview and his party in an ideological battle that had begun almost four decades earlier.[2]

Despite its triumphalist overtones, Cameron's statement betrayed a certain insecurity. It is not just that sentences starting with 'I think in a way' do not sound very self-assured. Cameron also added the caveat that 'it is inevitable that some people take a different view', which meant that he became tangled up in a contradiction: If the 'inevitable' voices of dissent were so strong that they were worth mentioning, how could he claim that there was a new consensus? The fact that Thatcher's death was met with street parties and soon triggered arguments about the official status and the public cost of her funeral also implies that there were far more opponents of Thatcherism among the British public than Cameron cared to suggest when he spoke of who 'we' are 'now'. The opinion polls concerning Thatcher's legacy conducted at the time support this view. 34 percent of respondents in an ICM poll thought that Thatcher's rule was 'bad' for Britain, and 50 percent 'good'.[3] Similarly, in a ComRes poll, 34 percent of respondents disagreed with the statement that 'Margaret Thatcher's policies were right for the country at the time', while 45 percent agreed.[4] The polls indicate that public opinion on Thatcher and her politics is deeply divided, even if a majority supports her.

---

1 Morris 2013. Cameron's statement is a (possibly accidental) quote of Tony Blair's close ally Peter Mandelson, who wrote that 'we are all Thatcherites now' in article published by the *Times* in 2002 (cf. Tempest 2002). Obviously, Cameron and Mandelson allude to the phrase 'We're all Keynesians now', which is attributed to Milton Friedman and Richard Nixon.

2 In a piece of journalistic commentary, Polly Toynbee argues convincingly that Cameron's coalition government is attempting to revive and deepen Thatcherism, as is evidenced by its attack on the welfare state (Toynbee 2012). In my own terms, the Cameron government resembles the Thatcher and Major governments in attempting to orchestrate an offensive step of the power bloc. I will explain in detail the meaning of these concepts in chapter 2.

3 Clark 2013.

4 Rentoul 2013.

The contentiousness of Cameron's 'new consensus' claim reveals that even though Margaret Thatcher resigned more than twenty years ago, it is still an open question as to what Thatcherism was, and the extent to which it continues to inform present-day British politics. In fact, we may not be able to understand the present conjuncture of British capitalism if we are not able to make sense of Thatcherism. This book is my stab at providing an explanation. In so doing, it critically comments on Cameron's claim and discusses how the Thatcherite era continues to 'haunt' contemporary Britain.

My starting point is the 'sea-change' – to use a metaphor popularised by James Callaghan – in British politics in the late 1970s. Against this backdrop, I discuss how the Thatcher and Major governments went about restructuring capitalism in Britain. In my view, this consisted in removing the institutional supports of the 'post-war settlement' – the fragile arrangement between capital and labour that traded state welfare provision and full employment for wage restraint and acquiescence at the level of production – inflicting a historical defeat on the organised working class, and replacing Keynesian with neoliberal economic policy.

In 1994, Tony Blair became leader of the Labour Party, which turned out to be perhaps the biggest political success of Thatcher and her associates: the main opposition party had been transformed into a broadly neoliberal force, and the main actors on the British political scene were now united behind much of the agenda set out by Thatcher and her followers – even if this did not translate into a broad popular consensus.

Today, it is clear that the shift towards neoliberalism, which took place in most of the centres of capitalism from the 1970s onwards, paved the way for a global economic crisis comparable in scale only to the Great Depression of the 1930s. Accordingly, I will not only discuss what neoliberalism means in the British context, and how it is linked to Thatcherism. I will also examine how Thatcherism contributed to sowing the seeds for the current crisis.

My analysis is based on Karl Marx's insight that capitalist relations of production are marked by an antagonistic relationship of domination between workers and capitalists, and that class antagonism and class domination are at the heart of the capitalist mode of production (CMP). I expand on this by also making use of the work of Poulantzas. He argues that capitalist relations of production are characterised by the private ownership of the means of production, which will only come into existence if there is a legal system and a state instituting and maintaining it. Against this backdrop, a specific agenda for political analysis emerges: it is dedicated to examining how political decision-making addresses the unstable relation of class domination at the heart of the CMP (which often happens indirectly), how capitalist class domination is reproduced in and through state apparatuses, and what this means for relations of forces between the working class and the capitalist class.

This agenda obviously departs from analyses of Thatcherism emanating from the political mainstream, which tend to disarticulate the issues of class domination and class relations of forces.[5] Standard operations in the literature on Thatcherism include asking

(1) how Thatcher managed to implement certain policies and win elections, that is, what her 'statecraft' consisted in;[6]
(2) whether certain policies 'worked', that is, whether their stated aims were reached;[7] and
(3) to what extent Thatcherite policies represented a break with existing patterns of policy-making, and whether they undermined existing configurations of political and economic institutions.[8]

Obviously, all of these operations can be carried out without ever touching upon the class issue, and in most cases authors either refrained from discussing it or mentioned it merely in passing.

An emerging theme in the mainstream literature, usually resulting from the extensive use of operation (3), is the historicisation and normalisation of Thatcherism. Authors belonging in this camp suggest that it was less of a rup-

---

5   For reviews of the literature on Thatcherism, see Jessop et al. 1988, pp. 22–51; Marsh 1995; and Bevir and Rhodes 1998.
6   Bulpitt 1985; Crewe 1988; and Crewe and Searing 1988. Anthony King (1988) does not use the term 'statecraft', but his account of Thatcher's style of leadership provides a similar form of analysis. For accounts highlighting the limits of Thatcher's 'statecraft', see Buller 1999 and 2000, and Stevens 2002. Note that Thatcher herself published a book on 'statecraft' in 2002.
7   Kavanagh 1990; Riddell 1991; and Marsh and Rhodes 1992.
8   An elaborate attempt to examine the historical continuities and discontinuities of British politics in the Thatcherite era can be found in Kerr 2001. Colin Hay (1996b) charts the changes in the British state triggered through Thatcherite interventions. In contrast, David Marsh and Rod Rhodes (1992) suggest that the successes of the Thatcher governments in terms of implementing Thatcherite policies were limited. A more specific version of this line of argument can be found in some of the industrial relations literature. John MacInnes (1987), Eric Batstone (1988) and, again, David Marsh (1992) claim that the changes in this area have been overestimated. John Kelly (1990) provides a variation of the industrial relations argument. He concedes that there have been profound changes in British trade unionism during the Thatcher governments, but adds that there were signs of a recovery in British trade unionism from the late 1980s. With the benefit of hindsight, none of this is very convincing, as demonstrated by the numbers on strikes and trade union membership and density quoted below.

ture than is often assumed.[9] This is unconvincing, especially if the field of labour relations is considered: the number of working days lost due to strikes fell from 29.5m in 1979, when Thatcher took office, to 235,000 in 1997, when Blair became Prime Minister; union density was reduced from 57.4 to 32.4 percent;[10] and collective bargaining coverage dropped from 83 to 48 percent.[11] Importantly, this was not simply the result of global economic developments outside the remit of the Thatcher and Major governments: As data provided by Brown et al. show, the trend in union density was somewhat more pronounced than the general trend in highly developed countries in the centre of capitalism at the time; and the trends in strike incidence and collective bargaining coverage were considerably stronger.[12]

In my view, the politics of Thatcherism play an important part in these developments. As I will explain in due course, the Thatcher and Major governments sought to systematically constrain organised labour. Thatcher's mentor and close ally Keith Joseph had published a pamphlet in February 1979 entitled *Solving the Union Problem is The Key to Britain's Recovery*. Once Thatcher had become Prime Minister, what followed was the stepwise tightening of trade union law, the careful preparation for a confrontation with the organisation spearheading militant trade unionism in Britain at the time, the National Union of Mineworkers (NUM), and an economic and monetary policy accelerating the decline of British industry. The 1984–5 miners' strike, the key instance of the confrontation between the government and the unions, was the longest mass strike in British history and cost approximately £28bn.[13] But this is just

---

[9] Some of the authors stressing the continuity of Thatcherite policies with traditional, pre-Keynesian conservatism or non-Welfarist and non-Keynesian elements in post-war British politics include: Brittan 1985; Bulpitt 1985; Riddell 1991; Green 1999; Fry 2008 and 2010; and Vinen 2010. Marsh, Rhodes and Batstone (see footnote 8) surely also belong to this group, but for a different reason: They doubt that the Thatcher governments managed to trigger profound changes. Colin Hay and Stephen Farrall argue that authors sceptical of Thatcherism's novelty are usually focusing on policy implementation, which tends to be a more protracted process than seismic shifts in the dominant ideology (2011, pp. 41–2).

[10] Statistical Table on 'Trade Unions' in Jackson and Saunders 2012, p. 272.

[11] From 1980 to 1994, according to Brown et al. 1997, p. 75.

[12] Brown et al. 1997, pp. 74, 75, 78. Brown et al. play down the importance of the changes in strike incidence, but this is not convincing considering the numbers they supply: Out of the 21 countries compared, only six had a higher number of working days lost due to industrial disputes per employee between 1981 and 1985. Between 1991 and 1995, there were 16 such countries.

[13] Estimate by Dave Feickert (2004), a former research officer of the National Union of Mineworkers (NUM).

one of many fiercely fought industrial disputes in the Thatcherite era in which the government had a stake – either because they took place in the public sector, or because political decisions and legal changes had paved the way for employer attacks. Kelly provides an apt description of the situation under which unions operated in the Thatcherite era: 'Unions were unable to stem a flood of closures and redundancies, they failed to prevent real wages falling in the depths of the recession, they could not prevent changes in working practices and they suffered a number of spectacular strike defeats: railways 1982, mining 1985, printing 1986, TV-AM 1987, teachers 1987, P and O ferries 1989'.[14]

Taking seriously the substantial changes in labour relations, I arrive at the key observation of my book: I contend that Thatcherism's success and novelty, indeed its unity as a political project, lie in the fact that Thatcher and her associates profoundly shifted class relations in Britain in favour of capital and restructured the institutions underpinning class domination in the country.[15]

Saying this, I do not claim that looking at Thatcherism through the lens of the politics of class domination is specific to my approach. There are other authors who have done so, notably Stuart Hall, Colin Leys, Simon Clarke, Werner Bonefeld and David Coates.[16] Hall and Leys examine how the Thatcherites produced consent across class lines by formulating an 'authoritarian populist' response to the organic crisis of capitalism in Britain in the 1970s. Clarke and Bonefeld argue that Thatcherism constituted the (botched) attempt to implement a monetarist agenda in Britain, which was formulated with a view to disciplining the working class. Coates argues that Thatcherism is a radical response to 'the crisis of labour'.

My account of Thatcherism is specific not because I ground political analysis in class analysis, but because I do so in a new way. My key theoretical intervention is to propose that in the *first* instance, capitalist class domination consists in the extraction of surplus labour in the process of production.[17] It follows that political leaders will always intervene in the sphere of production in some way.

Against this backdrop, I contend that the other authors, with the exception of Coates, neglect the extraction of surplus labour and instead focus on other fields, namely the production of consent (Hall and Leys) and monetary policy (Clark and Bonefeld).[18] In so doing, they make valid points, but neglect a

---

14   Kelly 1990, p. 42.
15   Compare Coates 1989, p. 117.
16   Hall 1983a; Leys 1989 and 1990; Clarke 1988; Bonefeld 1993 and 1995.
17   Compare Jessop 1982, p. 249.
18   Coates's account is the one closest to mine, and I share many of his observations. It differs,

key trait of Thatcherism: It was an integral part of the Thatcherite project to directly intervene in labour relations, to deprive workers of their ability to forge coalitions, and to smash militant trade unionism. As a consequence, the authors in question underestimate the degree to which Thatcherism was a frontal assault on the working class.

For example, Bonefeld states: 'After the abandonment of the "monetarist" economics, the British Prime Minister promised to "kill Socialism in Britain" and fought the miners in 1984–5'.[19] This sequencing of events reflects Bonefeld's primary concern with money, but it produces a distorted picture of what went on: it suggests that the Thatcherites chose to attack militant workers directly only after they had failed to discipline workers with an indirect measure, that is, a monetary policy based on monetarist assumptions.

I contend, in contrast, that the implementation of monetarist policies and the attack on militant unions went hand in hand. In line with my emphasis on production, my book contains a case study analysing four policy papers on labour relations commissioned by the Conservative leadership during the Callaghan era. Among them is the 'Final Report of the Nationalised Industries Policy Group' in the Conservative Party, which is only mentioned in passing in much of the literature on Thatcherism. This report, written in 1977 by Nicholas Ridley, an ally of Thatcher, laid out how a future Conservative government would deal with the nationalised industries. Its significance for the question at stake lies in refuting Bonefeld's claim. The annex to the report contains a detailed plan aimed at smashing militant trade unionism, which shows that leading circles in the Conservative Party were preparing for a direct confrontation with organised labour even before there was a Thatcher government. As my chapter on British class politics between 1979 and 1984 demonstrates, the

---

however, in that Coates does not use a systematic conceptual framework when he analyses Thatcherism. As a result, it is difficult to examine the temporality of neoliberalism on the grounds of his approach.

19 Bonefeld 1995, p. 65. In Bonefeld's monograph *The Recomposition of the British State*, this sequencing of events is less apparent, but he nevertheless overemphasises the importance of monetary policy for the Thatcherite attack on the working class. Accordingly, he characterises the Thatcher era by arguing that it was marked by a 'monetary decomposition of class relations' (1993, pp. 139, 149) and the prevalence of a 'monetarist framework', which was used for 'a deflationary attack on labour' (1993, p. 241). Undoubtedly, the Thatcherite interventions in the field of monetary policy had significant effects on the relations of forces between capital and labour. But Bonefeld's language covers up the fact that the Thatcherites triggered the 'decomposition' of the working class in a very direct sense, that is, in the form of a frontal attack on organised labour.

INTRODUCTION 7

Thatcher governments stuck to this course and followed the recommendations of the report closely. In a nutshell, my analysis is concerned with establishing the articulation between direct attacks of the Thatcher governments on militant workers and Thatcherite economic policy in a broader sense, not just with the effects of their economic policy on class relations.

My key analytical distinction reflects this concern. In my view, there are two modes of 'top-down' politics under capitalist conditions:

(1) *class politics*, that is, political activities aimed *directly* at securing the extraction of surplus value; and
(2) *economic order politics*, that is, interventions primarily aimed at establishing and securing the preconditions for economic growth, which affect class domination only *indirectly*.

In relation to my object, I contend that Thatcher and her associates implemented both a new *class political arrangement* and a new *economic-political order*. The class political arrangement combined a repressive approach to labour relations with the attempt to divide the working class by co-opting certain fractions. The economic-political order centred on the notion of the 'free market'. Thatcherite interventions aimed at inducing growth through market liberalisation, which was achieved partly with the help of authoritarian modes of decision-making. As a result, the British economy was exposed, to a much stronger degree than before, to competition in the world market. The class political arrangement and the economic-political order were fully compatible with each other. I thus speak of an overarching *neoliberal regime*.

The analytical value-added of these distinctions may not be immediately apparent. It lies in elucidating the uneven temporality of political developments during the Thatcherite era and beyond: Whereas the New Labour governments broke with the Thatcherite class political arrangement, they broadly retained the economic-political order established by their predecessors. Correspondingly, the terms Thatcherism and Blairism should be reserved for the respective class political arrangements. A key finding of my analysis is that the continuities and discontinuities of neoliberalism can be accounted for by distinguishing between class politics and economic order politics.

I propose to further elucidate this by taking up Poulantzas's terminology and describing Thatcherism and Blairism as offensive and consolidating steps of the capitalist class in class struggle. In other words, Thatcherism reasserted capitalist class domination by orchestrating a successful offensive against the working class, and Blairism managed to protect this advance. At this point, two further findings of my analysis come into sight: The failure of organised labour to successfully counter the Thatcherite onslaught is a result of its inability to understand the offensive nature of Thatcherism; and the long erosion of Thatcherism in the 1990s reflects the political inability of Thatcher et al. to make the transition from an offensive to a consolidating step in class struggle.

PART 1

*Thatcherism and the
Neo-Poulantzasian Approach*

CHAPTER 1

The Hall-Jessop Debate

Arguments over Hegemony

According to historian Richard Vinen, the term 'Thatcherism' was 'quite widely used' in the late 1970s.[1] It probably entered the lexicon of political analysis for good thanks to a famous article by Stuart Hall called 'The Great Moving Right Show', which was published in *Marxism Today* in January 1979. It is no surprise that it was a prolific Marxist author who coined the term: there is a long tradition in materialist social thought of arguing against the personalisation of politics (Marx's famous pamphlet from 1852, *The Eighteenth Brumaire of Louis Bonaparte*, is a case in point), and Hall acted as a standard-bearer of this tradition when he analysed the political conjuncture of his day.

Strikingly, Hall's account of Thatcherism was the trigger for a long-winded debate among Marxist intellectuals on both the characteristics of Thatcherism and the nature of materialist political analysis. This debate mainly took place during Thatcher's 1980s heyday, but was reignited in the 1990s and 2000s.[2] The protagonists were Hall, Martin Jacques and Colin Leys on one side,[3] and Bob Jessop, Kevin Bonnett, Simon Bromley and Tom Ling on the other.[4] Colin Hay also became involved but claimed not to take sides, attempting to provide a 'synthesis' between the two approaches.[5]

The bone of contention was the hegemony of Thatcherism, that is, the question regarding to what extent the political rule of Thatcher and her associates was sustained by popular consent. Hall et al. argued that Thatcherism was a successful hegemonic project securing active popular consent on a grand scale; the gang of four around Jessop (as they were called back in the day) denied this and stressed that passivity and division were as important, if not more important, for the political rule of the Thatcherites.[6]

---

1 Vinen 2009, p. 4.
2 The debate had a little-known epilogue in *Das Argument*, a Marxist academic journal from Germany, which published an analysis of New Labour by Hall (2004; 2005) and a response from Jessop (2004). To my knowledge, Jessop's article has not been published in English.
3 Hall and Jacques 1983; Jacques 1983; Leys 1989 and 1990.
4 Jessop et al. 1988 and 1990; Jessop 2002b.
5 Hay 1996b, p. 147.
6 For ease of presentation, I provide a stylised account of the Hall-Jessop debate. I refrain from

This divergence reflects the fact that each side focused on a different aspect of the social fabric: Hall et al. primarily examined how the Thatcherites conducted the 'battle for the hearts and minds'[7] of the population and stressed that their 'ideological offensive'[8] triggered a profound shift in political discourse. In contrast, the gang of four focused on investigating how the Thatcherites acted within and shaped 'the specific institutional form of the connections between the state, civil society and the economy, and the distinctive organization of the state system itself'.[9] Along these lines, Jessop et al. argued that Thatcherism was pervaded by tensions and contradictions, and that the Thatcherites were not able to establish broad popular consent for their policies. All in all, the analyses of Hall et al. displayed an ideational bias, while those of the gang of four showed an institutional bias.[10] In other words, Jessop et al. primarily operated in the field of political economy, and Hall et al. in that of political ideology.[11]

Hall et al. on the Political Ideology of Thatcherism

Hall's account of Thatcherism was focused on the characteristics and effects of Thatcherite ideology. He studied the 'organic crisis'[12] of British society in the late 1970s, and asked how 'a capitalist economic recession (economic), presided over by a social democratic party with mass working-class support and organized depth in the trade unions (politically) is "lived" by increasing numbers of people through the themes and representations (ideologically) of a virulent, emergent "petty-bourgeois" ideology'.[13] Hall and Jacques's emphasis is on the innovative nature of Thatcherite ideology. According to them, it resonated with the population because it took the form of 'authoritarian populism'[14] – a mode of addressing the public and responding to the crisis at the level of discourse

---

tracing all the shifts and divergences in the participants' lines of argument because this would render my descriptions unnecessarily complex.

7   Hall 1988b, p. 72.
8   Leys 1990, p. 127.
9   Jessop et al. 1988, p. 156.
10 I owe the distinction between the 'ideational' and the 'institutional' level of politics to Hay (2007, p. 188). The term 'bias' refers to a focus of research. It *does not* imply that areas outside this focus are disregarded or ignored, only that they are not analysed in detail.
11 Compare Jessop et al. 1988, pp. 75–83; Hall 1988a, p. 105; Kurzer 1990, p. 265.
12 Hall 1983a, p. 23.
13 Hall 1983a, p. 21.
14 Hall and Jacques 1983, p. 10.

whose novelty lay in articulating two distinct patterns of intervention. The first was the call for 'law and order',[15] which was articulated in the context of a 'moral panic',[16] that is, a narrative according to which Britain was on the brink of 'social anarchy' due to purported threats to the social order like immigration and the rise of the radical left after 1968.[17] The demand for law and order represented an authoritarian mode of discursive crisis management taken from the standard repertoire of British Conservatism. The Thatcherites, however, linked it to a second pattern of intervention: the attack on the corporatist state. This response was populist because it was presented as an intervention on behalf of the British 'people', directed against the social-democratic establishment and the state apparatuses under its control.[18] According to Hall, the ensuing discourse was based on the juxtaposition of 'state control' and 'freedom':

> It is 'the State' which has over-borrowed and overspent; fuelled inflation; fooled the people into thinking that there would always be more where the last handout came from; tried to assume the regulation of things like wages and prices which are best left to the hidden hand of market forces; above all, interfered, meddled, intervened, instructed, directed – against the essence, the Genius, of The British People.[19]

In addition, Hall contended that Thatcherite ideas resonated with people because of their discontent with being 'disciplined, limited and policed' by the Labour governments, which resorted to 'repressive' techniques of crisis management.[20] As a result, Thatcher et al. managed to win cross-class support – even among some of those unlikely to gain materially from their policies.[21] In short, the Thatcherites reinvigorated Conservative ideology by combining 'the resonant themes of organic Toryism – nation, family, duty, authority, standards, traditionalism – with the aggressive themes of a revived neo-liberalism – self-interest, competitive individualism, anti-statism'.[22]

In conclusion, Hall and Jacques sought to explain why and how Thatcherism won mass support, and why people found its radicalism attractive. Conversely,

---

15   Hall and Jacques 1983, pp. 10–11.
16   Hall et al. 1978, pp. 16–17; compare Hall 1983a, pp. 37–8.
17   Hall 1983a, p. 24.
18   Hall 1983a, p. 27.
19   Hall 1983a, p. 34.
20   Hall 1983a, p. 32.
21   Hall and Jacques 1983, p. 13.
22   Hall 1983a, p. 29.

they mentioned only in passing its internal contradictions and the systemic, institutional and political obstacles to the leadership and dominance of the Thatcherites. It is worth stressing that Hall was well aware of the resulting ideational bias and justified it by *restricting* the *field of validity* of his account. He rejected any claim to be exhaustive,[23] and implied that a restricted account of Thatcherism can still produce important analytical and strategic insights.[24] The 'ideational bias', however, involves more than epistemological choices and personal research interests: it also reflects the historical context of Hall and Jacques's work. The latter was largely developed during the initial stages of Thatcherism – when the academic left was puzzling over why such a profound 'swing to the right'[25] had occurred in the British population.

In contrast, Leys gave his account of Thatcherism when it had already become routinised, and thus paid closer attention to its contestations and its uneven development. He stressed that the first couple of years in government were a 'testing time'[26] for Thatcher: Her deflationary economic strategy triggered protests from the ranks of her own party and from the industrial fraction of capital.[27]

Nevertheless, Leys retained Hall and Jacques's ideational bias. He agreed that ideology accounted for the enduring impact of Thatcherism on British society. For example, he stated that

> The ideological movement which 'Thatcherism' represented was as important as its economic policies, and perhaps more so. Some observers argued that its long-run significance would lie primarily in the extent to which it succeeded in completing the break-up of the amalgam of ideas which composed the post-war social democratic consensus ... and only secondarily in what it achieved through economic policies in office. The campaign to link the pro-market, anti-state doctrines of Thatcherism to popular Conservative themes ... certainly gave it more popular appeal than the Labour Left's advocacy of the Alternative Economic Strategy ... which had no such 'populist' dimension.[28]

Against this backdrop, Leys argued against excessive concern with possible long-term limitations of Thatcherite economic policies and pointed out that

---

23 Hall 1983a, p. 38; 1988a, pp. 99, 105.
24 Hall 1988a, p. 105.
25 Hall 1983a, p. 19.
26 Leys 1989, pp. 104.
27 Leys 1989, pp. 104–6.
28 Leys 1989, pp. 101–2.

most governments fail to articulate coherent long-term strategies. Following him, Thatcherism's successes on the ideological plane compensated for such shortcomings: The Thatcherites might not have dealt with the 'long-term infrastructural needs of industry', but thanks to their 'successful ... ideological offensive', they managed to see off the threat posed by organised labour and re-establish 'the security of capitalist-class rule'.[29]

Following Leys, the Thatcherite hegemonic project was successful because it managed to disorganise contestations to capitalist class domination. He sees evidence for this in the changes in popular attitudes that left the Thatcherite vision of society without a serious challenger: support for the Labour Party rose in step with its gradual acceptance of the Thatcherite political agenda.[30] This suggests that Leys shared the ideational bias of Hall and Jacques: He seemed to agree with them that the ideological innovations of 'authoritarian populism' best explain the successes of Thatcherism.

The 'Gang of Four' on the Political Economy of Thatcherism

If Hall, Jacques and Leys portrayed Thatcherism primarily as an ideology, the gang of four described it as a strategy of political leadership and domination. They focused on political processes and paid close attention to the strategic shifts of the Thatcher governments and the political-economic contexts in which these occurred.[31] Their institutional bias was a reaction to the ideational bias of Hall et al. They focused more on the institutions that acted as supports of Thatcherite ideology than on the ideology itself. And just like their counterparts, they restricted the field of validity of their approach and conceded that their analysis was not exhaustive.

Along these lines, the gang of four portrayed Thatcherism as a response to the 'dual crisis of the British state'[32] in the 1970s, a term they introduced

---

29 Leys 1990, p. 23; compare Hall and Jacques 1983, p. 13.
30 Leys 1990, p. 127. In the 1987 *Socialist Register*, Bill Schwarz made a similar point (p. 140): 'although there certainly was no great popular upsurge for monetarism, it does seem all too likely that the negative and critical dimensions of Thatcherite philosophy – those which worked upon popular experiences of the statist and corporatist emphases of classic Labourism – did effectively seal the ideological destruction of the politics of the post-war system, and thus make it look for a time at least as if there really were no alternative' (1987, p. 140). Schwarz signalled that he broadly agreed with Hall and Jacques (see Schwarz 1987, p. 125), but he refrained from commenting much on Jessop et al. I therefore do not see his piece as a direct intervention in the Hall-Jessop debate.
31 Jessop et al. 1988, pp. 11, 80.
32 Jessop et al. 1988, p. 80.

to describe the crisis of parliamentarism and corporatism. They stressed that this crisis afforded the Thatcher governments with a new, radical mode of political decision-making: It 'created the opening for the enhanced decisional autonomy of the Thatcher government to pursue its programme'.[33]

Against this backdrop, the gang of four qualify the stabilising effect of populism on the political leadership of the Thatcherites that Hall et al. observe. They agree that Thatcher and her cohort resorted to populist interventions in order to retain control of government. However, they add that it was in the interest of the Thatcherites to contain the mobilising effect of populism because it posed a threat to the decisional autonomy of the government.[34] In other words, the Thatcherites did not try to rally large parts of the population around their beliefs but to propagate them in ways that kept most people in a state of passivity.[35] Their populist interventions were conducted in a calculated and limited fashion; they made '*strategic use of ideology*'.[36] From this, the gang of four inferred that the Thatcherites never seriously tried to build popular consensus around their politics:[37] their political leadership and domination was based not only on making discursive interventions that produce active popular consent, but also on employing techniques that were coercive or that generated passivity.

In order to capture the multi-faceted character of political leadership and domination under capitalist conditions, the gang of four mapped out a new conceptual framework for 'political analysis'.[38] This framework was based on the following concepts:

(1) 'Social base', which referred to the 'social forces'[39] needed to support a leading group;
(2) 'Accumulation strategy', which designated a 'pattern, or model, of economic growth'[40] framed by government policies and economic and state institutions;
(3) 'State strategy', which denoted the interventions targeting the boundary between the state and the economy in order to (a) facilitate the imple-

---

33 Jessop et al. 1988, p. 81.
34 Jessop et al. 1988, p. 82.
35 Compare Jessop et al. 1988, p. 79.
36 Hay 1996b, p. 149; compare Jessop et al. 1988, p. 78.
37 Jessop et al. 1990, p. 98.
38 Jessop et al. 1988, p. 156.
39 Ibid.
40 Jessop et al. 1988, p. 158.

mentation of the accumulation strategy, (b) provide the social base with material benefits, and (c) regulate political representation in ways that favour certain social forces over others;[41]

(4) 'Hegemonic project', which stood for a '*national-popular* programme of political, intellectual and moral leadership'[42] whose successful implementation[43] consists in the construction of a 'coherent whole'[44] out of (1) to (3).

In line with their 'institutional bias', the gang of four thus redefined the criteria for a successful hegemonic project. If the political leadership and dominance of a specific group was to be sustainable over the medium term, there had to be large-scale, open and active consent, which again was premised on constructing and assembling four 'building blocks':

(1) A 'natural' constituency of supporters in the population;
(2) The existence of a viable economic growth pattern;
(3) An ensemble of state apparatuses that allowed the group of leaders to take control, and which operated in accordance with (1) and (2);
(4) The articulation of the group's ideology with the present ensemble of economic and state institutions, which was facilitated by the existence of a political agenda connecting blocks (1) to (3).

In other words, Jessop et al. argued that successful hegemonic projects are sustained by the articulation of a truly 'popular' ideological formation with a corresponding institutional configuration. They implied that otherwise advances in the 'battle for the hearts and minds' would prove short-lived.[45] In sum, for them, the markers for the success of a hegemonic project were active popular consent on a mass scale at the level of ideology *plus* coherence at the level of institutions.

Against this backdrop, the gang of four qualified the alleged success of the Thatcherite hegemonic project. First of all, they remarked that the Thatcherites failed 'to consolidate a stable social base'.[46] If there ever was one, it was

---

41 Jessop et al. 1988, p. 159.
42 Jessop et al. 1988, p. 162.
43 Compare Jessop 1990, p. 209.
44 Jessop et al. 1988, p. 162.
45 Compare Jessop 1990, p. 210.
46 Jessop et al. 1990, p. 84.

house-owners, mainly in the South East, and these were hit hard by the housing downturn in the early 1990s recession.[47]

Second, the gang of four argued that the Thatcherite accumulation strategy was a neoliberal strategy, that is, it was focused on privatisation, deregulation, commercialisation, tax cuts, and internationalisation.[48] They added that it failed to address the chronic ills of British industry: 'Thatcherism might well be promoting a worldwide post-Fordist age by creating a rentier British economy, with a secondary industrial role in the world economy and a low wage, low-tech service sector at home'.[49] Jessop et al. observed that 'there is as yet no sign of any industrial renaissance that will be needed both to replace the chronic trade deficit in electronics, cars and other manufactures, and to replace the foreign exchange that will be lost as North Sea oil output declines'.[50] From all this, they inferred that the Thatcherites failed to establish a durable growth pattern,[51] which was a problem because it threatened their ability to make material concessions to their social base.[52]

Third, Jessop et al. contended that the Thatcherite state strategy was liberal and authoritarian, that is, it attempted to deal with the 'dual crisis of the state' by marginalising corporatist forms of representation,[53] concentrating power in the centre and resorting to repression against 'opposition' and 'dissent'.[54] With the help of this strategy, they managed to undermine the institutions that had triggered the 'dual crisis'. The gang of four concluded that in this area the Thatcherite advance went further than in other areas.[55] However, they qualified even this one 'success' of Thatcher et al:

> She and her neo-liberal colleagues have proved more adept at rolling back the frontiers of the social-democratic state and the gains of the post-war settlement than at rolling forward a new state able to engage in an international race for modernization in the next long wave of capitalist expansion.[56]

---

47 Jessop et al. 1990, p. 91.
48 Jessop et al. 1988, p. 171.
49 Jessop 1986, cited in Jessop et al. 1988, p. 171.
50 Jessop et al. 1988, p. 172.
51 Jessop et al. 1988, p. 180.
52 Jessop et al. 1990, p. 97.
53 Jessop et al. 1988, p. 175.
54 Jessop et al. 1988, p. 176.
55 Compare Jessop 2002b, p. 45.
56 Jessop et al. 1990, p. 98. This point was later taken up by Adam Tickell and Jamie Peck,

Jessop et al. imply that this was a problem for the Thatcherite hegemonic project because, for active consent to exist, there had to be an accumulation strategy that generated productivity gains through increases in the skill of workforces. Only this would allow for the establishment of a productivist arrangement where economic expansion was coupled with rising standards of living for workers. For such an arrangement to be created and reproduced, however, there had to be state institutions safeguarding it[57] – an issue that was not addressed by the Thatcherite state strategy. In conclusion, the gang of four suggested that the Thatcherites did not manage to produce the building blocks needed in order to construct a successful hegemonic project.

Following Jessop et al., the record of the Thatcher governments confirms this. The gang of four argued, with Antonio Gramsci, that the Thatcherite hegemonic project remained 'arbitrary, rationalistic and willed'.[58] It might have shifted the 'immediate balance of forces',[59] but it did not construct a supportive institutional configuration. According to Jessop et al., its design was such that it blocked the achievement of full hegemony. They described it as a 'two nations hegemonic project',[60] which mobilised the 'support of strategically significant sectors of the population' and transferred 'the costs of the project to other sectors'.[61]

The gang of four spoke of 'two nations'[62] because they believed that the Thatcherites divided the population and, more specifically, the working class by pitting a 'productive' against a 'parasitic' section. According to them,

---

who introduced the distinction between 'roll-back' and 'roll-out neoliberalism' (2003, pp. 174–5).

57   Compare Jessop 1990, p. 101.
58   Ibid.
59   Ibid.
60   Jessop et al. 1988, p. 177.
61   Jessop 1990, p. 211.
62   The term 'two nations' entered the British political discourse thanks to Benjamin Disraeli, a nineteenth-century Tory Prime Minister. Disraeli wrote a political novel called *Sybil, or the Two Nations* in 1845. In it, a character refers to 'THE RICH AND THE POOR' in Britain as 'two nations; between whom there is no intercourse and no sympathy; who are ignorant of each other's habit, thoughts, and feelings, as if they were dwellers in different zones, or inhabitants of different planets; who are formed by a different breeding, and fed by a different food, are ordered by different manners, and are not governed by the same laws' (Disraeli 1845, pp. 68–9). Dividing the British population into 'two nations' was common at the time. Friedrich Engels, for example, spoke of the working class and the bourgeoisie as 'two entirely different peoples, as different as only the difference of race could make them' (1957, p. 351, my translation). Along these lines, Tories subscribing to an 'inclusive' form of nationalism in the tradition of Disraeli tend to refer to themselves as

Thatcher et al. did so by attempting to restructure the economy in a way that ensured that 'the productive be rewarded *through the market* for their contribution to production' and that 'the parasitic ... suffer for their failure to contribute adequately (if at all) to the market'.[63] In sum, their hegemonic project might have secured the active consent of substantial parts of the population,[64] but, at the same time, it was premised on excluding other, equally substantial parts. If Thatcherism was hegemonic at all, it possessed 'limited hegemony'.[65] It brought a 'passive revolution',[66] that is, 'the reorganization of social relations ("revolution") while neutralizing and channelling popular initiatives in favour of the continued domination of the political leadership ("passive")'.[67]

This conception of hegemony differs profoundly from the one used by Hall and his associates. Jessop et al. imply that their counterparts are too vague with regard to hegemony, which leads them to mistake transitory, passive agreement for lasting, active consent.[68] In line with this, Jessop highlighted that there are forms of exercising political power that are not based on consent. Following Antonio Gramsci, he saw 'a continuum running from open class warfare through "force, fraud and corruption" and "passive revolution" to an integral, expansive hegemony'.[69] He conceived of hegemony as just one among a number of configurations of political leadership and domination, which suggests that it should not be equated with the plain capacity to rule.

This is also consistent with the gang of four's empirical assessments of the extent of active popular consent to Thatcherism. Jessop et al. saw no convincing evidence that Thatcherism ever enjoyed hegemony. They argued that 'even if there is considerable popular support for Thatcherism, it is not reflected in the economic and/or political organizations of the working class or the new middle class'.[70] They added that the election victories of the Conservatives were the result of people making pragmatic decisions triggered by material concessions;[71] that many Britons voted against a party they disliked, not for

---

'one nation conservatives', and Jessop et al. describe Thatcherism as a form of 'two nations' conservatism based on 'divisive' nationalism.
63 Jessop et al. 1988, p. 88.
64 Jessop 2002b, p. 46.
65 Jessop 1990, p. 211.
66 Jessop 1990, p. 212.
67 Jessop 1990, p. 213.
68 Compare Jessop 2002b, pp. 43–4.
69 Jessop 2002b, p. 43.
70 Jessop et al. 1988, p. 79.
71 Jessop et al. 1988, p. 138.

a party they liked,[72] and that under the first-past-the-post electoral system in use in Britain, it was possible to gain an absolute majority of MPs without an absolute majority of votes cast.[73] Finally, Jessop et al. observed a steady decline in popular support for the Thatcher governments over the course of the 1980s, as evidenced in opinion polls.[74] Overall, they demonstrated that Thatcherism was not successful on any of the three levels.

In conclusion, the Hall-Jessop debate is characterised by a single profound disagreement: the extent of popular consent to Thatcherism. Leys argues that the gradual acceptance of Thatcherite policies by the Labour Party is a good indicator of Thatcherism having attained hegemony; the gang of four see proof for the absence of Thatcherite hegemony in opinion polls, the nonexistence of Thatcherite popular organisations and, most importantly, the incapacity of the Thatcherites to roll out an expansive growth pattern and redesign state institutions accordingly. It is important to stress, however, that the disagreement does not extend to the two approaches in their entirety. Hall et al. always accepted the need to establish how the ideology of Thatcherism connected to political and economic institutions;[75] likewise, the gang of four never denied that studying institutions requires paying attention to ideology.[76]

Class Politics vs. Economic Order Politics: Reconciling the Two Approaches

In a little-known article from 1983, Michael Bleaney made an important but largely forgotten observation concerning critical analyses of Thatcherism, namely that they tend to take positions that seem to be diametrically opposed. Thatcherite economic policy is portrayed either as something 'fundamentally irrational'[77] or as 'an unusually energetic and forthright expression of the class interests of British capital'.[78] The Hall-Jessop debate is a case in point: The gang of four emphasised that the Thatcherites failed to develop a coherent long-term economic strategy, while Hall et al. highlighted that it managed to secure capitalist class domination.

---

72 Jessop et al. 1988, p. 137.
73 Jessop et al. 1988, p. 136. Note that neither Thatcher nor her successor John Major managed to win an absolute majority of votes in a general election.
74 Jessop et al. 1990, p. 83; compare Jessop et al. 1988, p. 46.
75 Hall 1983a, p. 24; Leys 1990, pp. 125–6.
76 Jessop et al. 1988, pp. 55–6.
77 Bleaney 1983, p. 132.
78 Bleaney 1983, p. 133.

I contend that this divergence does not just reflect the different conceptions of hegemony used by the two approaches. It also mirrors a more fundamental split concerning the durability of capitalist social orders. Following Jessop et al., the most important precondition for a durable capitalist social order is the existence of stable economic growth – at least over the medium term.[79] In contrast, Hall et al. imply that it lies in the disunity of social forces posing a threat to capitalist class domination.[80]

This suggests that the two sides choose different entry points for their respective political analyses.[81] In my understanding, the term 'entry point' describes the political field from which scholars of politics start their analysis. By selecting it, they determine what in their view constitutes the centre of the political topography. In my view, the entry point of the gang of four is *economic order politics*. I understand by this the politics of maintaining a capitalist social order by bringing the institutional structure of the state in line with the economy and vice versa, thus securing the institutional preconditions for economic growth and social cohesion. In short, economic order politics is an umbrella concept for political interventions directly targeting the relationship between the state and the economy.[82] Correspondingly, the gang of four primarily study the impact of Thatcherite policies on the institutional framework sustaining capitalism in Britain.

In contrast, I contend that the entry point of Hall et al. is *class politics*. By this term, I understand the politics of maintaining capitalist class domination, that is, of reproducing the ensemble of institutionalised power relations that effect the extraction of surplus labour from workers at the level of production and the appropriation of the resulting surplus value by capitalists. In short, class politics is concerned with safeguarding the 'exploitability' of workers. Along these lines, Hall et al. examine to what extent Thatcherite policies succeeded in terms of integrating the working class into the existing social order.

This fundamental divergence also means that the two sides differ in terms of their respective timeframes for assessing the successes and failures of Thatcherism: Jessop et al.'s line is that the Thatcherites might have enjoyed short-term success in terms of establishing political control, but that their economic

---

79   Jessop et al. 1988, p. 180.
80   Leys 1990, p. 123; Hall and Jacques 1983, p. 13.
81   I owe the term 'entry point' to Jessop. Compare Jessop 2008b, pp. 227–30.
82   'Economic order politics' echoes the German term 'Ordnungspolitik'. Unlike ordoliberal usages of 'Ordnungspolitik' (compare Vanberg 2004), however, it does not have normative connotations and makes no claims as to what constitutes 'good' or 'bad' economic policy.

policies posed a threat to social cohesion over the medium term. In contrast, Hall et al. take a short-term view and point out that the Thatcherites managed to fend off the threat that organised labour posed to capitalist class domination.[83]

Obviously, the two political fields in question overlap. The Thatcherite stance on industry, for example, concerns both. Correspondingly, the two sides of the debate quite often have something meaningful to say about one and the same policy highlighting different articulations. In other words, the difference between economic order politics and class politics is an analytical distinction. The two fields are created by observers who are looking at politics from two different angles.

This is nothing unusual in political analysis. After all, some of the fields that figure heavily in mainstream policy analysis overlap substantially too – for example, 'social policy' and 'economic policy'. Moreover, the term '*entry point*' highlights that starting off from one field does not necessarily mean remaining there. In fact, it leaves room for establishing the articulation of this field with others. Correspondingly, each of the two camps in the Hall-Jessop debate discusses policies that are connected to (but not primarily located in) the field mainly covered by their counterpart.

In any case, it is not obvious that the choice of different entry points leads to one analysis being superior to the other. Both sides can point to empirical evidence backing up their case: On the one hand, the Thatcherites smashed militant trade unionism and, by winning four elections in a row, contributed heavily to the political marginalisation of the Labour Party left. Undoubtedly, they thus managed to fend off the challenge posed to capitalist class domination by the more radical factions of the British labour movement and created institutional safeguards for the existing social order that proved durable, at least over the short term. On the other hand, Thatcher and her cohort also presided over economic policies that deepened the structural weaknesses of the British economy. In line with neoliberal ideology, they liberalised and internationalised British financial markets, which entrenched the leading role of the City of London, especially its international section, and the subordinate role of British industry. The resultant decline of industrial production rendered

---

83   I use the attribute 'short-term' when I refer to developments taking place at the level of the conjuncture (for example, during the 1970s crisis or under new labour), 'medium-term' when I refer to transitions across stages in capitalist development (from Keynesian interventionism to neoliberalism), and 'long-term' when I look at the transitions across socio-economic orders (from feudalism to capitalism).

productivist arrangements impossible. By the looks of today, Britain is comparatively ill equipped to weather the current global financial crisis, especially if compared to more production-oriented countries like Germany. This suggests that Thatcherism was a successful strategy in terms of class politics, but less so in terms of economic order politics.

Both observations enhance our understanding of Thatcherism. Hall et al.'s emphasis on the short-term successes of the Thatcherites in the field of class politics reveals an aspect of their rule that separated them from any other group of political leaders in Britain in the entire post-war era: They pursued a successful offensive against organised labour. In the case of the gang of four, it is less clear whether they laid their finger on anything specific. The jury is still out on what the medium-term effects of Thatcherism are – it has surely contributed to laying the foundation for the deepest economic crisis Britain has witnessed since the Great Depression, but the other strategies used in post-war Britain in the field of economic order politics were not particularly successful either. No matter how this debate will be settled by future historians, it is safe to say that the gang of four made an important political intervention: They demonstrated that the Thatcherite claim to have 'turned Britain around' was spurious, and they have broadly been proven right by the fact that the British economy proved brittle in the face of a global financial and economic crisis.

If both sides have a point, it seems that they were talking past each other when they were arguing over the successes and failures of Thatcherism. This suggests that there is potential for reconciliation – especially as neither side claims to give an exhaustive account of Thatcherism. To a degree, I concur with Colin Hay, who argued that a 'synthesis' of the two approaches is desirable.[84] It is far from clear, however, whether it can be achieved. In my view, a true synthesis of the two approaches would be premised on meeting three challenges:

(1) settling the issue at the heart of the debate, that is, the question of hegemony;
(2) developing an inclusive conceptual framework allowing for the articulation of the insights gained by both sides; and
(3) grounding this framework in a consistent theorisation of capitalism.

The first challenge arises because both sides disagree fundamentally about hegemony, which means that settling scores seems difficult without taking sides. The second challenge is related to the first because it requires one to

---

84   Hay 1996b, p. 147.

establish how the different factors accounting for the durability of capitalist social orders are articulated. The third challenge entails opting for a specific theoretical framework, which, again, is likely to result in a bias towards one side or the other. After all, any such framework is built around a specific 'theoretical problematic',[85] which creates a hierarchy of importance among the different aspects of the object studied. Social theories are biased towards certain instances of the social world, predisposing them to fall on one side of the dichotomy between the 'ideational' and the 'institutional'. Due to these difficulties, I contend that a synthesis of both approaches in the form of a merger between equals is not possible. Rather, it will always assume the form of a more or less friendly takeover of one approach by the other.[86]

---

85 Althusser 1970, p. 25. The concept refers to the fundamental assumptions about the social world guiding the researcher. Any approach to political analysis is informed by a theoretical problematic determining what can and cannot be said by the person making use of it.

86 Hay's analysis (1996b) is a good example of how a purported synthesis becomes a friendly takeover. His strategy is to accept Hall et al.'s assertion that Thatcherism was hegemonic, but rid it of its class political dimension and integrate it into a conceptual framework derived from the gang of four's. Hay argues that a political ideology is hegemonic when it has become naturalised, that is, when there is no alternative vision with a mass appeal (1996b, p. 130). He goes along with the gang of four in saying that a successful hegemonic project needs 'structural underpinnings' (ibid.), but departs from them by suggesting that coherence between the institutional and the ideational sphere can be achieved if there is passive consent. Put bluntly, hegemony is 'cheaper' in Hay's framework than in the gang of four's. I disagree with the substance of Hay's line of argument in two respects: First of all, Jessop (1990, p. 213) is right to argue that equating silent and passive support with hegemony results in an imprecise account of political leadership and domination. There is a fundamental difference between political settings in which governments can build on the open, active consent of great parts of the population, and those where this consent is substantial, but where it builds on silence and passivity. Second, I doubt that Hay's key argument regarding hegemony is valid. He derives the 'naturalisation' of Thatcherism from the homogeneity of the official political discourse, that is, from general agreement between the leadership of two main parties in Britain over the most substantive issues in economic policy (1996b, p. 130). In my view, one does not follow from the other. As is widely known, there is a first-past-the-post electoral system in Britain. This means that the success of a party in a general elections hinges on its ability to win the support of the highly specific group of non-aligned voters in a few contested constituencies. If Britain has become a 'one-vision democracy', this reflects the highly strategic way in which party leaders design political agendas in the light of the electoral system (compare Jessop et al. 1988, p. 171), but not necessarily the overall attitudes of people. In other words, a 'one-vision democracy' is not necessarily a 'one-vision society'. For a more detailed discussion of the merits and flaws of Hay's analysis, see Gallas 2014.

CHAPTER 2

Neo-Poulantzasian Political Analysis

A New Articulation: The Primacy of Class Politics

In this chapter, I will lay out my responses to the three challenges I discussed in relation to merging the approaches of Hall et al. and the gang of four. Unlike Hay, I will not attempt to produce a proper synthesis. In my view, the theoretical problematics of the two sides are incommensurable. Instead, I propose to move towards 'reconciliation', that is, towards a conceptual framework that articulates themes taken from both approaches. In other words, I will shift the terrain of the debate rather than take sides. The end result, however, will be closer to the approach of the gang of four than to that Hall et al. For Jessop et al. are right on a crucial issue: it is impossible to assess the effectiveness and 'stickiness' of an ideological formation without examining the institutional configurations underpinning it.

In relation to challenge (1), I contend that Hall et al. did not demonstrate convincingly that Thatcherism was a successful hegemonic project. There are good reasons to assume that their criterion for the success of Thatcherism – the complete dominance of a Thatcherite common sense in the British population – was not met. Opinion polls indicate that support for trade unionism grew during the Thatcherite era.[1] The right turn of the Labour Party under Neil Kinnock

---

1 In the 1985 British Social Attitudes Survey, approximately 10 percent of respondents said that unions have 'too little' or 'far too little' power. This number climbed to about 28 percent in 1990, and stabilised at around 22 percent and 20 percent in 1994 and 1998, respectively (BSAS I, 2009). The numbers indicate that there was a substantial section of British society that disagreed with the new right attack on organised labour, and that this group was significantly bigger at the end of the Thatcherite era than during its initial stages. Even more significantly, in the 1994 and 1998 surveys, 56 and 54 percent of people agreed with the statement 'Employees will never protect their working conditions and wages without strong trade unions'. In contrast, only 24 and 18 percent of people thought that 'There is no need for strong trade unions to protect employees' working conditions and wages' (BSAS II, 2009). This implies that at the end of the Thatcher era, a majority of Britons still supported trade unionism, and the share of people who were opposed to it remained relatively small. Ivor Crewe's detailed analysis (1988) of opinion polls from the 1980s on people's attitude towards economic and social policy, decisions taken by the Thatcher government, and the Thatcherite style of government show much the same picture: There was no unequivocal support for Thatcherism among the British. Crewe concludes that polling evidence shows that 'the public has not been converted

may be a reflection of the popular opinion in the contested constituencies, but not necessarily in the country as a whole.[2] This suggests that Thatcherite beliefs were not shared universally and that a substantial (and increasing) number of people remained sceptical. In contrast, Jessop et al. manage to show that – measured against their criteria ('active consent' and 'coherence') – Thatcherism was not a successful hegemonic project. And yet, Leys had a point when he questioned the validity of these criteria.[3] Most governments fail to produce 'active consent' and 'coherence'; in fact, it appears that all British governments from 1957 onwards failed to produce 'active consent' on a mass scale; and that all post-war British governments failed to produce a mode of institutional integration that was self-reinforcing and coherent.

It seems that Jessop was aware of this problem. He conceded that there are 'fundamental theoretical problems posed by the analysis of hegemony in terms of hegemonic projects'.[4] The main issue is that talking about a 'hegemonic project' and defining hegemony in terms of 'active consent' and 'coherence' seems to imply that 'hegemony is typical or normal in capitalist societies',[5] and that every government seeks to establish it. As the example of Thatcherism demonstrates, this is not the case. In fact, it seems that governments can exercise leadership and dominate the political process for extended periods without properly establishing hegemony or even trying to do so. It is questionable whether the success of Thatcherism should be assessed in terms of how close its hegemonic project came to attaining full hegemony – no matter whether this is measured by looking at the degree to which a Thatcherite common sense was dominant, or the degree to which there was institutional 'coherence' and 'active consent'.

In light of this, I suggest reframing the debate. Since there appear to be different ways of leading and dominating a population, I contend that the existence of a dominant pattern of leadership cannot be equated with the existence of a hegemonic project. In other words, there is no point in using the concept automatically whenever we analyse political configurations. Instead, I propose using the term 'mode of leadership and domination', which captures all sorts of ways in which political leadership operates – whether via hegemonic arrangements or not.

---

to Thatcherism – not to its priorities, nor to its economic reasoning, nor to its social values' (1988, p. 35).
2 See Chapter 1, n. 86.
3 Leys 1990, p. 123.
4 Jessop 1990, p. 211.
5 Jessop 1990, p. 213.

This may not conform to Jessop's terminology, but it is in line with the substance of his take on hegemony. As we saw earlier, he pointed out that there was a 'continuum' between different forms of political leadership and domination. Jessop elaborated on this by calling for a

> more detailed consideration of different forms of 'passive revolution' ranging from the transitional case of 'two nations' projects (which combine features of an expansive hegemony and 'passive revolution' but direct them towards each of the 'nations') through normal forms of 'passive revolution' ... to the use of 'force, fraud and corruption' as a means of social control (which can be considered as a transitional form between 'passive revolution' and 'war of manoeuvre').[6]

Against this backdrop, it is possible to develop a differentiated typology of modes of leadership and domination. Following Jessop, there are five such modes. Two are hegemonic projects ('one nation' and 'two nations'); the others are passive revolution, force-fraud-corruption and open class warfare. Subsuming the term 'hegemonic project' under the category of 'mode of leadership and domination' has two advantages over simply assuming that there is such a project and assessing its failure or success.[7] First of all, if the term is reserved for political projects that secure (broad or modest) active popular consent, it follows that 'hegemony' is no longer taken to be the standard form of political domination. Second, framing the issue in this way allows for a differentiated assessment of the successes and failures of political projects and for moving beyond the truism that just about every political project in Britain failed to secure full hegemony. Instead, modes of leadership and domination can be identified with the help of a set of criteria distinguishing them from one another:

- a successful 'one nation' hegemonic project secures active consent on a mass scale and establishes a structure of institutional supports;
- a successful 'two nations' hegemonic project produces active consent among its social base and passivity among the remainder of the population – again supported with an institutional structure;

---

6 Ibid.
7 Note that the gang of four was self-critical on this front: 'A general problem with accounts of Thatcherism is the lax use of the terms "hegemony" and "hegemonic project". Although we have criticized this in earlier work, we must also plead guilty' (Jessop, Bonnett and Bromley 1990, p. 83).

- a successful passive revolution creates institutions that foster political passivity in the population on a mass scale;
- a successful project based on corruption manages to muddle through by buying the favours of groups of people in key strategic positions; and
- a successful project based on open class warfare manages to undermine contestations to capitalist class domination by repressing organised labour on the economic, political and ideological level.

This suggests that a state of 'coherence' can be achieved in different ways. In a successful 'one nation' hegemonic project, institutions are configured in a way that triggers an 'expansive' dynamic, that is, a productivist arrangement allowing for continuously improving standards of living for the majority of the population.

In contrast, in a successful 'two nations' hegemonic project, there is a coherent institutional framework insofar as institutions mobilise key strategic sectors of the populations and channel material rewards to them.[8] This difference can be captured with the help of a distinction introduced by Jessop, that is, 'substantive unity' and 'formal unity'.[9] Whereas 'substantive unity' implies the existence of a self-reinforcing institutional arrangement, which is likely to be durable over the medium term,[10] 'formal unity' refers to a self-reproducing, short-term arrangement.

It follows from this framework that Thatcherism might not have been hegemonic, but it was still based on a successful 'two nations' hegemonic project: There was a social base supporting the Thatcher governments, and there were accumulation and state strategies securing this support. Otherwise, it would have been impossible for the Thatcherites to win four successive general elections and dominate the British political scene for a good fifteen years. However, if Thatcherism was a 'two nations' hegemonic project, it can be concluded that it was just premised on formal, but not substantive, institutional unity.

So far, I have shifted the terrain of the Hall-Jessop debate by elaborating on themes from Jessop's work. This also means that I have not yet integrated much from the Hall camp, which confirms my suspicion that there is little room for convergence between the two camps in relation to challenge (1). This also means that I have not yet achieved my goal of reconciling the two approaches.

---

8   Jessop 1990, p. 211.
9   Jessop 1990, p. 210.
10 Needless to say that thanks to the crisis tendencies inherent in the CMP, even expansive arrangements are likely to erode eventually.

Things look more promising in relation to challenge (2). After all, neither side claimed to have produced an exhaustive account, which implies that observations made using class politics as an entry point may be compatible with those using economic order politics. It seems there is no contradiction in arguing that the Thatcherites successfully marginalised organised labour *and* implemented a new accumulation strategy and state project that contributed to undermining social cohesion over the medium term.

Yet it is one thing to make this statement, and another to ground it in a consistent conceptual framework (challenge 2) informed by a theorisation of capitalism (challenge 3). Meeting these challenges requires a coherent account of the relationship between capitalist class domination and broader social cohesion. If one wants to analyse Thatcherism integrating the insights of both sides of the debate, some serious theoretical work is required.

I see four main aspects of the relation between class domination and social cohesion under capitalist conditions from a Marxian perspective. First of all, each of the two poles of the relationship constitutes a defining characteristic of any capitalist social order. Following Marx, capitalism always involves class domination. He implies that capitalist relations of production only exist if capitalists exercise control over workers at the level of production in order to extract surplus labour.[11] On a more general level, a similar point can be made for social cohesion. To borrow one of Thatcher's phrases: There is no such thing as society without a minimum degree of social cohesion. In sum, a capitalist social order is not capitalist if capitalist class domination is absent, and it is not a social order if social cohesion does not exist.

Second, in capitalist social orders, capitalist class domination is necessary for cohesion to exist.[12] Without it, the dominant way of producing ceases to function, which in turn renders the reproduction of the given ensemble of social institutions impossible. Yet class domination generates resistance because of the antagonistic relationship between capitalists and workers inherent in the capitalist relations of production.[13] Thus capitalist class domination contains potential threats to its own viability and, hence, to social cohesion. In short, it is prone to crises. At the political level, class politics is the mode of political intervention that addresses such crisis tendencies *directly*. In contrast, economic order politics may have an effect on the modalities of class struggles and the viability of capitalist class domination, but this is the *indirect* result of political interventions targeting social cohesion.

---

11   Compare Marx 1962a, p. 328.
12   Marx 1962b, p. 362.
13   Marx 1962a, p. 350, see below.

Third, while threats to capitalist class domination are also threats to social cohesion, the reverse is not necessarily true. The Great Depression posed a threat to social cohesion, but not to capitalist class domination: Thanks to unemployment, deprivation and the defeats suffered during the revolutionary conjuncture after World War I and the October Revolution, the organisations of the working class were on the defensive, and did not manage to stop the advance of fascism in Europe.[14] Furthermore, capitalist class domination appears to persist even in chaotic settings where social cohesion is absent. This is evidenced by the existence of peripheral 'failed states', that is, zones in the global capitalist system that lack a minimum degree of institutional integration and ideological formations with a 'centripetal' effect on the population. There are often rudimentary forms of capitalist class domination in these zones – for example, in the form of a drugs industry run by capitalists subjecting wage labourers to their control at the level of production.

This implies, fourth, that basic forms of political leadership and domination are at least conceivable in such settings – even if the separation between the economic and political is likely to be blurred. It follows that political leadership and domination under conditions of the global dominance of the CMP always involves protecting capitalist ways of extracting surplus labour, but not necessarily securing the stable accumulation of capital over the medium term. In other words, there appears to be a primacy of class politics over economic order politics. It is impossible to engage in economic order politics in any meaningful sense of the word whilst completely neglecting class politics, but the reverse is not necessarily the case. This does not imply, however, that social cohesion is unimportant: Political leadership and domination will endure only if there is at least a minimum degree of social cohesion.

In conclusion, political leaders operating in capitalist social orders have to work to secure both capitalist class domination *and* social cohesion. Thatcherism shows that what proves effective in relation to safeguarding the former might, at least over the medium term, threaten the latter. Accordingly, if one wants to assess Thatcherism, it is worth exploring both class politics and economic order politics. Yet as class politics alone directly addresses the foundation of political leadership and domination in capitalism, I propose to meet challenge (2) by starting from it.

---

14   Poulantzas 1974, p. 61.

Poulantzas on the Capitalist State

So far, my strategy of reconciling the two sides has been to stress the importance of both class politics and economic order politics. This has involved making concessions to each of the two camps at different points: I have rearticulated the concept of 'hegemony' along Jessopian lines and have followed Leys in prioritising class politics. My overall line of argument, however, resembles the gang of four's more than that of Hall et al. because I share the conviction of Jessop and his associates that analysing political leadership and domination requires a focus on institutions.

Regarding challenges (2) and (3), the main issue is to reconcile my assumption that there is a primacy of class politics in capitalism with my Jessopian leanings at the conceptual level. My strategy here is to identify a class political subtext in the account of the gang of four, and to show how it might enable us to meet these challenges. The subtext in question is most visible when Jessop et al. speak of Thatcherism as a 'counter-offensive' to the 'earlier economic-corporate gains of the labour movement'.[15] This clearly portrays Thatcherism as a response to a working-class offensive, and hence as an expression of class conflict at the political level. Indeed, Jessop has since confirmed this reading when he notes that the gang of four owes much to Poulantzas's method in *Fascism and Dictatorship*,[16] which is an analysis of the rise and consolidation of German and Italian fascism on the grounds of 'a periodization based on *the steps and the turns of the class struggle*'.[17]

In this spirit, I will re-read Poulantzas and develop a conceptual framework that brings together an analysis using class politics as its entry point with a general focus on institutions.[18] This is in keeping with my aim to foster reconciliation between the two sides because both of them view Poulantzas favourably. In the past thirty years, Jessop has been drawing upon Poulantzas's work extensively,[19] while Hall showed his appreciation for him by writing his obituary in *New Left Review* (1980).

This formal justification for returning to Poulantzas can be substantiated with reference to the content of his work. There are passages that foreshadow

---

15 Jessop et al. 1988, p. 77.
16 Jessop 2006, p. 329.
17 Poulantzas 1974, p. 54.
18 To avoid misconceptions, I would like to stress that I am interested in *Fascism and Dictatorship* because of the method of political analysis developed in the book. I do not claim in any way that Thatcherism is a variant of Fascism.
19 Jessop 1982; 1985; 1990, pp. 220–47; 1991a; 2007a, pp. 152–207; 2008b, pp. 118–39; 2011.

my arguments concerning class politics and economic order politics: Poulantzas argued that the state addresses both 'the conditions of production', that is, the extraction of surplus labour, and the overall cohesion of a social order.[20] This suggests that it may be possible to tackle challenge (2) by developing a conceptual framework in the Poulantzasian tradition. Moreover, Poulantzas drew heavily upon Marx's critique of political economy.[21] So challenge (3) can potentially also be met by deploying Poulantzas.

In the tradition of Marx, Poulantzas approached political analysis by both producing general determinations of capitalism that account for any capitalist social order, and also examining how these are articulated, in concrete cases, with contingent factors and remnants of other historical eras.[22] Along these lines, Poulantzas distinguished between the 'mode of production' and the 'social formation':

> The mode of production constitutes an abstract-formal object which does not exist in the strong sense in reality. Capitalist, feudal and slave modes of production, which equally lack existence in the strong sense, also constitute abstract-formal objects. The only thing which really exists is a historically determined *social formation*, i.e. a social whole, in the widest sense, at a given moment in its historical existence: e.g. France under Louis Bonaparte, England during the Industrial Revolution. But a social formation, which is a real-concrete object and so always original because singular, presents a particular combination, a specific overlapping of several 'pure' modes of production.[23]

According to Poulantzas, making this distinction is a necessary precondition of examining social orders: The theoretical construction of the dominant mode of production serves as the 'condition of knowledge' of any social formation.[24]

---

20 Poulantzas 1973, p. 50.
21 Compare Gallas 2011.
22 My account of Poulantzas's work is stylised for accessibility's sake, treating his two key works *Political Power and Social Classes* (1973) and *State, Power, Socialism* (1978) as broadly congruent – even though the former book is partly informed by a 'regionalist' conception of the state (1973, p. 12), which the latter rejects (1978, pp. 15–16). On the development of Poulantzas's thought, see Jessop 1985.
23 Poulantzas 1973, p. 15. This should not be taken to imply that the 'mode of production' is a mere heuristic. In my understanding, Poulantzas's proposition that it does not 'exist in the strong sense in reality' emphasises its real yet tendential character (see below).
24 Poulantzas 1973, p. 13.

Along these lines, Poulantzas starts examining capitalism at the level of the CMP. He shares Marx's assumption that capitalist relations of production entail an antagonistic relation between workers and capitalists. Following Marx, the commodification of labour power, a defining feature of capitalist relations of production, introduces a tendency for constant conflict into capitalist social orders. He implies that labour power is different from other commodities because the conditions of its consumption remain under-determined by the basic rules of commodity exchange. The capitalists as buyers are in the position to argue that they can do as they please with their purchase. The workers as sellers can claim that their status as free owners of labour power must not be compromised through overwork and exhaustion, that is, that they must be able to re-sell it if the existing labour contract is cancelled. Put differently, they can justifiably demand that their ability to reproduce their own labour power is not compromised. In Marx's words: 'What occurs here is an antinomy, right against right, both equally confirmed by the law of commodity exchange. Force decides between equal rights'.[25]

From this, Marx inferred that capitalist relations of production entail constant class struggle over the conditions of the consumption of labour power between capitalists and workers.[26] It follows that capitalist class domination is contestable on the grounds of the rules governing commodity exchange: workers can legitimately challenge the command of capitalists over production because labour power is not a commodity like any other. After all, its consumption directly affects its 'reproducibility', and it is not dominantly reproduced in a capitalist fashion: to a large extent, the reproduction of labour power takes place in the household and involves unpaid reproduction work.

The special status of labour power as a commodity means that the capitalist relations of production and the capitalist form of extracting surplus labour are inherently unstable: the class antagonism inherent in them is an ever-present potential for crisis. It follows that the existence of capitalist relations of production does not as such guarantee the reproduction of capital or capitalist class domination. The latter requires class struggle to take a specific trajectory that remains contingent to the relations of production as such.[27]

Marx exemplified this in the chapter on the working day in *Capital*. He jumps in his presentation from the level of the CMP to the level of a real-concrete capitalist social formation, that is, from analysing the characteristics of the consumption of labour power in capitalist production to industrial conflict

---

25 Marx 1962a, p. 249, my translation.
26 Ibid.
27 Compare Gallas 2011, p. 105.

in nineteenth-century Britain. His cases in point are the continuous battles between workers and industrial capitalists over work hours taking place at that time. He argues that they eventually resulted in a short-term alliance between workers and agricultural capitalists, triggering a decision in parliament to enforce a legal limitation of the working day.[28] Its introduction was of key importance for the stabilisation of class relations in Britain because it prevented capital from destroying itself by destroying labour power, that is, by depriving workers of the ability to reproduce their capacity to work. This had happened as long as competition had remained unfettered and individual capitalists had been trying to out-compete one another by extending the working day ever more.[29] One of the ironies in the history of capitalism is that worker resistance resulted in the creation of legal obstacles to competition via work hours, which in turn protected the conditions for the permanent extraction of surplus labour along capitalist lines.

Marx also argued that the ensuing struggles led to the emergence of the working class and the capitalist class.[30] This suggests that there is only a tendency for class formation at the level of the CMP: classes are constituted through the unifying effect of real-concrete class struggles at the level of the social formation. In other words, they represent *collective actors* that form in class struggle, not 'sociological' groups constituted by people simply sharing the same 'place' in society.

In conclusion, the specific historical circumstances of class struggle in nineteenth-century Britain resulted in the 'chance discovery'[31] of an institutional arrangement not inherent in capitalist relations of production yet conducive to the stabilisation of capitalist class domination. This was possible because the antagonism between capitalists and workers in principle leaves room for temporary settlements that trade the overall confirmation of the capitalists' right to control the process of production and make business decisions for its restriction in areas deemed a hazard to the reproduction of labour power.[32] It follows that the reproduction of capitalist class domination and relations of production require institutional innovation and an equilibrium of class

---

28 Marx 1962a, p. 300.
29 Marx 1962a, pp. 280–1.
30 Marx 1962a, p. 249.
31 Compare Lipietz 1987, p. 15; see also Marx 1962a, pp. 312–13.
32 These settlements may also be conducive to the establishment of productivist dynamics because they potentially shift the focus of capitalist competition from work hours to productivity, or, in Marx words, from 'absolute' to 'relative surplus value'. Compare Marx 1962a, p. 432.

relations of forces that allows for implementing stabilising arrangements. Said equilibrium exists if capital is strong enough to control production and weak enough to be prepared for settlements and, conversely, if labour is strong enough to achieve settlements and too weak to take control of production.

The connection of Poulantzas's theorisation of capitalism to this line of argument is revealed if we compare it with the gang of four's. Jessop's theoretical problematic is, in his own words, 'the inherent improbability of stable capital accumulation' and the need for the capital relation to be embedded in market as well as extra-economic institutions.[33] This reflects the gang of four's concern with social cohesion. In contrast, Poulantzas's problematic can be said to emphasise the 'inherent improbability of stable class domination' and the need for an institutional framework addressing this problem. He discusses social cohesion only in a *second* step, which corresponds to my emphasis on the primacy of class politics.[34]

Developing this problematic, Poulantzas argues that one of the conditions of existence of capitalist relations of production and capitalist class domination is the existence of the capitalist state. Accordingly, he sets out to supplement Marx's analysis at the level of the CMP with a 'theory of the capitalist state',[35] starting from the following question: 'why, in general, does the bourgeoisie seek to maintain its domination by having recourse precisely to the national-popular State – to the modern representative state with all its characteristic institutions?'[36]

Poulantzas provides an answer by highlighting the 'relative *separation* of the State and the economic sphere' under capitalist conditions, which did not exist to the same extent in pre-capitalist social orders.[37] The fact that workers are in a subordinate position in the process of production, and yet are equal to capitalists in terms of their juridical status, means that there are limits to the

---

33   Jessop 2002a, p. 1.
34   This is also the dividing line between Poulantzas and the regulation approach of Michel Aglietta (2000) and Alain Lipietz (1998). With their focus on the expanded reproduction of total social capital, the 'regulationists' tend to see the extraction of surplus labour as always already given. Poulantzas, in contrast, explores how it is secured.
35   Poulantzas 1978, p. 123. This is consistent with how Marx envisaged his project of a critique of political economy, which remained unfinished. He set out to analyse the 'system of bourgeois economy' by producing books on 'capital, landed property, wage labour; the state, foreign trade, the world market' (Marx 1969, p. 7). When he died in 1883, he had only managed to complete the first volume of *Capital*.
36   Poulantzas 1978, p. 12; compare Pashukanis 1978, p. 139.
37   Compare Poulantzas 1978, p. 18; 1973, pp. 29–32.

domination of the capitalists over the workers. In other words, those exercising direct control over production must be distinct from those exercising direct control over the law. Otherwise, there would be no independent instance that could safeguard formal equality before the law. Correspondingly, workers can only be free juridically if there is the rule of law, which rests on the existence of an ensemble of independent apparatuses monopolising 'legitimate violence'.[38] This instance is the state or, more precisely, the 'capitalist type of state', whose 'distinguishing features' are 'the relative separation of the economic from the political, and the relative autonomy of the State from the dominant classes and fractions'.[39] In sum, capitalist relations of production only exist if those who control production cannot legitimately use direct and immediate violence to enforce their control. Poulantzas concludes that 'state concentration of armed forces and the disarming-demilitarization of private sectors' is 'a precondition of established capitalist exploitation'.[40]

Yet the monopoly of legitimate violence resulting from this process of concentration can only be reproduced, over the medium term, if state apparatuses resorting to force also accept the rule of law.[41] This is normally ensured through the existence of universal suffrage,[42] which increases the accountability of political leaders to the population and allows voters to sanction behaviour of state officials that is deemed illegitimate or illegal. Universal suffrage also makes the state appear as 'the incarnation of the general interest of the people'[43] – and does so despite protecting the exploitation of workers by legitimising the control of the capitalists over production. Stanley W. Moore summarises this in his phrase: 'When exploitation takes the form of exchange, dictatorship may take the form of democracy'.[44]

---

38 Poulantzas 1978, p. 82; compare Weber 2005.
39 Poulantzas 1974, p. 313.
40 Poulantzas 1978 p. 82. In this context, Poulantzas also argues that capitalist relations of production are not purely economic. The state may be separate from production, but it is not fully detached from it. After all, capitalist production involves relations of ownership that only exist if the state guarantees people's right to own, sell and purchase labour power. Poulantzas states: 'What is involved here is not a real externality, such as would exist if the State intervened in the economy only from the outside. The *separation is nothing other than the capitalist form of the presence of the political in the constitution and reproduction of the relations of production*' (1978, pp. 18–19).
41 Poulantzas 1978, p. 80.
42 Poulantzas 1978, p. 226.
43 Poulantzas 1973, p. 230.
44 Moore 1957, p. 85.

In conclusion, Poulantzas gives a twofold response to his question. First, he engages in a retroductive argument, that is, he establishes that the existence of a capitalist state constitutes one of the conditions of existence of capitalist relations of production.[45] This implies that capitalists have little choice but to operate in and through state apparatuses. If they turned against the state, they would turn against the capitalist relations of production as well. Many capitalists may advocate 'small government', but very few wish to abandon government altogether.

Second, Poulantzas addresses the reproduction of capitalist relations of production and the capitalist type of state by arguing that representative democracy is best suited to safeguarding the separation between production and the state over the medium term. It is, to use Vladimir Illich Lenin's words, 'the best possible shell for capitalism'.[46] This implies that there is a strategic incentive for capitalists to accept representative democracy. Poulantzas expresses this by portraying this state form as 'normal' and distinguishing it from 'exceptional' regimes such as fascism and military dictatorship.[47]

The Capitalist State and Class Domination

How does Poulantzas's account of the capitalist state relate to his theoretical interest in the improbability of capitalist class domination, and how is this improbability dealt with in capitalist social orders? Poulantzas stresses that the capitalist state is the key instance rendering capitalist class domination durable. Accordingly, he describes his own 'task' as discovering how the separation between production and the state 'jointly sets up agents of production at the juridico-political level, as political and juridical

---

45   Retroduction is a type of inference that proceeds by asking 'what are the conditions of the possibility for the existence of object (x)?' (compare Gallas 2011, pp. 98–9; Sayer 1979, pp. 114–17). It can be distinguished from functionalist inferences that derive the existence of an object from the reproduction requirements of another (compare Gallas 2011, pp. 101–2).
46   Lenin 1977, p. 17.
47   Poulantzas 1974, p. 313. He qualifies this assessment somewhat in his later book *State, Power, Socialism* (1978). In his view, the 1970s crisis in the centres of capitalism is characterised by the rise of a new state form, 'authoritarian statism', in which 'fascistic elements or tendencies appear in the democratic form of the State to a much more marked degree than previously' (Poulantzas 1978, pp. 209–10; compare Jessop 2011).

"individuals-subjects", deprived of their economic determination and, consequently, of their class membership'.[48]

Following Poulantzas, the state's separation from production also implies that the tension between the juridical freedom of workers and their economic subordination at the level of production can spill over into the realm of the state.[49] He indicates that this tension only exists if the state is independent, to some degree, from the dominant class, which in turn implies that the dominated classes occupy positions within it.[50] They may even establish 'centres of opposition to the power classes in the State'.[51]

This is most visible, at least under 'normal' conditions, in the 'political scene' of parliament and government.[52] Here, parties with a mass base in the working class operate, which may make demands at odds with certain aspects of capitalist class domination.[53] As a result, the overall durability of capitalist social orders hinges on the capacity of the state apparatuses to ensure working-class representatives refrain from pursuing policies or altering the state's *modus operandi* in ways that go 'too far' in terms of infringing on the capitalists' right to control the process of production.[54]

Poulantzas concludes that the antagonism between workers and capitalists traverses not only production but also the state. Accordingly, the state is not a neutral instance expressing the 'general will' of the people – even if, under the rule of law and, potentially, universal suffrage, it presents itself in such a way.[55] Furthermore, as the presence of representatives of the working class in the state shows, it is neither simply an instrument in the hands of the ruling class. Poulantzas concludes that the capitalist state is both a site of class conflict *and* an instance suppressing, decelerating and deflecting it. This is captured in his most famous phrase, which articulates the *active* role of the state apparatuses in terms of containing the class antagonism with their *passive* role as a reflection of an equilibrium of class relations of forces. He argues that the capitalist state should be seen as 'the *specific material condensation* of a

---

48   Poulantzas 1973, p. 128.
49   Compare Poulantzas 1978, p. 19.
50   Poulantzas 1978, pp. 140–3.
51   Poulantzas 1978, p. 142.
52   Poulantzas 1973, p. 230.
53   Compare Poulantzas 1973, p. 220. In this context, note the attempt of socialist forces in the Labour Party to establish control over city councils, and the resultant attack of the Thatcherites on the local state (see below).
54   Compare Poulantzas 1978, p. 142; Marx 1973, p. 43.
55   Poulantzas 1978, p. 156.

relationship of forces among classes and class fractions'.[56] If these relations of forces, reinforced by the mode of operation of the state apparatuses, favour capital overall, the capitalist type of state has a stabilising effect on capitalist class domination.

The term 'material condensation' not only implies that the state reflects class relations, but also that it has effects actively shaping these relations. Accordingly, Poulantzas derives four aspects of capitalist statehood from the existence of the capitalist relations of production – again by partly resorting to retroductive arguments:[57] the division between manual and mental labour; citizenship; the rule of law; and the existence of nationhood. All these aspects of statehood are reflections of the 'institutional materiality' of the state,[58] and they all counteract the improbability of capitalist class domination.

First of all, Poulantzas stresses that ideological relations are present in the constitution of capitalist relations of production alongside their economic and political aspects.[59] Following him, capitalist relations of production entail a historically specific division of labour, that is, the division between manual and intellectual labour, or planning and execution.[60] This division has the effect of legitimising the hierarchies existing in production: it emphasises alleged differences in expertise. Against this backdrop, Poulantzas argues that the existence of the state has the effect of duplicating the division between manual and intellectual labour.[61] After all, bureaucrats mostly carry out intellectual labour. At the same time, state apparatuses safeguard this division by employing, producing and reproducing a 'specialized professional corps'[62] and monopolising knowledge – be it through co-ordinating the elaboration of economic and political strategies, running institutions of public education like schools and universities, establishing an integrated legal and administrative system or standardising language.[63] All in all, the state plays a key role in the production of knowledge that contributes to legitimising the existing division of labour.

Second, the rule of law has an 'effect of isolation' on the population by giving people the status of '"individuals" – that is juridical-political persons who enjoy

---

56 Poulantzas 1978, p. 129.
57 Poulantzas 1978, pp. 49–50.
58 Poulantzas 1978, p. 49.
59 Poulantzas 1978, p. 17.
60 Poulantzas 1978, pp. 54, 59.
61 Poulantzas 1978, p. 56.
62 Poulantzas 1978, p. 57.
63 Poulantzas 1978, pp. 32, 56–9, 75; compare Stützle 2011.

certain freedoms'.[64] This presents an obstacle to the formation of a collective identity for workers in their opposition to capital.

Third, the rule of law and the state's monopoly of legitimate violence alter the terrain of class struggle: They 'contribute to shifting the class struggle away from permanent civil war (periodic and regular armed conflict) towards those new forms of political and trade-union organization of the popular masses'.[65] If class conflict occurs within a legal framework, this potentially defuses the threat it poses for the reproduction of capitalist relations of production: the 'legalisation' of class conflict is conducive to negotiating settlements and disarticulating questions of domination. Moreover, it potentially reduces class struggle to an economic struggle over conditions of remuneration.[66] Both points reiterate Marx's argument that class struggle can contribute to the overall stability of a capitalist social order. Accordingly, Poulantzas speaks of 'capitalist law' as a 'framework of cohesion' that binds capitalist social formations together under the leadership of the dominant classes.[67]

Fourth, capitalist relations of production entail individualisation. They are accompanied by a historically specific spatio-temporal matrix, which reflects this 'atomization'.[68] Poulantzas argues that space under capitalist conditions is *'serial, fractured, parcelled, cellular and irreversible'*, and that time is *'segmented, serial, equally divided, cumulative and irreversible'*.[69] Both these characterisations mirror the fragmentation caused by the specific division of labour inherent in the capitalist relations of production. However, durable patterns of production only emerge if this tendency is countered through the existence of a state that homogenises space and time by turning them into territory and tradition,[70] and creating the spatio-temporal matrix of the nation.[71] In the process, a 'people-nation' is created.[72] Its existence counters the divisive results of the isolation effect and binds the population of a territory together, overriding the centrifugal effect of the class antagonism inherent in the relations of production.[73]

---

64 Poulantzas 1973, pp. 213, 189.
65 Poulantzas 1978, p. 82.
66 Poulantzas 1973, p. 132.
67 Poulantzas 1973, pp. 87, 88.
68 Poulantzas 1978, p. 63, 98.
69 Poulantzas 1978, pp. 103, 110.
70 Poulantzas 1978, pp. 99, 107.
71 Poulantzas 1978, p. 114.
72 Poulantzas 1978, pp. 112–14.
73 Compare Poulantzas 1978, p. 63.

In conclusion, Poulantzas explains how the existence of a state counteracts certain destabilisation tendencies inherent in the capitalist relations of production. For members of the dominant classes, this happens through the emergence of a 'power bloc',[74] which unites them behind the leadership of a hegemonic fraction. This fraction is capable of securing the consent of the members of other fractions of capital to an economic and political agenda in line with its own interests. Characteristically, state apparatuses are selective regarding the internal representation of economic and political strategies, that is, they reflect and present these strategies in particular ways and thus favour some over others.[75] Correspondingly, the hegemony of a certain fraction of capital relies on key state apparatuses working in its favour and successfully influencing other apparatuses.[76] But hegemony in this context does not just mean that the fraction in control is adjusting the competences and hierarchy of the state apparatuses to its own agenda. The formation of a 'functional trans-state network rising above and short-circuiting every level of state apparatus and branch' is just as important.[77] It fosters institutional integration and ensures that the 'hard core' of the state, that is, its key 'command posts', remain beyond the reach of the dominated classes.[78] The trans-state network achieves this by exploiting legal 'loopholes', which permit interventions that override democratic decision-making and even the rule of law.[79] This suggests that state

---

74 Poulantzas 1978, p. 127.
75 Poulantzas 1978, p. 135.
76 Traditionally, the City has been the hegemonic fraction within the British power bloc. Its 'anchors' in the British state system are the Treasury and the Bank of England. Compare Gallas 2008.
77 Poulantzas 1978, p. 137.
78 Poulantzas 1978, p. 143. The traditional hold of the British aristocracy over the state is a case in point. For centuries, there has been a network of aristocratic elements in the higher echelons of the civil service, parliament and government, which has stabilised capitalist class domination by controlling access to the key institutions of the state, most importantly the Bank of England and the Treasury, and of the civil service in general (Ingham 1984, pp. 139–42). Even today, many leading British politicians and civil servants have been educated in public schools and Oxbridge institutions (Cadwalladr 2008), that is, places whose ethos is traditionally informed by the gentlemanly values of the British aristocracy (Cain and Hopkins 2002, p. 45).
79 Poulantzas 1978, p. 84. An example is the relationship of command between the Thatcher government and the leadership of British police forces during the miners' strike, whose legality was dubious, and which was instrumental in cracking down on the strikers with brute force (see below).

managers may act both 'in accordance with the law and against the law',[80] giving them the opportunity to defend the status quo and sabotage working-class advances within the state. If all else fails, they can resort to legitimising their acts by invoking the '*higher interests of the state (raison d'Etat)*'.[81]

In contrast, for the dominated classes, state-mediated stabilisation works through numerous mechanisms of fragmentation that serve to disarticulate the divide between capital and labour, and weaken the organisational basis of the working class as a collective actor. Moreover, the capitalist legal system deflects, formalises and decelerates class conflict by tendentially confining struggles within the institutional limits of their originating context.[82] As a result, economic class struggle over the conditions of remuneration is prevented from spilling over into political class struggle over the control of the state apparatuses – and into ideological class struggle over the conditions of the production and distribution of science and knowledge.[83]

Poulantzas concludes that there is a tendency for the capitalist type of state to disorganise the dominated classes at the political level by constituting the population as a people-nation, and to organise the dominant classes by orchestrating the exclusion of subaltern groups from the core apparatuses of the state.[84] In sum, he contends that a capitalist type of state, ideally of the representative-democratic type, facilitates capitalist class domination by atomising and, at the same time, reuniting the population.

---

80 Poulantzas 1978, p. 85.
81 Poulantzas 1978, p. 84. An infamous example is the decision by Tony Blair in December 2006 to close an investigation by the Serious Fraud Office into alleged corruption at British arms manufacturer BAE Systems, which was said to involve the Saudi Royal family. Blair justified his move by arguing that it would harm British interests to upset the Saudis and lose their co-operation in security matters (Leigh and Evans 2006; 2007).
82 Poulantzas 1973, pp. 136–7. The history of the British labour movement provides many examples of industrial conflicts being weakened because workers did not manage to build political support for their aims. See, for example, my account of the 1984–5 miners' strike in this book.
83 Poulantzas 1973, p. 69; 1978, p. 45. A counter-hegemonic, socialist political project capable of threatening capitalist class domination will only emerge if such a spillover takes place. Put differently, a socialist transformation strategy will only be successful if there is a re-articulation of economic, political and ideological class struggle.
84 Poulantzas 1973, p. 189; compare 1978, p. 140.

The Field of Validity of Neo-Poulantzasian Political Analysis

Poulantzas provides a consistent account of capitalist statehood, but there is a fundamental problem with it. On the one hand, he presents the capitalist type of state as a 'class State',[85] which mirrors his theoretical problematic and his focus on the capitalist relations of production. On the other hand, he concedes that capitalist social formations are pervaded by non-class relations of domination, which are articulated with historically concrete states:

> Relations of power do not exhaust class relations and may go a certain way beyond them. Of course, they will still have class pertinency, continuing to be located, and to have a stake, in the terrain of political domination. But they do not rest on the same foundation as the social class division of labour, and are neither a mere consequence nor homologues or isomorphs of that division; this is most notably in the case of relations between men and women ... Now, although these power relations stretch beyond class relations, the State cannot keep aloof from them.[86]

Despite his awareness of non-class relations of domination and their articulation with historically concrete states, Poulantzas neither explains them at the level of the CMP nor establishes their articulation with class relations when analysing social formations.[87] This is unsurprising: at the level of theory, it is not possible to infer the existence of non-class relations of domination from the existence of capitalist relations of production. Consequently, there are limits to the explanatory power of Poulantzas's theory of the capitalist state. This becomes a problem when he examines capitalist social formations and indicates that his analyses are exhaustive. When he looks at the rise of 'authoritarian statism' in the 1970s, for example, his stated aim is to capture the 'present-day State' in the 'dominant ... capitalist countries'.[88] This suggests that there is a gap between his claims regarding the field of validity of his empirical analyses and the actual scope of his theoretical framework.

Poulantzas seems to recognise this problem and attempts to argue it away. He indicates that said gap does not exist because, in the last instance, non-class relations of domination are manifested inside class relations, which means that

---

[85] Poulantzas 1978, p. 44.
[86] Poulantzas 1978, p. 43.
[87] Compare Nowak 2011, p. 124.
[88] Poulantzas 1978, p. 204.

their link to the state does not require a separate explanation. He tries to show this by examining the relationship between gender and class relations:

> Through its activity and effects the State intervenes in all the relations of power in order to assign them a class pertinency and enmesh them in the web of class powers. The State thereby takes over heterogeneous powers which relay and recharge the economic, political and ideological powers of the dominant class. The power exhibited in sexual relations between men and women, which is certainly dissimilar to that of class relations, is nevertheless invested in the latter and is mediated and reproduced as a class relation by the State and the company or factory: class power therefore traverses, utilizes and gears down that other power, assigning to it a given significance.[89]

This line of argument appears flawed. Gender relations may be 'invested' in class relations, but it does not follow that they are 'mediated and reproduced as a class relation'. After all, the reproduction of labour power hinges on the performance of domestic labour. This suggests, at least under conditions of patriarchal relations of reproduction, that class relations are also 'invested' in gender relations. Similarly, if class domination 'traverses' and even 'utilises' gender domination, the reverse is also true. Hence there is no overall necessity that class domination 'gears down' gender domination or 'assigns to it a given significance'. In fact, Poulantzas's argument appears circular: the penultimate sentence of the cited paragraph implies that gender relations are reproduced as class relations because the relations of production have a primary role in capitalist social formations; the last sentence indicates that there is a primacy of the relations of production because gender relations are reproduced as class relations. As a result, I concur with Jessop who criticises Poulantzas for his 'class reductionism'.[90]

Some authors seek to defend Poulantzas from such charges by highlighting passages such as the 'anti-reductionist' one cited earlier and by extending his definition of the capitalist state as a material condensation of class relations to gender and race relations.[91] I contend that this does not resolve the problem: Poulantzas's definition of the state is no longer grounded theoretically if it is modified without substantiating this modification at the level of the CMP.

---

89 Poulantzas 1978, pp. 43–4.
90 Jessop 1985, p. 341.
91 Bruff 2008, p. 7; Bretthauer 2011, p. 85.

Put differently, simply redefining the state in a pluralist fashion leaves the gap in question wide open. It follows that upholding claims to generality would require a wide-ranging theoretical effort. The capitalist state would have to be constructed as a theoretical object in ways that go beyond the relations of production and, hence, beyond Poulantzas.

Even if such an endeavour were feasible, embarking on it would be beyond the scope of this book, which is focused on providing a political analysis of the Thatcherite era. Thus I have opted for a different strategy: I suggest closing the gap by retaining Poulantzas's theory of the capitalist state as it is, whilst limiting the field of validity of my empirical analysis to the class character of the (British) state (in the Thatcherite era). I will show in due course that despite this serious restriction, there is still value-added in looking at Thatcherism from a Poulantzasian perspective. It enables us to reconcile the two sides of the Hall-Jessop debate, and establish the continuities and discontinuities of neoliberalism in Britain. Furthermore, it needs to be emphasised that even if the resulting analysis is not exhaustive, it remains open to future extensions.[92]

In conclusion, Poulantzas develops a consistent theorisation of capitalism and of the capitalist type of state, but if we want to base our analyses of historically concrete states on his work, we have to restrict their field of validity. This also implies that a return to Poulantzas is premised on abandoning his implicit epistemological claim to be exhaustive both at the level of theory and empirical analysis. One reason why I describe my own approach as 'neo-Poulantzasian' and not just 'Poulantzasian' is to highlight its epistemological modesty: it provides an analysis that is limited in scope but still useful. Despite this revision, I contend that Poulantzas affords us with a theorisation of capitalism and the capitalist type of state, which, thanks to its internal coherence, meets challenge (3) – the challenge of providing a consistent theoretical grounding for the concepts of political analysis.

Class Politics, Economic Order Politics, Regime of Condensation: A Framework for Political Analysis

Poulantzas called for a research agenda concerned with how historically concrete states are reproduced in and through class struggle, that is, how state

---

92 Obviously, it follows from restricting the field of validity of my analysis that I cannot claim it is superior to all others in all respects. In fact, many of them are very useful for their purposes, especially those provided by Hall et al. and Jessop et al.

apparatuses produce and secure capitalist relations of production and capitalist class domination. Unfortunately, he never developed a concise account of how to transform this agenda into an analytical toolkit. If we want to build on Poulantzas, we have to distil a conceptual framework from his work by building on a range of different theoretical arguments and empirical observations.

In his 1985 book on Poulantzas, Jessop attempted to carry out this task. He identified a strategic theme in Poulantzas's work:

> His research agenda ... focuses on the micro-physics of power and the nature of the state form as a strategic terrain. It also treats hegemony much more in terms of the state's organisational form as a system of political class domination than in terms of a specific type of global political project. This confirms the importance Poulantzas attached to the idea that the state is a social relation – the material condensation of a balance among class forces.[93]

Jessop adds: 'Poulantzas also argues ... that the relative autonomy and class unity of the capitalist state should be seen as the resultant of the complex interaction of micro-policies and strategies'.[94] Jessop concludes that strategies are the hidden link between the abstract-formal determinations of the state at the level of the CMP and the political processes taking place within historically concrete states. He suggests that the tendencies of the capitalist type of state are brought to bear at the level of the social formation through individual and collective actors who are developing and implementing strategies. These strategies emerge – and are mobilised for the reproduction of the capitalist relations of production – due to the *modus operandi* of state apparatuses. Jessop thus recommends replacing Poulantzas's notion of a 'structural mechanism' creating hierarchical internal representations of exogenous information inside the state with 'strategic selectivity'.[95] He then introduces several '"middle range" concepts' that are strategic in nature.[96] These concepts can be used to analyse how political processes reflect, reproduce and undermine abstract-formal determinations of the capitalist type of state in historically concrete situations. Unsurprisingly, these concepts re-emerge in Jessop et al's

---

93   Jessop 1985, pp. 340–1.
94   Jessop 1985, p. 342.
95   Poulantzas 1978, p. 134; Jessop 1985, p. 349.
96   Poulantzas 1985, p. 344.

later analyses of Thatcherism. More generally, Jessop argues that by developing strategic concepts, Poulantzas developed a novel and innovative research framework, preparing 'the ground for a decisive break in Marxist political analysis'.[97]

In my view, Jessop's intervention is a useful way of elaborating on Poulantzas's claims that the construction of the abstract-formal object 'capitalist type of state' requires one to reflect upon real-concrete factors such as the status of the class relations of forces and specific institutions; and that analysing historically concrete states is premised on the construction of such an object. By introducing concepts such as 'accumulation strategy', 'state strategy' and 'hegemonic project', Jessop highlights the articulation between the forms that constitute the CMP, real-concrete institutions such as the legal limitation of the working day, and specific agendas of political leaders. Accordingly, I follow Jessop in terms of his emphasis on strategy.

And yet, I depart from Jessop's line at the point where the articulation of his concepts reflects his own theoretical problematic more than Poulantzas's. He focuses primarily on social cohesion and economic order politics and only secondarily on class domination and class politics. According to Jessop, the building blocks of a successful 'one nation' hegemonic project are a mutually reinforcing social base, accumulation strategy and state strategy. In his view, the accumulation of capital is the key issue to be addressed in the creation and reproduction of a durable capitalist social formation.

Following Marx, I want to turn this line of argument on its head. In *Capital*, Marx suggests that the extraction of surplus labour is a necessary (but not sufficient) condition for capital accumulation. Now, the ability to secure surplus extraction is exactly what capitalist control over production consists in. It follows that capitalist class domination cannot be seen as an effect of accumulation of capital. Rather, it is its precondition. In order for any of the fruits of production to be appropriated, they have to be produced first.

As a consequence of this insight, I will frame my own neo-Poulantzasian approach to political analysis by moving beyond Jessop and combining some of his concepts with novel ones. Operating on the grounds of Poulantzas's theoretical problematic implies that the politics of leadership and domination in capitalism is concerned with reducing the improbability of capitalist class domination by creating, protecting and modernising the institutions supporting it. This tends to be done at different levels.

---

[97] Jessop 1985, p. 342.

First of all, political leaders acting on behalf of the power bloc will be inclined to devise strategies that safeguard the continuous extraction of surplus labour. They will do this in part by directly addressing the class antagonism in production. For example, they will introduce legal regulations that concern the conditions of the consumption of labour power, 'juridify' industrial action or interfere with them with the help of repression or public proclamations. If there is a degree of coherence to these interventions, we can speak of an *extraction strategy*.

Second, political leaders will also try to make people consent to, or at least tolerate, policies that largely favour the capitalist class and entrench their control over production. If they do it, again, with a degree of coherence, I contend that they are governing via a *mode of leadership and domination* (see above). Both the *extraction strategy* and the *mode of leadership and domination* belong to the realm of *class politics* because they *directly* address class relations and class domination. If the strategies formulated in the fields are compatible (meaning that they do not undermine or cancel out one another), I speak of a *class political regime*.

Nevertheless, it is important to stress, in a Jessopian vein, that capital accumulation retroacts on class domination by potentially reinforcing it – especially when competition is mainly based on increasing relative surplus value. Hence successful interventions in the realm of economic order politics reduce the improbability of capitalist class domination, albeit *indirectly*. Like Jessop, I thus propose to speak of an *accumulation strategy*, which targets the institutional preconditions of the accumulation of capital at the level of production, and a *state strategy*, which addresses the institutional preconditions of the accumulation of capital at the level of the state. Again, if they are consistent with each other, I contend there is an *economic-political order*.

Finally, if the class political regime and the economic policy regime conform to each other, I refer to the result as a *regime of condensation*. This overarching concept refers to a global strategy of stabilising a capitalist social formation. It describes the active condensation of class relations of forces in and through the state, which has the effect of organising the power bloc and disorganising the working class (see Figure 1).[98]

By integrating concepts that address both the fields of class politics *and* economic order politics, I contend that my approach meets challenge (2), the

---

98   When I speak of 'consistency', 'conformity', 'coherence', 'compatibility' or 'correspondence' in the context of strategies, I refer to formal or substantive unity in Jessop's understanding of the terms (see above).

< Direct Effect on Class Domination >   < Indirect Effect on Class Domination >

Extraction Strategy	Mode of Leadership and Domination	Accumulation Strategy	State Strategy
↕↕↕	↕↕↕	↕↕↕	↕↕↕
Class Political Regime		Economic-Political Order	
↕↕↕		↕↕↕	
Regime of Condensation			

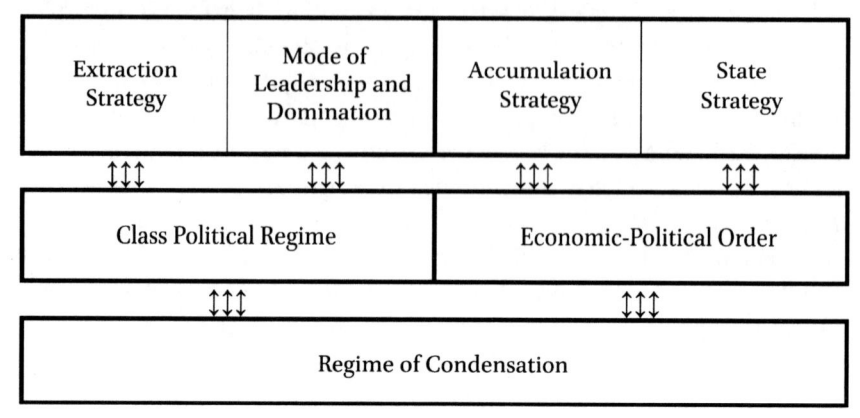

FIGURE 1   *Fields and levels of neo-Poulantzasian political analysis*

challenge of developing an inclusive conceptual framework. It may not provide a synthesis of Hall et al. and Jessop et al., but it does include themes from both sides. It rests on an account of hegemony akin to the gang of four's, yet it still chooses class politics as its entry point – just like Hall et al. Moreover, it is based on Poulantzas's theorisation of capitalism, which both sides hold in high regard.

The Cycle of Class Struggle

I contend that there is a strong link between the extraction of surplus labour and the overall subordination of the working class within a social formation. This is consistent with Poulantzas's theoretical problematic and my assumption that class politics has priority over economic order politics. At the level of the CMP, this says no more than that there is a link between economic order politics and class politics, and that the former should be examined in terms of its (indirect) effect on capitalist class domination, rather than just in its own right. At the level of the social formation, in contrast, the articulation between the two fields shifts constantly. It changes because decision-making and the implementation of policies change political agendas, and because new economic, political, and cultural developments reorder the priorities of political leaders.[99]

---

99   Around 1988, for example, class politics ceased to be the main concern of the Thatcherites because they had successfully marginalised organised labour by that time.

In line with my theoretical problematic, I assume that the historically concrete articulations between class politics and economic order politics reflect what I call the cycle of class struggle. This contention is based, once again, on Poulantzas. In *Fascism and Dictatorship*, he distinguishes between 'offensive' and 'defensive steps' of class actors. The former refer to collective efforts with the aim of making material gains; the latter refer to attempts to prevent the antagonist from doing so.[100] Apart from that, Poulantzas refers to 'turns' in class struggle, which occur when an advance of a class actor falters and is reversed.[101] Such turns can be explained with reference to three mechanisms inherent in the CMP:

(1) Thanks to competition, the material structure of capitalist production and the capitalist division of labour are constantly being reorganised,[102] which also means that class relations shift.
(2) The accumulation of capital is a crisis-prone process due to various obstacles (shortages in money capital, means of production or workers; working class resistance; technological change; a lack of demand), which are moved around rather than eliminated; economic crises tend to shift the conditions of class struggle.[103]
(3) The course of class struggle is unpredictable to a degree, because it is not fully determined by the mode of production but also reflects real-concrete institutional configurations and historically contingent choices by made by collective actors.[104]

In sum, the steps and turns in class struggle reflect shifting relations of forces, which are visible in the demands made by class actors, the mobilising force behind these demands, and the material outcome of class struggles. The fact that there are constant shifts in relations of forces also suggests that class actors are forced to continuously reformulate their strategies and start anew, which is why I refer to a 'cycle'.

---

100   Poulantzas 1974, p. 50.
101   Poulantzas 1974, p. 54.
102   'Constant revolutionising of production, uninterrupted disturbance of all social conditions, everlasting uncertainty and agitation distinguish the bourgeois epoch from all earlier ones. All fixed, fast-frozen relations, with their train of ancient and venerable prejudices and opinions, are swept away, all new-formed ones become antiquated before they can ossify' (Marx and Engels 1952, p. 465, my translation).
103   Harvey 2011, pp. 7–11.
104   Gallas 2011.

Class Leadership and Strategy

My description of the 'cycle of class struggle' implies that political leaders make strategic calculations and determine their agendas against the backdrop of class conflict and constantly shifting relations of class forces. If they represent the capitalist class, they are inclined to subscribe to political strategies preserving the capitalist status quo by organising the power bloc and disorganising the working class. If they represent the working class, they are likely to work on improving working conditions and defend gains against encroachment. In short, political decision-makers have a significant impact on class struggles and are often directly involved in them.

Obviously, this is a far-reaching claim concerning the political agency of individuals and groups. Sceptics may point out that political leaders usually do not use the terms my analysis is based on when they make strategic calculations or describe their positions. They rarely claim to be 'representatives' of 'the power bloc' or the 'working class', and they usually do not claim to orchestrate 'offensive' or 'defensive' steps. And crucially, many of them would object to the claim that they are involved in 'class struggle'. It follows that my analytical terms do not represent direct reflections of how most politicians experience their activities.

In light of this, some people may say that my framework is based on arbitrary attributions. In order to refute this claim, I want to address two questions in this section:

(1) What is the connection between political strategy and class struggle?
(2) How is this connection experienced by the individuals involved in political decision-making?

Regarding question (1), I would like to point out that my concepts reflect my Marxian understanding of capitalism: political leaders cannot escape the fact that they operate in an environment shaped by strategic selectivities based on tendencies inherent in the CMP – no matter whether or not they recognise this. In other words, the tendencies in question constitute conditions of their activities and have constraining or enabling effects. This becomes clear, for example, when we look at taxation. The capacity of governments to act is compromised if they are not able to collect taxes. Taxation in turn requires capitalist class domination to be intact and capitalist accumulation to take place. This creates a strong incentive for government representatives to engage in acts that have a unifying effect on the power bloc and a disorganising effect on the working class. In other words, there is a strong incentive for government representatives to exercise leadership on behalf of the capitalist class. This is done, most importantly, by identifying the needs of 'business' (or of certain key sectors of the 'business' world), prioritising some of these needs over others, and developing an according political agenda. As a result, the strategies I refer to emerge.

Under conditions of universal suffrage, exercising capitalist class leadership along these lines poses a challenge. After all, government agendas have to be based on a degree of popular consent. It follows that concessions to subaltern groups are part of the repertoire of techniques used by governments operating in a capitalist environment. Moreover, it can be inferred that governments do not necessarily always exercise capitalist class leadership, and that they can be divided along class lines.[105]

Nevertheless, if there is universal suffrage, government constitutes a privileged strategic point for the exercise of such leadership. After all, democratically elected governments are in a good position to claim that they represent the nation as a whole, not just the power bloc, which also means that their members are well positioned to mediate between the different fractions of capital and enforce unity.

Along these lines, Jessop argues that the strategic selectivity of state apparatuses is crucial for the unification and homogenisation of capitalist class activities into coherent strategies (see above). This implies that those who control state apparatuses play a key role in developing and controlling these strategies. Put differently, the strategic calculations of political leaders operating on behalf of the power bloc tend to trigger its offensive or defensive steps.

The prerequisites of successful working-class leadership are quite different. Due to the constraining effect of the CMP, government does not constitute a privileged strategic point for exercising it. Quite the contrary: governments of capitalist states are prone to pursuing a strategy focused on what is presented as the 'national interest'. Most of the time, this coincides with the interests of the power bloc, not least because governments are interested in implementing a successful accumulation strategy that secures their tax base. Accordingly,

---

[105] Accordingly, Poulantzas points out that there are multiple points within the capitalist state where capitalist class leadership can be exercised: 'Given the complex articulation of various state apparatuses and branches (which is often expressed in a distinction between real power and the conspicuous formal power of political arena), the formation of a Left government does not necessarily entail that the Left exercises real control over all, or even certain, state apparatuses. This all the more so in that the state institutional structure allows the bourgeoisie to meet a popular accession to power by permutating the sites of real and formal power' (1978, p. 138).

Labour governments in Britain have time and again acted in line with the interests of the City and against those of organised labour, most visibly by cutting benefits and reining in the welfare state. This served to deepen divides between the leadership and the rank-and-file, and between the industrial and the political wings of organised labour.

In other words, governments involving parties with mass support from workers are likely to have a divisive effect on the working class (unless there is a revolutionary situation). They often opt for rejecting working-class demands and undermine or at least outmanoeuvre working-class forces making these demands. The political leaders of the working class are faced with the difficult strategic task of organising working-class unity in the face of the existence of strong selectivities in the state that work against it.

In contrast to the level of government, the level of the production represents a privileged point for exercising working-class leadership. There is a tendency of workers to form coalitions in order to negotiate over the conditions of the consumption of labour power. After all, there is an incentive for workers to unify: the higher their degree of unity, the greater their capacity to cut out competition and exercise bargaining power. This can potentially be channelled into class organisation.

Obviously, there are counter-tendencies. Most importantly, there is an incentive for individuals or groups to formulate demands reflecting their specific position in production, not the overall position of the working class or the labour movement. If certain groups of workers are in a comparably strong bargaining position, a strategy focused on a single business or a sector of the economy may bring higher-than-average returns; if they are in a very weak bargaining position, it might allow them to win at least some concessions. Both scenarios may lead to workers being co-opted to management agendas and their leaders taking on a dual role also acting as co-managers.

When labour movements emerge, these tendencies and counter-tendencies rarely appear to cancel each other out. Rather, they tend to result in the prevalence of inconsistent and ambiguous strategic orientations: the tendency for class formation is evidenced by the existence of labour movements in almost all developed capitalist settings; the tendency for co-optation by the generally high degree of division among workers. In sum, working-class leadership is likely to appear in conjunction with individualism, sectionalism, nationalism, etc. – possibly within one and the same person or organisation.

Furthermore, there is an important qualification to be made regarding the strategic orientations of working-class leaders. If there is a capitalist state, the exercise of class leadership at the point of production usually takes place in a setting in which class struggles get institutionalised and juridified: there will be institutional forums for negotiations, as well as terms under which industrial action is considered illegitimate or even illegal. Under such conditions, working-class leadership may be exercised, but it is likely that challenges to the control of capitalists over the labour process remain confined to specific aspects of work, such as wages, work hours, training or health and safety. As a result, trade unions possibly act both as instances of working-class leadership and 'mass integrative apparatuses',[106] that is, institutions producing and securing consent among subaltern groups to the capitalist status quo.

Under these circumstances, it is not a given that trade union leaders exercise class leadership, but it is possible.[107] In the British context, the 'Battle of Saltley Gates' in 1972 constitutes an obvious instance of such leadership: a network of trade unionists from different industries orchestrated the shut-down of a coke depot in order to support striking miners, which was crucial in terms of forcing the government to offer a settlement on favourable terms.[108] In the Thatcherite era, many trade unionists adopted class-based strategic orientations almost by default: The clearer it became that Thatcher et al. were intent on destroying their organisations and, in some cases, their industries, the more obvious it was to them that it was necessary to resort to militancy at the level of the shop-floor.

In sum, there is a case to be made for deciphering both government and union activity as potential instances of the exercise of class leadership, and for assuming that the CMP is facilitating the emergence of class strategies. This is neither meant to say that such strategies cannot emerge out of class leadership exercised elsewhere, nor that every single government or union activity constitutes an instance of such leadership. Rather, I propose to examine the activities of governments and unions and to identify those aspects of their activities that can be interpreted as instances of class leadership and strategy. This especially makes sense in the case of the Thatcherite era, where there is substantial evidence for the exercise of class leadership on both sides.

This leads me to question (2), the question as to what are the experiences of the individuals involved. I contend that they do not have to fully grasp the class implications of their interventions so long as these interventions 'work' in terms of having an impact on class relations. This is in line with Marx's assertion that the tendencies and mechanisms constituting the CMP are not necessarily visible.[109]

---

106   Hirsch 1998, p. 78; compare Hyman 1985, p. 104.
107   Compare Hyman 1985, p. 118.
108   See also the case study on the miners' strike.
109   As Marx points out in *Capital* (1962a), there is a tendency for social relations in capitalism

I am not arguing, however, that class struggle is a wholly unintended effect of people's activities and takes place behind their backs. People tend to frame their intentions in terms that accord to the exigencies of everyday practice, not to those of systematic explanation. It follows that if they refer to class domination and class struggle, they tend to use language significantly different from the language of Marxist intellectuals. Yet in so doing, they make class issues addressable in a practical sense – which is not necessarily the same as understanding them fully or even explaining them. In British politics, there are a few obvious examples of this: in the Thatcherite era, industrialists and politicians linked to the power bloc often emphasised the 'right to manage', which was their way of justifying capitalist class domination and the fight against actors contesting it.[110] Similarly, politicians tend to stress that they aim to ensure economic 'growth', which is how they address the need for stable conditions of accumulation and, indirectly, exploitation. This implies that whenever they develop fairly consistent policies around these two themes, they are in the process of shaping the strategies of the power bloc in the fields of class politics and economic order politics, respectively. A similar argument can be made when union representatives speak of 'working people' or, simply, workers, which is often an attempt to facilitate working-class solidarity and organisation. And obviously, there are, to this day, union leaders in Britain who speak the language of class and pursue strategies that are explicit about their class content.[111]

In conclusion, there is no contradiction in saying that actors have intentions and make strategic calculations, and arguing that they do not necessarily speak of 'class struggle' when they partake in strategies invested in it. Materialist political analysis, in large part, consists in translating from the language used in the political scene to an analytical language highlighting the class character of politics in capitalism.

---

to take on fetishised, reified forms. His prime examples are the commodity, money and capital. According to him, actors tend to reproduce these social relations without fully understanding their form and functions. Consequently, they tend not to have a clear grasp of how their activities impact on and are connected to the CMP.

110 On the emergence of this discourse, see Gibbon 1988, p. 155.
111 An example is the recent attempt by Unite, the biggest British union, to get the Labour Party to select working-class candidates for the 2015 general election.

The Steps and Periods of Class Struggle

The fact that political leaders engage in strategic calculations against a backdrop of class conflict explains why they prioritise class politics in certain situations and economic order politics in others. If leaders acting on behalf of the power bloc have successfully facilitated an offensive, for example, they may choose to consolidate this rather than push even further. In such a situation, they will be inclined to concern themselves with economic order politics rather than class politics, because pushing too far may unite and strengthen the antagonist or even weaken labour so much that the reproduction of labour power is no longer guaranteed. Similarly, the political leaders of the working class may opt to consolidate rather than push further if there is a risk of plunging the entire social formation into crisis – especially if they are unwilling or unable to envisage a transition to socialism. Accordingly, it makes sense to supplement Poulantzas's two categories (offensive/defensive step) with a third one: the consolidating step, that is, a step aimed at 'freezing' the relations of forces in their given state and sustaining a situation where neither side makes substantial additional material gains.

This suggests that the accuracy of strategic assessments made by political leaders hinges on their ability to react adequately to a configuration of class relations in a specific conjuncture. There is no reason to assume that their strategies represent the best possible option in a given situation. In other words, strategies can fail and disintegrate – and even if political leaders happen to choose the 'optimal' strategy, the strength of their antagonists could still derail it. Hence, it is possible that a strategy is aborted before the completion of a step in class struggle. Moreover, political leaders sometimes successfully launch a strategy, but fail to co-opt other strategies through unification and homogenisation – a problem that is especially relevant for political leaders of the working class because they are faced with strategic selectivities detrimental to working-class organisation.

All of this calls for further differentiation of the concepts deployed. Poulantzas does so when he implies that each step in the cycle of class struggle can be broken down into component processes. He distinguishes up to four periods within a step:[112]

---

112   Poulantzas only makes these distinctions for offensive steps, which is why I have added their defensive equivalent. Consolidating steps correspond more or less to offensive steps with respect to their component processes, with the difference that material gains are replaced by institutional safeguards for the status quo.

(1) an initial period starting with the onset of the step and ending in the 'point of no return', that is, the point when the side making the step can no longer be prevented from making material gains (or from impeding their antagonist from doing so);[113]
(2) the period from the point of no return to these material gains coming into existence (or coming off the agenda);
(3) the period where the ensuing shift in the relations of forces is first reflected at the level of the state – 'a period characterized by particular instability and ambiguity' (or a return to the status quo ante);[114] and
(4) the 'stabilization' or consolidation of the new (or old) relations of forces.[115]

In the light of the fact that even successful political strategies disintegrate eventually, I would suggest adding a fifth period to this framework: 'erosion', which involves a marked loss of public support for the existing institutional arrangements and social forces sustaining a step and their subsequent fragmentation.[116]

Furthermore, I would argue that Poulantzas's distinctions do not capture very well conjunctures where strategies are already unravelling when they emerge, or where strategies are entirely absent because there is no political force capable of unifying and homogenising political activities. To describe these conjunctures, I propose to use the terms 'actionism' and 'passivity'. The first expression refers to activism for activism's sake, that is, activities that generate much noise but have little real effect. It can be applied to situations where an emerging strategy is already disintegrating. 'Passivity' speaks for itself and is associated with a lack of strategy.

Obviously, these are descriptive categories and, equally obviously, a step can be interrupted at any point. Nevertheless, they are useful: they invite us to identify key moments where the fate of a strategy is decided, and to think about the question as to when exactly an incomplete step has ended and a strategy connected to it has been abandoned.

It is important to stress that speaking of the cyclical nature of steps in class struggle does not imply a pre-determined course of development. It simply highlights the repetitive character of politics under capitalist conditions, where there is a constant process of the emergence, consolidation and disintegration

---

113 Poulantzas 1974, p. 66.
114 Ibid.
115 Poulantzas 1974, p. 67.
116 Note that Bastiaan van Apeldoorn and Henk Overbeek deploy a fairly similar sequence of periods when they discuss the 'life course of hegemonic projects' (2012, pp. 6–7).

of strategies, which reflects the instability caused by class antagonism and capital accumulation. It also emphasises the two-dimensional nature of the dynamic of class conflict: there are both changing relations of forces between the power bloc and the working class, and degrees of escalation expressed by the alternation between 'offensive' and 'consolidating steps'.

The Method of Periodisation

Inspired by Poulantzas's *Fascism and Dictatorship* and the class analytical subtext in Jessop et al's work, my conceptual framework is meant to capture historical developments: it describes the formation, implementation and disintegration of political strategies in different political fields. Accordingly, it will help me to develop a periodisation of the political strategies of the Thatcherites as the group of political leaders acting on behalf of the British power bloc from the late 1970s until the 1990s. This process-centred method of analysis allows me to relate Thatcherite policies to their pre-history and history, and to consider pathdependent features of capitalism in Britain, which explain why these policies appeared plausible, why the Thatcherites commanded large-scale popular support and lost it again, and how the Blairites built on Thatcherism and departed from it.

In line with my conceptual framework, this periodisation combines three threads: I will examine class politics, economic order politics, and their articulation in a regime of condensation. While the periodisation of class politics, by definition, follows the cycle of class struggle, the periodisation of economic order politics does not. After all, the CMP produces effects irreducible to the class relations inherent in it,[117] which creates a disjuncture between the temporality of class politics and economic order politics. Class politics maps neatly onto the cycle of class struggle because strategies in this area emerge as a direct response to this cycle, but strategies in economic order politics do not because they address the exigencies of capital accumulation, which entails a dynamic development different (but not separate) from class struggle.

The most striking illustration of this in recent British history is the course of the Callaghan government. It formulated an embryonic version of the accu-

---

117 These effects are most visible in economic crises, which always affect class relations, but are not necessarily triggered by them. Accordingly, Marx starts speaking about crisis tendencies within the CMP before he even introduces classes. He argues that there is potential for 'crises of production and trade' due to the possibility of a mismatch between money in circulation and payments to be settled (1962a, p. 151, my translation).

mulation and state strategies followed by the Thatcherites and Blairites, but refrained from moving towards similar strategies in the field of class politics. Britain's position in the global financial market made the government undertake a U-turn in economic, fiscal and monetary policy, but it refrained from openly attacking the unions, which may have to do with the apparent strength of the working class at the time (it had just launched an offensive) and the ties between organised labour and the Labour Party.

Consequently, my periodisations of class political regimes and economic-political orders are neither completely disjointed nor fully congruent. The sequence of class political regimes reflects all twists and turns of the cycle of class struggle, whereas that of the economic-political orders only mirrors broad shifts and does so with substantial time lags. This follows from the distinct dynamic of capital accumulation, combined with the specific temporality of class politics and economic order politics caused by path-dependent institutional features of capitalism in Britain. In Britain, the institutions embedding class struggle developed under the dominance of a 'liberal collectivist' extraction strategy, which meant that capital and labour negotiated not just over the conditions of work, but also over the institutions underpinning the labour process. State apparatuses were not involved directly in these negotiations and engaged in arbitration and conciliation instead.[118] Correspondingly, class politics in Britain has generally tended to be reactive, ad-hoc and short-termist. In contrast, given the experiences of the wartime planned economy and post-war Keynesianism, economic order politics in the last six decades has been oriented to more medium-term goals. Not even the Thatcherites tried to break with this tradition. They refrained from making a U-turn in economic order politics in the early 1980s recession despite strong protestations to their course from the industrial fraction of capital and intellectuals aligned to it (see below).

In sum, if my book were a picture, class politics and the overall condensation of class relations in the British state would be in the foreground, economic order politics in the middle ground and the course of economic development in Britain in the background. This reflects my theoretical problematic, which emphasises the fundamental importance of surplus extraction for capitalist production and the overall organisation of capitalist social formations. Accordingly, I start with the periodisation of class political regimes and map the periodisations of economic-political orders and regimes of condensation onto it, providing a more complete picture.[119]

---

118   Howell 2005, pp. 46–7.
119   In correspondence with this mode of presentation, I have decided to include in my book

Thatcherism as a Class Political Regime

My method of periodisation consists in examining the cycle of class struggle and mapping class politics, economic order politics and their articulation onto it. In line with the diverging temporalities of strategies in different political fields, I contend that the Thatcherites orchestrated an offensive step of the power bloc with the help of short-termist strategies in the field of class politics and the active entrenchment of a medium-termist regime in the field of economic order politics.[120] In my view, the corresponding economic-political order had emerged in embryonic form under Callaghan, and was extended and reinforced first by Thatcher and her allies and then by Blair and his associates.

---

two detailed case studies establishing the characteristics of the Thatcherite extraction strategy and mode of leadership and domination (see chapter 7), but none on economic order politics.

[120] Obviously, the novelty of my analysis does not lie in the claim that the Thatcherites conducted an offensive. My analysis is different from others because I am using a framework for analysis based on a new articulation of concepts that links class analysis with the analysis of accumulation strategies. In fact, it was pretty common among left-leaning academics and trade unionists in the 1980s and early 1990s to use the term 'offensive' with reference to Thatcherism. Accordingly, both Hall and Jessop et al. employ it in their respective analyses; Richard Hyman refers to an 'offensive' of the Thatcher government in the area of trade union law (1987, p. 97); David Coates mentions an 'employers' offensive … against working class power in industry' (1989, p. 143); Kelly speaks of an 'employer-government offensive' directed against the unions (1990, p. 56); Henk Overbeek uses term 'offensive' in the context of the 'all-out attack on the strongholds of the organized working class' orchestrated by the government (1990, pp. 187–8); Peter Nolan mentions that Thatcher launched 'a sustained offensive against the unions' (1992, p. 3); Evans et al. speak of 'Thatcher's offensive against labour' (1992, p. 583); and Bonefeld refers to a 'sustained offensive against the working class' (1993, p. 224). Similarly, several of the trade unionists contributing to a volume edited by Martin Jacques and Francis Mulhern use the term 'offensive' (1981, pp. 111, 117, 139). Furthermore, Francis Beckett and David Hencke quote Mick McGahey, vice-president of NUM at the time of the miners' strike, as saying that his union was involved in a 'class battle with the full offensive of the enemy around you' (2009, p. 81). In contrast, John MacInnes contends that there was a 'government offensive against employers' in the form of the anti-industrial economic strategy of Thatcher and her associates (1987, p. 94), which is in line with his 'heretic' account of Thatcherism. However, his claim is unconvincing in the light of the fact that the economic strategy was a form of indirectly reasserting the 'right to manage' (see below). Nevertheless, the fact that MacInnes felt the need to reverse the proposition that there was 'an employers' offensive' underscores that it was very common at the time to speak of an offensive against organised labour (1987, p. 92).

In other words, I argue that there was a class political regime specific to the Thatcherite era and an economic-political order that had been inherited and was passed on. I therefore confine the term 'Thatcherism' to the field of class politics and refer to 'free market authoritarianism' in the field of economic order politics. Since both configurations appear to have complemented each other, I contend that there was a 'neoliberal regime of condensation' integrating them.

Furthermore, I assume that this neoliberal regime remained in place in the Blairite era but that there was a rupture in class politics, reflecting a new step in the cycle of class struggle, which was consolidating the Thatcherite offensive. In other words, I understand neoliberalism, in the British case, as a regime of condensation comprising two successive class political regimes (Thatcherism and Blairism) and one economic-political order (free market authoritarianism). The passage from one class political regime to the next corresponds to the shift from an offensive and to a consolidating step in the cycle of class struggle. Accordingly, a key finding of my analysis is the proposition that *Thatcherism should be seen as a class political regime*, which has far-reaching implications for our understanding of the continuities and discontinuities between the Thatcherite and the Blairite era and temporality of British neoliberalism.

Against this backdrop, I contend that Thatcherism facilitated the successful completion of an offensive step by the power bloc. In this respect, it differs from the offensive steps of the power bloc in the preceding four decades. All these were derailed by working-class resistance, which was often boosted by strategic miscalculations on the side of the government. In contrast, the Thatcher governments were highly successful in taking on organised labour; notably during the miners' strike in 1984–5, but also during disputes at the Wapping plant of News International (1986–7) and P&O (1988). As a result, Thatcherism gave capitalist class domination in Britain a durability that it had not enjoyed since the early 1940s.[121]

---

121 Eric Hobsbawm (1981) famously argued that 'The Forward March of Labour' had been 'halted' in the immediate post-war era, and that this was due to the decline of manual labour. Hobsbawm's claim is hard to reconcile with the fact that union density and strikes reached record highs in the 1970s, and that the Heath government fell over a miners' strike. As I will demonstrate in chapter 3, the Thatcherite attack was a successful counteroffensive to 1970s union militancy, and not the pinnacle of a long retreat.

Periodising Government Strategies in the Thatcherite Era

In my view, the Thatcherite class political regime was based on a repressive extraction strategy and a 'two nations' hegemonic project, which was serving as the mode of leadership and domination. The extraction strategy involved repressive legislation, the appointment of executives of state-owned companies known for their hostility towards unions, the preparation of a plan aimed at attacking the National Union of Mineworkers as the spearhead of militant trade unionism in Britain, discursive interventions against the labour movement, and support to employers willing to take on the unions.

Correspondingly, the hegemonic project consisted in campaigns against 'welfare scroungers', the restructuring of benefits, the preparedness to shrug off the social costs of a free market accumulation strategy at the level of discourse, attacks on traditionalist sections of the power bloc and the supporting classes, and the promotion of individualism, which was carried out through the privatisation of social housing and the liberalisation of financial markets. Both the extraction strategy and the mode of leadership and domination converged in that they aimed at aggressively undermining organised labour.

As a class political regime that was linked to an offensive of the power bloc, Thatcherism formed part of the neoliberal regime of condensation, which in turn has characterised the British state from the late 1970s until today. Yet the Thatcher and Major governments[122] also shaped this regime of condensation by establishing a new economic-political order, which lasted well beyond their political rule. This order consisted in a finance-driven, free market accumulation strategy and an authoritarian-managerialist state strategy (see Figure 2).

The accumulation strategy in question entrenched the dominance of the financial fraction in the power bloc by prioritising monetary and fiscal policy over industrial policy. Its free market character lay in the attempt to improve Britain's competitiveness via privatisation and financial liberalisation. It was informed by the 'neo-Ricardian' assumption that if British corporations are forced to enter transnational competition for investment, they will focus on

---

[122] As there is a great degree of continuity between the Thatcher and the Major governments, both in terms of class politics and economic order politics, I contend that the Thatcherite class political regime survived Thatcher's resignation. In my view, it even remained intact during the first two years of Blair's first term because New Labour initially made no fundamental political changes in this area. As a result, the Thatcherite class political regime existed from the late 1970s up until 1999.

Direct Effect on Class Domination		Indirect Effect on Class Domination	
Repressive Extraction Strategy	Two Nations Hegemonic Mode of Leadership and Domination	Free Market Accumulation Strategy	Authoritarian Managerialist State Strategy

⇅ ⇅ ⇅ ⇅

Thatcherite Class Political Regime	Free Market Authoritarian Economic-Political Order

⇅ ⇅

Neoliberal Regime of Condensation

FIGURE 2   *Government strategies in the Thatcherite era*

their most productive activities, which will bring about allocative efficiency and sustained growth.[123]

The accumulation strategy was flanked by a new, authoritarian-managerialist state strategy. This consisted in centralising state power and introducing authoritarian ways of dealing with dissent, for example, by establishing a presidential style of government, abolishing local political institutions (which were often left-wing), expanding police forces and the prison complex, and tightening penal law. Moreover, the new state strategy was characterised by the introduction of 'internal markets' and managerial methods of administration in the more peripheral state apparatuses responsible for public healthcare and education.

My periodisation of Thatcherism as a class political regime divides it into five main periods plus a pre-history and an aftermath:

(1) Pre-history (–1977): An authoritarian, proto-neoliberal current had existed in the Conservative Party for a long time, not least embodied in the person of Enoch Powell, who was Minister of Health and Financial Secretary to the Treasury under Harold Macmillan. The key events that strengthened the new right were the victories of the NUM over the Heath government in the 1972 and 1974 miners' strikes and the subsequent

---

[123]   Like Jessop (2003), I use the attribute 'neo-Ricardian' when I refer to economic policies based on assumptions similar to those informing David Ricardo's theory of comparative advantage. Needless to say, I am not talking about Piero Sraffa and his approach to political economy.

defeats of the Tory Party in the two general elections that took place in 1974. Thatcher exploited the inability of the Tory moderates to rally behind one candidate and won the leadership in 1975.

(2) Emergence to point of no return (1977–9): By 1977, the Social Contract, an agreement between the trade unions and the Callaghan government concerning the development of wages, was practically dead. The government had effectively abandoned it when it had accepted the terms of an IMF loan in 1976; as a result, the workers had ditched wage restraint. In the political scene, voices grew in strength that were in favour of disciplining workers instead of seeking conciliation. The Winter of Discontent in 1978–9 marked the point of no return: the right-wing mass media successfully portrayed Britain as a country in a deep crisis triggered by organised labour; strong forces inside the power bloc now advocated a confrontational approach to labour relations. Operating in a mode of 'crisis exploitation',[124] Thatcher won the general election in 1979.

(3) Material gains (1979–84): During this stage, the Thatcherites penetrated the state and made considerable material gains. In the field of class politics, they restructured industrial relations law along repressive lines, privatised state-owned industries, prepared for major industrial disputes, and restructured benefits. These policies were reinforced through changes in the field of economic order politics. Thatcher and her associates tried (and in the end failed) to implement a monetarist monetary policy and maintained high interest rates in a recession, which had a procyclical effect: the interventions reinforced the slump and destroyed substantial sectors of British industry. Nevertheless, they had material effects working in favour of the government: There was a significant increase in unemployment, which badly weakened organised labour and thus created conditions more favourable to surplus extraction. In other words, class relations of forces started to shift in favour of capital.

(4) Unstable intermittent phase (1984–88): This stage was marked by large-scale industrial conflicts. The decision of the National Coal Board (NCB), instigated by Thatcher and her associates, to close mines deemed uneconomic led to the 1984–5 miners' strike, which brought the government close to defeat. The fact that Thatcher et al. prevailed over the NUM in the end signified that the most forceful section of organised labour could no longer mount a successful defence against government policy, and, more generally, that organised labour was no longer capable of halting the offensive by the power bloc. This was further underscored by the Wap-

---

[124] Boin et al. 2008.

ping and P&O disputes. Moreover, the Thatcherites introduced sweeping changes to financial market regulation, which reinforced divisions within the working class and modernised the City as the hegemonic fraction of the power bloc.
(5) Stabilisation (1988–92): The victory of the Thatcher government and the power bloc in major industrial disputes contributed to the normalisation of Thatcherism. Many now believed that the changes instigated by Thatcher and her allies were not temporary but enduring, perhaps even irreversible. This was underscored by the fact that the leadership of the Labour Party started to embrace many of the changes, and that Thatcher's resignation in 1990 did not trigger the implosion of the Thatcherite class political regime.
(6) Erosion (1992–9): The shift in public discourse that had begun in the late 1980s intensified in the 1990s as discontent grew over the social costs of Thatcherism. This was reflected, inter alia, in the resurgence of the Labour Party. The aggressive policies of the late 1980s were toned down and transformed; however, the constant arguments in the Tory Party over Europe betrayed a strategic inconclusiveness on the question of whether the next step would be a consolidating one or another offensive.
(7) Aftermath (1999–): From 1999, a distinct Blairite class political regime started to emerge. Nevertheless, Thatcherism still influenced government policies: the Blair government refrained from repealing the changes in employment and trade union law enacted under Thatcher and expanded the workfare programmes that been launched by the Major government.[125]

The descriptions of the periods show that class political projects and political projects more generally are not neatly defined sets of policies that follow a simple pattern of conception-implementation. As I will discuss in detail in chapter 6, the Thatcher government ditched monetarism once doubts grew about its practical feasibility, which meant that it abandoned a key plank of its agenda. Against this backdrop, David Marsh is surely on the right track when he stresses that short-term political exigencies contributed to shaping the course of the government, at times trumping ideological conviction.[126] However, I do not share his conclusion that ideology 'was not the driving force behind policy'

---

125 For other periodisations of Thatcherism, see Jessop, undated, p. 36; Kerr 2001, p. 186; Hay and Farall 2011.
126 Marsh 1995, pp. 595, 605.

and, by implication, that the Thatcherites were political pragmatists who did not pursue a clearly defined political agenda.[127] As early as July 1980, in an interview with Eric Hobsbawm, Tony Benn gave a surprisingly accurate description of what the Thatcherite project would be, which underscores that the politics of Thatcherism was not the accidental product of day-to-day political management:

> It looks at the moment as if the Government, far from trying to revive the British economy, is using this crisis in order to secure certain very clear political objectives. Namely, if possible, the destruction of trade union power in the land by three processes: by stimulating unemployment to frighten working people away from trade unionism; by legislation to make effective trade unionism very difficult, if not impossible; and by the utilization of the media in a very sustained campaign to persuade the British public that the trade union movement is responsible for our problems and has got to be weakened if we are to recover from them.[128]

Against this backdrop, I contend that there was a coherent Thatcherite agenda from the outset – undermine organised labour – driven by a specific ideology – free market liberalism – and pretty elaborate plans of how this agenda could be implemented, an important example being the Ridley Report. The Thatcher and Major governments never veered off this course and never made concessions that would have worked against this goal, at least not over the medium term. And, as the decline in union density, collective bargaining coverage and strike incidence demonstrate, they were successful in marginalising organised labour. This is why I contend that it is justified, against the normalising and historicising discourse discussed in the introduction, to see Thatcherism as a distinct and coherent class political regime.

This does not mean, however, that every aspect of this project was known to the Thatcherites before Thatcher even took government, that there were no set-backs, and that its implementation did not have to be reconciled with day-to-day political exigencies. As Hay and Farrall rightly point out, the existence of political projects does not imply that everyone involved in their implementation is absolutely clear about what they involve:

---

127 Marsh 1995, p. 612.
128 Benn 1981, pp. 75–6.

In the same way that rationality need not imply a conscious and deliberate strategy so much as behaviour that is rationalis-*able* after the fact, so the existence of a project might be discerned with the benefit of hindsight from a consideration of the degree of consistency exhibited by the strategic choices made. In this way, periodisation offers a way of testing the proposition that a project existed. If a periodisation can be developed empirically from a consideration of strategic choices in a range of related policy domains over time, then it is credible to speak of the existence of a distinct project.[129]

Taking up Hay and Farrall's line of argument, Thatcherism existed as a class political project because key strategic decisions by the Thatcher and Major governments in the area of class politics were consistent with one another, and because it is 'periodisable' as a result.

An additional, important point about my periodisation is an observation that holds for both the post-war and the neoliberal era: In Britain, ruptures in the class political regime and the economic-political order often do not coincide with changes of government. The first moves towards neoliberalism happened when the Callaghan government adopted a monetarist fiscal and monetary policy in response to the 1976 sterling crisis. Similarly, until 1999 New Labour very much operated along the lines set out by the second Major government. Two general points for analyses of British politics can be inferred from this observation:

(1) In Britain, there is a disjuncture between the electoral cycle and the sequence of class political regimes, economic-political orders, and regimes of condensation, which also means that the electoral cycle and the cycle of class struggle do not coincide.
(2) Shifts in these regimes occur in response to crises and intense struggles beyond the control of governments.[130]

Accordingly, my periodisation takes changes of government seriously but does not automatically equate them with turning points in class relations and the development of the state.

In conclusion, I argue that Thatcherism amounted to a successful class political regime insofar as it orchestrated an offensive step by the power bloc

---

129   Hay and Farrall 2011, p. 444.
130   Compare Jessop, undated, pp. 22–3.

that was completed, leading to the reassertion of capitalist class domination in Britain. In this context, it is important to stress that the Thatcherites paid a high price for this success. It was based on entrenching an economic-political order that laid the foundation for the Great Recession post-2007. Combining the analyses of Hall et al. and the gang of four, I contend that the short-term successes of the Thatcherites in the field of class politics are linked to their medium-term failure in the field of economic order politics.

PART 2

Class and Politics in Britain, 1977–99

CHAPTER 3

Method of Presentation

The following chapters represent the main body of my book. In them, I use my conceptual framework in order to examine the rise and fall of Thatcherism. I establish that Thatcherism can be seen as a class political regime, and demonstrate how the Thatcherite approach to economic order politics retroacted on the establishment, entrenchment, reproduction, and erosion of this regime. In so doing, I operate on the grounds of a periodisation that maps Thatcherism onto the cycle of class struggle. In my view, Thatcherism reflects a completed offensive step by the power bloc, which rolled back the gains of the labour movement made during the post-war era. This step can be divided into five periods: emergence, material gains, instability, stabilisation, and erosion. Furthermore, I discuss the prehistory and aftermath of Thatcherism in order to put my object into a historical context. Accordingly, the order of my argument follows my periodisation: Each step of the Thatcherite offensive constitutes a chapter, and in each chapter I explain why I contend that the events at the time show there was an offensive.

Crucially, my account includes three case studies. These address in greater detail than the other chapters key events in the formation of Thatcherism that constitute turning points. Each case study is included in the chapter covering the period to which it refers. All three cases studies build, to a larger extent than the remainder of Part II, on original documents and contemporary coverage of the events in the print media. As a result, the degree of detail of my observations in this part varies. This is in order to strike a balance between providing a reasonably straightforward account of the Thatcherite offensive and making sure the analysis is backed up by sound historical evidence and thorough explanations.

The analytical focus of my case studies is to show that Thatcherism can be seen as a class political regime. As I explained in chapter 2, I prioritise class politics because my theoretical problematic focuses on surplus extraction.

My first case study concerns four policy papers commissioned by the Conservative leadership, which were all completed between June and November 1977. The fact that only one was published and three remained confidential gives us a clear sense of what the Thatcherites thought at the time, and how their communication with the British public diverged from their thinking. The significance of the reports lies in showing that a coherent new right political agenda was emerging, both in the areas of class politics and economic order politics. In this sense, they mark a watershed: Thatcher and her allies on the Conservative frontbench transformed themselves from a group leading the opposition to the inner circle of a government-in-waiting.

The second case study covers the Thatcher government's role in the 1984–5 miners' strike, which was the defining industrial conflict of the era. I argue that the Thatcherite extraction strategy can be read off from the actions of the government: It deliberately sought to run down the coal industry in order to marginalise the NUM, which acted as the spearhead of militant trade unionism in Britain.

The third case study deals with financial liberalisation and, more specifically, with the liberalisation of the stock market. I contend that the government's 'two nations' hegemonic project crystallises in how it approached this area. The promotion of 'popular capitalism', that is, the attempt to entrench capitalist attitudes in the population, rested on dividing the working class by providing some of its members with access to securities markets and mortgages. The restructuring in this area also brought about the modernisation of the City as the leading fraction of the power bloc: barriers to employment in the City based on traditional, gentlemanly cultural patterns were removed, which strengthened the ties of the City to subaltern groups. In sum, 'popular capitalism' was about deepening intra-class divisions and strengthening inter-class links.

CHAPTER 4

Pre-History: Britain in Crisis (–1977)

A Catastrophic Equilibrium

I analyse Thatcherism as an ensemble of strategies directly targeting class relations, which form part of a broader neoliberal regime of condensation. To show the value-added of this approach, I will first of all describe the historical context of Thatcherism, and show how a deep economic, political, and ideological crisis prepared the ground for a profound ideological shift in the Conservative Party, which consisted in various elements of neoliberal ideology beginning to dominate the party discourse.

Following Hall et al., I use a Gramscian expression to capture the conjuncture of the 1970s: 'catastrophic equilibrium'.[1] The term refers to a situation in which class actors engage in their 'reciprocal destruction' because both sides are strong enough to launch attacks, but neither side is capable of defeating the other.[2] In other words, a catastrophic equilibrium is a conjuncture marked by several consecutive, aborted attacks by both capital and labour. In my view, the fierce class struggles in 1970s Britain followed this pattern. They were the product of all post-war governments failing to create a coherent institutional framework for capitalism in Britain or, in my words, to institute a durable regime of condensation.

All British governments between 1945 and 1970 tried in various ways to instigate a settlement between capital and labour, and to implement strategies conducive to stabilising capitalist class domination. At various points, there were compacts between capital and labour based on trading wage restraint and compliance in the sphere of production with full employment and the provisions of a comprehensive welfare state. However, the resulting class political regimes did not last very long. Corporatist institutions remained ineffective and failed to deliver substantial and consistent improvements to the standard of living of workers, who in turn frequently resorted to strike action.[3] The weakness of British corporatism reflected the traditional weakness of the British state, whose century-long evolutionary development had produced institutional het-

---

1 Hall et al. 1978, p. 262.
2 Gramsci 1971, p. 219.
3 Jessop et al. 1998, p. 165.

erogeneity and had resulted in the emergence of economic apparatuses with only limited interventionist capacities.[4]

In the field of economic order politics, political leaders grappled with corresponding problems. Initially, the early post-war governments appeared successful insofar as they managed to establish an economic-political order that combined a Keynesian accumulation strategy with an interventionist state strategy. However, they failed to instigate the restructuring of the British industrial base, whose 'competitiveness' had been eroding since the second wave of industrialisation in the late nineteenth century:[5] on the whole, there were only sluggish increases in productivity and economic growth.

This was further aggravated by the incapacity of corporatist institutions to enforce wage restraint. Under the conditions of limited growth, substantial wage increases posed a threat to profits. In this situation, employers resorted to fending off this threat by increasing prices, which stoked inflation and restricted the growth of real wages.[6] At the macro-level, this resulted in a cycle of stagnation, which usually followed a 'boom and bust' pattern: first, there was a brief phase of expansion; next, inflationary pressures emerged and the balance of payments started deteriorating; this then resulted in a currency crisis and, finally, in a contraction.

The application of inconsistent political techniques of economic crisis management complicated the macroeconomic issues. On the one hand, successive governments committed themselves to Keynesian demand management; on the other hand, they stuck to orthodox ways of stabilising the pound: they chose to react to the recurring currency crises with ad-hoc cutbacks in state expenditure, which stabilised the pound but undercut demand. Once stabilisation had been achieved, they reflated, which created new inflationary pressures. In other words, the application of Keynesian techniques had a pro-cyclical, not an anti-cyclical effect. Under these conditions, Britain never saw the emergence of a self-reinforcing productivist growth dynamic as witnessed in France and West Germany at the time. In light of this, Jessop speaks of 'Britain's flawed Fordism'.[7]

The shortcomings of post-war strategies in the field of economic order politics not only reflected the weakness of corporatist institutions. The fact that the dominant fraction of the power bloc, the City, did not have an interest in the resurgence of its industrial counterpart further compounded difficulties, as did

---

4 Compare Badie and Birnbaum 1983, pp. 122–3.
5 Hobsbawm 1968, p. 178.
6 Compare Panitch 1976, p. 242.
7 Jessop 1991b, p. 137; compare Overbeek 1990, p. 191; Kerr 2001, p. 196.

skills shortages and the widespread unpreparedness of management to invest.[8] As a consequence, there was a disjunction between dominantly corporatist, 'one nation' class politics and the rudimentary Fordism prevalent in economic order politics. Put more simply, compacts between capital and labour were not underpinned by sustained growth. Thus the 'post-war settlement' remained a project that never struck roots deep enough to become a regime of condensation – despite its initial popularity and the emergence of institutional supports.

Correspondingly, the prospects of a lasting arrangement looked bleak already by the late 1950s. Organised labour chose to resist the wages policy that the government tried to impose, and did so successfully. Over the next 15 years, there were various attempts to either revive the post-war settlement or replace it with a new regime, none of which worked. By the late 1960s, a dual impasse in terms of class relations of forces started to emerge in Britain. I call it 'dual' because it was both an impasse between capital and labour,[9] and between revivalist and modernising forces within the power bloc.[10]

By now, capitalism in Britain had entered a state of catastrophic equilibrium: The Wilson government's jab at creating a legal framework for labour relations, set out in a white paper called *In Place of Strife*, was derailed by working-class resistance, and so was Ted Heath's attempt, the *Industrial Relations Act*, a couple of years later. Had they been successful, both projects would have amounted to a rupture in British labour relations: under the traditional, 'liberal collectivist' system that had emerged in the late nineteenth century, trade unions and unionists did not enjoy positive rights, but they were protected by a system of immunities.[11] As a result, the activities of unions and employers were in large part based on procedural conventions rather than legal regulations.

Crucially, the Heath government was defeated in two miners' strikes (1972 and 1974), the second of which led the Prime Minister to call a general election asking 'Who governs Britain?'. Heath lost this election, which took place in February 1974, and another one in October 1974. The fact that the Wilson and Heath government were unable to defeat organised labour proves that the hold of the power bloc over the working class was weak.

The manifesto of the Labour Party for the February election was a pretty radical response to Heath's question, reflecting the influence of the party left

---

8   Nolan 1989, pp. 86–7.
9   Compare Jacques 1983, p. 48.
10 Jessop et al. 1988, p. 15.
11 Marsh 1992, p. 3.

around Benn and the strength of militant trade unionism. It demanded 'a fundamental and irreversible shift in the balance of power and wealth in favour of working people and their families' and the extension of public ownership in industry.[12] The fact that Labour managed to narrowly win the election on the grounds of such radical demands and that the Conservatives were unable get the backing of the voters in their confrontation with unions shows that a working-class offensive had started.

At the level of government, this played out in the form of 'a radical corporatist solution to Britain's industrial decline', which initially gave the unions an unusually high degree of influence over key policy decisions.[13] At its heart lay the Social Contract, an arrangement between the incoming Wilson government and unions, which traded acquiescence and wage restraint for improvements in healthcare and education, increased pensions, price controls and the promise of extending 'industrial democracy'.[14] But the working class offensive came to a halt soon after. The unions steadily lost ground because their leaders remained loyal to the government, which imposed several rounds of pay restraint while steadily loosening price controls.[15] The result was a fall in the standard of living for workers. In November 1976, a few months after Wilson had resigned and had been replaced by James Callaghan, the government openly showed that it was not prepared to allow a shift in the class relations of forces in favour of the working class. It reacted to the next currency crisis by siding with financial capital and prioritising its interests over those of working people: On behalf of the government, Chancellor Denis Healey requested a bailout from the IMF. In the end, the cabinet agreed to cut spending by £2.5bn and sell £500m worth of BP shares for a £2.3bn loan from the IMF.[16]

The failure of the working-class offensive deprived organised labour of a plausible narrative on how to advance towards socialism. At the same time, the trade unions were still in a strong position and the British economy remained unstable. This suggests that the conjuncture was characterised by a constellation of class forces where neither the restoration of full capitalist control over production nor a socialist transformation seemed genuine possibilities. At the time, Hall et al. gave an accurate description of the situation: 'Britain in the

---

12   The call for a fundamental power shift and the extension of public ownership are also in the manifesto for the elections in October 1974. See Labour Party 1974a, 1974b.
13   Coates 1989, p. 70.
14   Cohen 2006, p. 31.
15   Coates 1989, pp. 87–8.
16   Giles and Newman 2005.

1970s is a country for whose crisis there are no viable capitalist solutions left, and where, as yet, there is no viable political base for an alternative socialist strategy'.[17]

In my view, the catastrophic equilibrium reflected the absence of a viable regime of condensation, which had not existed since the war. Moreover, at this point state apparatuses were no longer capable of preventing the economic crisis, materialised in the perennial weakness of British industry, from spilling over into the realms of the state and civil society and producing political and ideological crises. In other words, there were mutually reinforcing crisis tendencies on all instances of the social formation.

At the economic level, the most visible symptoms were stagflation (stagnation plus inflation), rising unemployment and the instability of the balance of payments and the pound. All this occurred against the backdrop of a surge in industrial conflict in the metropolises and tensions in global capitalism. Most importantly, the Bretton Woods system of international finance broke down, which occurred after the US had suspended the dollar's convertibility into gold at a fixed exchange rate in 1971.[18] Besides, there was the oil crisis of 1973 – a surge in the price of oil engineered by the OPEC states as a reaction to the Yom Kippur War that pushed up inflation and dented the profitability of capital on a global scale.[19]

The economic crisis spilled over into politics in the form of a crisis of hegemony, a situation referred to above as 'dual impasse'.[20] In the late 1960s and 1970s, political leaders found it increasingly harder to bind the working class into arrangements that ensured submissiveness. Furthermore, conflicts within the power bloc intensified. This was most notable during the Wilson governments. Harold Wilson's famous invocation of the 'white heat of the technological revolution' formed part of his failed attempt to instigate a shift in the relations of forces within the power bloc in favour of industry.

As Jessop et al. point out, the economic and political problems also translated into, and were further reinforced by, a dual crisis of the state, that is, a crisis of corporatist institutions and a crisis of representation.[21] The corporatist remnants of the post-war settlement had proved dysfunctional for both sides of industry. For labour, they had been too weak to underpin a self-reinforcing

---

17 Hall et al. 1978, p. 308.
18 Compare Eichengreen 1996; Candeias 2004.
19 Compare Coates 1984, pp. 40–1.
20 Compare Poulantzas 1974, p. 60.
21 Jessop et al. 1988, pp. 81–2; compare Poulantzas 1974, pp. 63, 71; 1978, p. 234.

growth dynamic that could have sustained a steady increase in living standards. For the power bloc, corporatist institutions had not secured wage restraint via a viable wages policy.

This was flanked by a crisis of representation at the level of parliament. There was a marked drop in the share of votes for the party duopoly of Labour and Tories if the 1970 and 1974 general elections are compared. In 1970, 89.7 percent of votes went to the duopoly; in 1974, the numbers were 74.9 and 75 percent. This reflects the resurgence of the Liberal Party and the rise of Celtic nationalism, which brought an end to the two-party system that had dominated British politics throughout the 1950s and 60s.[22]

Finally, this ensemble of crisis tendencies also spilled over into the realm of ideology. The consensus ideologies that had informed the 'one nation' hegemonic project as the dominant mode of leadership and domination from 1940 were no longer plausible in a situation of heightened tension and deepening division.[23] One nation conservatism finally proved untenable under Heath, and so did social democratic corporatism: the Social Contract broke in the late 1970s thanks to pressures imposed on workers' living standards by the Callaghan government. Furthermore, it was no longer taken for granted by the general public that the Beveridgian welfare state constituted the adequate response to the divisiveness and the crisis tendencies of capitalism in Britain.

This crisis of 'mainstream' ideology was accompanied by a crisis of left-socialist ideology. In this area, the ossification of the socialist regimes in Eastern Europe made the prospect of a socialist alternative less plausible, and the emergence of new political actors such as the women's, the lesbian and gay, and the green movements challenged traditional assumptions regarding the political strategies and aims of the left. Hall captured the mood by stating: 'Socialist Man, with one single mind, one set of interests, one project, is dead. Who needs "him" now?'[24]

In conclusion, capitalism in Britain was in an organic crisis in the 1970s, which affected the economic, the political and the ideological level. This created a fertile ground for novel interpretations of the political economy of Britain that demanded drastic change and broke with the assumptions of the post-war settlement. At the same time, it was unclear where these novel interpretations would come from. For several years, neither conservative nor socialist forces provided political responses that garnered mass support.

---

22 Based on the numbers in Kaiser 2006, pp. 182–5.
23 Compare Hall et al. 1978, p. 322.
24 Hall 1988b, pp. 169–70.

Proto-Thatcherism: Enoch Powell, 'Selsdon Man' and the Heath Government

The weakness of corporatist apparatuses constituted the institutional dimension of the 1970s crisis. Its equivalent on the plane of ideology was the inability of capital and labour to build respective alliances around a convincing interpretation of the crisis. Part of this was the crisis of Conservative ideology, which was particularly visible in the Heath era. The Heath government embraced three different extraction strategies in the space of five years, that is, a repressive approach, corporatism and statism. None of these strategies worked, at least not in terms of containing militant trade unionism. The Heath government was the first in Western Europe brought down by a labour dispute: in 1972, the miners managed to force concessions from the National Coal Board (NCB); when they walked out again in 1974, Heath called an election and lost.[25] This experience paved the way for a radical break with one nation conservatism, and the development of an aggressive stance towards organised labour within the Conservative Party. It led to the formation of a distinct, new right faction in the party around Thatcher and her close ally Keith Joseph.

Thatcher's rise reflects the marginalisation of the formerly dominant ideology in the Conservative Party, and its replacement by a novel ideological formation that was based on economic liberalism and authoritarian calls for a strong state.[26] The ideas of the new right did not emerge out of the blue. Obviously, the demand for 'law and order' is a classical theme of British conservatism.[27] But the ideology of economic laissez-faire also never ceased to influence Conservative thinking, even if those sympathetic to state interventionism gained the upper hand after the war. In 1961, Harold Macmillan, the then leader of the Tory Party and Prime Minister, wrote in his diary that the cabinet was divided between those favouring 'old Whig, liberal, laissez faire traditions' and those 'not afraid of a little dirigisme'.[28] Macmillan sided with the 'dirigists' and got his way, but there was one prominent member of the cabinet who openly advocated economic liberalism and law and order politics, as well as opposing the interventionist turn of the Tory leadership: Enoch Powell, the then Minister of Health. Powell was 'the first heavyweight politician to mount a coherent attack

---

25 Darlington and Lyddon 2001, p. 69; Cohen 2006, p. 29.
26 See Gamble 1988, pp. 155–6, 173, and my critique of Gamble in Gallas 2014.
27 Hall 1983a, pp. 37–8; Hobsbawm 1989, p. 19.
28 Cited in Green 1999, p. 30.

on the post-war consensus politics from the Conservative right'.[29] Many of his themes were to reappear in the Thatcherite discourse, not least because some of his followers became leading Thatcherites, and because he found an admirer in Thatcher.[30]

Most obviously, Powell foreshadowed Thatcherism by being a free marketer and, more specifically, a proto-monetarist. He claimed that the only legitimate form of state interventionism consisted in controlling the money supply.[31] In 1958, he resigned from his post as financial secretary to the Treasury in protest against a government decision to increase public spending by £50m, which in his opinion would fuel inflation.[32] Moreover, he criticised exchange controls, nationalisation, incomes policy, planning, regional policy and high public spending and proposed the floating of the pound.[33]

But Powell also prepared the ground for Thatcherite authoritarianism, even if he was not a hardliner when it came to law and order issues.[34] In his notorious 'rivers of blood' speech in 1968, he described Britain as 'a nation busily engaged in heaping up its own funeral pyre' by allowing mass immigration, adding that looking into the future, he saw the 'River Tiber foaming with much blood'.[35] Powell's gory imagery contributed to a climate of fear in the British population, which Thatcher later exploited:[36] Taking a leaf out of Powell's book, she portrayed mass immigration as a danger. For example, she remarked that white Britons felt 'rather swamped'.[37] All in all, she time and again operated on the grounds of a politics of fear, fuelling moral panics by invoking perceived threats to the British nation that she then could use to legitimise authoritarian forms of social control directed against minorities and her political enemies.[38]

Powell's speech cost him his position in Heath's shadow cabinet and his political career. Nevertheless, he enjoyed substantial support for his anti-immigration stance. According to a Gallup poll conducted after the speech,

---

29   Evans 1997, p. 41.
30   Gamble 1988, p. 73; Vinen 2009, p. 46.
31   Vinen 2009, p. 51; compare Lane 1983, p. 175; Kavanagh 1990, p. 70.
32   Gamble 1988, p. 70.
33   Kavanagh 1990, p. 70; Vinen 2009, p. 51.
34   Vinen 2009, p. 48.
35   Powell 2007.
36   Compare Hall et al. 1978, p. 246.
37   Cited in Vinen 2009, p. 48.
38   Compare Saunders 2012.

25 percent of the population wanted to him to become the next Leader of the Tory party, and London dockers demonstrated in his support.[39] Against this backdrop, Powell claimed to air the views of the 'silent majority',[40] trying to use his popularity for furthering his economic cause: he soon after demanded the denationalisation of public enterprises and a reduction of taxes, albeit with limited success:[41] Visible displays of popular support remained limited to his stance on immigration; he did not manage to unsettle the dominance of one nation orientations in the Tory party and the country as a whole.

During the years of the Heath government, Powell became an outspoken critic of Heath's decision to take Britain into the European Economic Community (EEC). In the end, he decided to turn against his party: In February 1974, he urged his supporters to vote for Labour; in October 1974, he became an MP for the Ulster Unionists.

One could argue that Powell simply entered the limelight too early for him to undermine the Tory mainstream. But it is also pretty obvious that his downfall had to do with the fact that he differed from Thatcher in a crucial respect: he presented laissez-faire liberalism in a backward-looking manner, which made it appear as a traditionalist ideology. Powell subscribed to 'Little Englandism' at a time when leading forces in the Conservative party favoured a closer connection of Britain with the EEC. His populism was tinged with racism, his authoritarianism with a conservative stance on the constitution, and his economic liberalism with 'Manchesterian' views.[42] Furthermore, he was anti-American at the height of the Cold War.[43] And unlike Thatcher, he was highly reluctant to call for the transformation of traditional British institutions.[44] As a result, many saw him as an old-fashioned eccentric rather than as a moderniser capable of taking on Britain's economic and political problems, which contributed to the failure of his challenge to the Tory leadership.[45]

Nevertheless, Powell successfully influenced the mainstream political discourse: he highlighted the weaknesses of the post-war settlement and used them to bring far-right ideas into the public debate. In so doing, he sowed the seed for the Thatcherite interpretation of the organic crisis of British capitalism in the 1970s.

---

39   Gamble 1988, p. 71.
40   Kavanagh 1990, p. 73.
41   Gamble 1988, p. 72.
42   Jessop et al. 1988, p. 60.
43   Vinen 2009, p. 53.
44   Schofield 2012, p. 96; compare Vinen 2009, p. 56.
45   Compare Vinen 2009, p. 49.

Powell had been relegated to the backbenches by the late 1970s, but his ideas tied in with those of many party activists, who were convinced that the post-war settlement was beyond reanimation.[46] By 1970, attempts to revive it had been made for about a decade without tangible success. Both voluntary and statutory incomes policy had been tried out in order to tame inflation and stabilise the pound, and neither had delivered in terms of stabilising growth and disciplining workers. At the same time, the structural weaknesses of the British economy, especially its ailing industrial sector and the chronic pressure on the pound, had worsened. Consumption had not increased in the preceding years, and unemployment and inflation were increasing. As a result, there was a substantial degree of popular discontent over Wilson's economic policy.[47]

Against this backdrop, the shadow cabinet held a meeting at Selsdon Park Hotel in early 1970, whose purpose was to discuss ideas for the general election manifesto. According to Ewen Green, the discussions on the future course of the party were inconclusive, but the 'context of its reception' gave it a mythical status.[48] Both the Prime Minister and the press agreed that the Tories had made a decisive shift to the right. Wilson coined the term 'Selsdon Man', evoking memories of 'Piltdown Man', a skeleton found in 1912 that was initially assumed to date back to the Palaeolithic and later exposed as a hoax. He insinuated that a primitive species pronouncing Stone Age free market economics had emerged on the scene that was also, perhaps, the product of fraud.

Significantly, Heath and the leadership of the party did not choose to challenge the claim of a rightward turn.[49] This demonstrates that Wilson's intervention was not just a piece of political propaganda, but that the tectonic plates underneath the surface of British conservatism had started to shift. In retrospect, the fact that the move to the right was reluctant at first suggests that the crisis of Tory ideology was yet to climax.

Correspondingly, the Conservative election manifesto of 1970 reiterated that the party was intent on recreating Britain as 'one nation united in a common purpose', but also advocated free market and authoritarian themes. It pledged to end statutory incomes policy, cut government spending and taxation, halt the drive towards nationalisation, introduce industrial relations legislation codifying unionisation and disputes, and promote law and order policies

---

46 Green 1999, p. 38.
47 Stewart 1977, p. 117.
48 Green 1999, p. 35.
49 Green 1999, pp. 36–7.

including immigration control, the expansion of the prison complex, and a crack-down on 'welfare scroungers' and 'demonstrators'. Furthermore, it clearly anticipated a key theme of the Thatcherite discourse by advocating the liberation of the individual from socialist state control:

> Socialists believe in the extension of the power of the State: government today is trying to do too much, managing too much, bringing too much to the centre for decision. We plan to clear away from Whitehall a great load of tasks which has accumulated under Socialism; to hand back responsibilities wherever we can to the individual, to the family, to private initiative, to the local authority, to the people.[50]

Along these lines, Heath announced at the 1970 party conference, which took place just after his election victory, that his government would promote the free market and individualism. Heath wanted 'to provide room for greater incentives for men and women and to firms and businesses ... to encourage them more and more to take their own decisions, to stand firm on their own feet, to accept responsibility for themselves and their families'.[51] The discussions in the Conservative Party at the time can be seen as indications of a shift towards economic liberalism in the area of economic order politics.

This was flanked by a confrontational approach to class politics, which went against the corporatist orientations that dominated mainstream British politics back then: the incoming government chose not to consult with the unions over its political course.[52] Throughout the post-war era, governments had regularly met with union representatives for talks about pressing political issues. In addition, the Heath government attempted to create a legal framework for labour relations and, in particular, to legislate against militancy from the union rank-and-file. The purpose of the 1971 Industrial Relations Act was 'to bring about by *fiat* what no longer could be won by consent'.[53] It introduced an official registration procedure for unions, made them accountable for the activities of their members, and imposed cooling-off periods and strike ballots. Moreover, it established a National Industrial Relations Court (NIRC) and a 'Commission on Industrial Relations'.[54] Registered unions faced legal sanctions if the activities of their members did not conform to prescribed procedures.

---

50   Conservative Party 1970.
51   Cited in Green 1999, p. 36.
52   Middlemas 1990, p. 290.
53   Hall et al. 1978, p. 284.
54   Compare Crouch 1977, pp. 169–71.

Furthermore, the Heath government inched towards a divisive 'two nations' approach at the level of the hegemonic project. Leading conservatives foreshadowed Thatcher's theme of a socialist 'enemy within' threatening to undermine law and order.[55] Heath created a link between unrest on the shop-floors and the rebellion of students: 'Great factories, railways, airports are brought to a standstill by strike action ... Great seats of learning ... are disrupted by rebellious students'.[56] Similarly, Enoch Powell spoke of a 'conspiracy of liberal causes' for which he blamed a ubiquitous anarchic force directed against the status quo.[57] Following him, this force consisted of striking teachers, student rebels, demonstrators, troublemakers in Northern Ireland, people of colour, anti-apartheid campaigners, etc.

In sum, the activities of the Heath government can be seen as both an attempt to orchestrate an offensive of the power bloc against the working class and as indications of Thatcherism *avant la lettre*: they constituted a move towards a repressive extraction strategy and a 'two nations' hegemonic project. However, the government was faced with the difficulty that it had not united the power bloc behind its agenda. Support for the Industrial Relations Act was weak among industrial capital. The Confederation of British Industry (CBI) was in favour of its introduction, but the majority of individual industrialists ignored it out of pragmatic reasons.[58]

It was even more worrying for the government that resistance was forming outside the power bloc. The threat of repression invigorated the union movement. The TUC started to organise a range of protests, most notably a series of national one-day strikes between December 1970 and March 1971. Unsurprisingly, the Labour leadership exploited discontent in order to re-establish firm links between unions and the party. All members of the shadow cabinet decided to fight the act.[59] Despite the fact that organised labour was not capable of preventing the enactment of the new regulations, militant workers took no more than three months to derail them. An unofficial boycott by dockers against container work outside dock areas at lower pay was pivotal. The Transport and General Workers' Union (TGWU) was fined on the grounds that it was responsible for the industrial action. Nevertheless, the dockers continued their boycott and defied the NIRC, and the Court of Appeals found that there

---

55 Hall et al. 1978, p. 276.
56 Cited in Hall et al. 1978, p. 275.
57 Cited in Hall et al. 1978, p. 276.
58 Crouch 1977, p. 177.
59 Stewart 1977, p. 126.

were flaws in the design of the act. The NIRC reacted by targeting shop stewards. When a group of them were thrown into prison (the Pentonville Five), the rank-and-file of the union movement threatened a general strike. The General Council of the TUC decided to support the call for action.[60]

All of this suggests that working-class resistance to the act posed a threat to the rule of law. The economic crisis, embodied in shop-floor militancy, began to spill over into the state. In this situation, state officials could have caused a breakdown of the political and legal system if they had decided to uphold the rule of law by insisting on going by the book. Considering the chronic weakness of the pound, a general strike might have damaged the international position of the British economy badly. The government faced a dilemma: it could neither go against law and order and release the prisoners, nor risk a deep economic and state crisis. The way out was a legal trick, which allowed the government to make a face-saving retreat. The Official Solicitor, who held an ancient office with little importance for the British legal system, invoked an old and mostly forgotten regulation and ordered the release of the Pentonville Five.[61]

In the end, it was the archaism and inconsistency of the British constitution that allowed state officials to handle this crisis in a flexible fashion. They were able to defuse the tensions with the unions without formally undermining the rule of law. This meant that the constitution had been saved, but the government paid a high price: it had to sacrifice the Industrial Relations Act, which quickly became a dead letter.[62] Heath's attempt to move towards a new extraction strategy had been derailed.

Faced with fierce working-class resistance to his repressive extraction strategy, Heath undertook a U-turn and attempted to revive the old techniques of co-opting organised labour – first corporatism and then statism, neither of which worked. This shows that he remained pragmatic and flexible, and that he was not prepared to take risks in order to see through the restructuring of labour relations. In this respect, he clearly differed from Thatcher. But there were also divergences regarding the substance of Heath's and Thatcher's policies. Heath sought not to undermine organised labour, but to restrain it. Similarly, he did not attempt to privatise state-owned industries, but merely to prevent

---

60 Following Leo Panitch, this was an attempt by the leadership of the union movement to remain in the driving seat and retain its control over organised labour. Compare Panitch 1976, p. 224.
61 Compare Panitch 1976, p. 225.
62 Compare ibid.

nationalisation from being extended. In other words, the agenda of the Heath government was never as clear-cut and doctrinaire as the agendas of Thatcher governments – and this even includes the beginning stages of Thatcher's first premiership.[63] Heath attempted to implement neoliberal 'policy adjustments' rather than a wholesale 'regime shift'.[64]

Heath's U-turn and its aftermath, the two election defeats in 1974, fuelled disappointment with the status quo in the Conservative Party and deepened the crisis of Conservative ideology, which in turn was reinforced by increasing economic difficulties. Thatcher and her supporters thrived on both. Economic liberalism and the call for repression against organised labour had not been discredited by the Heath episode. This is unsurprising: the corporatist and statist extraction strategies trialled after the U-turn not only proved just as unworkable, but they had also a long history of failure to their name. The effect of Heath's string of defeats was the destabilisation of one nation conservatism. The majority of the party rank-and-file now agreed that 'negotiated, as distinct from legislated agreements with the TUC could deliver no significant goods', and that 'the whole notion that government could beneficially intervene in industrial reorganisation and detailed economic management' should be abandoned.[65]

Thatcher's Seizure of the Conservative Party Leadership

After Heath's defeat, the Conservative Party underwent a transition not only in terms of personnel, but also ideology. It found itself in a phase of reorientation, which reflected an ideological crisis. Accordingly, there was no coherent party line between 1974 and 1977.[66]

In 1974, Joseph, a member of Heath's shadow cabinet, emerged as spokesman of the opposition against the leader and one nation conservatism. He publicly denounced central planks of the post-war settlement and sought to re-establish a 'true' brand of conservatism. In the area of economic policy, he followed Powell's lead: his conservatism was anti-Keynesian, anti-welfarist and in favour of the free market.

---

63 The 1979 election manifesto contained plans to privatise British Aerospace and the state-owned shipbuilders (Conservative Party 1979). Behind closed doors, the Thatcherites were already discussing how to marginalise the NUM (see below).
64 Jessop 2002a, p. 85.
65 Lane 1983, p. 173.
66 Middlemas 1991, p. 193.

The most visible reflection of the fact that Joseph was actively fighting against the dominant forms of Tory ideology was the establishment of the Centre for Policy Studies (CPS) in 1974 – a think tank that he set up together with Thatcher and Alfred Sherman, who became its director of studies. The CPS was supposed to serve as an alternative to established party institutions like the Central Office and the Conservative Research Department.[67] Its aim was to spell out the strategic and programmatic implications of Heath's defeat as well as elaborating an agenda directed at dismantling the institutional remnants of the post-war settlement.[68] The new right around Joseph and Thatcher presented itself as a Conservative response to the simultaneous shift of Labour to the left.[69]

In February 1975, Heath chose to throw down the gauntlet and challenge the critics from his party by holding a leadership ballot. Joseph decided not to stand because he had been facing strong criticism for his proposition that the right to have children should be restricted for poorer Britons. Thanks to remarks like these, many doubted that he was talented enough a politician for the job.[70] Thatcher, who had become a close ally, decided to run in his stead. There were three factors that worked to her advantage. First, she had not been a central figure within the Conservative establishment.[71] This underscored her credentials as a candidate embodying a break with the ailing institutions of post-war Britain.[72] Second, there was substantial discontent with Heath among Conservative MPs because he had lost two general elections in a year.[73] Third, there was general dissatisfaction with one nation conservatism, especially among the grassroots of the party.[74] In the end, Thatcher prevailed in the leadership contest.

However, her victory should not be read as a reflection of widespread support for her ideological orientation, which was still evolving anyway. This is visible in the fact that she only undertook a limited reshuffle of the shadow cabinet when she became leader. At the same time, she chose not to include Heath.[75] In so doing, she signalled that she wanted a clear break with the Heath era.

---

67 Gamble 1988, pp. 80–1.
68 Kavanagh 1990, p. 89; compare Gamble 1988, pp. 80–1.
69 Compare Middlemas 1991, p. 194.
70 Gamble 1988, p. 81.
71 Gamble 1988, p. 82; compare Morgan 1990, p. 392.
72 Compare Middlemas 1991, p. 195.
73 Compare Evans 1997, p. 7; Gamble 1988, p. 83.
74 Morgan 1990, p. 392.
75 Gamble 1988, pp. 85–6; Middlemas 1991, p. 193.

A New Direction for the Conservative Party

Thatcher and Joseph quickly started steering the party in a new direction. In a secret paper for the Shadow Cabinet called 'Policy-Making, 1975', which was written a month after the leadership election, Joseph argued, with reference to Britain, that 'the frontiers of freedom have been forced back, and we now need to counter-attack rationally and articulately'.[76] Apart from suggesting that it was time to go on the offensive, the paper only made recommendations on how to organise the process of establishing a new party line. Joseph proposed setting up an 'Economic and Social Strategy Committee', which was supposed to co-ordinate the work of numerous policy groups that were in turn responsible for developing a Conservative agenda for their respective field.[77] Soon after, the Shadow Cabinet agreed with this plan,[78] meaning that Thatcher and Joseph had established an internal structure helping them to frame the debates on the Conservative frontbench.

In April 1975, soon after Thatcher took the leadership, Joseph used this structure in order to disseminate a confidential paper called 'Notes towards the Definition of Policy'. It was aimed at sketching 'a strategy for party renewal and national recovery' and was the first important contribution to the debate on the party line.[79] Thatcher had explicitly asked Joseph to produce this paper,[80] which can be seen as an attempt to control the discussions from the start.

In it, Joseph spelled out what he meant by 'counter-attacking': He made clear his intention to start a new political project that broke with one nation conservatism, calling for a 'long-term strategy' based on 'radical approaches' and arguing against slipping back to the 'policies of the past'.[81] His proposals contain all the key tenets of new right ideology. In the area of economic order politics, Joseph advocated a free market approach. He suggested

- restricting the money supply and cutting public expenditure in order to combat inflation;[82]
- exposing 'the public sector as much as we can to the market';[83]

---

[76] Thatcher Archive, 109980, p. 1.
[77] Thatcher Archive, 109980, p. 2.
[78] Thatcher Archive, 110091, p. 2.
[79] Thatcher Archive, 109980, p. 3.
[80] Thatcher Archive, 109952, p. 3.
[81] Thatcher Archive, 109980, pp. 3–4.
[82] Thatcher Archive, 109980, p. 7.
[83] Ibid.

- reducing subsidies for businesses and allowing the reduction of 'over-manning' through their exposure to competition;[84] and
- lowering direct taxes on 'earnings and investment'.[85]

Furthermore, Joseph left no doubt as to whom he saw as the main enemy of this agenda. He opined that 'we have a mulish trade union movement, with some malignancy'.[86] Whereas 'mulish' is a pretty harmless attribute, Joseph's reference to 'malignancy' in this context reveals his deep-seated hostility towards militant trade unionism: It evokes the image of a cancerous body, which can only survive if it receives aggressive treatment that possibly involves cutting out all the affected parts. This is also visible in Joseph's concrete recommendations concerning class politics, which are testament to a repressive approach. He proposed

- enforcing the law without hesitancy during industrial conflicts and enquiring into the creation of a legal framework specifically geared to union activities;[87]
- forcing unions by law to hold secret ballots;[88]
- stripping the 'dependents of strikers' of access to benefits and tax rebates, which were usually important sources of income for families during stoppages;[89] and
- considering to provide 'the forces of law and order' with 'supplementary support' in the event of a 'political strike' – probably a coded reference to using volunteers or troops.[90]

Moreover, the paper contains recommendations concerning the production of consent – most importantly, the sale of council houses.[91] Strikingly, all of

---

84   Thatcher Archive, 109980, p. 9.
85   Thatcher Archive, 109980, p. 10.
86   Thatcher Archive, 109980, p. 6.
87   Thatcher Archive, 109980, pp. 9, 12.
88   Thatcher Archive, 109980, pp. 12, 18.
89   Thatcher Archive, 109980, pp. 9–10.
90   Thatcher Archive, 109980, p. 9. This interpretation is building on the Carrington Report from 1977 (see below), which was the first major Conservative policy paper on labour relations after the leadership election. It contained a passage entitled 'Use volunteers or troops only in exceptional circumstances or for very specific purposes' (Thatcher Archive, 111394, p. 20).
91   Thatcher Archive, 109990, p. 14.

Joseph's recommendations were put into practice in some way or another during the years of the Thatcher and Major governments, which demonstrates that Thatcher and Joseph had a pretty clear idea back then of where they wanted to take the party.

At the time, however, Joseph's plans were met with fierce resistance by the remaining Heathites on the Conservative frontbench. Quintin Hogg, a member of the Shadow Cabinet, made notes during the meeting where Joseph's paper was discussed. According to these notes, Reginald Maudling, who had been home secretary under Heath, remarked that he did not agree 'with one little bit' of the tract. Francis Pym, another member of Cabinet under Heath, is quoted as saying that '[t]he Keith paper is a recipe for disaster'. The notes also indicate that Thatcher and her allies Geoffrey Howe and Angus Maude defended the main thrust of Joseph's argument.[92]

In February 1976, James Prior, a one nation Tory and the Conservative frontbencher with the closest relationship to the trade unions, presented a paper on labour relations to the Shadow Cabinet, which diverged widely from Joseph's. According to the minutes of the meeting, Prior proposed 'not taking the issue head-on as yet' because 'the healing process' between the unions and the Conservative Party was progressing. Furthermore, he suggested proceeding 'slowly and quietly' and taking advantage of 'the new willingness in the TUC to discuss policy with us'.[93]

The minutes reveal that Prior's paper was controversial. The views aired ranged from the suggestion to build up 'an effective working relationship with trade union leaders' to the observation that 'there was a danger of losing credibility' if the Shadow Cabinet 'ran away from everything', that is, if it avoided re-regulating labour relations. In one remarkable statement, an unnamed participant proposed an approach closely resembling the 'salami tactics' that would become the hallmark of the Thatcherite approach to labour relations: 'We should not give the unions a pretext for their contrived anarchy and we should have a range of legislative measures ready in the locker for use as and when the situation was [sic] seen to demand it. The best way to proceed was piece-meal, introducing single measures to deal with particular abuses when the moment was ripe'.[94]

All in all, the variety of opinion on labour relations on the Conservative frontbench at the time reflects the fact that Thatcher and Joseph did not have

---

92 Thatcher Archive, 111154, pp. 1–2.
93 Thatcher Archive, 110026, pp. 1–2.
94 Thatcher Archive, 110026, pp. 2–3.

full control over the course of the party yet. Quite the contrary: the first years of Thatcher's leadership were marked by deep (and deepening) rifts; Thatcher would only establish full control well into her first government.

In his notes, Hogg describes a meeting with Peter Carrington in March 1977. Carrington was a representative of one nation conservatism, a former defence secretary and a member of the Shadow Cabinet. He would become foreign secretary under Thatcher. According to the notes, Carrington confided to Hogg that he was disturbed by how the party was run, and that 'we are giving the impression of an extreme right-wing party'. He added that he blamed Thatcher and Joseph for this state of affairs.[95]

New Right Ideology

In contrast to the Conservative frontbench, the party grassroots were broadly supportive of the new party line. Thatcher and Joseph quickly managed to build a broad constituency for their politics. They did so with the help of public interventions translating the vague feeling among many Britons that things were going wrong into a dismissal of the fundamental assumptions guiding postwar politics. In line with Joseph's paper, they publicly denounced corporatism, incomes policy and alleged social democratic tendencies within the party; moreover, they promoted supply-side economic policies.[96] The different elements informing their political agenda converged in the wholesale rejection of 'collectivism' and 'socialism': Thatcher and her allies portrayed coalitions and collective action among workers as a distortion of the market that was to blame for Britain's economic decline; moreover, they dismissed socialism as an illegitimate and morally corrosive ideology advocating the levelling of hierarchies and the destruction of tradition.[97] Thatcher remarked at the time that 'What we are seeing in Britain now is not a crisis of capitalism but a crisis of Socialism'.[98] Needless to say, as far as the Labour leadership was concerned, the Social Contract was an attempt not to break with capitalism, but to resolve the economic crisis with the help of corporatist techniques.

In sum, Thatcher and Joseph were able to connect the widespread sentiment that there was a deep-rooted crisis with the equally widespread fear

---

95   Thatcher Archive, 111182.
96   Schwarz 1987, p. 123; Gamble 1988, p. 92; Middlemas 1991, p. 199.
97   Lawrence and Sutcliffe-Braithwaite 2012, p. 140; Saunders 2012, p. 32; compare Gamble 1988, p. 54.
98   Cited in Saunders 2012, p. 31.

of Eastern European-style socialism. Their public interventions exploited the 'ideological polarisation' that came with the catastrophic equilibrium.[99] Time and again, they claimed that 'the country has fallen victim to the stealthy advance of socialist collectivism', which chimed with people's experience of the rigidity of the bureaucracy that was caused by post-war state interventionism.[100]

Importantly, the attack of Thatcher and Joseph on socialism and the post-war settlement built on an interpretation of the crisis that disarticulated class. The two of them quite consciously chose to strengthen non-class ties and identities by blaming collectivist forces of all backgrounds for the decline of Britain.[101] Accordingly, Thatcher deployed a language juxtaposing the 'industrious' and the 'idle' without ascribing particular class backgrounds to either of the two groups. In Thatcher's worldview, the manual workers trying to 'get on' in life as individuals through 'hard work' deserved support, while those relying on benefits or trying to advance collectively by means of class organisation were at the receiving end of her scorn.[102] As such, this was nothing more than the nth rehashing of the Elizabethan distinction between the 'deserving' and the 'undeserving poor'.[103] But Thatcher gave it new life by using it in an innovative way: she aligned the 'deserving' group with the middle class by speaking of 'ordinary working families',[104] and she replicated the distinction at the level of the power bloc by heaping praise on the figure of the innovative and highly active 'entrepreneur' while attacking the 'vested interests' in the 'establishment'. Following Thatcher, the privileged groups concerned were defending underserved entitlements and – in the shape of Tory grandees supporting one nation conservatism and the post-war settlement – were making common cause with working class 'idlers'.[105] In other words, Thatcher constructed, with her rhetoric, two groups that divided the nation but cut across class lines. In my terms, she was starting to build a 'two nations' hegemonic project. Fittingly, Joseph revealed in a candid statement at the time that 'the objective of our lifetime, as I see it, is embourgeoisement'.[106] This suggests that he was in favour of a society where working-class identity,

---

99   Hall et al. 1978, p. 313; compare Saunders 2012, p. 30; Schofield 2012, p. 106.
100   Ibid.
101   Compare Hobsbawm 1989, p. 18.
102   Lawrence and Sutcliffe-Braithwaite 2012, pp. 134, 140.
103   Compare Hill 1952.
104   Lawrence and Sutcliffe-Braithwaite 2012, p. 134.
105   Compare Lawrence and Sutcliffe-Braithwaite 2012, pp. 134, 140.
106   Cited in Lawrence and Sutcliffe-Braithwaite 2012, p. 140.

in particular its collectivist and socialist traits, have been wiped out thanks to the dominance of a form of identity highlighting individualistic aspirations.

In conclusion, the pre-history of Thatcherism is marked by the emergence of a fairly coherent political agenda that combined a free market approach to economic policy with a deep hostility towards the labour movement, its organisations and ideology. In retrospect, elements of the class political regime and economic-political order that were to characterise the Thatcher era were starting to appear at the level of political discourse: The mid-1970s were a time when leading representatives of the Conservative Party started to see a free market approach to economic order politics and a repressive, 'two nations' approach to class politics as viable political strategies. However, it is important to note in this context that Thatcher was popular with the party rank-and-file, but that she had not yet won full control over the leading circles of the party. Accordingly, I contend that the first two years of Thatcher's leadership of the Tory Party still belong to the pre-history of Thatcherism.

CHAPTER 5

Emergence: A New Agenda for the Conservative Party (1977–9)

A Political Rupture

1977 was a turning point because the new leadership of the Conservative Party managed to streamline internal debates on its ideological orientation.[1] From this point onwards, Thatcher and her followers were able to position their party as a political force that broke with the status quo.[2] Conversely, one nation conservatism, the political face of the gentlemanly capitalist ideology that had dominated the British power bloc for so long, was becoming marginalised.[3] The Thatcherite class political regime and the free market authoritarian economic-political order began to emerge.

There are two reasons why I contend that there was a rupture in 1977. One was the Grunwick dispute, whose highpoint was reached in June of that year; the other the fact that four important reports were completed in the summer and autumn of 1977 that laid out elements of the new Conservative strategy and agenda.

Grunwick was a film-processing firm based in North London. It mostly employed immigrant workers, among them many Asian women with East African backgrounds, who were paid badly and had to work long hours. The attitude of the management was characterised by 'an undercurrent of racist and paternalist arrogance'.[4] Some of the workers began striking for union recognition in August 1976, which led to dismissals and a two year long strike for their reinstatement and the recognition of their union, the Association of Professional, Executive, Clerical, and Computer Staffs (APEX). The owner, George Ward, was not prepared to give ground; as a result, the conflict escalated and led to sympathy strikes by postal workers as well as mass picketing by trade unionists from all over the country and left-wing political activists. Eventually, the

---

1 Middlemas 1991, p. 199.
2 Middlemas 1991, p. 193.
3 For an account of gentlemanly customs and their economic political significance, see the case study on the 'Big Bang'. A detailed historical analysis of 'gentlemanly capitalism' and the formation of the British power bloc can be found in Gallas 2008.
4 Forbes 1978, p. 387.

Callaghan government set up a Court of Inquiry tasked with examining the dispute. It produced a report recommending that the sacked workers be reinstated and the union be recognised, but this was to no avail. Ward ignored the report, and the House of Lords ruled that he had the right to refrain from recognising the union.[5]

The significance of Grunwick for the emergence of Thatcherism lies in the fact that a pattern emerged that would reappear frequently in the era of the Thatcher governments: Whenever there were union-busting employers who sought confrontations with organised labour, they could count on the rhetorical and practical support of the Conservative frontbench and its networks. In fact, the link between hard line employers and the party leadership would prove instrumental in driving back organised labour during the Thatcher years.

At the level of public discourse, Joseph actively worked to de-legitimise the cause of the strikers at Grunwick. With reference to the mass picketing, he publicly spoke of 'blatant terrorism and illegality in the name of trade unionism', 'red fascism' and a 'make-or-break point for British democracy'.[6] Considering that the strikers were simply demanding the right to organise in their workplace, this can be seen as a conscious attempt to whip up hatred against the trade unions. Thatcher was not quite as strongly worded, but she also tried to publicly question the legitimacy of the strike.[7]

In terms of practical support, John Gorst, the Tory MP for Hendon North, played a crucial role. He got directly involved in breaking the strike: 'It was Gorst who at the critical moments of the strike stood beside Ward at every news conference and meeting, who carefully controlled the management's tactics, developing all the time a perverse litany of individual freedom, the right to work, the horrors of the corporate state'.[8]

Some of the operational work on the ground was also carried out by the far-right National Association for Freedom (NAFF). In early 1977, the NAFF had tried to undermine a boycott of British mail unions of phone calls and mail going to South Africa by seeking an injunction. Now the mail unions were trying to block mail going out of the Grunwick plant, which threatened to hit the company badly because it sent out developed films in the post. As a reaction, the NAFF launched an operation that consisted in breaking through the picket lines with lorries carrying the mail, which was then taken to post boxes all

---

5   Sivanandan 1977; Forbes 1978; Reid 2004, pp. 354–5; Cohen 2006, pp. 41–2.
6   Thatcher Archive, 111944, p. 2; 111944, pp. 1–2.
7   Hansard HC, 933, 1733–40; 934, 538–43.
8   Forbes 1978, p. 388.

over the country.[9] In her memoirs, Thatcher pronounced that she gave NAFF 'as much support' as she could.[10] In his biography of Thatcher, Hugo Young quotes an unnamed ally of Thatcher's as stating that '[i]n emotional moments she's said that NAFF is doing more for freedom in this country than anyone else in politics'.[11]

At the time, Prior was opposed to Joseph's aggression and quite in favour of the report produced by the Court of Inquiry.[12] But it is indicative of the tide turning against one nation conservatism that Thatcher and Joseph had their way and did not need to compromise their stance. This shift becomes even more visible if we look at the internal debate on the party line. In my view, 1977 is a watershed also because four of the working groups instituted by Thatcher and Joseph produced reports, and all four of these reports contained detailed recommendations in the areas of class politics and economic order politics that reflected, to varying degrees, Thatcher and Joseph's worldview. The working groups in question were:

– the 'Authority of Government Group' chaired by Carrington;
– the 'Nationalised Industry Policy Group' under Nicholas Ridley;
– the 'Stepping Stones' project of John Hoskyns and Norman Strauss; and
– a group around Joseph working on a pamphlet on economic policy.

Obviously, these reports were important because a fairly clear-cut Conservative agenda emerged. But it also appears that Thatcher and her allies sought to co-ordinate an offensive of the power bloc in a much more conscious way than past Conservative leaderships: in line with the attitude taken towards the strikers at Grunwick, the reports contained detailed recommendations on how to marginalise the British trade union movement.

∴

---

9   *The Telegraph*, 13 September 2010.
10   Thatcher 1995, p. 399.
11   Young 1989, p. 111.
12   Forbes 1978, p. 390.

Case Study: Preparing for Government – Conservative Policy Papers from 1977

The Carrington Report (June 1977)

The 'Authority of Government Group' was set up by the circle around Thatcher as early as May 1975, shortly after her election as party leader. The Carrington group was explicitly tasked with drawing up plans for emergencies like the 1974 NUM strike, where the government was faced with a direct, politically motivated challenge to its authority. It contained both proponents of a conciliatory approach and hardliners in favour of confrontation. The former, among them Carrington, had serious doubts about the ability of a Conservative government to defeat militant trade unionism; the latter were more optimistic.[13]

The final report, completed in June 1977 against the backdrop of the escalation of the Grunwick dispute, reflected these divisions. In line with the views of the faction around Carrington, it conceded that a future government 'might have to capitulate to an all-out miners' strike or a shut down of all power stations'.[14] Other passages read like a carefully crafted compromise between both sides:

> We are convinced that the government could win out in more challenges to its authority than in the past ... But we also recognise that in a highly interdependent society with specialised roles, there will always be groups with the power to successfully challenge government. In these cases the only possible course is for government to avoid confrontations.[15]

Despite the guarded prose of the document, it contained a number of recommendations that were clearly aimed at breaking strikes in sectors that were important for energy production. It advised:

- to institute a 'high-powered unit responsible to a Senior Minister' that was tasked with preparing 'constantly up-dated contingency plans';
- to design new power stations in a way that made 'picketing more difficult';
- to extend 'dual-firing' at power stations, making them less dependent on coal;

---

13 Dorey 2009, p. 139.
14 Thatcher Archive, 111394, p. 12.
15 Thatcher Archive, 111394, p. 4.

- to secure the supply of power stations with coal through an according stocking policy; and
- to actively manage public opinion and use it in order to undermine the legitimacy of a strike, possibly through the use of referenda.[16]

A highly contentious point, the use of volunteers and troops to break strikes, again brought out the divide between those seeking conciliation and those advocating a hard line:

> Some of us believe that both employers and unions have a tendency to exaggerate the mystery and craft involved in a particular occupation and that officials are so hypnotised by the limiting cases, such as nuclear power stations, that they discount unduly the scope for the use of volunteers or troops in cases where exceptional skills are not required. However, in practice the main constraint is probably not the availability of the required skills, but rather the fear that the use of troops or volunteers will exacerbate the situation leading to an escalation of conflict.[17]

It is a sign of the strength of the hardliners that breaking strikes with the help of the military, which would have been interpreted by the union movement as a deeply hostile act, was considered at all.

A spokesman of the British power bloc, Campbell Adamson, the director-general of the CBI, was interviewed by the Carrington group in January 1977. He openly sided with the hardliners, expressing his hope that 'the next Conservative government would not become so obsessed with the dangers of confrontation that they had to be avoided at all costs'.[18] Significantly, Thatcher claims in her memoirs that at a meeting a year earlier, representatives of the CBI had urged her and other members of the Conservative frontbench to support the incomes policy of the government.[19] Consequently, Adamson's statement is an indication that the support of the British power bloc for one nation conservatism and its more conciliatory approach to labour relations was receding, and that the more combative approach associated with Thatcher and her close confidants had found the backing of important sections of British capital. Leys observes that '[d]uring these years much of the CBI leadership, not just the small-business membership, came to believe that (as one industrialist

---

16 Thatcher Archive, 111394, pp. 8, 15, 18–23.
17 Thatcher Archive, 111394, pp. 20–1.
18 Cited in Dorey 2009, p. 144.
19 Thatcher 1995, p. 311.

expressed it) "Mrs Thatcher's government is all that stands between [us] and a rapid slide into a down-market version of the German Democratic Republic"'.[20]

The Ridley Plan (July 1977)

In April 1976, the Nationalised Industries Policy Group was constituted. It was tasked with drawing up a report on how to manage and privatise nationalised industries. The chair was Nicholas Ridley, an MP and former Powellite who was close to Thatcher.[21] But none of the members of the group were members of the Shadow Cabinet. The Ridley Plan, as it came to be known, was completed a month after the Carrington report and diverged substantially from the latter because it was less ambiguous and more combative in its message. The main part laid out recommendations for how a future Conservative government should deal with the nationalised industries and the public sector. The annex, which was aptly titled 'Countering the Political Threat', discussed how a Conservative government should prepare for major clashes with the unions over the envisaged restructuring. It provided detailed recommendations on to how confront and undermine organised labour and reverse the class relations of forces in favour of the power bloc. In other words, it contained a broad agenda with far-reaching implications for Thatcher's political line, laying out elements both of a new class political regime and a new economic-political order. Obviously, the plan was meant to be a secret strategy paper, but it was leaked to *The Economist*, which published an article mainly covering its annex.[22] The reaction in the media was, in many ways, one of ridicule: 'It all seemed utterly far-fetched'.[23] But the Thatcher governments would subsequently follow the recommendations closely, in particular those in the annex.[24]

In my view, the historical significance of the Plan lies in capturing a new regime of condensation in the making. It contains detailed recommendations on how to apply new right ideas both in the fields of economic order politics and of class politics, with a focus on nationalised industries and public services.

---

20 Leys 1985, p. 17.
21 Ridley would later serve under Thatcher as Minister at the Foreign Office, Financial Secretary to the Treasury, Transport Secretary, Secretary of State for the Environment, and Secretary of State for Trade and Industry. In his role as Transport Secretary, he would be directly involved in undermining the 1984–5 miners' strike.
22 *The Economist*, 27 May 1978.
23 Goodman 1985, p. 25.
24 Compare Wiles 1985, p. 172; Hain 1986, p. 33; Hyman 1987a, p. 213; Gamble 1988, p. 103; Coates 1989, pp. 128; Young 1989, p. 368; Middlemas 1991, p. 283; Marsh 1992, p. 120; Kerr 2001, p. 172; Dorey 2013.

Considering that Callaghan and Healey had already adopted a neoliberal fiscal and monetary policy, the recommendations pushing for privatisation amounted to sketching the contours of a new economic-political order replacing the post-war settlement. But notably, the authors also describe the corresponding class political regime by discussing how to deal with the unions and win over the population.

At the start of their paper, Ridley et al. alleged that the nationalised industries are run for the benefit of their employees, and not for the consumers of the goods or services provided.[25] In line with their free market thinking, they defined the latter not as 'the public', 'the people' or 'the population', but as 'customers'.[26] This suggests that they viewed nationalised industries and public services primarily as businesses operating on a market. They did not assess the public sector on the grounds of political criteria such as its effect on social cohesion or the quality of life of disadvantaged groups, but on the grounds of economic criteria, that is, how well they met money-mediated demand. Correspondingly, the long-term aim of Ridley et al. was to privatise all nationalised industries apart from 'true utilities' such as gas, electricity, water, the railways (including underground railways), the mail service and the telephone network.[27] Consequently, I see the Ridley Report as an attempt to set out a plan for a drastically reduced public sector and, hence, for a fundamental restructuring of the British state.

The report developed three closely connected strategic themes, which, bound together, were supposed to lead to denationalisation. The first theme was 'management'. Due to the limited scope and the technical character of recommendations in this area, Ridley et al. deemed them comparably easy to implement. The recommendations were:

---

25 Thatcher Archive, 110795, p. 1.
26 Ibid.
27 Ibid. The fact that the group made these exceptions is not the result of a belief that 'true utilities' should remain in public hands. Rather, the reasoning of Ridley et al. was strategic: They assumed that unions have a lot of leverage in the sectors in question because stoppages hurt the entire economy badly. According to them, the number of 'weeks of strike the nation can survive' in the sectors like water, electricity, gas and healthcare was 'zero' (p. 9). They concluded that '[t]here really is very little Government can do about these industries other than get them to price their wares correctly through a rate of return on capital policy' (p. 17). The activities of future British governments would show that Ridley et al. were pretty timid in this matter. Apart from the NHS, where privatisation is still ongoing (and the advice of Ridley et al. to operate 'by stealth' has been followed by all governments from Thatcher to Cameron), all the sectors in question have been privatised.

- introducing sanctions for management failure and rewards for successes in order to create incentives for better performance;[28]
- publishing unit costs in order to 'highlight inefficiency', that is, to put pressure on management and work forces;[29]
- instituting 'return-on-capital obligations' in order to restrain wages and fragment industries and pay levels;[30]
- setting up an accounting system that highlights uneconomic activities;[31]
- agreeing 'five-year rolling corporate plans' between industries and sponsoring government departments in order to control investment;[32]
- determining wage settlements on the grounds of manpower supply and vulnerability of the public to a strike in the respective industry;[33]
- separating the civil service and state-owned companies by forcing ministers to refrain from interfering with management, and introducing supervisory boards with the task of protecting management against 'ministerial and bureaucratic pressures';[34]
- ensuring that potential labour representatives on boards remain isolated;[35] and
- appointing board members sympathetic to the plans, that is, 'commercially-minded bankers and holding company chairmen'.[36]

Taken together, these measures did not amount to a comprehensive denationalisation. But they certainly aimed to make nationalised industries more similar to private sector companies. Hence, they can be seen as preparatory in character. This conforms to the recommendation of Ridley et al. to conduct denationalisation 'by stealth'.[37] Sheila Cohen describes this approach somewhat sarcastically as 'salami tactics'.[38]

The second theme was 'ownership'. Recommendations in this area consisted in pursuing a three-step approach:

---

28   Thatcher Archive, 110795, p. 1.
29   Thatcher Archive, 110795, p. 2.
30   Thatcher Archive, 110795, p. 12.
31   Thatcher Archive, 110795, p. 5.
32   Thatcher Archive, 110795, p. 6.
33   Thatcher Archive, 110795, p. 9.
34   Thatcher Archive, 110795, pp. 12–13.
35   Thatcher Archive, 110795, p. 13. According to the report, worker representatives can do 'little harm' if they are in 'a distinct minority' (ibid.).
36   Thatcher Archive, 110795, p. 14.
37   Thatcher Archive, 110795, p. 15.
38   Cohen 2006, p. 54.

(1) passing legislation to abolish public sector monopolies;
(2) fragmenting the relevant industries by creating a number of separate companies; and
(3) selling them to private investors.[39]

This is another instance of 'salami tactics', albeit on a much grander scale. The recommendations reveal that there were people around Thatcher with comprehensive plans in the field of economic order politics. In their report, Ridley et al. envisaged an accumulation strategy based on the free reign of the market, and their approach to implementing the desired changes reveals an authoritarian streak: they claimed to know which policies are best for the 'country' and thus felt entitled to implementing them whilst shielding them from public scrutiny. This is an indication that a state project based on authoritarian, top-down decision-making was emerging.

The third strategic theme, which is also a reflection of 'salami tactics', confirms that this is a valid point. It concerned the step-by-step preparation for a confrontation with the unions, and was based on the assumption that they would lead the resistance against denationalisation.[40] Ridley et al. were aware of the relation of forces between the power bloc and organised labour, and were keen on shifting them in favour of the former. The fact that they urged caution and chose to keep their recommendations confidential reveals that they were trying to draw lessons from the defeat inflicted on Heath by the miners.[41]

The Ridley Report delineated a new class political regime insofar as it outlined elements of a new extraction strategy and a new hegemonic project. Elements of a repressive extraction strategy are visible where Ridley et al. suggested seeking confrontation with the unions and inflicting defeat on them. In some ways, their observations resembled those in the Carrington Report aimed at breaking strikes in sectors relevant for energy production, but there is a shift both in tone and scope. The five main recommendations in this area were:

(1) making concessions in 'vulnerable industries', that is, those industries where strikes would massively impact on the everyday lives of the British population;

---

39   Thatcher Archive, 110795, p. 22.
40   Thatcher Archive, 110795, pp. 24–6.
41   Witness that there is a reference to 'the Saltley Coke-works mob' in the report (Thatcher Archive, 110795, p. 25).

(2) ensuring that the battle ground of the inevitable confrontation with the unions is shifted to a 'non-vulnerable industry, where we can win';[42]
(3) fortifying defences in vulnerable sectors, especially in coal mining;[43]
(4) cutting off funds to striking workers through 'legislation to deal with tax refunds and unemployment pay';[44] and
(5) recruiting, equipping and preparing mobile police forces to take on strikers, as well as asking haulage companies to recruit 'good non-union drivers ... prepared to cross picket lines, with police protection'.[45]

Moreover, Ridley et al. listed a host of measures directed at winning over workers and dividing the working class. In other words, they also outlined elements of a 'two nations' mode of leadership and domination. They argued that workers might consent to privatisation if they are told that wages will rise as its result – whether through increases in efficiency, the introduction of co-ownership schemes, or even outright concessions, which the authors see as an adequate response to resistance in 'vulnerable' industries.[46] The first two measures, they reckoned, could outmanoeuvre the Labour Party and create irreversible results.[47] Furthermore, they proposed to denationalise the British National Oil Company (BNOC) and turn this denationalisation into a 'coup de theatre [sic]':

> The assets of B.N.O.C. are worth approximately £1000m. We could offer them at at [sic] price, say, of half their value to the public at large ... This would be a positive act of giving public assets to the public, as well as making every man a capitalist.

In other words, Ridley et al. proposed to entrench pro-capitalist attitudes in the population by extending and popularising share-ownership. They argued that

---

42 Thatcher Archive, 110795, p. 24.
43 'Here we should seek to operate with the maximum quantity of coal stocks possible, particularly at the power stations. We should perhaps make such contingent plans as we can to import coal at short notice. We might be able to arrange for certain haulage companies to recruit in advance a core of non-union lorry drivers to help us move coal where necessary. We should also install dual coal/oil firing in all power stations, where practicable as quickly as possible' (Thatcher Archive, 110795, p. 25).
44 Thatcher Archive, 110795, pp. 10, 25.
45 Thatcher Archive, 110795, p. 26.
46 Thatcher Archive, 110795, pp. 17, 25.
47 Thatcher Archive, 110795, p. 17.

this could be achieved by converting state-owned companies into stockholding ones and discounting the stock to the general public. This can be seen as an attempt to divide the working class by creating a group of workers who are responsive in their action to the position of their company in the market because they are stockholders.

Finally, Ridley et al. also explained how they expected the different strategic themes to interlink. They said that the five recommendations directly relating to labour relations 'should enable us to hold the fort until the long term strategy of fragmentation can begin to work'.[48] This shows that they viewed the recommendations under the first and the third theme as interim measures aimed at facilitating the implementation of the recommendations under the second theme, which were portrayed as producing lasting changes to the political economy of Britain.

The main aim of the plan, denationalisation, became a central plank of the accumulation strategy pursued by the Thatcherites. The recommendations in this area were taken further than proposed. Thatcher and her allies managed to privatise two fifths of all nationalised industries, including some of the 'true utilities'.[49] The introduction of obligatory rates of return was crucial in the process.[50] However, they did not fully break up monopoly structures, which remained all but intact in the cases of BT and British Gas.[51] Peter Riddell concludes that rushed privatisation in many cases brought about 'inadequate industrial structures'.[52]

Similarly, the course of the Thatcher governments concerning the extraction strategy closely followed the Ridley Report. Thatcher and her inner circle carefully prepared for large-scale confrontations with the unions. During the first Thatcher government, they bought time by making concessions to some of the unions. At the same time, they restricted access to benefits for strikers and overhauled the policing of industrial conflict. Moreover, they fortified the infrastructure needed to deal with a miners' strike through stockpiling coal at power plants. When this strike came in 1984, Ridley was Minister of Transport and member of the Cabinet committee responsible for preparing and executing the government's response to it.[53] This indicates that there was a great degree of continuity between the formulation of the Ridley Report in 1977 and the

---

48   Thatcher Archive, 110795, p. 26.
49   Riddell 1991, p. 87; compare Marsh and Rhodes 1992, p. 38.
50   Riddell 1991, p. 91.
51   Riddell 1991, p. 109.
52   Riddell 1991, p. 108.
53   Milne 1995, p. 10.

class politics of the second Thatcher government at this decisive turning point. And Ridley's strategy brought the desired results: the NUM was defeated, and so were other militant trade unions in preceding and subsequent conflicts. Consequently, the restructuring of the public sector went ahead, and privatisation soon appeared irreversible.[54]

But the impact of the Ridley Report in the area of class politics was not restricted to the extraction strategy. Thatcher and her allies followed another piece of advice in the Ridley Report closely, that is, the idea of using the denationalisation of BNOC to popularise share ownership and 'making every man a capitalist'. This agenda was later pursued in the Thatcherite campaign for 'popular capitalism', which concerned all denationalised companies, not just one.[55] 'Popular capitalism' was a central plank of the Thatcherite 'two nations' hegemonic project insofar as it was an attempt to build and reinforce what was deemed the 'productive nation' – at the expense of the 'idlers' who were not part of it.

In sum, the Ridley Plan represents a key document of Thatcherism in ascendance. It shows that a learning process had been taking place in the leadership of the Conservative Party regarding class politics. This learning had been triggered by Heath's defeat and had led to the recommendations of the Carrington Report. But Ridley and his group, who had started work a year later than Carrington, were much clearer about their political aims: they designed building blocks of a new class political regime based on repressing organised labour and extending asset ownership, which demonstrates their willingness to orchestrate an offensive step of the power bloc. Moreover, their commitment to denationalisation, especially when viewed against the backdrop of the Callaghan government embracing monetarism, demonstrates that they were also prepared to push forward with a free market accumulation strategy.

The Right Approach to the Economy (October 1977)

Shortly after the Ridley Plan had been circulated, a group involving several Conservative frontbenchers, namely Joseph, Howe and Prior, presented an economic programme for a future Conservative government. It was called *The Right Approach to the Economy* and was published for the 1977 Conservative Party Conference. Its title indicated that it was meant as a sequel to an earlier paper, *The Right Approach*, which had been made available a year earlier.

---

54 Riddell 1991, p. 110.
55 Riddell 1991, pp. 114–26; compare Jessop et al. 1990, p. 91; Evans 1997, p. 35.

On the whole, *The Right Approach* was less concise than the later paper.[56] It contained only a short paragraph on labour relations, entitled 'Industrial Attitudes', which simply asked whether the 'existing institutions' were still adequate. Similarly, it mentioned only in passing inflation and the money supply, the key themes of Thatcher's approach to economic order politics in the first years of her government.[57]

In contrast, *The Right Approach to the Economy* contained a clear commitment to economic liberalism, and some indications of a repressive approach to labour relations. It was less radical than the Ridley Plan or the Carrington Report (after all, the latter mooted the possibility of using troops and volunteers in order to break strikes). But this is unsurprising given that it was a pamphlet published for the public domain. Significantly, the recommendations made were compatible with the more far-reaching shift envisaged in the secret papers, and the main thrust was to call for a 'new approach', which was a conscious (if tentative) turn away from the post-war settlement.

In the text, the authors state that 'our prime and over-riding objective is to unwind the inflationary coils which have gripped our economy and threaten to throttle the free enterprise system'.[58] The suggested response was a monetarist approach to monetary policy, that is, 'the strict control of the money supply'.[59] This was flanked by other proposals belonging in the tradition of economic liberalism,[60] namely, the calls for 'the removal of unnecessary restrictions on business expansion' and for the 'full explanation by Government and management of their economic aims in the light of the inescapable financial constraints within which a solvent nation – like a solvent company – must operate'. These demands were reflections of a supply-side approach to economic policy and a public-choice take on fiscal policy, respectively.[61] The recommendations in this area suggest that the Conservative frontbench had now agreed on a fairly coherent, free market accumulation strategy with monetarism at its heart.

In the area of class politics, the paper was not quite as outspoken. In fact, it flirted with reviving a corporatist arrangement to replace the Social Contract, but also contained repressive elements. It suggested:

---

56 Compare Young 1989, p. 107.
57 Thatcher Archive, 112551.
58 Thatcher Archive, 112551, p. 7.
59 Thatcher Archive, 112551, p. 11.
60 On the different schools within economic liberalism, see Gamble 1988, pp. 39–57.
61 Thatcher Archive, 112551, p. 6.

- the establishment of an economic forum tasked with discussing the fundamentals of economic policy with the trade unions and the employers, which resembled the 'Concerted Action', a tripartite corporatist forum in Germany;[62]
- a return to collective bargaining (as opposed to the incomes policy imposed on the unions under the Social Contract);[63]
- a (non-binding) code of practice for actors operating in the area of labour relations;[64] and
- the imposition of restrictions on the closed shop.[65]

The passage on the closed shop contained a statement stressing that '[t]he Conservative Party is against the closed shop', but also the qualification that 'a simple attempt to ban closed shop can be not only ineffective, but sometimes even harmful to the individuals concerned'.[66] A different passage dealing with trade union militancy was less ambiguous: 'If ... we should find some within the ranks of organised labour who are determined to mount a direct *political* challenge to a newly elected Conservative government, we say now quite plainly that they will be resisted firmly and decisively'.[67] This is indicative of how careful the Conservatives were at this point when it came to communicating their stance on labour relations, and that they wanted to avoid being seen as a political force aiming to marginalise the labour movement. Obviously, this was fully compatible with the 'salami tactics' recommended by the Ridley Plan.

Stepping Stones (November 1977)

The *Stepping Stones* report was the product of an initiative by two businessmen, John Hoskyns and Norman Strauss, who initially did not belong to Thatcher's inner circle. Sherman of the CPS introduced them to Joseph and Thatcher, who commissioned a strategy paper from them in the spring of 1977.[68] The *Stepping Stones* report was completed in November 1977 and remained secret.[69] According to her autobiography, Thatcher discussed it over dinner with the authors and Joseph, Maude and Willie Whitelaw, the Heathite Shadow Home

---

62   Thatcher Archive, 112551, p. 12.
63   Thatcher Archive, 112551, p. 13.
64   Thatcher Archive, 112551, p. 14.
65   Thatcher Archive, 112551, p. 33.
66   Ibid.
67   Thatcher Archive, 112551, p. 16.
68   Young 1989, p. 114.
69   Thatcher Archive, 111771.

Secretary.[70] Hoskyns then produced an abridged and less combative but possibly more coherent version taking up some of the discussions,[71] which was reviewed at a meeting of the Leader's Steering Committee (a circle of key members of the Shadow Cabinet) in January 1978. The minutes of the meeting show that there were serious disagreements over this paper.[72]

In line with Strauss's professional background in marketing, *Stepping Stones* was mainly concerned with winning over the 'hearts and minds' of the electorate. Accordingly, it contained a 'communications programme' for the Tory Party.[73] But the report did not stop there: Hoskyns and Strauss did not just want to ensure victory in the next election, but a victory on terms that would allow the Tories to meet the key challenge facing the next government.[74] According to them, this challenge lay in instigating 'a sea-change in Britain's political economy' that would reverse the economic decline of the country.[75] Importantly, they added that there was an obstacle blocking this reversal: 'the negative role of the trades unions'.[76] Their conclusion was that 'a radical change' in the 'political and economic role' of the labour movement was needed.[77]

All things considered, Hoskyns and Strauss, thanks to their systematic approach, did more than just give short-term recommendations on how the Conservatives should approach the next general elections. They linked them up with detailed remarks on what a new Conservative political project could be. This is why *Stepping Stones* would play an important role in shaping the political strategy and the class and economic order politics of the Conservative Party in the Thatcherite era. Correspondingly, Thatcher later remarked in her memoirs that she 'came to appreciate the depth and quality of John Hoskyn's analysis'.[78] Following Young, this was an understatement. He writes that she was 'tremendously excited by what she read'.[79]

At the heart of Hoskyns and Strauss's argument is the observation that a conciliatory approach to labour relations will not work, will deepen Britain's crisis, and will turn out to be detrimental for the Conservative Party: 'Any strategy

---

70   Thatcher 1995, p. 421.
71   Thatcher Archive, 109848.
72   Thatcher Archive, 109952, compare Thatcher 1995, p. 421.
73   Thatcher Archive, 111771, 1977, pp. 1–2.
74   Compare Thatcher Archive, 111771, p. 8.
75   Thatcher Archive, 111771. p. S-1.
76   Ibid.
77   Thatcher Archive, 111771, p. 5.
78   Thatcher 1995, p. 420.
79   Young 1989, p. 115.

which does not address this problem of the trades union role from the outset, ensures failure in office, even though it might, at first sight, appear to make electoral success more likely'.[80] As a consequence, Hoskyns and Strauss advocated going on the attack or – in my terms – orchestrating an offensive step of the power bloc. In their view, the deep crisis of the political economy of Britain made anything less than a direct confrontation with the trade unions unavoidable: 'once the system itself starts to show signs of fatigue, instability, disintegration, then we start to talk about discontinuity. In discontinuity, solutions can only be found by breaking constraints which we had assumed were unbreakable'.[81] Correspondingly, Hoskyns and Strauss proposed 'breaking rules', that is, going against the existing conventions and procedures in the area of labour relations.[82]

In line with their call for an offensive, Hoskyns and Strauss mainly covered class politics in their paper. The Ridley Plan had laid out elements of a repressive extraction strategy; in contrast, *Stepping Stones* focused on leadership and domination, and it developed elements of a 'two nations' hegemonic project. In a nutshell, Hoskyns and Strauss suggested that the Conservatives should work on creating divisions in the labour movement by driving a wedge between moderate rank-and-file members and their radical leaders.[83] In other words, they proposed operating through active attempts to split the working class.

Their method of choice in achieving this end was 'psychological warfare'.[84] Correspondingly, they proposed creating, at the level of discourse, a strong link between the Labour Party, the union leadership, socialism, dictatorship, impoverishment, injustice and Britain as a 'sick society'.[85] Furthermore, they suggested contrasting the bleak picture of the status quo thus created first with the situation in 'other European countries',

> whose policies, even under social democratic governments, turn out to be well to the right of the last Tory government; and then with the 'Healthy society', which we can build if we want it – fairness, tolerance, openness to new ideas, respect for the law, material and intellectual independence – all in all, maturity and responsibility.[86]

---

80   Thatcher Archive, 111771, p. 13.
81   Thatcher Archive, 111771, p. 9.
82   Thatcher Archive, 111771. p. A-4.
83   Hoskyns and Strauss, 1977, p. 42.
84   Hoskyns and Strauss, 1977, p. A-12.
85   Hoskyns and Strauss, 1977, pp. 29–30, 42.
86   Hoskyns and Strauss, 1977, p. 40.

In addition, Hoskyns and Strauss argued that the creation of these two contrasting discursive chains could be underpinned with 'symbolic policy' helping to 'disturb the mental sets' of the supporters of trade unionism.[87] Among other things, '[t]his could, for example, involve a role in a reformed second chamber, or a guaranteed legislated, non-majority on the Board of a company, or a shareowning role for union members, or a controlling role in a local authority, etc.'[88] Furthermore, Hoskyns and Strauss stressed that these policies 'are not simply cosmetic'.[89]

Given the fairly combative tone of the other passages quoted, it is surprising how much they seem to row back at this point. In fact, Hoskyns and Strauss here appeared to propose a new corporatist settlement where union leaders trade a restriction of their room for manoeuvre for legally protected but strictly limited access to policy-making and decision-making at the level of the company. Obviously, this raises the question as to how it would have been possible to achieve such a settlement if it had indeed been flanked by attacks on the union leaderships at the discursive level. It appears that Hoskyns and Strauss were still searching for a coherent approach. Tellingly, the abridged version circulated after discussions with the 'Steering Group' under Whitelaw no longer contains any recommendations that sound corporatist.

All things considered, Hoskyns and Strauss suggested that their class political agenda was necessary for reaching what they saw as the primary 'communication objective' of the Conservative Party: 'to persuade the electorate to reject Socialism, and also to reject its continued promotion by the trade union leadership'.[90] Due to their commitment to reversing Britain's decline, they supplemented their class politics with a number of recommendations located in the area of economic order politics. These were fully compatible with the combative approach to labour relations and the free market approach of *The Right Approach to Economy*:

– stabilising the pound through 'monetary discipline, balanced budgets, public sector wage restraint';[91]
– shifting the tax burden from earnings to consumption (that is, from direct to indirect taxes, which are regressive in nature);[92]

---

87 Thatcher Archive, 111771, p. 39.
88 Thatcher Archive, 111771, p. A-9.
89 Thatcher Archive, 111771, p. 39.
90 Thatcher Archive, 111771, p. S-2.
91 Thatcher Archive, 111771, p. 6.
92 Thatcher Archive, 111771, p. 7.

- deregulating the private sector;[93] and
- using the revenues from North Sea oil in order to cut public debt.[94]

In conclusion, *Stepping Stones* contained a comprehensive agenda for the new right. Its historical significance lies in making a case for an offensive against organised labour and sketching elements of a mode of leadership and domination facilitating such an attack. In this sense, it ties in neatly with the Ridley Plan, which also called for an attack, but focused on the extraction strategy of a future Conservative government. Furthermore, *Stepping Stones* was fully compatible with the accumulation strategy envisaged in *The Right Approach to Economy*.

In my view, 1977 was a rupture and the starting point of the Thatcherite offensive because the new right around Thatcher and Joseph now possessed a fairly coherent and comprehensive political agenda. This agenda included detailed strategic considerations concerning its communication to the general public. At the same time, it was still hotly contested, underscoring its emergent and provisional character. In her memoirs, Thatcher wrote about a Steering Committee meeting where *Stepping Stones* was discussed, in which she and her colleagues had argued themselves 'to a standstill'.[95] The minutes of the meeting confirm her description. Peter Thorneycroft, chairman of the Conservative Party, criticised the 'note of extreme antagonism to the unions' that characterised the first draft; Pym advised against 'being too insensitive and too controversial' when it came to the union issue; and John Davies, Shadow Foreign Secretary, remarked that the Conservatives 'should be extremely careful of trying to separate union members from union leaders'.[96] Thatcher spoke out in favour of the paper, remarking that appealing to union members 'over the heads of their leaders' was the right approach.[97] She added, however, that there was maybe 'too much bureaucracy' in the paper – possibly a comment on its corporatist leanings – and she agreed with a critical remark by Davies that the union issue could not be 'the centre-piece' of the Conservative election strategy.[98] In the end, the meeting agreed that the discussion would continue; that only

---

93 Ibid.
94 Ibid.
95 Thatcher 1995, p. 421.
96 Thatcher Archive, 109832, pp. 2–3.
97 Thatcher Archive, 109832, p. 2.
98 Thatcher Archive, 109832, p. 4.

Prior, due to his close links to the union movement, 'should deliver major speeches on the trade unions';[99] and that

> [i]t was important that we should campaign to win the support of union members and criticise, in an appropriate tone, some of the actions, speeches and policies of trade union leaders. But this should not be the centre-piece of our election strategy.[100]

Obviously, this statement on party strategy oozed the spirit of compromise, but it was also entirely consistent with the 'salami tactics' proposed by the Ridley Plan: It was a matter of choosing the right time and place for an attack on the unions. As Thatcher had made clear with her support for *Stepping Stones*, for her the issue was not whether a future Conservative government should attack them, but when this should happen. The fact that this was not necessarily the dominant view in the Shadow Cabinet reflects that the offensive launched by Thatcher's inner circle had not yet reached the point of no return.

A Regime of Condensation in Emergence

The historical significance of the four reports lies in showing – against the accounts of the 'normalisers' and 'historicisers' – that the circle around Thatcher had a pretty clear idea of where they wanted to go politically even before they won the elections; that this would amount to a break with the convictions guiding mainstream post-war politics; and that they viewed organised labour as the key obstacle in the way. The plans contained key elements of the accumulation strategy, the extraction strategy and the hegemonic project in place during the Thatcher and Major governments. In addition, they are authoritarian in spirit, which conforms to the state project later implemented. In this sense, they show that by 1977 the neoliberal regime of condensation, which would characterise the political economy of Britain for next decades, was in emergence.

Put differently, the plans reveal that the circle around Thatcher aimed from the outset to fundamentally restructure capitalism in Britain. Of course, their recommendations were not a master plan to which Thatcher and her associates stuck slavishly. Nevertheless, they reflect themes and ideas that would have a significant impact on the policies of the Thatcher and Major govern-

---

99   Thatcher Archive, 109832, p. 5.
100   Thatcher Archive, 109832, appendix.

ments. Accordingly, the political course of these governments was not just the product of trial-and-error, 'muddling through' and opportunism under favourable circumstances. Rather, it was the result of all of this on top of careful short- and medium-term strategic planning. The politics of Thatcherism combined a 'series of non-negotiable precepts',[101] strategic assumptions about the implementation of the according policies, concessions and adaptations to specific situations, and ad-hoc decision-making revealing a willingness to improvise and gamble.

∴

The Winter of Discontent as a Point of No Return

In 1978–9, Britain witnessed the peak of the first stage of a new working-class defensive – the 'Winter of Discontent'. The unions decided to abandon wage restraint, which was a component of the Social Contract struck between the Labour government and trade union leaders after Wilson's re-election in 1974. Subsequently, the defensive would grow into a broader movement against the offensive of the power bloc orchestrated by the incoming Thatcher government.

In the two years before the Winter of Discontent, workers had experienced a fall in real wages not seen since the Great Depression. It was caused by government measures taken in response to the 1976 currency crisis. Under the deal with the IMF, the government reduced state expenditure by increasing taxation and decreasing the social wage in the form of cutting the subsidies for state-produced energy.[102] Furthermore, the wage ceilings now imposed on the unions under the Social Contract were substantially below the rate of inflation.[103]

Apart from administering a cut in real wages, the government decided to take a hostile approach to the TUC's agenda, which weakened its link to trade union leaders and disrupted the established channels of communication and negotiation.[104] As a result, by the winter of 1978–9, workers no longer accepted restraint, and the Social Contract ceased to have a binding effect. A wave of

---

101 Evans 1997, p. 3.
102 Middlemas 1991, pp. 156–7.
103 Hay 1996a, pp. 259–60.
104 Compare Middlemas 1991, pp. 165–6.

strikes, many of which took place in the public sector, led to 29,474,000 lost working days – by far the highest number recorded after the war.[105]

The political significance of the 'Winter of Discontent' lies in the fact that it was the point of no return for the Thatcherite offensive.[106] For a significant part of the population swung behind the Conservative leadership, who presented themselves as a new political force prepared to break with the conventions of post-war politics. Their discursive interventions were centred on claiming that organised labour was destructive and the Labour government inept, especially in terms of stabilising economic fundamentals, and on articulating such claims with the widespread fear of the domestic radical left and Soviet-style authoritarian socialism. Correspondingly, Thatcher put the blame for the crisis on organised labour:

> We have been through a period of increasing trade union power. The unions have had unique power and unique power requires unique responsibility. That responsibility has not been forthcoming. That is the reason for the position in which the country finds itself today – about which they [sic] can be no dispute.[107]

The Thatcherites presented the population with a simple, all-embracing yet flawed explanation for the state of the country, which crystallised in the famous slogan used in the 1979 general election campaign: 'Labour isn't working'.

This explanation overlooked that the weakness of Britain's industrial base, as well as the institutional underpinnings of corporatism, had created a flawed form of Fordism.[108] There were serious attempts, not least under Wilson, to modernise British industry and create competitive forms of mass production, but they did not bring lasting successes. The corporatist institutions supporting the post-war settlement were weak and did not prevent inter-firm competition over costs and work intensity: owners often responded to competitive pressures by cutting input costs, putting pressure on wages and intensifying production rather than investing in technological modernisation.[109] As a result, wages and productivity in Britain remained low compared to other countries

---

105 NatStats I, 2009. The year with the second highest number after the war was 1972, which was the height of the conflict over the Industrial Relations Act. This number was 23,909,000 (ibid.).
106 Jessop et al. 1988, p. 62.
107 Thatcher Archive, 103924.
108 Burgi and Jessop 1991, p. 175.
109 Nolan 1989, pp. 87–90; compare Nolan 1992, pp. 7–9.

belonging to the core of global capitalism.[110] A defining feature of Fordism was missing: There was no self-reinforcing productivist cycle of investment, productivity increases and subsequent improvements to the living standard of workers. Instead, workers bore the brunt of the recurrent economic crises and made comparably small advances during upswings. This suggests that union militancy was not an expression of 'irresponsibility', but a rational response to a crisis-ridden arrangement under which compliance with the dominant accumulation strategy had time and again resulted in the stagnation or even deterioration of workers' living standards.

Nevertheless, the Thatcherite interpretation of the conjuncture was taken up by many of the media, which popularised and disseminated it: 'The Myth of the Winter of Discontent, with its images of closed hospitals, rubbish piling up in the streets, and dead bodies rotting unburied in graveyards, was a masterpiece of selective news management in the Conservative interest'.[111] The papers portrayed the strikers as people without moral qualms about the dire consequences of their behaviour on other people's lives. Hay describes in detail how this style of reporting played out:

> The *Mirror* identifies the 'STRIKE THREAT TO BONE BOY', describing the predicament of 'seven-year-old Anthony ... hoping for a life-saving bone marrow transplant' as 'cleaners and porters at London's Westminster Hospital ... walked out'. This rhetorical strategy of adopting the subject position of a child cancer patient ... is placed in a somewhat different light when the story is analysed in greater detail. A close scrutiny of the news text reveals that 'Anthony' is not in fact a patient at the London Westminster Hospital at all, but at the 'nearby Westminster Children's Hospital' to where 'the strike is *expected* to spread' (emphasis added).[112]

The anti-union discourse soon dominated the entire political scene, which is demonstrated by the fact that Callaghan and TUC leader Len Murray felt it necessary to publicly denounce the strikers.[113]

The strikers did not manage to counter this discourse efficiently. The unions were still able to mobilise workers in force, but the Winter of Discon-

---

110   Nolan 1989, pp. 83–4.
111   Gamble 1988, pp. 94–5; compare Blackwell and Seabrook 1985, p. 144; Hay 1996a; Reid 2004, p. 396.
112   Hay 1996a, pp. 263–4.
113   Cohen 2006, p. 50.

tent brought 'fundamental ... divisions within the British working class' to the fore.[114] Fault-lines emerged on all fronts – between workers in different sections of industry, between fractions of the working class representing different places within the division of labour, between different levels in the organisational hierarchy of trade unions, and between the industrial and the political wing of the labour movement.

Cohen reports how oil tanker and lorry drivers walked out at roughly the same time without co-ordinating their respective actions: 'It remains a puzzle why, given the enormous "muscle" of two groups of workers without whom the country could not function, these strikes were conducted separately and almost in ignorance of one another, like ships passing in the night'.[115] This is an obvious case of sectionalism.

Apart from a lack of co-operation and co-ordination, there was also disagreement within the ranks of organised labour over aims – even though the actual demands made were mostly plainly economic. This reflected the different places occupied by different groups of union members within the social division of labour. Low-paid public sector workers – like nurses, hospital ancillary workers, ambulance personnel and gravediggers – played an important role in the strike wave.[116] Their representatives attacked differentials within public sector pay and argued for freedom from restraint in wage bargaining. Unions representing better-paid public sector workers, however, refused to support their demands.[117]

Furthermore, there were the divides between the rank-and-file and the leadership of organised labour, and between the industrial and the political wing of the labour movement. The first divide was nothing new: the 1950s had seen the rise of a shop-stewards movement in Britain whose members advocated and organised grassroots industrial action.[118] What was new was a Labour government that had given up on integrating organised labour in the state through corporatist or statist-corporatist arrangements. The leading circles in the Labour Party no longer presented themselves as ambassadors of the working class in the political scene.

Finally, there was also the division between workers as providers and as consumers of public services, which could well concern one and the same person.

---

114   Middlemas 1991, p. 167, compare p. 327.
115   Cohen 2006, p. 50.
116   Reid 2004, p. 355.
117   Middlemas 1991, p. 166.
118   Morgan 1990, p. 412.

EMERGENCE: A NEW AGENDA FOR THE CONSERVATIVE PARTY (1977–9)   119

Hain notes that public sector walkouts always create a strategic dilemma that in this particular case proved to be the Achilles heel of the action:

> Strikes in the 1978–9 'Winter of Discontent' could easily be portrayed as the product of union 'self-interest' and 'callousness', even though workers involved were among the poorest in the country, and their militancy sprang from the failures of Labour's income policy. This was because it was fellow members of the working class who were most badly hit: people, especially the old, who could not afford private treatment and depended upon strike-hit hospitals, parents (mainly women) penalized by striking caretakers closing schools and teachers refusing to supervise lunches. Savings could actually be made by local health and council services from unpaid wages, releasing the pressure on public finances and managers. The dilemma for public sector trade unionists is that, while strikes are aimed at those in authority, it is working-class people most dependent upon state services who suffer most from their withdrawal.[119]

It appears a paradox that an unprecedented number of workers turned out during the Winter of Discontent whilst organised labour was highly divided. On the one hand, this reflects the fact that union density had reached a peak, so that there was a large pool of people to draw from.[120] On the other hand, the increase in membership mostly occurred in sectors of the economy with already strong unions, which means that it did not lead to a shift in the social composition of the trade union movement and left existing divides intact.[121] Moreover, the strike wave came at a point when both the political projects to which trade unionists had dominantly aligned themselves – social democratic (neo-)corporatism and socialism in the Bennite vein – had just been defeated. Add to this the traditionally economistic outlook of British trade unions, and the result was a comparably apolitical movement.[122]

This is also demonstrated by the trajectory of the strike wave: The cause for unrest was that restraint under the Social Contract had not paid off, and the trigger was that successful industrial action for pay rises in some sections led others to follow suit.[123] Cohen points out that workers started taking control

---

119   Hain 1986, pp. 303–4.
120   Compare Western 1997, p. 146.
121   Compare Hain 1986, p. 260.
122   Compare Poulantzas 1973, p. 183; Hobsbawm 1981, p. 18; McIlroy 1988, p. 234.
123   Compare Cohen 2006, p. 48.

of parts of the public sector by deciding how emergency services should be run and which activities could be stopped temporarily and which ones had to continue. In my view, the political significance of these events should not be exaggerated: the self-organised provision of basic public services by workers on strike was not aligned to a project of political transformation; it was an attempt to deal with the dilemma of hurting one's own 'natural' constituency, not an act of rebellion against the hold of the power bloc over the political economy of Britain.

Conversely, the fact that workers mostly stuck to making economic demands explains the brittleness of their action. A political project was needed that could have given organised labour relative unity and could have addressed structural obstacles to solidarity, but this political project no longer existed. As a consequence, organised labour was not able to communicate a positive vision of a transformed society with their action, which might have made it easier to justify its disruptive effects to the general public.[124] The apolitical nature of the strike wave, combined with the critical state of the British economy, made it easy for the enemies of organised labour to portray unions as a force of destruction.

The consequence of the institutional and strategic weaknesses that were covered up behind the strikers' numerical strength was that the new right was able to turn substantial parts of the public against organised workers. Thatcher's claims that her confrontational stance towards unions 'is the only one for Britain', and that 'we have heard no alternative' resonated with the mood of large parts of the population.[125] A situation had arisen where it was no longer possible to contain or even stop the momentum behind Thatcherism, all the more because Wilsonian neo-corporatism and Bennite socialism had been defeated.

The demise in popularity of both options reflected that strategies aimed at implementing a Fordist growth dynamic had always clashed with the path-dependencies of capitalism in Britain, namely, the dominance of the City over the power bloc, the prevalence of economistic orientations in the working class, a state with limited interventionist capacities, and the weakness of corporatist institutions. Moreover, in the countries committed to productivist models, the 'crisis of Fordism' had already emerged, so that strategies aimed at moving Britain into this direction looked even less plausible to many.[126]

---

124 Compare Hyman 2001, p. 103.
125 Thatcher Archive, 103924.
126 Compare Jessop 2002a, p. 81.

Thatcher's contention that there was 'no alternative' exposed the fact that there was no coherent non-neoliberal narrative on how to address the crisis and move away from 'muddling through' on the political plane.

By imposing their interpretation of the crisis on the public, the circle around Thatcher galvanised the forces in the power bloc prepared to go on the offensive. They created a mandate for a new government 'to curb the growth of trade-union power'.[127] A contemporary poll in *The Times* found that approximately 80 percent of the population thought unions were too powerful and should be restrained by law.[128] The Winter of Discontent marked the 'point of no return' in the formation of Thatcherism:[129] It was the point when Thatcher and her associates had managed to turn public opinion against organised labour.

More broadly speaking, the circle around Thatcher responded to the organic crisis of capitalism in Britain with a politics of fear. The author of an internal paper on 'Themes' for elections argued that 'Fear is more potent than hope', and that the Conservative Party should start from making 'clear the threat'.[130] Correspondingly, the circle around Thatcher advanced the authoritarian claim that Britain faced an all-encompassing social crisis, which could only be resolved by taking a hard-line approach to 'law and order' issues. Along these lines, the 1979 Conservative election manifesto lamented the 'growing disrespect for the rule of law', which was described as 'THE MOST DISTURBING THREAT to our freedom and security'. According to the manifesto, there was an ensemble of enemies of the law, who came from all sections of society. It included 'Labour', 'the criminal', 'violent criminals and thugs', 'hooligans at junior and senior levels', 'immigrants', 'the young unemployed in the ethnic communities', 'the government', 'strike committees and pickets', 'terrorism' and 'convicted terrorists'.[131] All these people apparently had their part to play in creating a threat to the existence of British society. No explanation was given for how the activities of these highly diverse groups had come to intersect. It was enough to insinuate

---

127 Reid 2004, p. 396. The leading Conservative politician Kenneth Clarke remarked in 1985 that 'when we returned to office in 1979 one very major reason was that we were elected to curb excessive trade union power – of the trade unions over Government – and abuse of trade union power vis-à-vis employees within trade unions. The background was that a good Government had been swept out of power in 1974 by a political miner's strike, and the Labour government in the late 1970s had been firmly controlled by trade union bosses' (cited in Riddell 1991, p. 44).
128 Hain 1986, p. 124.
129 Jessop et al. 1988, p. 62; Jessop, undated; compare Hay 1996a, p. 253.
130 Cited in Saunders 2012, p. 30.
131 Original emphasis, Conservative Party 1979.

that there was an enemy, however vaguely defined, in the process of bringing down the country.

A year earlier, Hall et al. had provided an apt description of how the construction of a public enemy worked, and how this was linked to a rise in authoritarianism in public political discourses:

> [I]n its varying and protean forms, official society – the state, the political leadership, the opinion leaders, the media, the guardians of order – *glimpse*, fitfully at first, then (1968 onwards) more and more clearly, the shape of *the enemy*. Crises must have their causes; causes cannot be structural, public or rational, since they arise in the best, the most civilised, most peaceful and tolerant society on earth – then they must be secret, subversive, irrational, a plot. Plots must be smoked out. Stronger measures need to be taken – more than 'normal' opposition requires more than usual control.[132]

Thatcher and her circle were successful in shaping a new agenda with mass appeal for the Tory Party because they provided a simple (and simplistic) explanation for the economic crisis, which they portrayed as an aspect of a wider social malaise caused by the advance of socialism. Part of the appeal of the new agenda was that it was premised on, to use Hall's words, an 'authoritarian-populist' response to Britain's decline.[133] Thatcher and her circle styled themselves as politicians breaking with the old ways, and not shunning away from tackling the perceived problems head-on by taking an uncompromising stance. In a situation of catastrophic equilibrium, this message struck a chord with substantial parts of the population – especially with petty capitalists and owners of small capital, who felt threatened by the strength of organised labour. These fractions of capital constituted the social basis of Thatcherism.[134]

The advance of new right ideology was facilitated by the fact that it partly overlapped with the approach to monetary and economic policy embraced by Callaghan and his Chancellor Denis Healey in the wake of the IMF crisis. Healey had consented to the monetarist premises of the IMF loan and had accepted the social cost of monetarism in the form of increased unemployment.[135] It was the leadership of the Labour Party who had acted as pioneers of neoliberalism at the level of government in the mid-1970s. However, there was a key difference

---

132 Hall et al. 1978, p. 320.
133 Hall and Jacques 1983, p. 53.
134 Jessop et al. 1988, p. 96. Giles and Newman 2005a; 2005b.
135 Giles and Newman 2005a; 2005b.

between the proto-neoliberals in the Labour Party and the new right around Thatcher, which concerned the depth of their convictions. For the Labour leadership, embracing neoliberal fiscal policies was a tactical reaction to a currency crisis.[136] For the Conservative leadership, it was desirable out of principle.

All in all, new right ideology was successful precisely because it went against the political convictions that had informed the project of a post-war settlement:

– it was anti-corporatist, denying organised labour a role in economic and political decision-making;
– it was anti-welfarist, questioning the legitimacy and feasibility of social policy;
– it was anti-Keynesian, questioning the legitimacy and feasibility of demand-orientated economic policy; and
– it was anti-interventionist, questioning the state's role in directing the economy.

On this platform, Thatcher won the general elections. This was only the delayed political manifestation of the fundamental shift in the relations of class forces that had occurred during the Winter of Discontent.

---

[136] 'Healey had little confidence in the money supply as a guide to policy, but understood well enough that to restore the confidence of the financial markets the Treasury needed a visible lodestar for its economic policy. In his own words, Healey was an "unbelieving" monetarist – an opportunist rather than a convert to the new economic fashion. Once he had left office, he was to comment laconically of his flirtation with [monetarism] ... that "[a] government takes great risks when it flies in the face of market opinion ... however misguided that opinion may be"' (Stephens 1996, p. 11).

CHAPTER 6

Material Gains: Conducting Class Politics by Stealth (1979–84)

Economic Order Politics in Plain Sight, Class Politics by Stealth

Thatcher's first years in government saw the materialisation of both a free market authoritarian economic-political order and a distinctly Thatcherite class political regime based on a repressive extraction strategy and a 'two nations' hegemonic project. The emergent economic-political order was highly visible because decision-making in this area took centre stage in government announcements. The contours of the class political regime were much harder to spot. Its elements were mainly implemented by stealth.

Probably the most visible shift in economic order politics was that the new government openly embraced monetarism.[1] The Thatcherites were obsessed with creating 'SOUND MONEY' by capping the expansion of the money supply.[2] They believed that monetary stability, under conditions of the free reign of market forces, would eradicate economic imbalances and lead to a state of equilibrium.[3] Accordingly, they considered establishing a stable currency and securing unbridled competition as the main task of a government, and assumed that prosperity would follow. This, at least, was the theory.

For the Thatcherites, creating economic freedom required a laissez-faire regime to foreign trade and the transnational movement of capital. They assumed that the removal of trade barriers and capital controls would result in the reinforcement of the competitive strengths of the British national economy. In the tradition of David Ricardo, they alleged that this would force actors to make rational decisions about the use of their resources, which in turn would

---

1   The term 'monetarism' is often used with reference to strategies in monetary policy prioritising the fight against inflation. In fact, orthodox monetarism à la Milton Friedman is a more specific approach: It targets inflation but requires that this be done via directly controlling the *quantity* of money in circulation, that is, by restricting the creation of new money to the amount needed to meet higher output. It follows that targeting inflation via '*qualitative*' interventions, such as pushing up interest rates, is *not* monetarism in the strict sense of the term (compare Stephens 1996, p. 9).
2   Conservative Party 1979, capitalised by the authors.
3   Compare Joseph, Thatcher Archive, 110607.

result in allocative efficiency and sustained growth. Correspondingly, I contend that the Thatcherites inaugurated a free market or 'neo-Ricardian' accumulation strategy.[4]

Furthermore, Thatcher and her associates also implemented a new state strategy. They expanded repressive state apparatuses and promoted state centralisation at the same time as limiting state intervention in the economy. In other words, the emergent strategy was authoritarian and competition-oriented. Accordingly, I speak of a new, free market authoritarian economic-political order.

The shifts in class politics were less visible. They broadly followed the hidden agenda laid out in the Ridley Report. Initially, Thatcher et al. chose to make concessions to organised labour in the public sector. At the same time, they shifted the ground of industrial action by introducing repressive trade union laws. In this area, the contours of a new regime that would combine a repressive extraction strategy with a 'two nations' hegemonic project were still pretty blurred. With the benefit of hindsight, however, it is clear that the Thatcherites broadly knew where they were going. They opted for 'salami tactics', shielding their agenda very carefully from public scrutiny by initially focusing on a rather technical issue: labour law. Prior, the Secretary of Employment from 1979 until 1981, later conceded that the government's strategy involved 'changing the law gradually, with as little resistance, and therefore as much by stealth, as was possible'.[5]

In conclusion, there was a specific arrangement concerning political decision-making in the second period of Thatcherism. Although Thatcher won the election in 1979 thanks to the Winter of Discontent, the Thatcherites chose to drag economic order politics to the foreground and push class politics into the background. They had assessed where potential pitfalls of facilitating a shift in class relations lay: As the Heath episode had shown, beginning the crackdown on organised labour with a war of manoeuvre was likely to unite workers and undermine the government. Against this backdrop, the Thatcherites chose a strategy that consisted in a war of position followed by an open attack on militant trade unionism.[6] As a consequence of these strategic choices, my order of presentation in this chapter will reverse the hierarchy between class politics and economic order politics at the level of the CMP. I will first investigate Thatcherite economic order politics and then Thatcherite class politics.

---

4   Jessop, undated.
5   Cited in Dorey 1993, p. 28.
6   Compare Middlemas 1991, pp. 311–95; Howell 2005, p. 146.

Economic Order Politics 1: Monetarism

The Thatcherites assumed that under conditions of 'sound money', the disciplining effect of competition would in the long run ensure economic growth – even if the new focus of monetary policy would initially have a pro-cyclical effect and deepen the recession Britain had entered in 1980. Their accumulation strategy was premised on a version of economic liberalism that regarded the restriction of inflation as the foundation of economic policy.[7]

Accordingly, the discourse of Thatcherism in ascendance revolved around not just the threat of the 'trade unions', but also monetary stability. On the eve of the second election in 1974, Joseph delivered a speech that defined inflation as *the* problem of the age. He stated that it was 'the most important issue before the country', adding that it was 'threatening to destroy our society'.[8] Inflation not only figured heavily in *The Right Approach to the Economy*, but was also the first issue discussed in the 1979 election manifesto, which meant that it was in a more prominent position than 'trade unions' and the lessons from the Winter of Discontent. The manifesto reiterated the points made two years earlier by stating: 'Inflation is now accelerating again ... Inflation on this scale has come near to destroying our political and social stability.'[9]

The assumption that high inflation was an evil that had to be defeated did not just reflect the widespread fear that, given the chronic weakness of the pound, investors would withdraw capital from Britain – as had happened during the recurring balance-of-payments crises in the preceding decades. Joseph argued that if nothing was done to control inflation, a 'catastrophic' economic crisis would occur that would destroy savings and the 'working capital' of businesses, and would lead to mass unemployment.[10] The Thatcherites claimed that Britain was headed for economic meltdown, stressing that inflation was one of the root causes.

The material basis for these claims was that inflation in the mid-1970s was exceptionally high (see Table 1). It fell in the last two years of the Callaghan government, but was still substantial compared to later years. The inflationary pressures reflected the attempts by the unions to counter the pressure on living standards with forcing high nominal wage increases, which the owners set off by raising prices.[11] It reveals that the Social Contract remained a weak arrangement that did not lead to a lasting drop in inflation.

---

7 Tomlinson 2012a, p. 62.
8 Joseph, Thatcher Archive, 110607.
9 Conservative Party 1979.
10 Joseph, Thatcher Archive, 110607.
11 Compare Busch 2006, p. 418.

TABLE 1   *Retail Price Index (RPI), UK*

	Inflation (annual change in percent)
1974	16.1
1975	24.2
1976	16.5
1977	15.8
1978	8.3
1979	13.4
1980	18.0
1981	11.9
1982	8.6

SOURCE: JACKSON AND SAUNDERS 2012, P. 271

The Thatcherites laid the main blame for inflationary pressures on the Keynesian economic policy dominant in the early post-war era. This policy had attempted to keep unemployment at bay by expanding demand, but it had failed to curb the wage inflation caused by the resultant steady and strong demand for labour power, which in turn boosted the bargaining power of organised labour. Accordingly, Joseph blamed the reflationary aspect of Keynesianism for the crisis. Reiterating his monetarist beliefs, he argued that inflationary pressures were caused by the 'creation of new money – and the consequent deficit financing – out of proportion to the additional goods and services available'.[12] He added that incomes policy did not work because governments were never able to control wage increases in all sectors of the economy. Finally, he stated that reflation tended to result in rising imports and according pressure on the pound, which in turn led governments to opt for cutbacks in order to avert currency crises. This, he implied, did nothing to strengthen the productive base of the British economy.[13]

---

12 Joseph, Thatcher Archive, 110607.
13 Joseph invoked the experience of 'wage drift', that is, the expansion of wages at individual plants above sectoral and national standards, which was common in Britain at the time. This underscores that corporatist institutions remained weak insofar as they struggled to enforce binding standards.

Once the Thatcher government had been formed, the new Prime Minister and her inner circle followed Joseph's lead. Nigel Lawson, the then Financial Secretary to the Treasury, stressed in 1981 that the government sets 'as the overriding objective of macro-economic policy the conquest of inflation'.[14] In the view of the Thatcherites, this could be achieved by pursuing a monetarist approach to monetary policy. They subscribed to the monetarist belief that inflation reflects an expansion of the money supply beyond the expansion of production at a given point in time. For them, the obvious remedy was to introduce strict controls. Along these lines, the 1979 manifesto called for the introduction of targets for the growth in the money supply, cuts in government spending, and the abandonment of expansionary fiscal policies and price controls, which were assumed not to work.

In a way, monetarism sat uneasily at the centre of the emerging economic-political order. Supply-side economics suggested that markets should be deregulated and liberalised as far as possible. If the monetarist orthodoxy was taken seriously, this surely did not hold for the money market: It demanded caps on monetary expansion, whose imposition amounted to a form of tight market regulation. This created tensions at the level of ideology. Christopher Johnson is right in stressing 'the incompatibility of abolishing controls and restrictive practices in markets such as those for credit, foreign exchange, securities, housing and labour, yet seeking to retain strict official curbs in one key market – that for money'.[15]

Due to these tensions, the Thatcherites struggled to develop a coherent political practice informed by monetarism. The Thatcher government announced targets for the growth in the money supply in 1980, but it was unclear how these would be achieved.[16] There were marked disagreements both within the economic state apparatuses and the power bloc about whether targeting the money supply was an adequate instrument for curbing inflation, and what the pivot of anti-inflationary monetary policy should be.

According to Johnson, there existed at least three competing strategies in the field of monetary policy in the early 1980s that were supported by the key state apparatuses.[17] The first was orthodox monetarism, which was upheld by the inner circle of the government, that is, Thatcher, Howe and Lawson, her first and her second Chancellor. Thatcher et al. at first appeared successful in

---

14   Cited in Leys 1989, p. 27.
15   Johnson 1991, p. 32.
16   Johnson 1991, p. 33; compare Middlemas 1991, p. 241.
17   Johnson 1991, p. 34.

imposing their course on the Treasury. The latter produced a green paper on 'Monetary Base Control', that is, the idea to check the expansion of the money supply by limiting the quantity of money made available to commercial banks by the Bank of England and of notes and coins in circulation. However, under the influence of academics and City economists, Treasury and Bank officials subsequently rejected this approach as unworkable.[18] Monetary base control required the stipulation of fixed targets for the money in circulation, which in turn would have transformed interest rates and exchange rates into dependent variables fluctuating according to supply and demand.[19] This was considered a potential source of instability because rates would become unpredictable. Hence, monetary base control failed to win the backing of the practitioners from the Treasury and the Bank, who were not prepared to cede control over interest rates and the exchange rate; of the ideologists of the power bloc (that is, mainstream economists); and, most importantly, of the City as its dominant fraction.[20] Unsurprisingly, monetary base control did not reach the implementation stage.

The second approach was supported by the Bank of England and was anti-monetarist in character. It regarded the quantity of money as a dependent variable to be determined by the demand for money, that is, output mediated by prices and interest rates. Since attempting to steer output or prices was incompatible with Thatcherite economic liberalism, this approach amounted to controlling the money supply via manipulating interest rates.[21]

The third approach, dominant in the Treasury, also diverged from monetarist orthodoxy. It saw the money supply as a dependent variable that reflected fiscal policy, external flows and bank lending. Accordingly, Treasury officials, like their counterparts at the Bank, regarded interest rates and exchange rates as primary levers when it came to restricting the money supply.[22]

Against the backdrop of the diversity of views on inflation in the economic state apparatuses, it is not surprising that the monetary policy pursued by the Thatcherites did not develop in a linear fashion. Initially, they flirted heavily with orthodox monetarism, whilst paying tribute to the dominance of the Treasury over state institutions in Britain by accepting that the latter followed course three. During this period, which lasted from 1979 until 1981, the

---

18   Johnson 1991, p. 34; Stephens 1996, p. 20.
19   Browning 1986, p. 290; Stephens 1996, p. 20.
20   Compare Johnson 1991, p. 34.
21   Johnson 1991, p. 34.
22   Johnson, p. 35.

government's monetary instrument of choice was cutting the public sector borrowing requirement (PSBR).[23]

Nevertheless, government policies remained inconsistent, which reflected the contradiction between the push from the 'supply siders' for a free market economy and the monetarist call for a heavily regulated money market. One of the first interventions of the incoming Thatcher government, which was consistent with the commitment to the 'free market', was to cut income tax. The Thatcherites claimed that this would reward the population for 'hard work, responsibility and success'.[24] The top rate fell from 83 to 60 percent, and the basic rate from 33 to 30 percent. In order to make up for the resultant losses in taxation revenue, the government increased VAT from 8 to 15 percent.[25] The tax cuts in effect amounted to a redistribution of the burden of taxation from earners of high incomes to earners of lower incomes; the power bloc and its supporting classes and class fractions gained materially at the expense of the working class.[26] Lower income tax rates were in line with an offensive of the power bloc and the idea of a 'free economy', but they clashed with a primary aim of the Thatcher government: They fuelled inflation, which shot up to 21.9 percent in May 1980.[27] The government intervened by increasing interest rates, pushing them up from 12 to 17 percent within the space of six months.[28] This was a significant move insofar as it went against monetarist convictions and amounted to the government embracing the conventional instruments of monetary policy favoured by Treasury officials.[29] Accordingly, monetary and fiscal policy under Thatcher did not fully conform to monetarist ideology from the start. The Thatcherites responded to the pressures of day-to-day policy-making

---

23   Johnson 1991, pp. 35–6; Riddell 1991, p. 18.
24   Conservative Party 1979.
25   Johnson 1991, pp. 110–12.
26   Compare Middlemas 1991, p. 240; Kavanagh 1990, pp. 230–1.
27   Johnson 1991, p. 113.
28   Gamble 1988, p. 100.
29   The arch-monetarist Milton Friedman did not hide his disappointment over the pragmatic course of the government. Commenting on a green paper on *Monetary Control*, he wrote: 'I could hardly believe my eyes when I read ... "the principal means of controlling the growth of the money supply must be fiscal policy ... and interest rates". Interpreted literally, this sentence is simply wrong. Only a Rip van Winkle, who had not read any of the flood of literature during the past decade and more on the money supply process, could have possibly written that sentence. Direct control of the monetary base is an alternative to fiscal policy and interest rates as a means of controlling monetary growth' (cited in Johnson 1991, p. 41).

by remaining pragmatic and bowing to a path-dependent feature of the British system of government: the dominant position of the Treasury.

Nevertheless, in this period, the circle around Thatcher still appeared to assume that the switch to orthodox monetarism would come sooner or later. Howe announced in the 1980 budget speech that there would be targets for the increase of the money supply, which would fall year by year in line with corresponding cuts to the PBSR. The targets constituted the 'medium-term financial strategy' (MTFS) of the government.[30] The aim of the MTFS was supposed to make monetary and fiscal policy less flexible and restrict the government's room for manoeuvre in the area of short-term economic interventions.[31] The MTFS was not only supposed to serve as a benchmark for state expenditure, but also as a signal to organised labour that there were limits to wage increases because there was limited additional money available, and that the money supply would be tightened.[32]

This second attempt to put monetarism into practice also failed: the MTFS soon proved unworkable. Once again, 'supply-side' economics and monetarism clashed. In line with 'supply-side' thinking, the Thatcherites had decided to remove both exchange controls and restrictions on bank lending. This meant that the government had ceded control over flows of money into and out of Britain, which in turn thwarted attempts to control the money supply.[33] In other words, the liberalisation of capital markets undermined the monetarist course in monetary and fiscal policy.

As a result of this experience, the Thatcherites undertook a U-turn. In 1981, they abandoned the idea of 'monetary base control' and quietly accepted the management of sterling's exchange rate through the manipulation of interest rates.[34] In the budget of the same year, the emphasis of the MTFS shifted from controlling the money supply to reducing the PSBR over the medium term.[35] In the 1982 budget, the targets for the money supply were relaxed – unsurprising given the fact that they had not been met in the preceding years.[36] In 1985, they were finally abolished.[37] With this decision, the government conceded that the attempt to put monetarism into practice had failed and showed that

---

30   Gamble 1988, p. 100; Stephens 1996, p. 10.
31   Gamble 1988, p. 100; Busch 2006, p. 420.
32   Kavanagh 1990, p. 227.
33   Stephens 1996, p. 13.
34   Compare Middlemas 1991, p. 255; compare Johnson 1991, p. 46.
35   Stephens 1996, p. 21.
36   Compare Johnson 1991, p. 274.
37   Riddell 1991, p. 21.

it approved of the Treasury's decision to revert back to a style of monetary and fiscal policy last practised in the 1950s.[38]

All in all, Thatcher's course in monetary policy demonstrates that policies designed in the political scene do not necessarily feed through to other state apparatuses unchanged. Rather, they are adapted and modified according to both the relations of forces within the power bloc and the institutional contexts into which they are transferred. In this case, the Treasury had its way: it ensured that the monetarist doctrine was sacrificed for the more far-reaching goal of implementing a free market course in economic policy.[39]

Economic Order Politics II: The Free Market

Although monetarism had technically been abandoned, the Thatcherites still broke with a fundamental assumption that had guided monetary and fiscal policy during the post-war years. This was the Keynesian assertion that, faced with a downturn, state apparatuses should reflate. Despite presiding over a recession – gross domestic product growth shrunk by 2.0 percent in 1980 and 1.2 percent in 1981 – the circle around Thatcher resisted pressure from the 'wets', the remaining upholders of one nation conservatism in the cabinet and on the conservative frontbench, to return to a Keynesian strategy.[40]

Instead of making anti-cyclical interventions, the government increased interest rates, which reflected the fact that it prioritised the fight against inflation. It showed disregard for the economic cycle and used conventional instruments of monetary policy at a highly unusual point. This had a pro-cyclical effect: the pound appreciated, which made British exports unprofitable and accelerated the decline of British industry.[41]

The destructive effect of high interest rates was aggravated by supply-side interventions that reflected the neo-Ricardian belief in the allocative efficiency of open, unfettered markets. The Thatcherites decided to abolish exchange

---

38   Middlemas 1991, p. 256.
39   Bonefeld's contention that '[t]he MTFS failed ... because of the presence of labour in and against capital' (1993, p. 167) is unconvincing. It suggests that the British working class was in a position of strength at the time, which is not backed by the events in the field of class politics in the early 1980s (see below), and it appears to discount the possibility that political leaders make strategic mistakes because they misunderstand the workings of the economy and the state.
40   Figures from Johnson 1991, p. 265.
41   Johnson 1991, p. 38.

controls, which meant that investors could withdraw their capital from Britain and reinvest it elsewhere. This forced British industry to compete for investment on a global scale; individual companies had to realise returns in line with international profit rates.[42] Given the 'productivity gap' between Britain and other western industrialised countries, this shift further contributed to putting British industry out of business.[43]

The combination of a recession, a pro-cyclical approach to monetary policy and financial liberalisation had a devastating effect on the industrial sector.[44] In the early 1980s, employment in manufacturing declined rapidly (see Table 2); between 1979 and 1981, output fell by 14 percent.[45] In line with their neo-Ricardian belief in the beneficial effect of unbridled international competition, the Thatcherites presented the demolition of substantial parts of British industry as a necessary process.[46] They argued that it would eventually benefit the British economy by enhancing competitiveness, not least because rising unemployment would undermine organised labour's capacity to force high wage increases and resist changes in the organisation of work.[47]

The drive to increase competitiveness through the disciplining effect of open markets on companies and workers was also evident in the nationalised industries. In line with the Ridley Report, the Thatcherites pressed for the introduction of a profit-oriented, private sector approach to managing state-owned companies and for their outright privatisation. They appointed new chairmen renowned for their hard line on industrial relations and their penchant for cost cutting.[48] Furthermore, and again just as Ridley et al. had recommended, they imposed tight limits on borrowing and targets for rates of return on investment.[49]

This in turn brought nationalised corporations into conflict with the government. They could no longer rely on meeting rising wage costs with borrowed money, which posed a problem in a situation where inflation stoked wage

---

42   Johnson 1991, p. 37.
43   Jessop 1991b, p. 137; compare MacInnes 1987, p. 80.
44   Bonefeld 1993, p. 162.
45   Gamble 1988, p. 125.
46   Ibid.
47   Along these lines, the 1979 manifesto had stated: 'Too much emphasis has been placed on attempts to preserve existing jobs. We need to concentrate more on the creation of conditions in which new, more modern, more secure, better paid jobs come into existence' (Conservative Party 1979).
48   Kavanagh 1990, p. 221.
49   Hain 1986, p. 129.

TABLE 2   *Jobs in manufacturing, UK*

	Annual change, in percent
1980	−4.4
1981	−10.4
1982	−5.8
1983	−5.9

SOURCE: BUSCH 2006, P. 422

demands and a recession dented profitability. For the Thatcherites, privatisation was an attractive option in this situation. As well as reducing the PSBR, it was in line with the idea of creating unfettered, open markets and took the problem of management off the government's back.[50]

Against this backdrop, the government opted for privatising state-owned companies in waves of increasing magnitude. First, the National Enterprise Board was ordered to sell £100m worth of assets, and the BNOC was instructed to sell stakes in North Sea oil fields.[51] Second, the government sold shares in British Petroleum, British Aerospace, the British Sugar Corporation, and Cable and Wireless.[52] Third, they put 51 percent of shares in British Telecom on the market.[53] After 1983, Conservative governments expanded privatisation far into the area of 'true utilities' that Ridley et al. had declared untouchable.

The flipside of the retreat of the economic state apparatuses from production was that they also started to neglect infrastructure, that is, the preconditions of production whose creation and reproduction was not dominantly co-ordinated via markets. The government cut spending for universities and science in general, and it also allowed the physical infrastructure of production to crumble. In a situation of chronic under-investment, it insisted that it was the responsibility of the private sector to fund improvements.[54] Taken together with the accelerating de-industrialisation of Britain, this aggravated deficiencies in innovation and reinforced the 'low-skill, low-wage, low-productivity

---

50   Compare Johnson 1991, p. 145; Riddell 1991, pp. 91–2.
51   Gamble 1988, p. 99.
52   Gamble 1988, p. 104.
53   Johnson 1991, p. 159.
54   Gamble 1988, p. 125; compare Jessop 1991b, p. 157.

character of the British economy', entrenching the weaknesses of the capitalism in Britain.[55]

The push for market liberalisation through de-nationalisation, as well as the abolition of exchange controls and the deflationary course in monetary and fiscal policy, demonstrate that the Thatcherites were in the process of installing a new accumulation strategy. This was centred on the neo-Ricardian notion of boosting growth through open, transnational competition. Obviously, the ideology of minimal state involvement in markets sat uneasily with actual government activities, but these were justified with reference to the need to remove barriers to unbridled competition.

Similarly, the economic realities on the ground diverged heavily from the lofty visions of prosperous, free market Britain. Even if growth soon started to stabilise, there was another deep recession in the early 1990s. Importantly, the refusal to develop an industrial policy and the active dismantling of British industry further entrenched the traditional dominance of the City over the power bloc.[56] It facilitated financial expansion and made the whole British economy more dependent on the City, which at the same time increased its exposure to the volatility of financial markets. Today, this is visible in the destructive impact of the global financial crisis post-2008 on Britain: the country experienced a deep recession and several years of sluggish growth. It weathered the crisis badly in comparison to Germany, a national economy of a comparable size and degree of development with a considerably stronger industrial sector (see Table 3).

Besides, industrial decline and financial expansion deepened social inequality and thus boosted centrifugal tendencies in British society. As companies with low levels of productivity went bankrupt, unemployment shot up, in particular in 'traditional' manufacturing sectors like heavy engineering and chemicals.[57] In contrast, employment in and around the financial sector increased, and wages in this area would soon explode. Differences in wealth across the whole population grew substantially. Between 1979 and 1985, the number of people living below the poverty line increased by 55 percent, to 9.4m.[58] In 1979, the top income decile earned 3.9 times more than the bottom decile; in 1989, this number had gone up to 5.53.[59] Moreover, divisions within the working

---

55   Jessop 1990, p. 90.
56   On the traditional dominance of the City over the British power bloc, see Gallas 2008.
57   Compare Middlemas 1991, pp. 492–3; Gamble 1988, p. 194.
58   Riddell 1991, p. 156.
59   Johnson 1991, p. 313; compare MacInnes 1987, p. 84.

TABLE 3   *Real GDP growth rate, Germany and UK*

	Germany	UK
2007	3.3	3.4
2008	1.1	−0.8
2009	−5.1	−5.2
2010	4	1.7
2011	3.3	1.1
2012	0.7	0.3
2013	0.4	1.7

SOURCE: EUROSTAT I, 2014

class deepened: Unskilled workers were hit hard by redundancies, while skilled workers often managed to retain their jobs and enjoy rising wages.[60]

Similarly, regional disparities within Britain increased. Scotland, Wales and the North of England were hit hard by the demise of traditional industries, whilst the South and East of England profited from booms in the financial sector, high-tech industries and retail.[61] This led to a regional concentration of unemployment, which trapped the people affected in a vicious circle. Joblessness made them immobile, which in turn confined them to places where the chances of re-employment were much lower than elsewhere.[62] Consequently, their status was perpetuated.

In conclusion, the Thatcher government instituted a neo-Ricardian accumulation strategy based on the notion of the 'free market', which undermined social cohesion and did not bring sustained growth. There were two recessions within the space of a decade; in contrast to the predictions of the Ricardian model, industrial restructuring induced by international competition did not benefit the British economy in its entirety but entrenched its existing deficiencies, in particular in the areas of skills, innovation and investment. It led to an economy heavily dependent on financial services, which was badly exposed to turbulences in the financial markets.

---

60   Compare Riddell 1991, p. 151; Middlemas 1991, p. 262.
61   Riddell 1991, pp. 158–61.
62   Riddell 1991, p. 165.

Economic Order Politics III: Authoritarianism

Following Jessop et al., the British state was in a dual crisis when Thatcher took office – a crisis of corporatism and a crisis of parliamentary representation. Corporatist arrangements such as the Social Contract had lost their credibility in terms of binding organised labour into agreements. Similarly, neither Labour nor the Tories had managed to move the country towards a coherent regime of condensation, so that electoral support for the party duopoly was declining.

The Thatcherites responded to the weakness of the link between parliamentary parties and the population by loosening it even more. They circumvented parliament and claimed to speak directly to, and on behalf of, 'the people'. Moreover, they stressed that they were prepared to take on the political establishment and the state apparatuses supporting it.[63] The populist mode of communicating with the population is evident in the 1979 election manifesto: 'No one who has lived in this country during the last five years can fail to be aware of how the balance of our society has been increasingly tilted in favour of the State at the expense of individual freedom. This election may be the last chance we have to reverse that process, to restore the balance of power in favour of the people'.

Corresponding to the claim to speak directly to the 'people', Thatcher adopted a presidential style of leadership. The Thatcherite inner circle assumed that the Prime Minister's mandate granted them a monopoly on conceiving the remedies for the perceived ills of British society.[64] Similarly, Thatcher attempted to direct political processes in a top-down fashion. She sidelined cabinet and operated with ad-hoc groups and subcommittees instead, so that decision-making was centralised.[65] Her supreme role was supported institutionally by a network of state apparatuses, that is, the Cabinet Office, the Treasury, the Foreign Office, and the Defence Policy Unit.[66] Thatcher established a strong link between her inner circle and the Treasury in the form of a Cabinet subcommittee called the 'E committee'. It was controlled by Thatcher loyalists and oversaw the implementation of Thatcherite economic policy. Conversely, the involvement of Cabinet in economic policy matters was minimal.[67] Similarly,

---

63 Compare Jessop et al. 1988, p. 83.
64 Compare Middlemas 1991, p. 464.
65 Schwarz 1987, pp. 132–3; Kavanagh 1990, pp. 259–61.
66 Middlemas 1991, p. 458.
67 Schwarz 1987, p. 133.

Thatcher et al. pushed the Department of Trade and Industry (DTI) to the margins. This was consistent with the Thatcherite neglect for industrial policy and the more general decline of corporatist institutions.

The centralisation of state power taking place under Thatcher, however, went beyond establishing new channels of government decision-making.[68] Thatcher and her allies also restructured the workings of the state bureaucracy. By 1983, they had cut the number of civil servants by 100,000.[69] Furthermore, they modified the internal structure of the civil service, limiting the decisional autonomy of individual departments. They abolished the Civil Service Department, which meant that they were able to sideline a group of influential civil servants critical of the government's course.[70] Finally, they started the 'Financial Management Initiative', which imposed cash limits on departments and obliged them to monitor their activities and expenditure constantly.[71] Government institutions were forced to adopt private sector-style cost-effectiveness models.[72]

All in all, the changes amounted to the 'managerialisation' of the civil service and reinforced the dominant position of the Treasury over the state.[73] The centralised system of government resulting from the restructuring of the bureaucracy shielded Thatcherite policies from criticism and obstruction by officials. Keith Middlemas comments: 'Mrs Thatcher and her Treasury team ensured that the regime could not be questioned in official circles. Whether or not civil servants thought it was correct (and the majority did not, before the mid-1980s) they accepted it as their framework of reference'.[74]

The push to centralise state power was mirrored at the level of the political scene: Thatcher sidelined the 'wet' tendency in the cabinet and the parliament, which was sceptical of her radicalism.[75] The popularity of the new right interpretation of the Winter of Discontent, the mandate given to Thatcher in 1979 by the electorate and the degree of control her faction had secured over the Conservative Party allowed the new Prime Minister to install a Thatcherite rather than a Conservative government: The Prime Minister's inner circle

---

68   Jessop, undated.
69   Evans 1997, p. 55.
70   Middlemas 1991, p. 421.
71   Middlemas 1991, p. 422.
72   Johnson 1991, p. 82.
73   Jessop, undated; compare Middlemas 1991, p. 457.
74   Middlemas 1991, p. 259.
75   Vinen 2009, p. 117.

occupied the Cabinet posts dealing with economic issues from the start.[76] The only exception was Employment, which was held by Prior.

One of the areas where there were profound disagreements and deep divisions between 'wets' and Thatcherite 'drys' was monetary policy.[77] In fact, Thatcher's monetarist course did not have a majority in Cabinet.[78] But Thatcherite control of the key economic state apparatuses equalled dominance over the decision-making of the government.[79] Accordingly, the majority group in cabinet was not able to prevent Thatcher et al. from pursuing monetarist policies. The twists and turns of the government in this area during the first Thatcher term resulted less from the arguments between 'wets' and 'drys' than from the flaws and inconsistencies of the monetarist agenda.

This is unsurprising given that the 'wets' remained divided and weak.[80] They failed to capitalise on Thatcher's difficulties during the recession. There were misgivings within the CBI about high interest rates and low returns on capital, and some leaders of industry openly supported the 'wets'.[81] Nevertheless, industry as a whole did not enter an outright alliance with them – partly because many members of the industrial fraction favoured 'two nations' over 'one nation' conservatism in most of the other political areas, and partly because of divisions between small and big industrial capital. After the 1981 budget, the CBI swung fully behind the Thatcherites and turned away from the 'wets'.[82] The more Thatcherite control over government became normalised, the more cabinet was brought into line. Thatcher exercised her right as Prime Minister to decide cabinet membership by purging it of purported dissenters. Step by step, key figures of the 'wet' faction were removed.[83]

The composition of the Conservative Parliamentary Party also increasingly reflected Thatcherite dominance and the marginalisation of one nation conservatism.[84] Conservative MPs increasingly replicated the social basis of Thatcherism; they decreasingly had close ties to the gentlemanly institutions that had traditionally supported the power bloc and British conservatism (and were

---

76   Schwarz 1987, pp. 132–3; Middlemas 1991, p. 236; Vinen 2009, p. 119.
77   Schwarz 1987, p. 138; Kerr 2001, p. 167.
78   Evans 1997, p. 43.
79   Schwarz 1987, p. 133.
80   Kavanagh 1990, p. 261.
81   Gamble 1988, p. 191.
82   Middlemas 1991, pp. 252, 352.
83   King 1989, p. 59; Evans 1997, p. 46.
84   Evans 1997, p. 51.

now associated with the 'wets').[85] The share of Conservative MPs educated at public schools declined by two thirds between 1974 and 1987. Similarly, whereas the figure for Conservative parliamentarians educated at Oxford and Cambridge decreased from 56 to 44 percent, the number of those with degrees from 'provincial' universities doubled to 26 percent. Moreover, there was a higher share of self-made businessmen.[86]

The authoritarian streak revealed by the Thatcherites' centralised style of decision-making and their streamlining of the Tory Party are also revealed by their stance on the parliamentary opposition. They aimed to establish an anti-socialist political consensus, under which there would be no place for a Labour Party with a strong party left. In 1983, Thatcher was quoted as saying that she wanted a duopoly of parties operating 'within the same framework of free enterprise', which was a view echoed by some of the organic intellectuals of Thatcherism.[87] Two years later, she added: 'I have always regarded part of my job as ... killing socialism in Britain'.[88] To that end, the Thatcherites went on to dismantle the institutions of corporatism, undermine organised labour and cut the ground from under the feet of the socialists in the Labour Party.

Yet most importantly, the Thatcherites remained in control because there was no obvious alternative for the power bloc to supporting them. The 'wets' were a feeble force, the Labour Party was in disarray after being defeated, and the Social Democratic Party (SDP), a breakaway organisation of former Labour politicians with a centrist orientation founded in 1981, did not garner stable popular support.[89] Moreover, the power bloc and Thatcherites were united in their hostility towards organised labour. The City as a dominant fraction appeared to swallow Thatcher's petty capitalist anti-elitism and her resentment towards its gentlemanly traditions because it shared the goal of undermining the trade unions.[90]

All in all, the Thatcherites exploited the weakness of their opponents and made material gains by creating institutional supports for their politics in the state. They installed an authoritarian mode of government, which was based on the small circle around the Prime Minister making decisions and implementing them in a top-down fashion. The gentlemanly ethos still pervading parts of the Conservative Party and the civil service was sidelined by a 'competitive ...

---

85 Vinen 2009, pp. 117–18.
86 Vinen, p. 48.
87 Hain 1986, p. 274.
88 Cited in Schwarz 1987, pp. 144–5.
89 Gamble 1988, pp. 118–19.
90 Compare Middlemas 1991, pp. 312–14.

business ethic'.[91] In so doing, the Thatcherites instigated a recomposition of the state and of the Conservative Party that undermined some of the remnants of feudalism in Britain, namely, the control of long-established upper-class networks over the civil service and the 'natural' party of government. This was in line with Joseph's assertion that it was the historical task of the new right to complete Britain's transition from feudalism to capitalism.[92]

The Thatcherites' approach to internal state restructuring was mirrored in their stance on reorganising the external relations of the state. In line with its authoritarian leanings, the Thatcher government strengthened the repressive state apparatuses. Despite its hostility to state spending, it raised police wages, bought new equipment and increased the number of officers.[93] There was a 20 percent increase in police staff between 1980 and 1989, and a real-term rise of the Home Office budget by 55 percent.[94] In 1980, after a riot in Bristol and a steel strike, the Thatcherites also decided to modify the police command structure and the strategies for dealing with 'public disorder'. Under the banner of 'mutual aid', police officials were now invited to seek support from forces outside of their region immediately if they needed it.[95]

The repressive approach of the Thatcherites is also visible in the area of criminal law. They encouraged judges to pass 'tough' sentences and introduced new custodial types of punishment for under 21s.[96] Furthermore, they took a hard line on hunger strikes by Republicans in Northern Ireland that took place in the early 1980s. These were called off after Thatcher had refused to make concessions and some strikers had died.[97]

It is ironic that Thatcher was able to present herself as a champion of the people who took on the detached and elitist political establishment. She led a small coterie of convinced neoliberals at the very top of the executive who formulated an authoritarian state strategy. Their project was premised on attempting to establish complete control over the state and the political scene, albeit broadly within the confines of the British constitution, that is, without suspending parliament or the rule of law.[98] Their capacity to establish this form of authoritarian rule resulted from the catastrophic equilibrium. The trade

---

91   Evans 1997, p. 49.
92   Joseph 1975.
93   Gamble 1988, p. 107.
94   Riddell 1991, p. 169.
95   Hain 1986, pp. 178–9.
96   Gamble 1988, p. 134.
97   Gamble 1988, pp. 107–8.
98   Compare Jessop et al. 1988, p. 83.

union movement and the traditionalists in the City were paralysed, as were the forces representing continuity in the political scene, that is, the Labour Party and the 'wets'. All these actors were perceived as aligned with the post-war settlement and its sclerotic institutional supports. This created a vacuum in the political scene, which the Thatcherites filled by presenting themselves as the only political force capable of leading the country out of the crisis.

In conclusion, the Thatcherites implemented a state project which, in truly authoritarian fashion, addressed the crisis of representation in the British state by marginalising the representation of forces dissenting to the Prime Minister's course. It aimed to build an anti-socialist consensus in the political scene, created channels of decision-making that bypassed parliament and cabinet, sidelined traditionalist elements in the power bloc, and fortified repressive state apparatuses, allowing them to crush social and political forces opposed to the new political course.[99]

The emergence of the Thatcherite authoritarian state strategy roughly coincided with the formation of their free market, 'neo-Ricardian' accumulation strategy. Both complemented each other: The push for privatisation and market liberalisation amounted to a rollback of the institutions that supported the project of a post-war settlement. This warranted an uncompromising style of government that was premised on exploiting the repressive force of state institutions and reorganising the state in a way conducive to top-down control. At the same time, the centrifugal forces unleashed by the 'free market' approach to economic policy undermined social cohesion, which the government was able to use as a justification for bringing the repressive state 'back in'. In other words, the accumulation strategy and state project implemented by the Thatcherites corresponded to each other, which suggests that a new economic-political order was emerging. I propose to call this order 'free market authoritarianism'.

Class Politics I: Repression and Division

Having examined the economic order politics of the Thatcherites, I will now use this analysis to contextualise their class politics. The fact that class politics did not take centre stage during the second period of Thatcherism does not mean that Thatcher and her associates ignored it. Quite the contrary: They consciously tried to avoid a tactical mistake that they attributed to Heath, namely, using the momentum of taking office to launch an open attack on

---

[99] Compare Gamble 1988, p. 31.

organised labour. They believed that this had invigorated and unified the trade union movement in the early 1970s. Instead, they followed the cautious recommendations of the Ridley Report. This advised carefully preparing for an open war against organised labour and making concessions if this was conducive to undermining the enemy over the medium term. Of course, the Thatcherites did not follow the report in every detail, but they took its main recommendations very seriously – especially those dealing with organised labour. Consequently, Thatcherite class politics at this point can be described as determined but watchful.

Although the Thatcherites took power on the back of a campaign against organised labour, once in government they refrained from declaring industrial relations their primary area of concern. Behind the scenes, however, they actively worked to shift class relations in favour of the power bloc by carefully advancing against the unions. Cohen speaks of 'salami tactics' in this context; Anthony Ferner uses the French words 'reculer pour mieux sauter' [flip to fry better].[100]

The fact that there was a main thrust to Thatcherite class politics does not mean that it was uncontroversial in the Cabinet and the Conservative Parliamentary Party. Prior did not share the Thatcherite hostility towards unions. He was in favour of retaining and reforming, not abolishing, the Social Contract.[101] Unsurprisingly, his green paper on labour relations was rejected by the Thatcherites. Thatcher and her inner circle were suspicious of the Employment Secretary, who in their view remained too conciliatory in his approach to labour relations.[102] In 1981, Thatcher decided to strip him of his office; he became the new Secretary of State for Northern Ireland. This also meant that the channel of communication between the Cabinet and the union movement had been shut off.[103]

During the period in question, the key sites of class politics were (1) trade union law, whose coercive dimension was strengthened; and (2) social policy, which was restructured according to a 'two nations' understanding of society. The Thatcherites introduced three new acts in the area of trade union law, all of which created institutional obstacles to exercising class power from below: the 1980 Employment act, the 1982 Employment Act and the 1984 Trade Union Act. The 1980 act banned flying pickets and secondary action.[104] It attempted

---

100   Ferner 1989, p. 13.
101   McIlroy 1988, p. 46.
102   Schwarz 1987, p. 132.
103   McIlroy 1988, p. 49; compare Adeney and Lloyd 1986, p. 76.
104   The 1980 Act covered labour law in general, not just trade union law. It also weakened

to undermine the efficiency of picketing by restricting it 'to the point where the only pickets not open to legal challenge were those attending in small numbers where they themselves worked, who kept out of everyone else's way and who, consequently, were virtually impotent'.[105] The 1982 act narrowed the definition of a trade dispute and made unions liable for illegal action taken by their members.[106] This amounted to a restriction of the immunity of unions from being sued due to industrial action.[107] The 1984 act obliged unions to hold secret ballots when they elected officials and took decisions regarding industrial action or political funds.[108]

In addition, the Thatcherites amended laws and regulations in other areas, again with the aim of undermining the strength of organised labour. In line with one recommendation of the Ridley Report, the 1980 Social Security (No. 2) Act restricted the access of strikers' families to benefits by assuming that they disposed of £12 a week in strike pay. Similarly, in 1982 income tax rebates to strikers were frozen until they had returned to work, and the supplementary benefit strikers could claim for adult dependants was declared taxable. All these means were effective in depriving strikers of economic resources because most of the time their unions did not provide them with strike pay.[109] This was especially the case in industrial conflicts of long duration like the 1984–5 miners' strike.

Similar in spirit, and close to another Ridley Report recommendation, was the policy of strengthening the police capacity of dealing with public disorder. Not only were command structures and operational plans altered in general, but also specific tactics targeting strikers. All this contributed to containing industrial conflict.[110]

Moreover, the Thatcherites increased the stocks of vital resources, again following a recommendation of the Ridley Report. Coal stocks rose from 37m to 57m tonnes between 1981 and 1984. Moreover, energy policy changed, again in order to shield the country from shortages in coal caused by a strike. Oil imports were increased drastically, and so was the capacity of facilities for oil-

---

workers' protection from unfair dismissal (Saville 1985, p. 300), which means it de-regulated labour markets whilst re-regulating industrial action.
105 Hain 1986, p. 124.
106 Leys 1989, p. 108; Clark 2000, p. 107.
107 Compare Cohen 2006, p. 55.
108 Hain 1986, p. 125; Shackleton 1998, p. 586.
109 Hain 1986, pp. 128–9; compare Middlemas 1991, p. 284.
110 Hain 1986, p. 179.

fired power generation.[111] These are examples of how the government actively attempted to shift class relations of forces by modifying the battleground of industrial conflict. Cohen comments:

> The government's 'salami tactics' effectively concealed, at the time, the real seriousness of the Thatcherite threat. Yet, from the beginning, its effect was deadly. Some of the provisions of the 1980 Employment Act … seemed almost benign to those unaware of the implications. But the Act's restrictions on picketing and, still worse, its attack on 'secondary' (solidarity) action, began the long process of nailing strikers to the ground.[112]

Thatcherite policies targeting industrial relations were consistent in that they aimed at reshaping the battleground of industrial conflict to the disadvantage of organised labour by constraining its room for manoeuvre. They aimed at safeguarding the capitalists' control over the process of production, which was no longer to be achieved via using corporatist institutions aimed at co-opting organised labour, but by the repression of challenges to the 'right to manage'. Accordingly, I speak of a repressive extraction strategy.

Outside industrial relations, the government introduced measures that were intended to reshape people's lived experience of their position in society by turning them into asset-owners: The 1979 election manifesto promoted 'property-owning democracy'; in 1984, Lawson, the then Chancellor, coined the phrase 'popular capitalism'.[113] In particular, the first term insinuated that political participation should flow from economic status. By invoking the image of the good citizen as the property-owning citizen, it replicated the socio-economic division between the 'haves' and the 'have-nots' at the political level.

The most important aspect of this agenda was housing policy. The 1980 Housing Act instructed councils to sell council houses if their tenants had occupied them for more than three years.[114] The houses were sold at prices up to 50 percent lower than their market value. This was flanked by the decision to decrease the number of council houses to be built and to withdraw rent subsidies. As a result, rents increased by 66 percent between 1980 and 1981, giving tenants a strong incentive to buy.[115] This policy was presented as an act of individual liberation from the shackles of state control, which connected to

---

111   Hain 1986, p. 134.
112   Cohen 2006, pp. 54–5.
113   Jessop et al. 1988, p. 65.
114   Evans 1997, p. 59.
115   Hay 1992, p. 56.

the traditional economism of British workers, who had often preferred direct improvements of their economic status to advancement through the 'institutionalisation' of aspects of their lives.[116] At the same time, it disguised the fact that the government was setting in train a whole set of political measures at roughly the same time that were aimed at the authoritarian suppression of organised labour.

Unsurprisingly, liberation from state control was by no means the result of the policy in question. Rather, it replaced the dependence on state-subsidised housing by dependence on the state through the Mortgage Interest Tax Relief.[117] The aim of the new law was not to drive back the state, but to reshape the battleground of industrial conflict and alter class relations of forces again. It attempted to co-opt better-off groups within the working class into supporting the government's course. At the same time, it was intended to institutionalise compliance: If going on strike now meant that people risked losing their property rather than being evicted from rented accommodation, the 'opportunity costs' of walking out increased considerably. As a result, the expansion of house-ownership within the working class had a disciplining effect.[118] Moreover, it undermined working-class support for the welfare state because fewer workers depended on it for their housing. Besides, they were also transformed into potential 'players' on the real estate market, which reinforced individual aspirations at the expense of collective advancement.

In sum, the Thatcherites aimed to weaken the working class as a collective force by reinforcing its internal divisions and creating ties between some of its sections and other classes. In other words, they strengthened intra-class divisions whilst covering up inter-class antagonism.[119] This matched their image of Britain as a society marked by a *'single, vertical cleavage* stretching from top to bottom of society which opposes the productive to the parasitic'.[120] 'Property-

---

116 Compare Lane 1983, p. 183.
117 Hay 1992, p. 56.
118 In Andy Danford's ethnography of industrial action at a car factory in South Wales in the 1990s (1997, p. 127), for instance, one of the interviewed shop stewards portrays mortgages as one major factor that deters people from voting for strike action.
119 Compare Hobsbawm 1989, p. 17; Lawrence and Sutcliffe-Braithwaite 2012, p. 134.
120 Jessop et al. 1988, p. 88. The Thatcherites did not speak of a 'parasitic nation', but insinuated its existence by consistently dividing the population into two camps. They portrayed 'hard work' as a 'moral value' (Conservative Party 1987) and attacked certain sections of the population as not sharing this value. These sections were (1) unproductive members of the working class or 'shirkers' living off benefits; (2) workers in nationalised industries and militant trade unionists; (3) inefficient bureaucrats; (4) professionals in traditional trades

owning democracy' and 'popular capitalism' were expressions of a 'two nations' hegemonic project.

Crucially, this hegemonic project corresponded to the new extraction strategy in terms of entrenching disunity within the working class. Thus I contend that there was a coherent class political regime in the Thatcher era. This had not been the case for a long time. From around 1967, which marked the end of Wilson's wages policy, until 1977, when the Ridley Report was written and Thatcherism emerged, class politics in Britain was marked by incoherence, which is revealed by the constant shifts in the assumptions guiding policies in this field and the 'muddling through' of the actors involved.

Since both the repressive extraction strategy and the 'two nations' hegemonic project were aimed at shifting the class relations of forces in favour of capital, I argue that Thatcherism orchestrated an offensive step by the power bloc. This step had now reached a second period and was characterised by the power bloc making material gains, which took the form of changes to the institutionalisation of the wage relation and the reproduction of labour power.

Class Politics II: War of Position

The first Thatcher government tried hard to prevent open class war from breaking out, and, through a mixture of concessions and repression, succeeded in doing so. Nevertheless, the election of a government that blamed the unions for Britain's decline and was hostile to trade unionism, at least as long as unions were committed to a class-based approach,[121] pushed the labour movement to fortify defences almost by default. However, the resultant defensive did not enjoy the momentum that had been behind the last successful one from 1967 to 1974. During the Winter of Discontent, support for the unions in the wider population had crumbled. Moreover, the strike wave had revealed deep fault lines within their movement. As a consequence, class relations of forces were already shifting in favour of the power bloc when the first Thatcher government entered office.

Moreover, trade unions struggled with responding to mass unemployment and the weakening effect it had on their capacity to exercise bargaining power. Unemployment had risen from about 5 percent in 1979 to about 13 percent in

---

like finance, education and the law, enjoying privileges entrenched through restrictive practices; and (5) gentlemanly capitalists presiding over anti-competitive oligopolies (compare Jessop and Stones 1992, p. 183).

121 Compare Middlemas 1991, p. 318.

1983, and 2.2m jobs in manufacturing had been lost.[122] This constituted not only a contraction of the pool of workers that the unions had traditionally organised, but also led to a deepening of internal rifts in the working class. The wages of more highly skilled core workers were rising, whilst 'peripheral' workers were laid off and fell even further beyond the reach of the unions than before.[123] Consequently, the unions had to grapple with the difficulty of being forced into mounting a defensive against the power bloc in a situation of deep division and waning bargaining strength.

This in turn partly explains why the Thatcherites chose to entertain a pro-cyclical monetary and fiscal policy. According to Leys, 'the main weapon to weaken solidarity was the unemployment produced by the 1979/81 deflation'.[124] The destabilising effect of the new accumulation strategy in the field of economic order politics proved stabilising in the field of class politics.

In sum, the unions were still strong in quantitative terms during the first Thatcher government, but no longer in qualitative terms. Combined with the still fresh memories of the victory of 1974, this led many trade unionists to misconceive the conjuncture. There was a widespread feeling that the Thatcher government would prove short-lived, that the Prime Minister did not mean what she said, and that she would eventually be forced into a U-turn just like Heath.[125] Accordingly, the TUC fought the anti-union legislation, but only in a half-hearted fashion. Union leaders struggled with formulating an adequate response to the 'salami tactics' of the Thatcherites, and their strategy was marred by contradictions. They engaged in campaigns against government policy, especially against the changes in trade union law, and yet continued to participate in now marginalised tripartite bodies like the National Economic Development Council in the hope that the government would make a U-turn. Middlemas comments: 'It was ... obvious to the government that the TUC was trying to ride two or maybe three horses at once, a dilemma of which Norman Tebbit and the Cabinet took every advantage'.[126] This dilemma reflected both the disunity of organised labour and the political and ideological 'paralysis' of its leaders,[127] which was reflected in their inability to grasp what was at stake.

---

122   Middlemas 1991, pp. 346, 492–3.
123   Middlemas 1991, pp. 263, 335–6.
124   Leys 1989, pp. 152–3; compare Bonefeld 1993, p. 146.
125   Cohen 2006, pp. 53–4.
126   Middlemas 1991, p. 327.
127   Middlemas 1991, p. 326.

The Thatcherites in their turn remained cautious and exploited their opponents' weakness. Despite their 'two nations' rhetoric, they left the welfare state largely untouched and refrained from instigating a fundamental rollback in this area.[128] The changes introduced centred on cutting the link between growth in earnings and growth in unemployment benefits. Despite these cuts, overall social security spending expanded greatly after 1979, which mostly reflected rising unemployment.[129] Thus the government failed to achieve spending targets and postponed them.[130]

In line with the Ridley Report, the Thatcherites avoided strikes in critical infrastructural sectors. In 1979–80, they made concessions to oil tanker drivers, power workers and workers in the water supply industry. Around the same time, Thatcher forced Joseph to bail out British Leyland. This was not just for financial reasons – breaking up a nationalised corporation during a recession could have proven costly. It was also because it would not have paid off politically, as it might have caused conflict with the unions and Labour.[131] Finally, in 1981 the government decided against taking up the gauntlet thrown down by the miners, who had gone on strike after the National Coal Board (NCB) had announced a programme of pit closures. The government retreated quickly, and provided extra funding to keep the pits open. Moreover, the Treasury condoned above average wage settlements with the miners.[132]

Nevertheless, the Thatcherites continued to press for increases in coal stocks and to prepare for a major confrontation. The then Secretary of State for Energy, David Howell, conceded in November 1984 that the retreat in 1981 had been 'entirely tactical'.[133] He added:

> Neither the Government nor I think society as a whole was in a position to get locked into a coal strike ... In those days stocks weren't so high. I don't think the country was prepared, and the whole NUM and the trade union movement tended to be united on one side.[134]

---

128 Leys 1989, p. 105.
129 Kavanagh 1990, p. 214.
130 Johnson 1991, p. 82.
131 Compare Middlemas 1991, pp. 291–2.
132 Adeney and Lloyd 1986, p. 76; Hain 1986, p. 134.
133 Cited in Hain 1986, p. 134.
134 Cited in Saville 1985, p. 304. Francis Beckett and David Hencke's claim that 'the need to back down in 1981 helped convince both Thatcher and Joseph that they must ultimately take on the miners and defeat them' (2009, p. 33) is unconvincing. As both the quotes

In her autobiography, Thatcher confirmed this account of events. Speaking about the strike, she remarked that 'there is no point in embarking on a battle unless you are reasonably confident you can win'.[135]

Among the miners and their supporters, the government climb-down was commonly interpreted to reflect their continuing strength.[136] In an interview conducted just after the conflict, Arthur Scargill, who was soon to become NUM president, recognised that the government's course was a tactical retreat and only claimed a 'qualified victory'. However, he still described its decision to grant concessions as 'pre-mature', stated that a working-class movement against the Thatcherites was about to emerge, and even argued that the newly brought-in legislation had been undermined already: 'Their new legislation has effectively been shattered and shown to be impotent by the resistance of the dockers and the miners in recent months'.[137] Scargill appears to have assumed that the strength of organised labour was not affected by the legal changes.

This sentiment is also present in contemporary journalistic essays by pro-union intellectuals. John Harrison recognised how mass unemployment was damaging TUC membership – numbers had fallen by 5m in 1981 – and how, combined with the changes in trade union law announced at the time, it was shifting relations of forces in favour of the power bloc. Nevertheless, he portrayed the government retreat as a 'major victory' for the miners, and argued that the trade union movement had remained 'organisationally intact'.[138] Vic Allen went even further. He described the government's reaction to the threat of a long-drawn conflict with the miners not as a careful tactical move, but as a hysterical reaction caused by fear:

> Then, in February, 1981 the present Conservative government responded to a partial, unofficial miners' strike against pit closures by agreeing to meet the strikers' demands. This response contained all the elements of hysteria which had marked Heath's behaviour in 1973. It was unexpected, dramatic, an unashamed reversal of policy for the benefit of miners only. It was as if Mrs Thatcher had suddenly recognized the route which Mr Heath had followed in 1974.[139]

---

presented here and the strategy papers discussed above show, the decision to take on the miners had been taken years earlier.
135   Thatcher 1993, p. 141.
136   Compare Middlemas 1991, p. 291.
137   Priscott 1981.
138   Harrisson 1982, pp. 22–3.
139   Allen 1982, p. 17.

MATERIAL GAINS: CONDUCTING CLASS POLITICS BY STEALTH (1979–84)   151

The perception that the position of organised labour had not changed in principle was surely welcomed by the Thatcherites, who were buying time in order to reshape the battleground for future confrontations.

The defensive character of industrial action during this period is revealed by the fact that when unions engaged in industrial conflict, they were either trying to avert the effects of industrial decline or to prevent changes in work organisation.[140] The first major industrial confrontation during the Thatcher era, the 1980 steel strike, illustrates both. Overproduction in the sector had been going on for years – not just in Britain, but also in Europe and beyond. As a result, the European Commission had decided that there should be reductions, and the chairman of the British Steel Corporation (BSC), Charles Villiers, negotiated 'agreed' redundancies with the Iron and Steel Trades Confederation (ISTC). The deal ended in 1979, and Villiers failed to broker a new one. Due to the cash limits imposed by the Thatcherites on the public sector, he made an offer which was viewed as not being worth considering by the ISTC. Villiers reacted by starting a new round of restructuring without consulting the union. The ISTC's answer was to walk out. 100,000 workers took part in a strike, which at the time was the longest in post-war British history.[141]

The strikers' strategy was centred on mass picketing. This worked in some cases – the workforce of private producer Hadfields walked out after 2,000 of their public sector colleagues had assembled outside their plant – but it led them to neglect the need for alliances with private sector steel workers and workers in other sectors important for the steel industry. The police, encouraged by the government, responded to mass pickets with their newly developed, aggressive tactics. These involved special forces like the Special Patrol Group (SPG), which tried to make picketing as an activity as uncomfortable as possible for those involved, for example, by carrying out baton charges against unarmed strikers.[142]

In the end, the momentum was with the BSC board. The strikers failed to garner unconditional support from their colleagues in the private sector. Workers at Sheerness Steel in Kent reacted with resentment to a mass picket; the workers at Hadfields returned to work quickly, and the union leadership wavered over how to bridge the divide between the two groups of workers it represented.[143] After three months, the ISTC settled with the board of the

---

140   Compare Ferner 1989, p. 10; Middlemas 1991, p. 288.
141   Middlemas 1991, pp. 289–90; Cohen 2006, p. 57.
142   Cohen 2006, pp. 58–9.
143   Accordingly, the union president had at first granted, then withdrawn and finally re-established dispensation to the private sector (Cohen 2006, p. 59).

BSC and agreed to a 16 percent wage increase, 90,000 redundancies and the introduction of 'productivity "strings"' that would result in further job losses.[144] What some interpreted as a victory – the initial pay offer had been 2 percent[145] – amounted to the first heavy defeat inflicted by the Thatcherites on organised labour: the settlement resulted in de-manning to a degree that stripped the ISTC of its power base and turned it into a toothless force.[146]

Although the Thatcherites had played their part in triggering the conflict by imposing cash limits on the BSC and promoting aggressive police tactics, they appeared to have been careful to avoid using a maximum degree of repression at this point. They refused to grant Villiers an injunction against secondary picketing at private-sector plants, which he had requested in case the 1980 Act would pass through parliament on time.[147] In so doing, they obviously tried to prevent the conflict from escalating. Accordingly, their tactics can be seen as aiming to contain the momentum behind the strike, but not actively repressing it, which again reflected that they were following a cautious strategy informed by the Ridley Report.

The aftermath of the strike demonstrates that the settlement amounted to a victory for the Thatcherites. They used it as a pretext for the fundamental restructuring of the BSC, culminating in privatisation in 1988. Villiers was forced into premature retirement and replaced by Ian MacGregor, who was known for his hard-line approach to industrial relations.[148] MacGregor was instructed to rationalise the whole corporation. He instigated a process of 'remorseless change'. By 1986, manual production had decreased from 21.5m tonnes to 15m tonnes, and productivity had risen considerably: the time needed to produce a tonne of steel had dropped from 18.2 to 6 man-hours. At the same time, the BSC board took the lead in decentralising wage bargaining,[149] thus deepening rifts in the workforce and further weakening institutional supports for coalition-building among workers.

The fact that disunity among workers started to translate into splits in the union movement is exposed in union responses to the legislation enacted by the Thatcherites. In 1982, the TUC held a 'Special Conference' at Wembley to discuss what to do about it. One of the topics debated was a provision of the 1980 Employment Act, which made public funds available to unions

---

144 Middlemas 1991, p. 290; Cohen 2006, p. 62.
145 Johnson 1991, p. 227.
146 Compare Middlemas 1991, p. 290.
147 Middlemas 1990, p. 290.
148 Ferner 1989, p. 15.
149 Middlemas 1990, p. 291.

in order to allow them to hold secret strike ballots[150] – clearly an attempt to formalise and decelerate the build-up to strikes with the aim of undermining their momentum.[151] It was decided that member unions accepting government money for ballots should be expelled. Moreover, the 1982 Employment Act limited organised labour's immunity from being sued, to which the Special Conference responded by stipulating that unions under the threat of the law should receive financial backing.[152] However, the corresponding resolution was phrased in a way that allowed for revoking the entitlement to support. It contained an amendment stating that the latter was not the automatic result of unions being threatened with legal action.[153] Accordingly, the 'Wembley Principles' of 1982 amounted less to a declaration of war on Thatcherite class politics, and more to an indicator of the disunity of organised labour.

The divided nature of the trade union movement was also revealed in how the TUC leadership under Len Murray disciplined, on various occasions, member unions engaging in militant action. The Associated Society of Locomotive Engineers and Firemen (ASLEF) struck in order to prevent British Rail (BR) from introducing 'flexible rostering', which would have increased productivity and reduced the manpower required. Their approach displayed an economistic and 'conservative' attitude rooted in the traditions of organised labour in Britain, which the TUC leaders saw as inappropriate in this situation. BR had come under fire from the government, which was inclined to downsize its network substantially and extend the road and motorways. The TUC was conciliatory to the government's plans and pressurised its member unions successfully to give up resistance to the changes. They still hoped for a reversal of fortunes for trade unionism under a different government and wanted to appear respectable.[154]

The conflict at *Stockport Messenger* in 1983 not only brought out a new degree of disunity within the ranks of organised labour, but also demonstrated that the changes in trade union law had begun to bite and deepen the divide between legalistic and militant trade unionists. This conflict was one of the first instances of a union suffering hefty fines for industrial action illegal under the new laws.

---

150 Shackleton 1998, p. 586.
151 Compare Hyman 1987b, p. 107.
152 Middlemas 1991, p. 326.
153 Compare Cohen 2006, p. 55.
154 Middlemas 1991, pp. 294–5, 327.

Stockport Messenger, as most companies in the printing industry at the time, operated under a pre-entry closed shop agreement, which excluded non-unionised workers.[155] Despite this, Eddie Shah, the owner, decided to set up two non-unionised print works. When workers at the existing plants were ordered to handle material produced in the new shops, they walked out. Shah decided to sack six workers and expand the capacity of his new plants so that they could accommodate all his papers.[156]

As a response, the National Graphical Association (NGA) picketed the new plants and blacklisted Shah's business, to which he responded by going to court. Consequently, Manchester High Court issued two injunctions against the NGA, which reacted by stepping up picketing. Now the government got involved. Several ministers openly declared their support for Shah.[157] He turned to the court again, which imposed a £50,000 fine on the NGA. The union continued picketing, and the government responded by urging the police to use their new strikebreaking tactics. The police complied, and the right-wing press reported on the subsequent confrontations in a heavily biased fashion. By covering 'the clashes from behind police lines', they presented a 'one-dimensional picture which completely distorted responsibility for the violence and left the pickets to take the full blame'.[158] Accordingly, they stirred resentment within the population against the union by reiterating the theme of the unions as irresponsible troublemakers, which had emerged during the Winter of Discontent.[159]

Eventually, the NGA decided to back down, withdraw the pickets, and call for negotiations through the Advisory Conciliation and Arbitration Service (ACAS). Shah reacted by going to court once more; the court ordered that the NGA pay £525,000 for two cases of contempt of the earlier injunctions. The NGA turned to the TUC and asked it to back a one-day national print walk-out and for general support under the 'Wembley Principles',[160] whose vagueness was revealed by the incidents to follow: The TUC's Employment Policy and Organization Committee voted in favour, but was overridden by Murray, who

---

[155] Hain 1986, p. 130.
[156] Cohen 2006, p. 72.
[157] During a session of Prime Minister's Questions in December 1983, Kinnock, the new leader of the opposition, attacked Thatcher for having met Shah in October. According to Kinnock, two photos of the two in 'deep conversation' were published in one of Shah's papers, the *Sale and Altrincham Messenger*. Thatcher did not comment on the meeting (Hansard HC, 49, 983–7).
[158] Hain 1986, p. 131.
[159] Ibid.
[160] Hain 1986, p. 132; Cohen 2006, p. 72.

insisted that unions were bound by the law and urged the General Council to overturn the decision. The NGA had little choice but to climb down. All in all, it had to spend about £1m in fines and legal costs.[161]

This situation showed that the Thatcherites' decision to take class politics to the terrain of law was a clever strategic move. Thatcher brushed off allegations of bias against organised labour by stating that she was not taking sides in an industrial conflict, but upholding the rule of law. She commented:

> This dispute is about an attempt to impose a closed shop on employees, who did not want it, by a process of union intimidation, and further to prevent that company from producing a newspaper by unlawful picketing under the criminal law. The employer has rightly sought the protection of the courts. The protection of the law is there for every citizen in the land and it is to be used. *The law is wholly separate from politics*.[162]

Thatcher here invoked a key ideological effect of the law form under capitalist conditions: its apparent neutrality.[163] The inherent bias of Thatcherite class politics was covered up by couching it in the law form.

The ASLEF and the NGA strikes illuminate the contradictions in which trade unions were entangled at the time. The leadership of the labour movement miscalculated the durability of the power bloc's offensive and did not want to undermine supposed chances of a neo-corporatist settlement by confronting the state head-on. Hence, they were caught between reiterating the role of trade unions as 'mass integrative apparatuses' and transforming them into class-based organisational vehicles of the opposition against Thatcherism. Individual member unions of the TUC were forced by the Thatcherite onslaught to defend jobs in outdated industries. They resorted to the traditional economistic outlook of organised labour in Britain almost by default and, as a result, struggled with garnering support from other sections of industry and the wider population. Consequently, trade union strategy at the time was marred by inconsistencies. The TUC leadership embraced 'new realism' after Thatcher's re-election in 1983, which was premised on the assumption that economic and political change could only be achieved through changes to the law, and that this was only possible with the help of a Labour government. 'New realism' was

---

161 Hain 1986, p. 132.
162 Hansard HC, 49, 983–7, added emphasis.
163 The notion that the law is neutral stems from the formal equality of individuals before it and covers up its intrinsic connection to capitalist class domination as a constitutive element of the capitalist relations of production (see above; compare Marx 1962a, pp. 190–1).

a miscalculation as regards the fierceness of the Thatcherite attack, which set out to weaken the working class irreversibly.[164] But it was not an act of class treason, as Cohen has it.[165] Rather, it reflected that even before the biggest industrial conflicts of the Thatcher era took place, organised labour already found itself in a weak position.

Conversely, the Thatcherite combination of a cautious approach to industrial conflict, draconian trade union laws and a pro-cyclical strategy in monetary and fiscal policy appeared to be working. The unions were tricked into mistaking the government's caution for weakness and their own weakness for caution; they overlooked the fact that the enactment of repressive laws meant that the relations of forces were shifting, and that the power bloc was making substantial material gains. In other words, the Thatcherites had successfully prepared the ground for escalating the onslaught on organised labour and making the transition from a war of position to a war of manoeuvre. Middlemas describes as follows what Tebbit, Employment Secretary from 1981–3, achieved by restricting unions' immunity from tort action: 'It seemed that he had put trade unions in a slave collar, an iron noose which tightened the more they struggled, but which did not relax, even if they did'.[166]

All in all, the Thatcherite class political regime was centred, at the time, on carefully preparing for an open war against organised labour. In line with the Ridley Plan, Thatcher and her associates concentrated on reshaping the battleground and refrained from attacking institutions and arrangements with a high symbolic value for the working class – such as the welfare state and collective bargaining. Michael Bleaney describes their approach as such: 'The government has adopted a strategy towards the trade union movement akin to that of a guerrilla war: to mount continuous attacks without getting involved in a major confrontation with the big battalions which might serve as a focus to mobilise opposition'.[167]

The Political Scene: De-Stabilisation and Re-Stabilisation

During the Winter of Discontent, the Thatcherites had come to dominate the political scene, even if this dominance resulted more from the popularity of Thatcher's authoritarian stance on organised labour than from the popularity

---

164 Hyman 1987b, p. 99.
165 Cohen 2006, p. 76.
166 Middlemas 1991, p. 324.
167 Bleaney 1983, p. 139.

of her neoliberal worldviews. This is demonstrated by the volatility of support for Thatcher during her first term. The recession in 1980–1 dented it on all fronts: the cabinet, the party, the power bloc, and the electorate. Especially the backing of the skilled workers proved unstable. They swung from the Conservatives to Labour, from Labour to the SDP, from the SDP back to the Conservatives and, to some extent, back to Labour. All of this reflected discontent with the pro-cyclical effect of the new accumulation strategy.[168] The wavering support for the Prime Minister was articulated with the more fundamental crisis of representation in the political scene insofar as there was infighting in the Parliamentary Conservative Party between the 'wets' and the 'dries' (or Thatcherites).

A further sign of this crisis was that the opposition was divided and unable to exploit discontent with the government. There were deep rifts in the Labour Party, which reflected its fundamental contradiction, that is, the contradiction between being a 'national' and a socialist, working-class party. This contradiction now took on the form of rows between left and right over how to counter the Thatcherite advance. Both wings engaged in what was effectively an argument over whether the party should attempt to formulate an offensive of the power bloc with an alternative path, or orchestrate another working-class offensive with the aim of triggering a socialist transformation. They found themselves deadlocked, which mirrored the catastrophic equilibrium of the conjuncture as a whole: neither side could claim that its respective project had delivered material gains in the last period in government, and neither side could afford to make concessions. After all, the agendas of the two camps were irreconcilable: Proto-neoliberalism and neo-corporatism were premised on restraining organised labour, and socialism was based on demanding the opposite, that is, the removal of any such restraints.

The deadlock and the impossibility of a compromise were revealed in the early 1980s when the party began to break up along the fault line between 'nationalists' and socialists. Initially, the Labour left seemed to gain the upper hand, which reflected the discontent of the party rank-and-file with the policies pursued by Callaghan and Healey.[169] Healey lost the 1980 leadership elections and was replaced by Michael Foot, who was popular with the left. Moreover, constitutional changes, aimed at democratising the party and strengthening the influence of the rank-and-file and the unions, were put into practice.[170]

---

168 Jessop et al. 1988, pp. 64, 74, 85.
169 Compare Kavanagh 1990, p. 164.
170 Compare Gamble 1988, p. 108.

The shift in favour of the socialist wing, however, soon proved a Pyrrhic victory. Senior party members around former Chancellor Roy Jenkins decided to form a breakaway organisation. The SDP claimed to depart from Labour's alleged socialist course and wanted to sever the ties between the political centre-left and trade unionism.[171] Despite initial successes in by-elections and an alliance with the Liberal Party, enthusiasm for the SDP evaporated after 12 months.[172] Nevertheless, the 'Alliance' appeared to attract many former Labour voters. In the general elections of 1983 and 1987, it gained 26 and 23 percent, respectively – results significantly higher than any of the post-war results of the Liberal Party.[173]

In light of internal rifts in the parliamentary opposition, it is not surprising that the Thatcherites were able to reassert their control over cabinet and party and win back supporters lost during the recession. Apart from the disunity of Labour, two other factors helped Thatcher ride out the temporary erosion of popular support. First, the recession ended and was followed by a cyclical economic upswing.[174] Second, there was the Falklands War, which began in May 1982. The government orchestrated a successful nationalist mobilisation,[175] which created 'euphoria' once the islands in the South Atlantic had been recaptured.

Like any 'successful' military campaign, the Falklands War was highly functional for consolidating the status quo and producing consent. It offered an escape route out of economic and political problems by triggering a process of ideological closure: Conflicts within British society were superseded by nationalist appeals to unity.

The purely ideological character of these appeals is demonstrated by the fact that 'for the British government, the Falklands were about as low as they could be on its list of priorities'.[176] Before Argentine troops invaded the Falklands on Good Friday 1982, the islands had been of no political or geopolitical interest whatsoever to the Thatcher government. In fact, it had downsized a small defence force that had existed there. Once the Argentine occupation had started, Thatcher opted for war – despite efforts by the Reagan administration and the UN to produce a negotiated settlement.[177] Considering the pre-history

---

171 Compare Hall 1983b, p. 316.
172 Gamble 1988, pp. 119–20.
173 Compare Kaiser 2006, p. 185.
174 Jessop et al. 1988, p. 64.
175 Hobsbawm 1983, p. 263.
176 Hobsbawm 1983, p. 258.
177 Morgan 1990, pp. 458–9.

of the conflict, it appears that the government insisted on a military intervention in order to bolster its popularity.

The trigger for actual physical confrontations was a similarly 'suspicious' episode.[178] In early May, the Argentine battleship 'General Belgrano', which appeared to be returning to the Argentine mainland, was torpedoed by a British submarine. As a result, 360 people were killed. Clive Ponting, a civil servant, later claimed that the War Cabinet had decided to sink the vessel in order to undermine a Peruvian peace plan.[179] Once more, the government brushed aside all efforts to resolve the conflict peacefully, fuelled nationalist sentiment, and went ahead with the invasion.[180] British armed forces quickly recaptured the islands, and about 1,000 people died in a war waged over a territory with a population of 1,800.[181]

The Falklands War has to be put into the context of the recurring crises that marred the post-war period and, more specifically, the 1970s catastrophic equilibrium. Hobsbawm argues that the Argentine invasion caused a feeling of 'national humiliation', which was tied to a general sentiment that Britain was in decline.[182] Thatcher exploited these themes by conjuring up images of national 'greatness',[183] taking an aggressive stance and deploying a 'purely military logic'.[184] This in turn allowed her to depoliticise the conjuncture and strengthen her grip on the government.[185] The 'successful' war effort contributed to her winning the 1983 general elections comfortably.[186]

The election result reveals that the social basis of Thatcherism was formed of small owners of capital, 70 percent of whom voted Conservative.[187] Thatcher's

---

178 Morgan 1990, p. 460.
179 Evans 1997, pp. 99–100.
180 Compare Morgan 1990, pp. 458–9. Robert Gray comments: 'With the commitment of forces to combat, identification with the men became a compelling motive, even for people who had reservations about the initial dispatch of the task force ... This atmosphere of national emergency and danger inevitably strengthened the authority of Government' (1983, p. 273). He concludes: 'This was in many ways the ideal war – short, sharp, "successful", directly involving small professional armed forces and their families, but consumed vicariously through press and TV – for cementing a reactionary chauvinist consensus' (Gray 1983, p. 274).
181 Freedman 1988, pp. 14, 116.
182 Hobsbawm 1983, p. 260.
183 Compare Gray 1983, p. 275; Hobsbawm 1983, p. 261.
184 Gray 1983, p. 273.
185 Gray 1983, p. 270.
186 Compare Freedman 1988, pp. 100–4.
187 Kavanagh 1990, p. 303.

constituency also consisted in a sizeable number of skilled workers, who in many cases lived in south, owned their own cars and homes, worked in the private sector, and were not union members.[188] Many skilled workers had been alienated from previous governments through incomes policy and wage restraint, and were in favour of income tax cuts and battling inflation.[189] Only 39 percent of unionists voted for the Labour Party, whose social base was among workers in the North and in Scotland, public sector workers in general and inhabitants of council houses.[190] The divisive nationalism of the Thatcherite 'two nations' hegemonic project, which juxtaposed 'productive' and 'parasitic' elements of society, had paid off: It was deepening the political disunity of the working class and created a 'new cross-class alliance against those identified with the post-war settlement and its self-evident failures'.[191] In conclusion, the Thatcherites were able to consolidate their dominance over the political scene during their first term, even if this did not reflect their strength as much as it mirrored their opponents' weakness.

The Neoliberal Regime of Condensation

The second period of Thatcherism was characterised by the active attempt of the new government to roll back the institutional supports of the post-war settlement, and to alter class relations of forces in favour of capital by undermining organised labour – in particular through the use of trade union law. Accordingly, the period in question was the second period in an offensive of the power bloc, which was characterised by the latter making substantial material gains. A new economic-political order was implemented – free-market authoritarianism – as well as a new class political regime – Thatcherism. They were compatible with each other:

– The pro-cyclical character of the new accumulation strategy reinforced the divisions in the working class, which weakened working-class resistance to the enactment of repressive trade union legislation and created the foundations for a 'two nations' hegemonic project;

---

188   Kavanagh 1990, p. 181.
189   Jessop 1991b, p. 141.
190   Kavanagh 1990, p. 181.
191   Jessop 1991b, p. 142.

- The authoritarian character of the state project underpinned the similarly authoritarian character of the repressive extraction strategy, and paved the way for police repression against the allegedly 'parasitic' nation;
- The repressive extraction strategy removed obstacles to deregulation, liberalisation and privatisation by attacking the unions, and further deepened the authoritarianism of the state strategy; and
- The 'two nations' hegemonic project stabilised the neo-Ricardian accumulation strategy and created discursive constructions which served as justifications for authoritarianism.

In light of the formal unity between the Thatcherite approaches to class politics and economic order politics, I contend that the Thatcherites created a new regime of condensation. Since all the strategies in question were informed by neoliberal thinking, I propose to call it the neoliberal regime of condensation and to see it as the result of a neoliberal regime shift. In other words, I argue that capitalist class domination was now institutionalised in and by the state in a dominantly neoliberal form.

The results of this new regime in terms of economic fundamentals were not all bad, but far from impressive. The recession ended after 1981, and on some fronts, the economy stabilised. Growth recovered from −2.0 and −1.2 percent in 1980 and 1981 to 1.7 and 3.8 percent in 1982 and 1983.[192] Similarly, inflation fell from 18.0 percent in 1980 and 11.9 percent in 1981 to 8.6 percent in 1982 and 4.6 percent in 1983.[193] Finally, wages consistently rose, even after inflation, with the rate of increase starting to rise substantially after 1982: 0.7 percent in 1980, 0.9 percent in 1981, 0.6 percent in 1982 and 3.6 percent in 1983. However, these numbers cover up the substantial divergences in the rate of wage increase over different sectors.[194] In general, it needs to be considered that Britain profited, at the time, from two developments outside the realm of economic-policy making at the national level: the discovery and exploitation of North Sea Oil, and decreasing commodity and raw materials prices in the world market.[195]

The neo-Ricardian character of Thatcherite industrial restructuring is underscored by two countervailing trends: Overall productivity was raised by 10 percent between 1980 and 1983, whilst corporate investment fell by over 35 percent between 1980 and 1981.[196] This indicates that increases in productivity were the

---

192   Johnson 1991, p. 266.
193   NatStats 11, 2009.
194   Maynard 1988, p. 123; MacInnes 1987, pp. 82–3.
195   MacInnes 1987, pp. xii–xiii.
196   Maynard 1988, p. 91; Middlemas 1991, p. 262.

result of putting low-productivity companies out of business, not so much of modernising production and increasing relative surplus value.[197]

Accordingly, the upturn from 1982 onwards seems to have been driven by an international economic upswing and by consumer spending and a housing boom, and not by investment in the industrial sector.[198] Total consumer credit rose from £13.4bn to £18.9bn between 1981 and 1983,[199] which implies that the recovery was facilitated by personal debt. This in turn led to a substantial increase of imports and an increasing trade deficit.[200]

Besides, unemployment not only remained high, but rose considerably: from 5.4 percent in 1980 to 10.7 percent in 1983. The Thatcherites saw this development as a necessary adjustment process. Ridley, for example, remarked in 1981 that 'the level of unemployment is evidence of the progress we are making'.[201] Those unemployed and those with low-paid jobs fell behind better-paid workers and professionals, which leads Middlemas to conclude that 'the beginnings of a two- or three-tier society emerged'.[202] The policies of the Thatcherites produced sharpening social inequality without improving the productive base of the British economy.

Moreover, the higher degree of inequality became entrenched as Thatcher and her entourage successfully created additional obstacles to working-class organisation: Mass unemployment drove a wedge through the working class, making coalitions across class fractions harder to achieve. Whereas the (newly) unemployed lost out in this situation, those keeping their jobs suffered less or even benefited from wage gains.[203] Moreover, the changes in trade union law made it harder to engage in effective industrial action. Along these lines, Jessop et al. discuss 'Thatcher's economic experiment' under the header 'Economic Failure, Political Success'. They state:

> Thatcher has failed to be a monetarist ... Inflation has dropped as a result of lower commodity prices in the world recession, massive unemployment, capital's inability to raise prices as competition intensified, and the huge collapse of economic activity as Britain has hastened into recession at least a year ahead of other nations ... This has obvious strategic

---

197 MacInnes 1987, p. 85; Overbeek 1990, p. 195.
198 Middlemas 1991, p. 262.
199 Middlemas 1991, p. 564.
200 Johnson 1991, pp. 210–11.
201 Cited in MacInnes 1987, p. 57.
202 Middlemas 1990, p. 262.
203 Compare Leys 1989, p. 107.

implications as workers' power is devastated and the senile areas of British industry suffer involuntary euthanasia – there is no real means of ensuring productive restructuring, investment and innovation to secure sustained recovery and growth.[204]

In my own terms, the Thatcher government at this point had succeeded in the area of class politics and had failed in the area of economic order politics. It had laid the foundation for the subsequent marginalisation of trade unionism, but it had not improved the prospects for a medium-term revival of the British economy.

---

204 Jessop et al. 1988, pp. 84–5.

CHAPTER 7

Instability and Confrontation (1984–8)

Class Politics Moves into the Foreground

In the 1979–84 period, the Thatcherites made material gains in their pursuit of a neoliberal regime of condensation, and their course won electoral approval: Thatcher secured a second term in 1983. The year 1984 marked a turning point because class politics moved to the foreground and became the field of politics that dominated public debates. After having changed the terrain of class struggle in the preceding years through changing the law, the Thatcherites now chose to start a war of manoeuvre against the leading fractions of organised labour, most importantly the NUM. This led to fierce and drawn-out confrontations between some of the more militant trade unions on one side and the power bloc and the repressive state apparatuses on the other. Economic order politics faded into the background in terms of public attention, but the Thatcherites, with their new political focus, were able to build on what they had achieved in this area in the preceding years.

In 1984, industrial conflict reached a scale unknown since the Winter of Discontent. 27,135,000 working days were lost, which was not far short of the post-war record of 29,474,000 in 1979.[1] The 1984–5 miners' strike was the defining industrial confrontation of the Thatcher era. Coal was still a nationalised industry, which meant that the strike amounted to a direct confrontation between the government and the most militant and best-organised fraction of the labour movement. For a while, the stoppage brought the government close to defeat – a result that would have weakened the hold of the Thatcherites over the political scene and would have derailed their attempt to undermine organised labour. In other words, the stakes were high in this conflict, and the strategy sketched out in the Ridley Report was by no means invincible. The repressive nature of the Thatcherite extraction strategy and its limitations crystallised in the miners' strike. The reaction of Thatcher and her associates to the stoppage leaves no doubt that they were intent on orchestrating an offensive of the power bloc against organised labour. For all these reasons, I have included a detailed case study on the strike in this chapter.

---

1 NatStats I, 2009.

The confrontation between the NUM and the Thatcherites, however, was not the only major industrial conflict in this period. It was followed by two confrontations in which different branches of privately-owned industrial capital co-operated closely with the government and managed to damage militant trade unions beyond repair. This further entrenched the shift in the relations of forces in favour of the power bloc – not least thanks to the changes in trade union law and their impact on organised labour's room for manoeuvre. The first was the conflict between Rupert Murdoch's News International, a media corporation with close ties to the government, and the printers' unions in 1986–7. It was triggered by Murdoch's decision to open a new plant in Wapping (East London), which was manned by members of the 'yellow' Electronic, Electrical, Telecommunications and Plumbing Union (EETPU), and led to workers in Murdoch's old plants being laid off. Under the constantly intensifying threat of court proceedings, the workers' resistance faltered. The other confrontation was the 1988 P&O strike. It led to the sequestration of the funds of the National Union of Seamen (NUS) for secondary picketing and made the union bankrupt.

The Thatcherites flanked their direct confrontations with organised labour by entrenching their 'two nations' hegemonic project. Financial liberalisation was the device with the help of which they divided Britain into a purportedly 'productive' and an allegedly 'parasitic' nation. It linked the interests of better-off workers keen on buying a house and investing in stock with those of the City firms that pushed for internationalisation and expansion, and associated the gentlemanly capitalists presiding over an oligopoly at the Stock Exchange with those workers who were dependent on social housing and other benefits. In sum, the liberalisation of financial markets enabled the Thatcherites to deepen divisions within the working class and cover up class antagonism.

The centrepiece of liberalisation was the 1986 Big Bang at the stock market, which resulted in the expansion, internationalisation and 'de-gentrification' of the City, and which marginalised the 'gentlemanly' groups still dominating it. The power bloc was modernised through the fundamental changes in the City, and its new, international character matched the neo-Ricardian accumulation strategy initiated in the preceding years. Furthermore, financial liberalisation also brought the liberalisation of the mortgage market, which extended the availability of credit for the population and flanked the privatisation of council housing, thus deepening the rifts in the working class. All in all, financial liberalisation had far-reaching implications for class domination in Britain, which is why it merits detailed investigation. I have thus included another case study in this chapter, which looks at Big Bang and the effects of liberalisation.

∴

Case Study: Attacking the Union Movement – The 1984–5 Miners' Strike

The Centrepiece of the Thatcherite Offensive

There is a normalising and historicising discourse not only on Thatcherism in general, but also on the miners' strike in particular. According to this discourse, the ferocity of this year-long industrial conflict and the degree of polarisation it caused can be explained with reference to the intransigence and radicalism of its protagonists, namely Scargill, the president of the NUM, and MacGregor, who had left the BSC to become chairman of the NCB in September 1983. An oft-heard story is that the clash between two similar personalities located at different ends of the political spectrum prevented a settlement, which would have had less disastrous consequences for the industry than the all-out victory for the NCB in March 1985.[2]

In my view, this account of events is personalising the strike dynamic and thus covering up its economic-political circumstances. For one, the strike itself and Scargill's leadership had mass support among the miners, at least outside the 'working' mining communities in South Derbyshire, Nottinghamshire and Leicestershire. In fact, the strikers held out for a year, and did so despite being faced with police repression, media vilification and serious economic hardship for themselves and their families. These facts sit ill with the claim that Scargill was simply exploiting the strike for his own political agenda and being prepared to sacrifice his own constituency in the process, which is relayed in the normalising and historicising literature.[3] Second, MacGregor was appointed by Thatcher in the full knowledge that he was a 'union buster', and that civil servants warned against his appointment.[4] Despite the fact that there were some misgivings about how he communicated with the media and general public,[5] the government was behind him during the entire strike. Thatcher knew that MacGregor planned to downsize the industry considerably and was in favour of privatisation,[6] and there are no records of her protesting against this course. In any case, MacGregor's stance was fully consistent with the plans laid out for the coal industry by the Conservative Party and the Thatcher

---

[2] Goodman 1985, pp. 61; Adeney and Lloyd 1986, pp. 5, 31, 201; Beckett and Hencke 2009, pp. 31, 42, 266–7; Vinen 2009, pp. 158–9, 162.
[3] Compare Goodman 1985, pp. 33–4; Adeney and Lloyd 1986, pp. 34–5; Beckett and Hencke 2009, pp. 42, 265.
[4] Goodman 1985, pp. 57–8; Saville 1985, p. 328; Adeney and Lloyd 1986, pp. 27, 55.
[5] Beckett and Hencke 2009, pp. 151–2.
[6] Goodman 1985, p. 28; Thatcher Archive, 133568, p. 7.

government, and with the general thrust of Thatcherite strategy to attack organised labour and marginalise militant trade unionism. In light of this, I propose a different interpretation of events: The miners' strike was the centrepiece of the offensive against the working class orchestrated by the Thatcher government.

Phase 1: The Point of No Return

The miners were an obvious target for the Thatcherite inner circle. The Ridley Report had warned that the 'most likely area' for a confrontation with organised labour over privatisation was coal.[7] This echoed the experiences of the Heath government, which had failed to contain the organisational strength and militancy of the NUM. The Thatcherites saw the union as the '"leading arm" of the labour movement' and decided to follow a 'calculated plan' in order to defeat it.[8]

Their hostility towards the miners' union was confirmed when it elected Scargill, a left-leaning militant, as its president in 1981. Scargill was one of the people behind the successful, militant strike tactics adopted by the Yorkshire NUM in the late 1960s and early 1970s. These tactics heavily relied on 'flying pickets', that is, on activist strikers continuously moving between places deemed strategically important in order to form picket lines. This proved highly effective in terms of extending stoppages geographically and increasing their impact. They were a key factor behind the miners' victory in 1972.[9]

The defining incident of that strike took place at Saltley coke depot just outside Birmingham city centre. The depot, which was the last large-scale distribution centre to operate during the strike, was closed by a mass picket in February 1972. The blockade was carried by a coalition between miners from all over the country and local industrial workers, and was orchestrated by Scargill and a local network of Communist trade unionists.[10] Due to the sheer number of workers involved and their capacity to act together despite hailing from different fractions of their class, the Battle of Saltley Gates acquired 'an almost legendary significance in the mythology of the coalfields'.[11] In turn, the new right saw Scargill as their archenemy. Ridley relays in his memoirs that he saw the events at Satley 'with scorn'. According to him, Thatcher 'always knew, even

---

7   Thatcher Archive, 110795, p. 25.
8   Hain 1986, p. 226.
9   Compare Milne 1995, pp. 15–16; Cohen 2006, p. 75.
10 Darlington and Lyddon 2001, pp. 57–8; Cohen 2006, p. 20.
11 Morgan 1990, p. 328; compare Darlington and Lyddon 2001, p. 61; Cohen 2006, p. 75.

as far back as 1978, that she would face a pitched battle mounted by Arthur Scargill'.[12]

Correspondingly, the Thatcherites followed the Ridley Report closely in preparing for a confrontation with the NUM. In 1981, they decided to back down in a dispute over pit closures in order to avoid a clash before their arrangements for containing a large-scale strike in the mining industry were in place. In the aftermath of that dispute, Thatcher decided to set up a 'group on coal' (MISC 57) – a secret Cabinet Committee tasked with preparing for a full-on confrontation with the NUM. In keeping with the spirit of the Ridley Plan, the group discussed in great technical detail what could be done to increase the 'endurance' of power stations and protect industry in the event of a miners' strike.[13] Its key recommendation was to increase coal stocks, which is indeed what happened right away: stock rose from 37m tonnes in 1981 to 57m in 1984. The other main options discussed had also already been mentioned in the Ridley Plan: the extension of dual firing at power stations and the increase of coal imports.[14]

Apart from working on the technical aspects of the power supply, the government also prepared for a strike by increasing its control over the infrastructure. In 1982, Walter Marshall, a supporter both of Thatcher and of nuclear power, was appointed chairman of the Central Electricity Generating Board.[15] Furthermore, the government restructured policing and modified laws in ways that systematically disadvantaged strikers.[16]

Soon after the battleground had been prepared, the Thatcherites entered into confrontation with the NUM. One day after her re-election in 1983, Thatcher is reported to have said privately: 'We're going to have a miners' strike'.[17] The point of no return was reached when Thatcher appointed Ian McGregor to head of the NCB in September 1983. He replaced Norman Siddall, who had closed 20 pits and cut 23,000 jobs in mining without causing a lot of publicity.[18] McGregor had earned his reputation as a 'union buster' when he had been at British Leyland, British Steel and at the American corporation AMAX. Unsurprisingly, the NUM saw McGregor's appointment as a deliberate provocation by

---

12 Ridley 1991; pp. 66–7.
13 CAB 130/1228; CAB 130/1260; compare Adeney and Lloyd 1986, p. 73.
14 Ibid.; Saville 1985, p. 306.
15 Goodman 1985, p. 25; Saville 1985, p. 306; Hain 1986, p. 134.
16 Beckett and Hencke 2009, p. 36.
17 Cited in Saville 1985, p. 305; Hain 1986, p. 134.
18 Ferner 1989, p. 15.

the government.[19] By now, it was pretty obvious that an open conflict was no longer avoidable. In other words, the government preparations for the conflict had ended.

In contrast to the Thatcherites, the NUM lacked a clear direction during this phase. Despite Scargill's election, members were not convinced that a confrontational stance towards the NCB and the government was the right approach. In January 1982, they voted against walking out in a national ballot over a pay offer from the NCB of 9.5 percent.[20] The mainstream press, supported by a Scargill's predecessor Joe Gormley, a right-winger, had successfully campaigned against a national strike.[21] There was a second vote against going on strike in October 1982, when another ballot was held over pit closures and a pay offer.

A third ballot came in March 1983 when the South Wales Area, backed by Scotland and Yorkshire, voted for a strike over the closure of the Ty Mawr-Lewis Merthyr pit. Scargill invoked rule 41 of the NUM statutes, which authorised regions to engage in autonomous strike action if the executive committee agreed. However, the right wing successfully pushed for a national ballot, and members again decided against walking out.[22]

The fact that South Wales was outvoted reveals rifts between different area organisations of the NUM, which were divided over strategy and general political outlook.[23] The institutional basis of these divisions was the 1977 pit incentive scheme, which Gormley had pushed through despite the fact that it was rejected in a national ballot. Areas gained the right to negotiate local wage agreements, which, according to differentials in productivity, produced pay gaps between miners in different areas.[24]

Phase II: Early Gains and Tactical Mistakes

MacGregor was seriously trying to shrink the British coal industry from the start. There is a secret document from September 1983 providing the minutes of a meeting attended by, among others, Thatcher, Lawson, Peter Walker, the Energy Secretary, and Tom King, the Employment Secretary. In this meeting, Walker reported that MacGregor planned to shut 75 (out of 186) pits and reduce manpower from 202,000 to 138,000 within the space of three years.[25]

---

19 Compare Hain 1986, p. 135; Saville 1986, p. 306.
20 Saville 1985, p. 304.
21 Hyman 1985, p. 332.
22 Saville 1985, pp. 305, 308; Adeney and Lloyd 1986, p. 22.
23 Compare Burgi and Jessop 1991, p. 178.
24 Cohen 2006, pp. 75–6. Thatcher Archive, 133121.
25 Thatcher Archive, 133121, p. 2; Beckett and Hencke 2009, p. 255.

In response to this plan, Walker stated that it could cause 'considerable problems', but no critical comments from the other participants were recorded.[26] A second meeting between Thatcher, Lawson, Walker, King and others took place in January. It discussed a new proposal by MacGregor, which was in keeping with the old plan, and consisted in ridding the industry of 45,000 jobs over the course of two years.[27] This was accepted by everyone present.

Against this backdrop, MacGregor embarked on a collision course straight away – not only with the NUM, but also with the fractions of the NCB bureaucracy that were still committed to a corporatist approach to industrial relations.[28] One of his first acts in office was to announce that he would eradicate 'uneconomic' output. Soon after, he decided to offer the NUM a 5.2 percent pay rise, which – even if in line with other public sector pay offers – amounted to a reversal of the lenient regime of previous years. The NUM leadership reacted by holding an emergency national conference, which instituted an overtime ban and allowed the leadership to hold a national ballot whenever they saw fit.[29] Within two months of his appointment, McGregor had managed to get both sides of industry to assume battle positions. Crucially, however, he had not gone on the attack yet. In all likelihood, his was a calculated hesitance: The impact of a coal strike was harder to contain in winter, when demand was high.

Similarly, the NUM leadership was not convinced that it was the right time to walk out. They were hesitant because after three defeats at the ballot box they were not sure whether members would vote for a national strike. Consequently, they opted for a course of action that appeared to buy them time: the overtime ban, which succeeded insofar as it diminished coal stocks during the following winter.[30] Middlemas alleges that the NUM was planning to 'move beyond the overtime ban ... to a short decisive campaign without a ballot, culminating in a settlement'.[31] In hindsight, however, this appears a miscalculation. Neither side made the first move at this point, which in the end would help the NCB.

The eventual trigger for battle was a series of announcements made by the NCB in March 1984 shortly after the government had decreed that the coal industry would have to manage without subsidies by 1986. First, the Coal Board announced its decision to close Cortonwood Colliery in South Yorkshire, followed a day later by the declaration that they would also shut nearby Bullcliffe

---

26 Thatcher Archive, 133121, p. 2.
27 Thatcher Archive, 133712.
28 Compare Ferner 1989, p. 15.
29 Hain 1986, p. 135; Saville 1985, p. 305.
30 Middlemas 1991, pp. 298–9; Milne 1995, p. 18.
31 Middlemas 1991, p. 299.

Wood. Just a few days after that, they revealed that they were planning to close five pits straight away and then embark on a programme of closures that would shut another 20 pits and cost 20,000 jobs.[32]

Francis Beckett and David Hencke state that the closure announcement concerning Cortonwood was a mistake by the South Yorkshire Coal Board Director, George Hayes. Apparently, the NCB had not decided to close the pit at that time.[33] But this matters less than the fact that the NCB decided not to own up to the mistake, but instead pressed ahead with announcing a programme of closures. In other words, it was ready for the battle with the NUM.

Crucially, the real extent of the planned closures as agreed at the meeting in January 1984 was never revealed during the strike. Scargill had been accusing the NCB of possessing a 'hit-list' of 75 pits earmarked for closure from 1982. He renewed this claim during the strike, but was rebuffed by the NCB. In fact, at a later stage of the stoppage, Thatcher agreed to MacGregor sending a letter to every miner's home in the UK, denying the claims categorically.[34]

But even the 'official' line amounted to a conscious break with the status quo: It meant that the NCB had annulled the 'Plan for Coal' – an 'outline scenario' agreed by the Labour government, the NCB and the NUM in 1974, which had led to new investment in the industry and new pits opening up. According to the agreement, it was possible to avoid pit closures if there were increases in output.[35]

The government legitimised its confrontational stance by presenting the British coal mining industry as inefficient. Throughout the strike, Walker would repeat this claim. He alleged that the mining industry had cost taxpayers £1,334m in 1983–4 – a claim that shaped the public perception of the issue and was never challenged successfully, either by the miners or the opposition in parliament. Investigations by the economists and accountants would later reveal that the government's numbers were inaccurate. Furthermore, British pits were highly productive compared to those in other Western European countries. This was revealed by NCB numbers that compared the levels of subsidies across Europe: in 1984, these were £19.19 a tonne in France, £12.06 in West Germany, and £4.11 in the UK. But the NUM failed to capitalise on these findings.[36]

---

32 Hain 1986, p. 136; Middlemas 1991, p. 298; Milne 1995, p. 18.
33 Beckett and Hencke 2009, p. 47.
34 Jones 2014.
35 Hyman 1985, p. 353; Leys 1989, pp. 118–19; Beckett and Hencke 2009, p. 26.
36 Saville 1985, pp. 308, 316–17; Adeney and Lloyd 1986, pp. 24, 252–3.

According to Hyman, the union's hesitancy reflected its fear that arguments over economic efficiency could easily backfire because they implied that the NCB was right in principle to base its assessment of the viability of mines on their profitability.[37] Avoiding this debate was, in all likelihood, a first tactical mistake of the NUM. Had the general public understood that the government's economic claims were contestable, it may have been easier to garner support for the stoppage.

In any case, the NUM saw the accidental choice of Cortonwood as a provocation: It was generally expected that the pit would remain open for another five years, and only two weeks before workers had been transferred there from other pits. Moreover, it was located in the union's heartland, Yorkshire, where a third of Britain's 180,000 miners were based.[38] This was Scargill's homeland; it was a stronghold of the left wing of the NUM. All of this meant that the stakes were high from the start: victory for the government would require breaking the NUM's organisational backbone.[39]

In the end, it was not only the place but also the timing of events that drove the dynamics of the conflict: Spring was the worst possible season to go on strike. Along these lines, Milne argues that a 12-week strike could have sufficed to interrupt the country's electricity supply had the overtime ban continued until autumn.[40] In hindsight, the NUM leadership's decision not to press for immediate strike action in autumn 1983 may have been a second tactical mistake.

After the Cortonwood announcement, the NUM took up the gauntlet. On 8 March 1984, the NUM national executive authorised the areas of Yorkshire and Scotland to strike, where there had been spontaneous stoppages already. It invoked rule 41, which enabled it to make local strike action official.[41] The expectation was that there would be, in the words of the president of the Scottish NUM, Mick McGahey, a 'domino effect'.[42] The assumption was that the other areas would, one after the other, follow suit and go on strike.

However, this expectation did not fully materialise. Two weeks into the strike, 80 percent of miners in Britain had stopped work, and yet, some of the dominoes did not topple. Ballots in the smaller areas revealed split workforces or, in some cases, clear majorities against strike action. Crucially, Lancashire,

---

37   Hyman 1985, p. 341.
38   Saville 1985, p. 306.
39   Hyman 1985, p. 306.
40   Milne 1995, p. 18.
41   Saville 1985, p. 308; Cohen 2006, p. 78; Beckett and Hencke 2009, p. 51.
42   Cited in Cohen 2006, p. 78.

Derbyshire and Nottinghamshire voted against the strike; the Lancashire miners would later change their mind when they became the target of pickets. The material substratum to the 'pit culture of cooperation with management' in the Midlands was that pits were more modern, and pay was higher than elsewhere.[43] Pay differentials were a product of the 1977 incentive scheme.[44]

The NUM's decision to operate under rule 41 was also a decision not to employ rule 43, which required a successful national ballot before strike action.[45] Scargill attempted to avert demands for calling one by insisting that miners did not enjoy a right to vote their colleagues out of their jobs.[46] The tactical reasoning behind such a principled statement was the worry that the leadership could not mobilise a majority for a strike, which the ballots in the preceding years appeared to show. This was surely a defensive move, all the more so because some opinion polls suggested that a majority of miners were behind a national strike.[47]

Considering that the issue of the ballot would haunt the NUM leadership during the next months, the refusal to go to the members was its third tactical mistake. Even if the leaders' motives were reasonable, they underestimated how disregarding this specific democratic procedure would undermine the strike's legitimacy in the eyes of the public. In July 1984, Gallup conducted an opinion poll according to which 78 percent of respondents deemed the methods of the miners irresponsible.[48] Moreover, the decision provided working miners with a justification for strikebreaking. Likewise, it weakened the position of Nottinghamshire and Derbyshire miners who supported the strike.[49]

Finally, the refusal to ballot granted the committed authoritarian Thatcher, who pushed for the abolition of the democratically elected but left-leaning Greater London Council at the time of the strike, the opportunity to portray herself as a champion of democracy. Once again, she invoked the threat of left-wing totalitarianism – this time embodied in the leadership of the NUM. In a speech in July 1984, she declared the union to be 'the enemy within' that had to be fought just like the 'enemy without', that is, the Argentine army in the Falklands War, in order to preserve 'liberty'. Furthermore, she accused Scargill

---

43 Howell 2012, p. 154.
44 Hain 1986, pp. 128, 229; Milne 1995, p. 19; Darlington 2005, p. 78; Cohen 2006, p. 78; Howell 2012, p. 153.
45 Saville 1985, p. 308.
46 Cohen 2006, p. 78; Scargill 2009.
47 Hain 1986, p. 299; Beckett and Hencke 2009, p. 67.
48 Cited in Khabaz 2006, p. 235.
49 Compare Hyman 1985, p. 335; Hain 1986, p. 229.

of circumventing democracy[50] – despite the fact that he had acted in line with the NUM rulebook by invoking rule 41. With her speech, Thatcher took sides on the issue of the ballot and deepened divisions in the NUM. Thatcher's grossly distorted account of the situation was willingly taken up and disseminated by most of the mainstream press, whose reporting was marked by a deep hostility toward the miners' cause.[51]

In sum, the tactical mistakes of the NUM gave the Thatcherites the upper hand at this early stage of the conflict. The ballot was a theme that helped them to build bridges with certain groups of miners and to campaign against the NUM leadership. They were making early material gains through entrenching divisions among the mineworkers and winning public support for their hostile stance towards the NUM.

Phase III: Full Mobilisation, Polarisation and Instability
Rifts among the Miners

The third phase of the strike was marked by the Thatcherites mobilising the full force of the repressive state apparatuses against the miners, and the latter in turn mobilising the full force of a militant industrial stoppage. This led to polarisation on all fronts: polarisation between the NUM and the state; between those in the labour movement supporting the strike and those who were ambivalent or critical; and between striking and working miners. The rifts in the working class obviously assisted Thatcherite efforts to smash the NUM. And yet, the stakes remained high. The militancy and tenacity of the strikers made defeating the government a real possibility at two points at least. The frontline in this war of manoeuvre was constantly redrawn; the overall situation was highly unstable.

Thatcher and her entourage decided to keep playing the 'democracy' card, which deepened the rifts among different groups of miners. The most prominent division was the one between the militant regions that had started the strike – Yorkshire and Scotland – and Nottinghamshire, where the strike was least popular.[52] As a result, rank-and-file militants from Yorkshire decided to

---

50 Haviland 1984.
51 Khabaz 2006, pp. 207, 227–31.
52 Miners from Nottinghamshire were notorious for breaking strikes and exploiting the competitive advantage of their mines by accepting localised settlements. During the general strike of 1926, the leader of the Notts miners, George Spencer, struck a deal and ensured his members would return to work despite the fact that the stoppage was still ongoing. Subsequently, he even set up a 'yellow' union funded by the employers (compare

'picket out' workers in Nottinghamshire pits,[53] to which Thatcher reacted by raising, once again, the spectre of left-wing totalitarianism. A few weeks into the strike, she stated:

> My right hon. and learned Friend the Home Secretary explained to the House last week the measures that the police are taking to combat the disgraceful intimidation that has been used against working miners. It is ironic that although trade unions were formed to protect their members from threats of intimidation, those who could stop these attempts at intimidation fail to do so and refuse to condemn them. In the meantime, the police continue to exercise their powers with regard to picketing to enable miners who wish to go to work to continue to do so.[54]

The reality on the ground was, of course, more complex. It is far from clear as to how far Notts miners at this point felt intimidated by the strikers on the picket lines. According to David John Douglass, a co-ordinator of the Doncaster pickets, whose area of operation included Nottinghamshire, the fact that less committed miners did not turn up for work as long as there was picketing, and returned once the police had started to crack down on strikers, had nothing to do with intimidation: 'The pickets did enjoy considerable success in Nottingham whenever they were allowed to picket and show their determination. It was only as the police determined that Nottingham men would work, and picketing would stop that the waverers lost their excuse not to cross the line and went to work'.[55] Cohen confirms this view by pointing out that the pickets in a lot of cases gained active support from Nottinghamshire miners – hardly a reaction that can be solicited from people feeling intimidated: 'Yorkshire militants flooded Nottinghamshire to "picket out" the pits, gaining significant success with the help of fellow-activists in the area. At the start of the dispute, hundreds of Notts miners were out; one pit, Creswell, was shut down completely for several weeks'.[56] Even in the minutes of a MISC 101 meeting, the Cabinet Committee tasked with co-ordinating the government response to the strike,[57] there is evidence that claims of intimidation were overblown at the start of the

---

Pelling 1971, p. 187; Reid 2004, p. 316). Similar incidents were to happen further into the 1984–5 strike and shortly after it had terminated.
53   Hain 1986, p. 229; Douglass 1993, p. 15.
54   Thatcher Archive, 105484.
55   Douglass 1993, p. 26.
56   Cohen 2006, p. 79.
57   See below.

strike. According to the minutes, Leon Brittan, the Home Secretary, stated on 14 May 1984: 'In response to claims of intimidation, which had so far been hard to substantiate and prosecute because of the difficulties of obtaining evidence and the pressures on those affected, the police were attempting to maintain an active presence, not solely at the collieries but also in neighbouring villages'.[58]

Once the police escalated the situation by attempting to repress picketing, the pickets' stance towards strikebreakers hardened – all the more so since the vast majority of miners in the country had walked out, pit closures threatened the livelihood of the mining communities affected, and coal-rich Nottinghamshire was of strategic importance for an effective stoppage in terms of cutting supply.[59] This in turn increased opposition to the strike in general and the NUM leadership in Nottinghamshire in particular. The result was a rank-and-file revolt within the Notts NUM and the establishment of 'Working Miners' Committees'.[60]

These events provided the NCB and the Thatcherites with the opportunity to deepen divisions among the miners. The 'Working Miners' Committees' were supported and advised by the NCB and were set up and funded by a businessman close to Thatcher, David Hart.[61] At the level of public political discourse, the Prime Minister exploited the divisions further by making a distinction between strikers, whom she portrayed as violent, nihilistic criminals, and working miners, whom she saw as heroes who cared for their families, their industry and the country as a whole:

> We heard moving accounts from two working miners about just what they have to face as they try to make their way to work. The sheer bravery of those men and thousands like them who kept the mining industry alive is

---

58 CAB 130/1268.
59 Compare Cohen 2006, p. 78.
60 Compare Hyman 1985, p. 345.
61 Hain 1986, p. 143; Milne 1995, p. 365. In December 1985, nine months after the strike had ended in total defeat for the NUM, the split between militant and moderate miners was formalised. The breakaway Union of Democratic Mineworkers (UDM) was founded. The UDM was a 'yellow' organisation in the Spencer tradition. In Parliament, Conservative MP Andy Stewart and Thatcher praised its establishment as a victory for 'democracy' (Thatcher Archive, 106195). Soon, the UDM managed to win 30,000 members and a wage increase that was not available for the miners in the NUM. In the end, however, the UDM's acquiescent course did not pay off: In subsequent years, the NCB granted the UDM no favours (Middlemas 1991, p. 552). It pressed ahead with running down the industry, which, in 1994, was privatised with no more than 8,000 miners in employment (Cohen 2006, p. 121).

beyond praise. 'Scabs' their former workmates call them. Scabs? They are lions! What a tragedy it is when striking miners attack their workmates. Not only are they members of the same union, but the working miner is saving both their futures, because it is the working miners, whether in Nottinghamshire, Derbyshire, Lancashire, Leicestershire, Staffordshire, Warwickshire, North Wales or Scotland, it is the working miners who have kept faith with those who buy our coal and without that custom thousands of jobs in the mining industry would be already lost.[62]

Statements like these held back the information that the vast majority of miners initially supported the strike, and that it was the government, as evidenced by the appointment of MacGregor, that had decided to run down the coal industry, not the striking miners.

The events around the Notts NUM show that the NUM leaders erred in basing their strategy on a domino theory. Despite broad support for the strike, the Thatcherites managed to drive a wedge through the miners by exploiting the fact that there was one area of strategic importance that had decided to step out of line. A national ballot might not have brought a majority for a strike in Nottinghamshire, but it would have made it harder for working miners to justify their opposition to the course of the national leadership.

The NUM's strike effort was dented not only by internal rifts, but also by the leaders' inability to mobilise a broad alliance. There was some solidarity action, but it remained limited. The National Union of Railwaymen (NUR) and the ASLEF instructed drivers not to handle coal, which led to disruptions in Leicestershire and Nottinghamshire. Moreover, the NUS interrupted the shipping of coal from Northumberland and Durham for months, and dockers refused to handle imported coal. The patchy character of solidarity action reflected the fact that other militant sections of the labour movement, for instance, the steelworkers, had already been demoralised by earlier defeats.[63]

Furthermore, the TUC was hesitant in its support. After the Labour Party had campaigned on a left-wing platform in the 1983 general elections and suffered a devastating defeat, the TUC leadership had embraced 'new realism' – a strategy based on the assumption that a moderate approach would 'calm down' the Thatcherites,[64] and that the only way forward was to negotiate with whichever

---

62   Thatcher Archive, 105763.
63   Compare Darlington 2005, pp. 87, 92; Cohen 2006, pp. 77, 80.
64   Cohen 2006, p. 73.

government was in power.[65] Similarly, the support from the frontbench of the Labour Party remained lukewarm, which reflected the fact that the new leadership under Kinnock had also opted for a centrist course.[66] Both the TUC and the party misjudged the conjuncture: There was no longer a government willing to trade material concessions for acquiescence, as its appointment of MacGregor and its endorsement of his closure plans showed.[67] As a result, both organisations were on the defensive throughout the conflict, which neither helped them nor the NUM.

Things were made even harder for the striking miners by biased reporting on the strike within the mainstream media, which contributed to undercutting popular support for their action. According to D.V. Khabaz, the stoppage triggered 'the most partisan press campaign in the modern history of the British media'.[68] Even Labour-supporting papers like *The Daily Mirror* and *The Guardian* painted the NUM in an unfavourable light.[69]

Obviously, the government did not exercise direct control of the media. Khabaz indicates that two interlinked economic developments account for the uniformity in the media coverage of the strike. The 1980s witnessed a strong degree of concentration in the press. By 1987, 75 percent of the national dailies and 83 percent of the national Sundays were controlled by just three people: Rupert Murdoch, Robert Maxwell, and David Stevens. All three had business interests well beyond the press sector.[70] Khabaz concludes:

> The growing business interests of the press industry in modern Britain ... has [sic] created a delicate network of cooperation between the press and other conglomerates. The similar social origins, shared educational patterns and close working relationships amongst modern press barons – in the internal sphere – and other top directors and captains of industry – in the external sphere – has given way to [read: 'given rise to'] a new ideological and business culture shared by the press industry and other businesses.[71]

---

65   Hyman 1987b, pp. 99–101.
66   Hain 1986, p. 241; Hyman 1987b, 101.
67   Compare McIlroy 1988, pp. 54–5; Coates 1989, p. 133; Dorey 2013, pp. 186–7.
68   Khabaz 2006, p. 197.
69   Khabaz 2006, p. 199.
70   Khabaz 2006, pp. 131–2; 155.
71   Khabaz 2006, p. 156.

INSTABILITY AND CONFRONTATION (1984–8) 179

In other words, a political and economic environment had emerged where the press was integrated, to a large degree, into the neoliberal power bloc in formation. Correspondingly, the Prime Minister enjoyed a close personal relationship with both Murdoch and Maxwell.[72]

Consequently, public opinion was broadly in favour of the NCB. According to a Gallup poll, 51 percent of respondents stated, in December 1984, that they were sympathetic to the board, while only 26 percent sided with the striking miners.[73] Support for the strikers remained limited even within the working class. A National Opinion Poll in September 1984 claimed that 69 percent of workers were unwilling to strike out of sympathy with the miners.[74]

State Repression

In line with the aim of undermining the NUM, Thatcher and her allies in the government and the NCB exploited the divisions within the working class. State officials found it relatively easy to circumvent solidarity action and contain the wider effects of shortages in the supply of coal sourced in Britain – at least for most of the time. Just as the Ridley Report had recommended, they transferred the movement of coal from the railways to the road. This was not difficult because there were small haulage companies with non-unionised lorry drivers who were willing to take over, and some TGWU members were also prepared to move coal.[75] Moreover, officials resorted to importing coal in order to compensate for shortages. Imports came through smaller ports, which employed non-unionised dockworkers prepared to do the unloading.[76]

Another plank of the government's strategy was to exploit the repressive capacities of the state and impose an extensive police operation on the striking miners. As a result of the successes of militant trade unionism in the 1970s, the government had put into place measures to deal with 'public disorder'. The most important one had been the establishment of a National Reporting Centre (NRC) in 1972 – a direct result of the Battle of Saltley Gates.[77] The NRC assembled all Welsh and English Chief Constables whenever there were events with significant implications for 'public order'. The president of the Association of Chief Police Officers (ACPO) acted as its head.[78] The official purpose of

---

72   Milne 1995, p. 242; Khabat 2006, p. 136.
73   Cited in Khabaz 2006, p. 233.
74   Cited in Hain 1986, p. 255.
75   Goodman 1985, p. 94; Adeney and Lloyd 1986, pp. 142–4.
76   Cohen 2006, p. 80.
77   Hain 1986, p. 176; Beckett and Hencke 2009, p. 36.
78   Kettle 1985, pp. 23–4.

the NRC was to 'maintain full details of the availability of police throughout England and Wales ... and deploy it to places where it is needed'.[79] Only when its role in the miners' strike was discussed did the wider public learn of its existence. According to official pronouncements, the NRC never went beyond co-ordinating mutual aid. Those involved denied that it was directing police operations, and that the government controlled the police with its help.[80]

However, there is strong evidence to the contrary: First of all, there is an internal document showing that 'in 1982 the Home Office secretly revised the confidential circular governing the operation of the NRC so that it could be much more proactive in policing emergencies'.[81] Second, an *Observer* journalist, Nick Davies, visited the NRC in the second week of the strike. He reported that he overheard an official at the centre passing on registration numbers of coaches full of pickets to the representative of a Midlands force and asked this man to monitor their movements.[82] Third, the Chairwoman of the Merseyside Police Authority, Margaret Simey, publicly stated that the NRC had overruled local forces during the strike, adding that the ACPO had 'become an executive arm of the state, without any authorisation and without public control'.[83] Fourth, a report of the Chief Inspector of Constabulary to the Home Secretary said that the NRC was 'operated by a team under the direction of the President of the ACPO, my representative and one your officials'.[84] Fifth, there is a document relating to a meeting in the Home Office in May 1984. The background of the meeting was that there were arguments between the government and local authorities concerning who should pay for the police operations caused by the strike. According to the document, David Hall, the ACPO president, commented on this question by relaying that police authorities were 'starting to ask the question, "Who is directing the control of the NRC?" (and this is a most worrying aspect)'.[85] Beckett and Hencke see this as 'a reference, no doubt, to the fact that the Home Secretary could direct the NRC'.[86]

If the Home Secretary had the opportunity to influence policing, the Prime Minister was in a position to co-ordinate all the efforts by state institutions directed against the strike. Just after the stoppage had started, Robert Armstrong,

---

79 Kettle 1985, p. 26.
80 Kettle 1985, p. 27; Saville 1985, p. 310; Hain 1986, p. 189.
81 Beckett and Hencke 2009, p. 36.
82 Kettle 1985, p. 31; Bunyan 1985, p. 298.
83 Cited in Hain 1986, p. 189.
84 Tendler 1985.
85 Cited in Beckett and Hencke 2009, p. 90.
86 Beckett and Hencke 2009, p. 90.

the Cabinet Secretary, suggested 'setting up a ministerial group in the MISC series to consider all aspects of the situation which may be of concern to Ministers: industrial relations, law and order, power station endurance, the effect on the economy, the scope for mitigating action by the Government, and the handling of the media'.[87] Thatcher agreed to this plan.

MISC 101 involved all the members of Cabinet with briefs affected by the coal strike – a group heavily overlapping with the Thatcherite inner circle. Among those regularly attending were: Lawson, the Chancellor; Walker, the Energy Secretary; Brittan, the Home Secretary; King, the Employment Secretary; Tebbit, the Secretary of Trade and Industry, and Ridley, the Transport Secretary. Michael Havers, the Attorney General, was also present on numerous occasions.[88]

Meetings, which usually took place twice a week, tended to start with Walker describing the status quo in the coal industry and the other industries relevant for energy production. This was followed by reports from the other members of Cabinet. The group then discussed the current situation, with the Prime Minister summing up the debate and thus steering the course of the government. The existence of MISC 101 disproves the official government line that it was not involved in the dispute.[89] It meant that the government could play an active role in undermining the strike, for example, by devising strategies that addressed coal shortages and secured energy production, co-ordinating the use of legal means aimed at undermining the strike, and developing patterns of communication with the general public that undermined support for the strike among the population. More specifically, MISC 101 was also used to make sure that police operations were in line with the government strategy: the Home Secretary usually gave detailed updates on police activities.[90]

The existence of a chain of command from the inner circle of government via the NRC into the locally operating police forces was of crucial importance for the implementation of the government's anti-strike strategy. Thatcher and her associates decided against using the changed trade union law as their main weapon against the unions – even if there were arguments about this decision at MISC 101 meetings.[91] Instead, they opted for the 'criminalisation

---

87 Thatcher Archive, 133142.
88 CAB 130–12; compare Bunyan 1985, pp. 299–300.
89 Compare Young 1989, p. 370. In her autobiography, Thatcher admits as much. Discussing the government's role in the strike, she remarked: 'so much was at stake that no responsible government could take a "hands-off" attitude' (1993, p. 347).
90 Ibid.
91 CAB 130/1268.

and isolation of the strikers'.[92] This more individualised approach had three advantages. First, it allowed the Thatcherites to present the policing of the strike as a 'law-and-order issue',[93] which helped to demonise their opponent and de-politicise the dispute. Second, it meant that repression was focused on police operations, which, in contrast to court action, could be adapted to changed situations quickly. Third, it avoided the extensive invocation of contentious legislation, which could have united the labour movement.[94]

At the start of the strike, the home office ordered the police via the chain of command to inhibit picketing with roadblocks.[95] The police forces complied and stopped pickets from entering Nottinghamshire, invoking their power under the common law to prevent 'breaches of the peace'. According to police numbers, around 290,000 people were turned away in the first six months of the strike. Pickets who did not accept this were faced with the confiscation of their car keys or arrests. If arrests occurred, people usually had conditional bail imposed on them. This barred them from picketing or demonstrating outside their workplace.[96] One infamous event took place on 18 March 1984, at Dartford Tunnel in Kent: the police tried to stop everyone crossing the Thames and travelling north who looked like a miner – despite the fact that the tunnel is about a hundred miles away from Nottinghamshire.[97]

In sum, the police strategy, devised by the Thatcherite inner circle in collaboration with leading police officers, was 'to prevent picketing by taking pickets out of circulation – not by violent confrontation, but by sophisticated methods of control'.[98] It was not the simple result of the enforcement of unambiguous laws, but was based on strategic calculations that exploited police discretion for political purposes.[99] The Thatcherites managed to convince the police to play an active role in undermining the strike, rather than just decelerating its momentum by securing the legality of the activities of striking miners. Unsurprisingly, this caused frictions: John Alderson, the former Devon and Cornwall Chief Constable, complained that the police had been 'pulled into backing a political choice by the government'.[100]

---

[92]   McIlroy, p. 84. CAB 130/1268.
[93]   McIlroy, p. 85.
[94]   Hain 1986, pp. 190–1.
[95]   Bunyan 1985, p. 298.
[96]   Blake 1985, pp. 112–13.
[97]   Goodman 1985, pp. 120, 128; Adeney and Lloyd 1986, p. 100.
[98]   Christian 1985, p. 120.
[99]   Compare Blake 1985, p. 111.
[100] Cited in Hain 1986, p. 190.

The biggest battle between the strikers and the police took place in May and June 1985 at the British Steel Coking Plant in Orgreave near Sheffield. Over several weeks, strikers formed a mass picket to close it down, the trigger for which were convoys of coke moving from Orgreave to a steel plant in Scunthorpe. The NUM leadership sought a repeat of the Saltley incident in 1972, that is, a show of collective strength and determination visible for the general public, which would force the government to back down.[101]

The strategy worked insofar as supplies for the Scunthorpe plant threatened to dry up. In a secret letter to Andrew Turnbull, Private Secretary at No. 10, Michael Reidy, Private Secretary at Energy, provides details of a gathering involving the Energy Secretary, the Home Secretary, the Trade and Industry Secretary and the chairmen of the NCB and the BSC on 5 June 1984, which had been set up at an earlier MISC 101 meeting. Reidy explains that coke stocks at Orgreave were running out, and that the participants of the meeting had decided to move the remaining coke as quickly as possible to Scunthorpe. The letter reveals that the government ordered the police to contain the picketing at Orgreave, which confirms that there was indeed a chain of command: 'It was ... agreed that British Steel would immediately write to the Chief Constable of South Yorkshire, to inform him of their plans to empty the Orgreave site. The police would then, as necessary, be in a position to demonstrate that they were part of a carefully conceived and well executed operation'.[102]

The NUM strategy also gave the police the opportunity to attack the most committed and militant members of the union. On 18 June 1984, the police drew together forces, concentrated the pickets in one spot in front of the plant and surrounded them. What followed was 'one of the classic police "riots" in modern British history', which involved 'cavalry charges followed by attacks from the riot police on foot and lasted for three hours'.[103]

The 'Battle of Orgreave' became a seminal victory of the government and the police over the strikers, which consisted in breaking the mass picket at the site decisively. To add insult to injury, the mainstream press gravely distorted what had happened. According to Gareth Peirce, a defence lawyer for arrested miners, the TV news reversed the real sequence of events and portrayed miners throwing stones as the cause for the charge.[104] One picket, a Barnsley miner, was quoted in the *Guardian* as saying:

---

101   Hyman 1985, p. 336; Saville 1985, p. 324.
102   Thatcher Archive, 133366.
103   Saville 1985, pp. 324–5.
104   Ibid.

Armoured men attacking lads with basket ball boots on, T-Shirts and jeans, and then they're charging with horses. And when lads resort to the only weapons they've got, throwing stones, oh it's terrible. But it's OK when they're bashing you about the head with a bit of wood.[105]

The accusation that the police sought to demoralise the pickets by attacking them is also confirmed by the fact that most arrests did not lead to convictions.[106] All in all, Orgreave was a turning point in that it revealed three truths that were inconvenient for the miners: They did not enjoy the support within the working class and the wider population that they had enjoyed in the early 1970s; the police were more difficult to beat due to changes in organisation and strategy; and '[i]n general the media acted as another agency of the state in the dispute', which had not been the case a decade earlier.[107]

Despite the decision to opt for repressing the strike through policing it rather than resorting to trade union legislation, there was one area in which the changed legislation had a substantial material effect on the strike. The enactment of legislation under the Social Security (No. 2) Act, which reduced benefits to striking workers, significantly increased the pressure on striking miners and their families and left some without income.[108] The Citizens Advice Bureau estimated in April 1984 that a family of four with a striking father and a stay-at-home mother had to live off £26.75 a week.[109] The president of the Chorley Trades Council, a Lancashire town with a small population of miners, described the local situation as such: 'The majority of the area's 250 miners are now suffering severe hardship. The immediate problem facing many miners' families is knowing where their next meal is coming from'.[110]

The mining communities on strike responded by establishing an alternative welfare system, which was based around public kitchens and distribution centres for food and other urgently needed goods. In setting up and running this network of alternative institutions, the wives and partners of the striking miners played a key role. They organised themselves and became politicised, which both challenged traditional gender relations and stabilised families by

---

105   Cited in Lloyd 1985, p. 67.
106   Compare Saville 1985, p. 324.
107   Hain 1986, p. 232; compare Khabaz 2006, pp. 269–70.
108   Hain 1986, p. 128.
109   Figures cited in Adeney and Lloyd 1986, p. 220.
110   Cited in Beale 2005, p. 131. Beale remarks that the figure of 250 miners is probably wrong and estimates that about 100 is more accurate.

uniting them behind the stoppage. Hence, the network was crucial for sustaining the strike effort.[111]

Last but not least, the judiciary also played an important part in sustaining the government's strategy. On the whole, it accepted the extension of police powers during the strike, and did not hesitate to use the repressive capacities of the law in order to undermine the strike effort. Most of the time, sentences against militant miners were hefty; if a striking miner landed in court, it was difficult for him to obtain legal aid.[112]

The most notorious case of a series of court interventions in the strike occurred in autumn 1984. Guided by Hart, the Conservative businessman behind the working miners, two miners opposed to the strike requested the High Court to declare the strike unofficial under NUM rules – a court case that could have taken a long time to resolve. As a result, the plaintiffs sought an injunction under which the NUM leadership was barred from declaring the strike official. This was granted by the judge, which was a case of making new law: Whereas injunctions are usually used in emergencies, the strike had by now been going on for seven months. The judge used his discretion, thus making a political decision and mobilising the force of the law against the strike.[113]

The NUM leadership refused to accept the injunction, leading to contempt proceedings that ended with fines of £1,000 for Scargill and £200,000 for the union – at the time, the highest ever fines for disobeying a court order. Again, Scargill et al. refused to accept the decision, so that the High Court ordered the sequestration of the NUM's funds. The NUM trustees were replaced by a 'receiver', who now legally controlled the union's property.[114] This was a case of an ally of Thatcher attempting to destroy the NUM with the help of the courts.

The NUM had expected attacks from this side. Roger Windsor, its chief executive, set in train various bank operations to protect union funds by transferring £8.5m abroad. However, the sequestrators tracked down the hidden money easily. After this incident, Scargill took the handling of union funds into his own hands and began to deal with all NUM financial operations with the help of secret accounts and cash payments. He thus managed to prevent the sequestrator from getting hold of even more money. Scargill's secret funding system was never tracked down and broken up.[115]

---

111   Goodman 1985, pp. 162–3; Adeney and Lloyd 1986, pp. 222–3; Hain 1986, p. 237; Beale 2005, p. 126; Suddick 2005, p. 3.
112   Blake 1985, p. 118; Hain 1986, pp. 217–18.
113   Hain 1986, pp. 218–19.
114   McMullen 1985, p. 219; Hain 1986, pp. 218–19; Milne 1995, pp. 367–8.
115   Milne 1995, pp. 204–6, 350, 419.

Importantly, the judiciary, like the press, was not directly controlled by the government. This raises the question as to why the legal establishment was willing to act in line with the Thatcherite aim of breaking the strike and undermining the NUM. One reason is the actual overlap between the political and legal system. The best illustration of this is the position of Attorney General, who represents both sides. Havers, the office holder during the strike, regularly took part in MISC 101 meetings and publicly called for the imposition of hefty fines on the NUM for contempt. Hain comments: 'As is frequently the case, it was not obvious whether he was acting in his role as one of the highest law officers of the land or as a senior Conservative government minister'.[116]

A second reason for the judiciary falling in line with the government is the class background of its members. Hain observes: 'Perhaps it should come as no surprise that judges should have been hostile to unions and strikers when account is taken of their class background and political leanings. They are overwhelmingly middle- or upper-class, white, male and elderly, with political attitudes that range between the centre and the far right'.[117] If one adds to this the hostile press coverage of the strike, it is hardly astonishing that the judges, on the whole, turned out to be reliable partners of the government.

Two Critical Junctures

The Thatcherites mobilised a vast array of repressive measures against the strikers, who nevertheless managed to keep up their militant tactics throughout the dispute and sustained the stoppage in most of the country for months. On two occasions, they almost defeated their opponents, which shows that the economic-political conjuncture was open at the time. The victory of Thatcherism was not the unavoidable result of an ensemble of institutionalised, medium-term trends, but the contingent outcome of the articulation of these trends with the strategic decisions taken by key actors at critical junctures.

The first of the two critical junctures was reached when dockworkers went on strike in July 1984. Out of solidarity with the miners, unionised dockers had already been refusing to handle imported iron ore and coal in the months before. Now, at the port of Immingham in Hull, employers resorted to using workers for the job who were not registered under the National Dock Labour Scheme, which regulated working conditions in 71 registered ports across the country.[118] The decision to use unregistered dockers was perceived as a threat

---

116   Hain 1986, p. 219.
117   Hain 1986, p. 221.
118   Hunter 1994, p. 98; Cohen 2006, p. 81.

to the scheme by registered ones. The TGWU called for a national strike that found widespread support in the industry.

The stoppage threatened Britain's energy supply – both because imported coal compensated for shortages caused by the miners' strike, and because TGWU members working in oil distribution warned that they might join the action.[119] Furthermore, '[t]here was an early prospect of ... serious difficulty for industry ... arising from the interruption of both exports and imports', as Tebbit, the Trade and Industry Secretary, remarked at a MISC 101 meeting taking place just after the dock strike had started.[120] In this situation, the pound came under pressure and interest rates shot up,[121] which indicates that actors in the financial markets saw a joint strike effort by miners and dockers as a real danger to the British economy. A scenario emerged in which the power bloc would put serious pressure on the government to settle with the NUM out of concern for the infrastructure and the economic position of the country.

This scenario made the Thatcherite inner circle nervous. The minutes of a meeting in No. 10 Downing Street on 14 July 1984 attended by Thatcher and key members of the Cabinet reveal that there was detailed discussion over whether to use troops and even declare a state of emergency.[122] The fact that seeking assistance from the army was considered at all shows how dangerous a joint strike by miners and dockers would have been for the government;[123] the strike had reached a critical juncture.

In the end, however, the leadership of the TGWU decided to refrain from extending the strike effort. Instead, they called it off after a few days and settled.[124] The exact implications of the settlement, however, remained unclear. In August, employers resorted to using unregistered workers again, which triggered another stoppage. This time, support was weaker, especially at the unregistered ports. In September, the TGWU agreed to a new 'deal', which amounted to a victory for employers because they made few concessions. Obviously, this was a serious blow for the striking miners.[125]

---

[119] Hunter 1994, p. 98.
[120] CAB 130/1268, 12 July 1984.
[121] Adeney and Lloyd 1986, p. 141; Darlington 2005, p. 88.
[122] Thatcher Archive, 133424.
[123] There are reports that soldiers were part of picket-line police operations (Beckett and Hencke 2009, p. 98), but it is not clear from the evidence whether this was an exception or the result of a systematic effort to assist the police. Thatcher Archive, 133424.
[124] Darlington 2005, p. 88.
[125] Compare Hunter 1994, pp. 101–2.

Given the shaky support for industrial action among the non-registered dockers,[126] the TGWU leadership's decision to settle for very little is not surprising. However, their decision was shortsighted: The National Dock Labour Scheme was abolished in 1989.[127] It appears that the TGWU officials did not understand what was at stake in the mid-1980s – neither in terms of their industry's future nor in terms of the future of the British trade union movement. In hindsight, it seems that escalating the strike would have been a gamble, but it could not have produced worse results.

In sum, the TGWU leadership did not appear to grasp that the future of their own industry was linked to the miners' fate, and that a miners' victory was a precondition for halting the ongoing shift in the class relations of forces in favour of capital.

A similar scenario arose in October 1984, when the National Association of Colliery Overmen, Deputies and Shotfirers (NACODS) voted for a strike. The trigger was a tactical mistake by the NCB, which had cancelled an agreement that guaranteed payments to pit deputies even when they were picketed out. As it was illegal to keep pits open without deputies present, a NACODS strike would have extended the miners' strike by default – according to MacGregor, possibly even to working areas like Nottingham, which would soon have brought the NUM close to victory.[128] Correspondingly, Thatcher was keen to ensure that the NCB and NACODS agreed a settlement and put considerable pressure on MacGregor to achieve the desired result.[129] The strike had reached a second critical juncture.

The NACODS was a conservative managerial union with no tradition of industrial action; it had never voted to go on strike before. After 137 hours of negotiations with the NCB under the guidance of the Advisory Conciliation and Arbitration Service (ACAS) and at the very last moment, it called off the planned stoppage. A settlement was reached. It included a promise from the NCB to review the process of pit closures – a vague announcement with no direct consequences, which in the end failed to keep a single mine open.[130] Back in the day, Geoffrey Goodman observed that 'the union settled for less than it might have squeezed out of the coal board'.[131]

---

126   CAB 130/1268, 30 August 1984; compare Adeney and Lloyd 1986, p. 142.
127   Hunter 1994, p. 102.
128   Darlington 2005, p. 89; Cohen 2006, p. 82; Beckett and Hencke 2009, p. 147.
129   Beckett and Hencke 2009, p. 149.
130   Saville 1985, p. 314; Milne 1995, p. 23; Cohen 2006, p. 82.
131   Goodman 1985, p. 144.

It appears that NACODS leaders were the second group of trade union officials unwilling to shoulder the potential repercussions of escalating industrial conflict at a critical juncture. Possible motives are that their organisation traditionally did not resort to strike action, and that both the Thatcherites and the mainstream media had openly criticised the fact that they considered walking out.[132] Once again, however, acquiescence had consequences no better and possibly worse than those that militancy would have produced. The mining industry would be run down by the NCB in the ensuing years, which meant that deputies' jobs vanished with those of ordinary miners. Just like their counterparts at the TGWU, the leadership of the NACODS had misread the conjuncture. The Thatcherites were determined to phase out coal mining, which means that joining forces with the NUM would have been the only strategic option available to the NACODS that could have saved its members' jobs.[133]

---

132 Hain 1986, p. 230.
133 Both Cohen and Saville see flaws in the NUM's tactics during the NACODS episode. Cohen argues that the NUM did not do enough to ensure that NACODS members would walk out via exploiting 'family and neighbourhood connections'. According to her, Scargill did not intervene to convince them to do so, and rank-and-file members lacked information about the situation and remained immobilised (Cohen 2006, p. 82). It is doubtful, however, that an intervention by a divisive figure like Scargill would have helped secure a strike by the deputies. More important is Cohen's second point, the lack of information and mobilisation around the issue among the rank-and-file. Douglass's account of events in the Doncaster area in the autumn of 1984 (1993, pp. 57–63), for example, makes no mention of the NACODS episode, which is indicative of its minor importance for debates among rank-and-file. Considering the tightly knit nature of personal relations in mining communities, Cohen seems right to argue that a more co-ordinated attempt to connect to NACODS members could have brought different results. John Saville makes an entirely different point. He notes that in the negotiations, the NACODS insisted that the NUM be included in a potential settlement. The NUM, however, refused to accept the terms at which the NACODS settled. Saville sees this as a lost opportunity for the NUM to avoid total defeat (1985, pp. 314–15). Of course, a settlement involving all three parties would have made it much harder for the NCB to continue running down the industry without making concessions, as would eventually happen. And it might have bought time for the NUM. However, it is doubtful whether, in the long run, the end result would have been different. A settlement involving the NUM leading to closures could only have been interpreted as a defeat for the miners, and it is questionable whether they could have regrouped and maintained their defences after the event. Scargill, in any case, later claimed that Thatcher was prepared to settle on the unions' terms when she learned of the threat of a joint action by NUM and NACODS, and was even willing to withdraw the closures plan. According to him, it was only NACODS's decision to agree to a settlement on considerably worse terms that allowed her to retreat from this course. Consequently,

In sum, the Thatcherites did not just have institutional factors on their side, that is, the repressive force of the state, the media bias and the divisions within the labour movement. They were also plain lucky. Had the leaders of the TGWU or NACODS understood what was at stake, history might have taken a different course. In the end, the NUM's inability to forge durable alliances with other trade union forces paved the way for the victory of Thatcher and her associates.

Phase IV: Disintegration

The settlement between the NACODS and the NCB was the final turning point in the strike.[134] By seeing off the threat of a joint action, the Thatcherites stabilised their advance, while the defences of the NUM began to crumble. Unsurprisingly, the 'deal' shattered hope on the side of the striking miners that they could still win. Moreover, it made a face-saving retreat impossible: The NACODS had wanted the NUM to be included in the settlement, which the latter had refused on the terms negotiated. Consequently, the strikers found themselves in an 'all or nothing' situation, with the odds stacked against them.

In the month after the NACODS settlement, 16,000 miners returned to work, motivated by 'financial bribes' from the NCB.[135] The fact that money offers were taken up indicated that the NUM was close to losing, which the Thatcherites appeared to recognise. Hart started to lobby MacGregor to ensure that there would be no settlement with the NUM. Similarly, in January 1985 the Prime Minister's office actively undermined talks between the NCB and the NUM. People close to Thatcher announced via the press that talks were a waste of time and put pressure on the NCB not to settle. In the end, they were successful: The remaining strikers returned to work in March 1985 with no concessions from the NCB.[136]

Part of the material substratum of the defeat was that even though the strikers had managed to sustain their action for almost a year, at no point were they close to shutting down Britain's energy supply.[137] There were moments of nervousness – Tebbit,[138] for example, wrote a letter to Thatcher on 25 July

---

he sees the NACODS's behaviour as an act of 'betrayal' (Scargill 2009). Goodman's record of a conversation between Walker and Kinnock, the Labour Leader, in October 1984 appears to corroborate Scargill's claim (1985, p. 144). Against this backdrop, it is no surprise that the NUM leadership was not prepared to agree to a three-party settlement.

134   Goodman 1985, p. 150; Cohen 2006, p. 83.
135   Saville 1985, p. 314.
136   Goodman 1985, pp. 173–4; Hain 1986, pp. 143–4; Milne 1995, p. 370.
137   Jones 2013.
138   Thatcher Archive, 133446.

1984 expressing his doubts that things would work out favourably – but on the whole, the government strategy worked: the decision to build up coal supplies, import coal through smaller, unregistered ports and makeshift wharves, and resort to dual firing made up for the losses in coal production caused by the strike. Moreover, it was crucial for the government's success that the NUM had failed to unite all mineworkers, the trade union movement and the working class behind the strike. As John Saville observes, there is an important aspect of the conflict directly related to this issue: the co-optation of power workers to the line of the Central Electricity Generating Board was crucial in terms of containing the effect of the coal supplies diminished by the strike:

> What most observers underestimated was in fact the ability to import coal at dozens of small ports and improvised wharves along the east and south coasts, and the technical ability of those in charge of the power stations, with the willing co-operation of the power workers, to produce record levels of electricity. Without the co-operation of the power workers with management the output of electricity could not possibly have been maintained, and most commentaries on the miners' strike failed to appreciate the crucial contribution to the Government's victory that was being made by the workers in the generating plants.[139]

In sum, working-class divisions, successfully sustained and deepened by the Thatcherites, were the key factor explaining their victory.

Strategic Assessment

There are few other events that so clearly bring out the repressive character of the Thatcherite extraction strategy as the miners' strike. The intent of the Prime Minister and her associates was not to turn around an ailing industry. After all, the numbers they presented in order to demonstrate the 'uneconomic' character of coal mining in Britain were torn apart by economists.[140] Moreover, they kept closing coalmines on a grand scale in subsequent years until there were few open pits left. In my view, their aim was to phase out the industry because it was the base of the organisation spearheading militant trade unionism in Britain.[141] They prepared the confrontation with the NUM meticulously, fought their opponents with any means necessary, and were not prepared to foster

---

139 Saville 1985, p. 315. Thatcher confirms this view in her autobiography: 'it was the power workers whose attitude was most crucial' (1993, p. 350).
140 Saville 1985, pp. 317–20.
141 Compare Coates 1989, p. 132.

reconciliation after they had won, which is visible in their active prevention of a settlement in January 1985.[142] Indeed, the Thatcherites regarded the NUM as one of the main obstacles to the reassertion of management's control over the labour process and as a potential threat to their dominance over the political scene.[143] Thus I view the miners' strike as a conflict over capitalist class domination.

The main strategic successes of Thatcherism consisted in deepening the rifts in the working class, which contributed to creating a material substratum for their 'two nations' hegemonic project. At the same time, these rifts helped the Thatcherites to reinforce their control of the political scene. The leadership of the Labour Party wavered over their support for the strike, which meant that an alliance between the industrial and the parliamentary opposition in the country was not possible.

Furthermore, the Thatcherites benefited from the fact that the politics of the NUM and its supporters remained vague. The strike started out as an economic strike aimed at defending the pits and mining communities and, thanks to the degree of hostility and repression the miners were faced with, it quickly became a political strike with the goal of bringing down the government.[144] However, this was not articulated with an elaborate critique of neoliberalism and a positive vision of a socialist Britain. This made it hard for the strikers to refute claims that they were lawless and had a penchant for violence.

It is indicative of a lack of politics on the side of the NUM that Douglass's account of the Doncaster militants includes detailed descriptions of strategic and tactical debates among them, but next to nothing on political goals. In other words, the practical radicalism of the pickets and their preparedness to enter confrontations with the repressive agencies of the state did not appear to translate into a political project. Its absence meant that rifts within the working class reflecting material differences in the living conditions of its members could not be bridged.

The ideological weakness of the strikers was further aggravated by strategic mistakes of NUM leadership made in the run-up to and during the strike. 'Right-wingers' within the NUM were probably right to insist on a national ballot, even if for the wrong reasons. Similarly, militant rank-and-file activists who criticised mass pickets and favoured a 'guerrilla' approach also appear to have had a point, as the events at Orgreave show.[145]

---

142   Compare Dorey 2013.
143   Compare Young 1989, p. 368.
144   Compare Hain 1986, p. 224.
145   Compare Douglass 1993, p. 42.

But obviously, the NUM leadership did not operate in a vacuum. There were economic-political impediments to uniting the working class behind the strike, and challenging these was beyond the reach of a single, sectional union, even one with the organisational strength of the NUM. For one, there were the differences in productivity within the coal industry, which made it difficult to secure support for the stoppage in certain regions.[146] Furthermore, the overall economic and political trends were working against the NUM. Most importantly, the British labour movement found itself in a situation of crisis even before the strike had started. At the time of the strike, its political arm had to deal with the establishment of the SDP and the defeat of the Labour Party at the general election of 1983, while its trade union arm was weakened by the rifts in the working class caused by the economic upturn and the defeats suffered since the Winter of Discontent. The ideological void described extended far beyond the NUM and concerned the British left in its entirety. If one adds to this that the NUM only represented a fraction of the labour movement and was facing an offensive by the power bloc as a whole, it becomes clear that the union was facing a Herculean task when it took on the Thatcherites. Given the circumstances, it is a surprise that the NUM managed to bring the government close to defeat on at least one occasion and pose a serious threat at another. This implies that its strategy cannot have been all wrong.

In sum, the miners' strike constituted a lethal blow for the trade union movement in Britain. It meant that the best organised militant fraction of the British working class had been defeated. There were still other militant fractions, which also posed a certain threat to the Thatcherite project. However, they neither had a history of successful struggles with far-reaching political repercussions to their name, nor did their economic bases play a pivotal role for the British political economy as a whole. The Thatcherites had won the main battle against organised labour, but they had not, as yet, won the entire war.

∴

The Last Chapters in a War of Manoeuvre

The miners' strike resulted in the smashing of the strongest fraction of the British working class. In hindsight, it was the industrial conflict which defined class relations in the Thatcherite era. The defeat of the miners motivated big capitalists with close ties to the Prime Minister to exploit anti-union sentiment

---

146 Compare Howell 2012, p. 164.

and press ahead with the attack on militant trade unionism. They surely were spurred on by the fact that Thatcher had won a third term in 1987,[147] which could be interpreted as a substantial part of the population condoning the onslaught. Nevertheless, there were major confrontations even then, which demonstrates that the victory over the NUM had not as yet produced resignation and fatalism on all fronts. Moreover, the organisational networks among workers in other branches of industry were still intact. In other words, the conjuncture was still marked by instability, and the offensive against the working class had not as yet been completed.

On the front of trade union and employment legislation, the Thatcherites introduced further changes aimed at institutionalising the shift in class relations of forces in favour of capital, which confirms that the decision not to make use of some of the new provisions in the field during the miners' strike was entirely tactical. The 1984 Trade Union Act made secret ballots over the election of union executives and industrial action obligatory; the 1986 Wages Act restricted the role of wages councils, which negotiated remuneration in branches of industry with a low degree of union representation; and the 1988 Employment Act granted union members the power to seek injunctions in order to prevent stoppages, established a commissioner who was supposed to prevent unions from infringing on the rights of individual members, and imposed separate strike ballots for each workplace.[148]

All measures were anti-union in character apart from the 1984 Act, which was more ambiguous. Nick Blake argues that it was aimed at undermining unions because its aim was 'to lure workers away from trade union meetings where issues are discussed, and turn them instead into passive consumers of the mass media, participating in the affairs of the union by postal ballot'.[149] Furthermore, the bureaucratic procedures that balloting involved under the act contributed to undercutting the momentum behind strike movements.[150] Then again, one could argue that in spite of the motivations of the legislators, the act in effect may have strengthened militant workers, at least in cases when they were able to obtain a majority at the ballot box. After all, this increased the legitimacy of industrial action in the eyes of the public, which is demonstrated by the debates around balloting during the miners' strike.[151]

---

147 The Conservatives did not lose much of their share of the vote (from 42.4 to 42.3 percent) and returned with a majority of 102 (from 144) (Kaiser 2006, p. 185).
148 Compare Shackleton 1998, p. 586.
149 Blake 1985, p. 108.
150 Compare Danford 1997, p. 127.
151 The act became law during the strike. While the decision to grant an injunction against

Another legal change, located at the level of the mode of leadership and domination rather than that of the extraction strategy, concerned housing once more. The push to privatise council housing was reinforced by the 1986 Housing and Planning Act. This not only promoted owner-occupation but also resulted in the sale of council houses to private landlords en bloc, in particular of the remaining higher quality homes. Hay comments:

> This has further de-legitimised council housing, reinforcing its perceived associations with inner-city deprivation and high crime rates now firmly enshrined within the dominant ideology, and strengthening the indoctrinatory power of the New Right's ideological elevation of the private home for the independent 'nuclear' family.[152]

The 1986 Act was part of an attack by the Thatcher government on the positions of the working class within the British state. These consisted of local authorities dominated by the Labour Party, which in some of the bigger cities were controlled by its socialist current.[153] Colin Leys calls them the 'institutional bases of "socialism"',[154] and Michael Lavalette and Gerry Mooney speak of 'local municipal socialism'.[155] The Thatcherites hit these projects by forcing local authorities to adopt new right policies, thus redirecting discontent from the national to the local level. Under the 1982 Social Security and Housing Benefits Act, Thatcher and her associates had already forced local authorities to implement cuts in council housing, which started to drive a wedge between the latter and the working class. The 1986 Act can be seen as a continuation of this strategy.

Yet this was only part of the attack. By the mid-1980s, Thatcher and her allies were prepared to take things further. They had abolished the six metropolitan councils and the GLC by 1986, and had taken control over the overall spending

---

the strike referred to the NUM rulebook, not the 1984 act, debates around the latter and its enactment may have influenced the public perception of the strike (compare McMullen 1985, p. 219).

152   Hay 1992, p. 59.
153   The prime examples are Liverpool, controlled by the Trotskyite Militant Tendency under the leadership of Derek Hatton, Sheffield under David Blunkett, and the Greater London Council (GLC) under Ken Livingstone (compare Middlemas 1991, p. 197; Lavalette and Money 2000, p. 206).
154   Leys 1989, p. 120.
155   Lavalette and Mooney 2006, p. 206.

of local authorities and local levels of taxation a year later.[156] In so doing, they could once again build on the rifts within the labour movement. The Labour leadership under Kinnock was ambiguous at best in its support for councils that took a radical stance and had ensured that the refusal of some local authorities to set rates in 1984–5 was taken back.[157] Moreover, Kinnock went on to purge the party of the radical left Militant Tendency, which for a time had controlled Liverpool City Council.[158] In sum, the Thatcherites rescaled the state by redividing the capacities of national and local government, thus expelling the organised working class from a number of positions in state institutions.

Around the same time, the industrial conflict over the new News International printing plant at Wapping in the East London docklands began to flare up. The importance of this conflict for class politics in Britain lies in its similarity to the miners' strike – both in terms of its trajectory and the type of opponents it pitted against each other.[159] Despite the defeat at Stockport Messenger, printing was still a stronghold of militant trade unionism. Conversely, News International was run by Murdoch, an associate of Thatcher, who had been able to count on her support when he acquired *The Times* and *The Sunday Times*.[160] Accordingly, the Wapping dispute was a confrontation between defenders of the status quo ante in the area of industrial relations and an arch-Thatcherite capitalist and supporter of the government's onslaught on organised labour, who wanted to repeat Shah's success at Stockport Messenger and get rid of a closed shop.[161]

Murdoch had acquired the site of the new plant as early as 1977 and had announced that he planned to use it in order to produce a new London newspaper. It later became clear that his true intentions were to move all his papers to the new facility.[162] In 1981, talks between management and the company's employees began over the new site and its role for the corporation. In 1984, the construction of the plant was completed. Around the same time, a round of negotiations with the unions over working conditions at the plant commenced. These led to no agreement because management demanded a drastic reduc-

---

156 Leys 1989, p. 120.
157 Lavalette and Mooney 2000, p. 207.
158 Kavanagh 1990, p. 305.
159 Compare Cohen 2006, p. 84.
160 Khadaz 2006, p. 136. This is not meant to imply that Thatcher instructed Murdoch to go on the attack. My point is that Murdoch shared Thatcher's political vision, and thus acted in accordance with her extraction strategy.
161 Marsh 1992, p. 99.
162 Ibid.

tion, compared to the standard of company, in the level of manning at the new plant. At the same time, Murdoch began to devise a plan for how to recruit and run the plant without an agreement with the printing unions, that is, the NGA and the Society of Graphical and Allied Trade (SOGAT), which still enjoyed a closed shop agreement.[163] Moreover, Murdoch began recruiting with the secret assistance of the EETPU,[164] whose leadership agreed to a '"sweetheart" deal',[165] under which workers were obliged to cross picket lines and were barred from walking out.[166]

In October 1985, management invited the printing unions to new negotiations and tabled a document demanding the abolition of the closed shop, a no-strike agreement, the 'right to manage', and the introduction of legally binding agreements. The unions rejected this document and interpreted the demands as a sign that management was unwilling to settle.[167] The leadership of the printing unions figured they were on the defensive and tabled a compromise which accepted technological changes to production and binding arbitration, but not the abolition of the closed shop. Management refused and terminated the negotiations.[168] This demonstrates that management was determined to smash the existing arrangement of industrial relations at their corporation.

In January 1986, Murdoch and his associates shocked the unions by starting production at Wapping. He staged a successful production and distribution run of the *Sunday Times*. The unions reacted with a strike ballot, which they won comfortably.[169] This was precisely the reaction that Murdoch had wanted. Responding to the walkout, he transferred the production of all his papers to Wapping, and also dismissed all his striking workers, some 5,000 people. He was able to exploit the fact that, by law, striking workers were not entitled to redundancy payments and could not claim unfair dismissal.[170] Moreover, he had prepared for this move by recruiting enough staff to run the production of all his papers without the workers laid off.[171] All of this suggests that Murdoch had lured the unions into an ambush.

---

163   Ibid.; Khabaz 2006, p. 166.
164   Marsh 1992, p. 100.
165   Cohen 2006, p. 84.
166   Khabaz 2006, p. 168; Marsh 1992, p. 100.
167   Khabaz 2006, pp. 168–9.
168   Marsh 1992, p. 99.
169   Khabaz 2006, p. 171.
170   Marsh 1992, pp. 99–100.
171   Khabaz 2006, p. 171.

Thatcher explicitly approved of Murdoch's approach. She said about him in the Commons: 'He is, in fact, trying to get rid of restrictive practices which should have been got rid of years ago, as they affect the future of some of Britain's most distinguished newspapers'.[172]

A yearlong dispute ensued, with the unions again resorting to mass picketing. Management, once more with the explicit support of Thatcher,[173] successfully requested injunctions on the grounds of the new trade union legislation. These barred the unions from picketing at the plant, which the latter refused to accept. As a result, the High Court fined SOGAT for contempt and ordered the sequestration of the union's funds, which were worth £17m.[174] Nevertheless, mass picketing continued. The police responded with repression: it prevented pickets from advancing to the plant, and there were mass arrests.[175] The battles fought were ferocious, but the pickets did not manage to seriously threaten the production and distribution of the papers.

In May 1986, after new negotiations, management made an offer of compensation worth £50m to the dismissed workers, which union members rejected in a ballot. This was not surprising given that the dismissals were not due to looming bankruptcy, but rather resulted from the determination of management to smash the existing industrial relations arrangement. Mass picketing carried on, which brought new injunctions. By August, another round of talks between the unions and management had started. Management offered £58m if the unions accepted an open shop at Wapping and works committees elected by the workers at the plants that would negotiate over pay and working conditions. Again, a ballot rejected the offer because, again, accepting it was tantamount to conceding defeat and accepting redundancies. The militants kept picketing, and the courts tried to act against them. It took until February 1987 for the conflict to come to an end. News International decided to seek the final sequestration of the SOGAT's funds; as this was considered a real threat to the existence of the union, its leadership decided to request that its members withdraw from the action, and the NGA had little choice but to follow suit.[176]

---

172   Thatcher Archive, 106313.
173   On the issue of legal intervention in the dispute, Thatcher stated: 'I wish those newspapers well in their efforts to print on the latest equipment. Management and everyone else, including trade unions, are entitled to take full advantage of the law' (Thatcher Archive, 106322).
174   Khabaz 2006, pp. 172–3.
175   Cohen 2006, p. 85; Khabaz 2006, pp. 173, 175.
176   Khabaz 2006, pp. 175–9.

INSTABILITY AND CONFRONTATION (1984–8) 199

During the Wapping dispute, patterns re-emerged that had already been visible during the miners' strike: a degree of disunity within the working class, which was reflected in the preparedness of the EEPTU to collude with management and thus undermine other unions and existing agreements; police repression against picketing; the close relationship between the Prime Minister and the head of the corporation in dispute; the ruthlessness with which management sought to smash the unions on strike; and the fact that the unions suffered total defeat. What was different was that the new trade union law was now employed to attack the unions, and that militancy did not bring management close to defeat. Both facts suggest that the Thatcherite attack had advanced, and that the unions had been forced to retreat even further. In sum, the working-class defensive against the Thatcherite onslaught was crumbling and the class relations of forces had begun to shift decisively.

The defensive terminated with the seamen's strike at P&O ferries in 1988–9. Again, both sides resorted to the familiar tactics and, again, the result was disastrous for organised labour. The P&O management, whose owner Jeffrey Sterling enjoyed close personal ties with Thatcher, had requested from workers drastic increases of work hours and a reduction in earnings. Moreover, it announced that 500 people would be made redundant – despite the fact that profits had soared to record levels. Accordingly, the onslaught on working conditions was not a direct response to competitive pressures, but was an attempt to exploit the anti-union sentiment of the conjuncture in order to attack organised labour. The workers responded by walking out; and just like News International, P&O responded by laying them off. Against the backdrop of rank-and-file disquiet about the events, the NUS called a national ballot. As a reaction, ferry owners requested an injunction against it on the grounds of the ban on secondary action introduced by Thatcherites. The courts complied with the request, stipulated that the dispute concerned P&O alone and, on this basis, threatened sequestration of the NUS's funds, which resulted in the union leadership calling off the ballot.

Thanks to the repressive effect of trade union legislation, the P&O workers were forced to continue with their action on their own. Again, they resorted to mass picketing, which brought battles with the police, but had a discernible effect on the ferry operator: Operations came to a halt for two months. The dispute escalated further when management announced that it had de-registered the NUS and had withdrawn from the National Maritime Board agreement, which meant that it was no longer bound by industry-wide bargaining. As a response, NUS workers at Sealink, the main competitor of P&O in Britain, chose to engage in sympathetic action, because they saw this move as a threat to their working conditions. The management of Sealink responded with the familiar pattern: it took the NUS to court accusing it of secondary picketing, which led the court to order the sequestration of the unions' funds. A week after the court ruling, the NUS backed down and instructed members who were not at P&O to return to work. Left to their own devices, the P&O workers still continued with their action, but they no longer stood a chance of winning. The strike was formally abandoned after 16 months, and 872 workers lost their jobs.[177]

In conclusion, the repressive effect of Thatcherite trade union legislation became apparent in the disputes that took place after the miners' strike, and the unions involved were not able to formulate an adequate response. It was obvious by now that the organised working class no longer possessed the means to halt or protract the offensive of the power bloc. Its defences had been pushed to the side.[178]

∴

Case Study: Dividing the Nation – The 'Big Bang' and the Liberalisation of Financial Markets

Financial Liberalisation and the 'Two Nations' Hegemonic Project
The liberalisation of financial markets was a plank of the neo-Ricardian accumulation strategy instituted by the Thatcherites. It aimed to strengthen the competitiveness of the City by exposing it to the pressures of the emerging world market in finance. This was done by removing institutional obstacles to the exportation and importation of capital, opening up access to the securities market and removing institutional obstacles to the expansion of the retail banking and mortgage markets.

Although financial liberalisation formed part of the Thatcherite agenda in economic order politics, the focus of this case study is not economic order politics as such, but its *indirect* effect on class domination. I contend that financial liberalisation underpinned the Thatcherite 'two nations' hegemonic project by entrenching 'divisive' nationalism. Moreover, I argue that insofar as financial liberalisation removed entry restrictions to the stock market, it tackled the internal organisation of the City as the leading fraction of the power bloc. Consequently, it can also be seen as having a *direct* effect on class relations. In other words, there is also an aspect of class politics to financial

---

177 Leys 1989; Metcalf, 2006.
178 Compare Leys 1989, p. 154.

liberalisation. Just as the miners' strike should be seen as a manifestation of the repressive extraction strategy of the Thatcherites, financial liberalisation should be viewed as a reflection of their 'two nations' hegemonic project.

The hegemonic effect of financial liberalisation may not be immediately obvious. After all, liberalisation on the whole benefited the power bloc and damaged the working class. It led to the expansion of finance as the leading fraction of capital and at the same time weakened labour through entrenching industrial decline and boosting individualist attitudes among workers. At first sight, this appears to be at odds with the Thatcherite 'two nations' hegemonic project because the latter required a minimum degree of consent across class lines.

Yet this assessment does not take into account the specific nature of 'two nations' hegemonic projects. These are based on the consent of specific sections of the working class, but not of the vast majority of its members. Obviously, it is possible that a certain set of policies is detrimental to a class as a collective, but does not have a uniform effect on all its members. A 'two nations' hegemonic project can potentially produce consent from some quarters of the working class *and* deepen the divide between labour and capital.

Correspondingly, the effect of financial liberalisation in terms of class domination was not just that it shifted class relations of forces in favour of the power bloc. It also had significant effects on internal relations *within* the capitalist class and the working class and created links across class lines:

- The liberalisation of the London Stock Exchange (LSE) profoundly affected the internal composition of the City as the leading fraction of the power bloc. The LSE was converted from a closed-entry market with restricted competition run by an oligopoly of traditional London gentlemanly capitalists into an open, internationalised, competitive market run by international financial corporations. This was articulated by the Thatcherites as 'competitive' financial enterprises sidelining 'vested interests'; they thereby insinuated that liberalisation amounted to the 'productive' nation turning against the 'parasitic' nation.
- The liberalisation of the mortgage market created the financial basis for the government's housing policy, which in turn re-drew the dividing line between working-class owner-occupiers and tenants. This again was presented as an act of enabling 'aspiring', 'hard-working' Britons to fulfil their dream of individual advancement and leave behind those who were allegedly incapable or unwilling to take care of themselves.
- The overall expansion of the City also re-drew the dividing lines among members of the working class. It entrenched the dominance of the City,

which was to the detriment of those working in industry, but it also improved the living conditions of certain groups of non-industrial workers by creating clerical jobs needed to sustain the infrastructure of finance. At the ideological level, this again was in line with presenting some workers as 'productive', and others, especially those employed in nationalised industries and involved in militant trade unionism, as trouble-making and unproductive.

In sum, financial liberalisation was highly functional to the political leadership and domination of the Thatcherites because it shifted class relations by strengthening the power bloc and deepening the divisions among workers.

The Institutional Context: The Close-Entry System of the London Stock Exchange

Financial liberalisation assembled two main processes: The liberalisation of the securities trade, as well as the liberalisation of the retail banking and mortgage markets. As a consequence of each having its own temporality, it is far from evident where this case study should be placed in the course of events I delineate. In the public perception, the defining event of financial liberalisation was the 'Big Bang', that is, the abolition of fixed commissions at the LSE in 1986. Moreover, the effects of the liberalisation of banking on class are less complex and easier to discern than the liberalisation of the stock market. As a result, my case study is built around the sequence of events at the stock market while presenting the developments in the banking sector as an 'interlude'.

The workings of the LSE before the 'Big Bang' exemplify two path-dependent features of capitalism in Britain:

(1) the absence of state regulation at the LSE illustrates the comparable weakness of the British state; and
(2) the fact that the internal cohesion of the City resulted from a 'gentlemanly' code of conduct underscores the importance of cultural patterns originating during feudal times for social relations internal to the British power bloc.[179]

Accordingly, the workings of the stock exchange also reveal how financial markets in Britain were traditionally embedded in a set of customary procedures whose functions were closure, that is, securing privileged access for a small group of people, as well as regulation, that is, imposing operational restrictions with the aim of preserving the efficiency and functionality of financial markets.

---

179 Gallas 2008.

The LSE was founded in the early eighteenth century. Around 100 years later, the organisational structure prevalent up until the 'Big Bang' came into being. The Exchange was a 'close-entry system'.[180] The City firms operating in it were based on the partnership model, that is, a hierarchical, paternalistic association of members. The public had no access, and non-members were not allowed to carry out transactions. Until 1972, new members had to be nominated by retiring ones. Moreover, membership was pending on passing a highly demanding written examination.[181]

However, it was not just the formal requirements that created barriers to membership. The nominations system ensured that there were considerable cultural barriers to be surmounted. Acceptance within the City was dependent on being acquainted with gentlemanly customs, which usually could only be acquired by family background or attendance at elitist educational institutions: 'The City's institutions and values reflected three of the pillars of conservative England: the public school, the gentleman's club and the country house'.[182] This was reflected in the way people presented themselves and how they interacted: 'Everything from the way people dressed, spoke and ate to the buildings and rooms in which they worked was derived from the standards of the English upper and upper middle classes: the gentleman's club lived on'.[183] The City in general and the Exchange in particular remained a tight-knit network closed to outsiders.

This was reinforced by the fact that the marginalisation of agriculture and the democratisation of the political scene through universal suffrage had marginalised the landed aristocracy.[184] Many of its members found refuge in the City and became fully integrated into it. As a result, in the early 1970s, 26 of the 27 major City firms disposed of 'a highly integrated kinship network of individuals' who appeared in registers of the British aristocracy. The aristocratic roots of many 'City dwellers' also ensured there were informal channels of communication between different City firms.[185] In conclusion, gentlemanly customs functioned as an instance producing internal cohesion and closure within the City.

---

180 Reid 1988, p. 45.
181 Thomas 1986, p. 14; Augar 2000, pp. 20, 48, 368.
182 Augar 2000, p. 33.
183 Augar 2000, p. 35. A certain Lord Poole of Lazards merchant bank was asked in 1974 how he had managed to avoid being entangled in a speculative boom allegedly caused by an 'arriviste' group in the City in the early 1970s. He answered: 'Quite simple, I only lent money to the people who had been at Eton' (cited in Ingham 1984, p. 139).
184 Gallas 2008, pp. 282–5.
185 Ingham 1984, p. 138.

Apart from producing internal cohesion, these customs also had a regulatory function. They embedded a code of conduct which was partly laid down in the rulebook of the Stock Exchange and was partly a product of the existence of certain conventions of interaction. Philip Augar describes the resultant system of self-regulation:

> In the market, those who did not play by the rules were ostracized. This was most evident on the Stock Exchange floor where there was a very strict code of behaviour, both formal and informal. The Stock Exchange rulebook set out clearly what was and what was not permitted and the system was operated in a meticulous manner. Disciplinary hearings did occur but the informal policing system was even more impressive. Word spread quickly when individuals or firms were consistently misbehaving and such parties very suddenly found it hard to get liquidity or to be shown business.[186]

The gentlemanly code of conduct and the tight-knit character of the business community around the LSE generated trust among the individuals involved, which meant that they were prepared to enter deals with each other without much external oversight.[187] It also created an image of trustworthiness in the eyes of parts of the public, which was one of the keys to explaining why the City was able to survive as the dominant fraction within the British power bloc despite the recurring crises of the twentieth century.[188]

The closure of the Exchange meant that it was next to impossible for outsiders to gain entry. Before Big Bang, there were no foreign firms, and almost no recently established British ones.[189] As a consequence, the Exchange was dominated by an oligopoly, and competition remained restricted. On the eve of Big Bang, the combined number of the two main types of firms operating at the Exchange was only 225.[190] These firms had a little more than 10,000 employees overall, so that the Exchange remained 'smaller than some of the larger American firms of the day'.[191] The small size of the LSE meant that it was possible to run it on the grounds of personal relationships.

---

186   Augar 2000, p. 20.
187   Ibid.; compare Leys 2001, p. 59.
188   Compare Ingham 1984, p. 138.
189   Reid 1988, p. 45.
190   Augar 2000, p. xvi.
191   Augar 2000, p. 19.

In this environment, a system of dealing emerged that was codified by the Exchange in an act of self-regulation in 1912.[192] It was based on 'single capacity', that is, a division of labour between 'brokers' and 'jobbers'. Investors in securities who were not members of the Exchange had to turn to a broker, who acted as their agent and made money by charging them a commission. Brokers were not allowed to hold shares and had to contact jobbers in order to make transactions. Conversely, jobbers possessed a 'book' of shares and made money by buying from and selling to their counterparts.[193] They operated as 'market makers', whilst brokers acted as 'intermediaries' between them and the outside world.[194]

'Single Capacity' had operational and regulatory functions. The former lay in ensuring that there was a secondary market in securities, that is, that transactions of already issued papers were always possible. This was secured by the operational rationality of jobbing. Jobbers cut a profit just like any other merchants: They sold their commodities at a retail price ('ask price') higher than its purchase price ('bid price').[195] In other words, they did not trade on rates, but on marketability, which means they were always prepared to buy or sell.[196] Augar concludes: 'The jobber was simply there to provide liquidity and make a profit'.[197]

The regulatory function of single capacity consisted in preventing jobbers from acting against the interests of the investors. Under this system of securities trade, actors at the Exchange were divided into three separate categories, that is, brokers, jobbers, and outside investors. This way, conflicts of interest were avoided, which would have occurred had the investors had direct contact with the jobbers. In that case, jobbers could have tried to offload loss-making

---

192 Thomas 1986, p. 6.
193 Reid 1988, p. 24. Augar gives a detailed description of how brokers made transactions for their clients under the old system: 'Execution of the [broking] firm's business through jobbers involved the broking firm's agency dealers, who worked on the Stock Exchange floor ... The crux of the dealers' job was to find the jobber who was most prepared to execute the firm's business on the best terms. The dealers would go round the market floor from pitch to pitch, asking "What are xyz co?", being careful not to reveal whether they were buyers or sellers, before deciding to which jobber they would give their business' (2000, p. 24).
194 Thomas 1986, pp. 9, 111; Augar 2000, pp. 16, 368.
195 Compare Thomas 1986, p. 4.
196 Ingham 1984, p. 147.
197 Augar 2000, p. 12.

positions on their book by talking clients into buying them or persuading them to sell profitable shares.[198]

Single capacity was institutionalised indirectly, that is, via the existence of fixed commissions for brokers. These undercut price competition and entrenched the oligopoly of the existing broking firms. Moreover, they prevented securities dealers from circumventing single capacity by employing 'dummy brokers'. These were brokers who acted as nominal intermediaries in transactions they in fact had not facilitated – either because they were associates of the dealer, or because their firm had been separated from a jobbing firm just for the purpose of making such transactions happen. By forcing clients to pay a commission to the broker, it was not cheaper to trade with a dealer acting in dual capacity, that is, as a jobber and a broker.[199]

In conclusion, the Exchange before Big Bang remained exclusive to a small, paternalistic coterie of people from privileged families, many of whom had aristocratic backgrounds. It was a restricted and oligopolistic market embedded both by proto-legal regulations logged in a rulebook and by cultural norms.[200] The observation of these regulations and norms was secured through the existence of a gentlemanly code of conduct, whose effectiveness in terms of producing cohesion rested on the comparably small size of the market and the face-to-face character of transactions.[201] The fact that this form of self-regulation did not lead to market breakdown was due to the restraints imposed by this pre-capitalist code, and not due to some miraculous 'invisible hand' steering a market left to its own devices.

The exclusive character of the Exchange coterie and the traditional weakness of the regulatory state in Britain led politicians and representatives of the power bloc to believe that self-regulation was possible and indeed desirable. It was seen as superior to state regulation because the tasks involved were conceived of as being 'esoteric', from which it was inferred that only practitioners (as opposed to civil servants or politicians) were able to carry them out well. The 'ideology of self-regulation' remained dominant up until the Thatcher era. As a result, the Exchange was an institution which for a long time escaped direct government interference.[202]

---

198 Compare Augar 2000, p. 12.
199 Compare Thomas 1986, pp. 5–6.
200 Compare Ingham 2002, p. 155.
201 Compare Augar 2000, pp. 19–20.
202 Moran 1991, pp. 61–2.

The Political-Economic Context: Restrictive Practices Legislation, World Market Pressures and Jobbing Problems

In the 1970s, the operational structure of the Exchange – institutionalised in 'Single Capacity' – came under fire. It had to face attacks from three quarters: the world market, the trading floor itself, and the legal sphere.

Most important was the last. Changes in law directed at undercutting restrictive business practices proved to be the lightning rod for the 'Big Bang'. The Restrictive Trade Practices, Services Order, introduced under the Wilson government in 1976, stipulated that the Exchange, among other financial institutions and service sector corporations, register its rulebook with the Office of Fair Trading (OFT) and make changes to offending rules.[203] Otherwise it faced having the rulebook declared null and void by the authorities. The Exchange chose to register it, which meant that the case would be referred to the Restrictive Practices Court if the OFT came to conclusion that it contained restrictive provisions.[204] At this point, it became clear that there would be a liberalisation of the securities trade in Britain, even if its exact form was still to be determined.

About the same time, the Exchange also came under pressure from the world market due to disintegration of the international financial architecture. By 1973, the Bretton Woods system had broken down under the strains caused by increasing capital mobility, which reflected the difficulty of enforcing capital controls after current account convertibility had been reintroduced at the end of the 1950s and Euro-currency markets had emerged.[205] Under the new regime of floating exchange rates, which no longer required capital controls,

---

203 Moran 1991, p. 69.
204 Thomas 1986, pp. 36–7.
205 Eichengreen 1996, p. 134. The post-war decades brought a massive influx of dollars into Europe, first as a result of the reconstruction effort financed by the US (compare Clark 2000, pp. 30–1), then due to American multinationals operating in Europe and European firms starting to export their products on a mass scale to the US (Ingham 1984, p. 52). This development was further reinforced by 'Regulation (Q)'. Under it, domestic interest rates in the US were kept down, and banks had to hold a non-interest-bearing reserve account at the Fed (Hamilton 1986, p. 54). This made investing in Europe attractive to holders of US dollars. The City exploited this situation by transforming its traditional business of financing trade and arranging loans through simply replacing sterling with offshore dollars. This created the so-called 'Eurocurrency' markets, which made offshore foreign currencies such as the US dollar available to borrowers, with City firms taking on the role of the intermediary. Exporting money to the UK was possible because by law, non-residents were exempt from exchange controls (Ingham 1984, pp. 52–3).

the liberalisation and transnationalisation of financial markets had become a genuine possibility.[206]

At the international level, the first move towards liberalisation was May Day 1975, when fixed commissions for brokerage at the New York Stock Exchange (NYSE) were removed.[207] Thanks to the absence of controls on the importation of capital in the US, foreign investment started to flow there. This gave New York a competitive advantage over the other main financial centres (including London) overnight. There was a plausible threat that the LSE would be reduced to a second-rank stock exchange dealing in domestic securities.[208]

Furthermore, the Exchange's internal workings came under strain. This was felt specifically by the jobbers, many of whom struggled to stay afloat. The number of jobbing firms fell from 179 in 1951 to 12 in 1984. This reflected, first, their under-capitalisation, which was a product of taxation and the frequent losses of capital due to the deaths of partners. Second, the rise of big institutional investors, at the expense of private ones, aggravated problems. It undercut jobbing firms' profitability because the decrease in investor numbers meant more one-way movements and less diversity in market transactions. Moreover, it increased 'put through' deals where the broker possessed both buying and selling orders and paid the jobber a reduced remuneration to execute the deal. Obviously, such deals were to the detriment of jobbers and undermined the regulatory framework by departing from the principle of single capacity.[209]

The decision of the Labour government to press ahead with market liberalisation and establish 'free competition' was in line with its proto-neoliberal economic order politics at the level of monetary and fiscal policy. It can also be seen as an attempt by the government to modernise its 'one nation' hegemonic project, which suggests that it had class political aspect. Going against restrictive practices in the City potentially meant weakening the hold of gentlemanly capitalists over it, which potentially opened space for another productivist experiment. Unsurprisingly, the approach of the government exposed a rift

---

[206] Lütz 2004, p. 175.
[207] Moran 1991, pp. 39–40.
[208] Ingham 2002, p. 153. This threat was reinforced by the rapid development of ICT, enabling the conduct of security trades without a physical market place (Hamilton 1986, p. 134; compare Plender 1987, p. 44). Again, the US made the first move in this direction: In 1971, a national automated quotation system, the NASDAQ, was established, which was a securities market based on a network of offices linked through a computer system (Thomas 1986, pp. 99–100; Reid 1988, p. 54).
[209] Thomas 1986, pp. 24–5; compare Reid 1988.

within the state: the Exchange and the Bank, that is, the main representative of the City in the State, protested against its course.[210]

With the Exchange rulebook being scrutinised by a state agency and the government intent on fostering 'free competition', it was obvious that the stock market would be liberalised. Considering the wider economic context of the changes in legislation, that is, the competitive pressures weighing on the City and the decline of jobbing, it is not surprising that the government chose to go down this path. After all, the Exchange was one of the key stock markets in the world, and it was part of the reason why the City still enjoyed a prominent position in the world market.

Phase I: Ruptures and a U-turn

The initial reaction of the Exchange to the threat of legal sanctions from the OFT was to avoid them by offering to review the system of self-regulation. Moreover, the threat of sanctions mobilised the Bank to lobby for its inclusion in industries exempted from restrictive practices legislation. Yet the government, represented through the Department of Prices and the OFT, refused to give in. In 1979, the Director of the OFT announced that he would refer the case to the Restrictive Practices Court. The OFT's main criticisms of the Exchange's rulebook were the existence of minimum commissions, the fact that under 'Single Capacity' brokers were not allowed to trade in securities, and the obstacles to gaining membership.[211]

The pressure on the Exchange grew with the rupture in the political scene caused by 1979 general elections. An early measure of the incoming government was to abolish exchange controls, which reflected its commitment to a neo-Ricardian accumulation strategy. This led to the biggest outflow of capital from Britain since the mid-nineteenth century. Just like then, the City was to become an exporter of capital again.[212]

As a result, City firms found themselves in competition with foreign institutions over British acquisitions in overseas shares. In this situation, American 'dual capacity' firms benefited because they could make offers on more favourable terms for investors than their British counterparts. Consequently, only about five percent of British acquisitions of overseas securities were channelled through City firms, which added to fears inside the power bloc that the City was about to lose its status as an international financial centre.[213]

---

210   Compare Moran 1991, p. 70; Thomas 1986, p. 37.
211   Thomas 1986, pp. 36–7; Reid 1988, pp. 27, 32.
212   Plender 1987, p. 43; Middlemas 1991, p. 382.
213   Compare Hamilton 1986, pp. 130–1; Reid 1988, pp. 33–4, 45.

Against this backdrop, the City became divided over the future of the Exchange. Some began to see bowing to the pressures and merging with multinationals as the only way of surviving the transnationalisation of securities markets that had been triggered by the liberalisation in the US.[214] Others believed that domestic business was generating enough revenue.[215] The existence of this rift illuminates a point made by Jessop and Rob Stones, who argue that the City was divided into an 'international' and a 'domestic' district.[216]

The division between 'transnationalist' advocates of restructuring and 'nationalist' traditionalists ran right through the Exchange. According to Michael Moran, it 'itself was internally deadlocked between reformers and opponents of change'.[217] With Thatcher taking office, the tide started to turn against the traditionalists. In 1980, she declared herself unprepared to exempt the Exchange from restrictive practices legislation. She thus overrode John Nott at Trade who a couple of weeks earlier had hinted at the possibility of a negotiated resolution of the issue in a meeting with Nicholas Goodison, the chairman of the LSE.[218] Thatcher appeared unhappy that the Treasury spent considerable sums on commissions for the issue of gilt-edged securities, that is, fixed-interest government papers.[219]

Thatcher's dismay was not simply the reflection of a frugal attitude on her side. It tied in with her neo-Ricardian beliefs in the field of economic order politics, that is, her support for transnational 'free competition'. Moreover, there was also a class political theme to Thatcher's dismay, which reflected her commitment to a 'two nations' hegemonic project. Joseph had indicated that it was the task of the new right to complete the capitalist transformation of Britain.[220] Accordingly, the Thatcherite onslaught on the Exchange can be seen as an attempt to eradicate feudal remnants in the City by expanding access and removing the privileges of the gentlemanly capitalists.[221] If, according to the 'two nations' imaginary, there was a division between a productive, hard-working nation of entrepreneurs and 'aspiring' workers and a parasitic nation of 'vested interests' hostile to competition, then substantial parts of the City belonged to the latter.

---

214   Compare Morgan 1990, p. 74.
215   Reid 1988, p. 45.
216   Jessop and Stones 1992, p. 172.
217   Moran 1991, p. 85.
218   Reid 1988, pp. 35–6.
219   Hamilton 1986, p. 132.
220   See above.
221   Compare Jessop, undated.

Obviously, due to the financial sector's pivotal role in the British power bloc, the Thatcherites could not deal with this state of affairs as they had with industry, that is, by waiting for transnational competition to put weaker City firms out of business. In other words, the City as a whole had to be forced to become part of the 'productive' nation. Under these circumstances, it was obvious that the Thatcherites would do what they could to sideline the defenders of the status quo at the Exchange and push through liberalisation.

By 1982, it had become clear that Thatcher and her associates would have their way. The Bank made a U-turn and accepted restructuring, which meant that the defenders of the status quo in the City had been deprived of their most important position in the state. There no longer appeared to be a way around the restructuring of regulation and the abolition of the closed-entry system at the Exchange. In other words, the point of no return had been reached.

The Bank's turn was unsurprising given that the economic environment in which the City operated had changed drastically thanks to the breakdown of Bretton Woods and the subsequent liberalisation of the NYSE. The Exchange was losing ground in terms of capitalisation: In early 1983, the combined capital of all stock exchange firms across the UK was less than the capital of Merrill Lynch, the largest US broker.[222]

And yet, assuming that there was just one possible reaction to this development underestimates the complexity of the conjuncture. In the City, the strategy of bowing to competitive pressures through liberalisation was still competing with the agenda of preserving the status quo by fortifying the defences against outside intruders. The fact that the Bank in the end embraced liberalisation reflects how its strategic prerogative was shifted by the Thatcherite advance. The Thatcherites successfully steered the Bank on course by entering an alliance with one of its key officials, David Walker. Walker, a proponent of liberalisation, had started his career at the commanding heights of the British state, the Treasury. In 1982, he was appointed Bank Director, and his responsibility was 'City organisation'.[223] It appears that Walker triggered the U-turn of the Bank after having had informal discussion about the matter in Whitehall.[224]

Walker's move heralded an inversion of the Bank's institutional function within the state: It no longer primarily represented City interests in the state by negotiating with the government on behalf of the financial sector. Instead, it started acting as a transmission belt which transferred the government's

---

[222] Reid 1988, p. 44.
[223] Reid 1988, pp. 220–1; Moran 1991, p. 76.
[224] Moran 1991, p. 76.

agenda into the City.[225] This was also revealed when the Prime Minister, true to the authoritarian spirit of the dominant state strategy, appointed Robin Leigh-Pemberton governor of the Bank in 1983. She had chosen him over other competitors because of his political 'reliability' – not least because he was a party member and had been leader of Kent County Council.[226]

Phase II: Shifting Institutional Conditions
Negotiations and a Settlement

The U-turn of the Bank altered the institutional conditions under which the Thatcherites operated. It opened the possibility for an out-of-court settlement, which for them had two advantages over court-imposed sanctions. First, it would allow government officials to directly influence the outcome of the process, which was not the case if a court had the final say. Second, there would be less of a polarisation, so that the City traditionalists would be less inclined to become alienated from the government.[227]

Accordingly, in the winter of 1982–3, representatives of the Treasury and Trade held secret talks with Bank officials, thus bypassing the OFT. The government's decision to seek a settlement reflected that the relations of forces within the City had changed in favour of the international City, and that the Thatcherites had been successful in pressing their case.[228] In the end, the Exchange agreed to abandon restrictive practices. In July 1983, a deal was announced between Cecil Parkinson at Trade and Goodison. In substance, it was a declaration of capitulation from the Exchange. Fixed commissions would be abandoned, and a range of measures would be implemented to end the closed-entry system: non-members would be allowed to become non-executive directors of City firms and to enter the Council, that is, the governing body of the Exchange. The only 'concession' Parkinson had made was that the government guaranteed that the court case be called off.[229]

What on the surface looked like a defeat for the OFT – after all, the court case against the Exchange had been prepared for years – was in fact a victory. Most of what the OFT had demanded in the name of 'free competition' had materialised. In effect, the government had achieved outside court what would have been interpreted as a resounding victory for it had it been the result of a court case. The representatives of the Exchange had agreed to the changes

---

225 Compare Moran 1991, p. 86.
226 Reid 1988, pp. 221–2.
227 Compare Reid 1988, p. 46.
228 Compare Reid 1988, pp. 45–8; Jessop and Stones 1992, p. 182.
229 Reid 1988, pp. 48–9; Moran 1991, pp. 70–1; Jessop and Stones 1992, p. 182.

not because they had adopted the viewpoint of the Thatcherites or the OFT, but because they wanted to avoid court orders enforcing restructuring.[230] As subsequent events would show, the settlement removed the main pillars of the traditional regulatory structure of the Exchange, that is, 'Single Capacity', closed entry and fixed commissions.

The Prime Minister could not hide her satisfaction over how her government had managed to overcome the resistance of the domestic City, and how it had forced the Exchange to liberalise its operational structure. In a speech at the Lord Mayor of the City's banquet, Thatcher stated:

> The world is full of surprises. What was unthinkable yesterday is commonplace and conventional today ... Not even the most hallowed of your institutions is immune from change. I believe even the Stock Exchange is undergoing one or two adjustments.[231]

By 1983, the Thatcherites had managed to formulate an approach to financial markets that was consistently neo-Ricardian. It was guided by the assumption that in order to increase the competitiveness of the City, financial markets had to be exposed to the world market and governed by 'free competition' all round.[232] Accordingly, 'liberalisation' was the order of the day. The first step towards liberalising financial markets had been the abolition of exchange controls; now, the operational structure of the Exchange underwent a shake-up. Nigel Lawson's budget speech of 1986 confirms this reading of events:

> Competition in financial services nowadays is not continental, but global. The City revolution now under way, due to culminate in the ending of fixed commissions, the so-called big bang, on 27 October, is essential if London is to compete successfully against New York and Tokyo. If London cannot win a major share of the global securities market, its present world pre-eminence in other financial services will be threatened.[233]

Parallel to this, the government had also embarked on liberalising the mortgage and the retail banking markets, whose restructuring in some ways mirrored the reorganisation of the securities markets.

---

230 Compare Reid 1988, pp. 48, 50, 53.
231 Thatcher Archive, 105472.
232 Compare Jessop and Stones 1992, p. 183.
233 Thatcher Archive, 109503; compare Overbeek 1990, p. 197.

Interlude: The Retail Banking and Mortgage Markets

Obviously the removal of exchange controls in 1979 drastically changed the conditions under which bankers in the UK operated, because it allowed them to import and export capital. They could now circumvent the 'corset' – a regulation which aimed at reining in bank lending by making it costlier – by issuing loans to customers via foreign subsidiaries. This in turn led to the abolition of the now redundant measure in 1981.[234] Both decisions increased the supply of the British population with loans. By taking them, the government entangled itself in contradictions because the resultant expansion of credit money rendered the meeting of the newly introduced targets under the MTFS impossible.[235]

As a result of the abolition of the 'corset', banks now operated under the same conditions as mutual societies, which had seen guidelines restricting mortgage lending scrapped in 1979. This increased competitive pressure on the latter, which was visible in a substantial increase in the market share of banks involved in mortgage lending: their share shot up from 8 to 36 percent between 1980 and 1982, and never went back below 13 percent in the next decade.[236]

The 'corset' had been accompanied by an arrangement under which building societies were allowed to form an 'interest-fixing cartel' that had kept the mortgage rate at an artificially low level.[237] In 1983, the increase of competition in the mortgage market led to the breakdown of this cartel. At the same time, controls on unsecured lending were removed, and the coverage of the government's subsidy for house buyers, the mortgage interest tax relief, was extended by increasing the value of loans covered from £25,000 to £30,000. Furthermore, the restrictions on equity withdrawal were abolished, which enabled house-owners to borrow against their property if its price rose. These measures prepared the ground not only for the expansion of private house-ownership, but also for the extension of private consumption, both by inflating personal debt.

In 1986, the changes in regulation were codified with the enactment of the Building Societies Act.[238] Besides, the act also allowed building societies to enter markets which partly had been controlled by banks, that is, money transfers, pensions, insurance and estate agency. Moreover, it gave them the opportunity to demutualise and transform themselves into PLCs. Some senior

---

234 Compare Leyshon and Thrift 1993, p. 230.
235 Compare Reid 1988, pp. 212–13.
236 Gentle and Dorling 1994, p. 186.
237 Muellbauer 2002, p. 11.
238 Ibid.; Gentle and Dorling 1994, p. 187.

managers saw this as a real opportunity because PLCs operated under less restrictive regulations. In sum, the act resulted in the establishment of full competition between banks and building societies.[239]

The government's interventions were consistent with its dominant orientations in the field of economic order politics, most importantly its neo-Ricardian accumulation strategy. They amounted to an act of liberalisation by de-segmentation. Controls underpinning restrictive practices in the two markets were removed, which led to closer integration.[240]

Furthermore, liberalisation in this field also formed a plank of the Thatcherite class political regime. It was informed by the ideas of 'property-owning democracy' and 'popular capitalism' and formed part of the 'two nations' hegemonic project. Its contribution to the latter lay in creating the financial environment in which the privatisation of council housing and transformation of tenants into owner-occupiers could take place. In other words, liberalisation deepened divisions within the working class by expanding the group of owner-occupiers and fostering the illusion that wealth was universally attainable. In actual fact, the 'nation of house-owners' envisaged by the Thatcherites turned out to be, over the medium term, a 'nation of debtors'.[241]

The interventions, along with the simultaneous privatisation of council housing, laid the foundations for a real estate bubble and a debt-fuelled consumer boom, which created the preconditions for the deep recession in the early 1990s.[242] According to Vinen, '[i]n the ten years to November 1988 non-housing loans given by UK banks increased from £4 billion to £28 billion; during the same period, housing loans increased from £6 billion to £63 billion'.[243] This in turn made itself felt through a substantial rise in unemployment, a fall in house prices, a hike in repossessions and widespread 'negative equity'.[244]

These effects of liberalisation reveal the short-termism of the Thatcherites. They were attempting to counter the tendency of capitalism to increase overall wealth whilst distributing it in an increasingly inequitable way by encouraging subaltern groups to go into debt in order to 'keep up'.[245] The crisis of the early

---

239 Marshall et al. 2003, pp. 739, 741.
240 Gentle and Dorling 1994, p. 186.
241 Gentle and Dorling 1994, p. 181; compare Konzelmann et al. 2013, p. 15.
242 Middlemas 1991, p. 381; Backhouse 2002, pp. 329–32; see below.
243 Vinen 2009, p. 205.
244 'Negative equity' occurs when 'the (estimated) market price of a house has fallen below the original mortgage advance that was used to buy that house' (Gentle and Dorling 1994, p. 182).
245 Compare Marx 1962a, p. 790.

1990s revealed the limits of this approach to class politics: It proved impossible to ensure consistent increases of wealth for the whole of the 'productive' nation, let alone the 'parasitic' nation.

Phase III: The Effects of Restructuring
The End of the Oligopoly

The Parkinson-Goodison agreement triggered a process of liberalisation that fundamentally overhauled the internal workings of the Exchange and its relationship to outside social actors and institutions. Liberalisation was accompanied by three parallel developments – centralisation, internationalisation, re-regulation – which effectively undermined the oligopoly of the existing City firms.

The measures taken by the Exchange directly after the agreement amounted to a three-step modification of its rulebook, which established a new system of trade compatible with flexible commissions. In October 1983, *all* member firms were allowed to trade in foreign papers, which was the beginning of the end for 'Single Capacity'. In April 1984, an even more far-reaching shift occurred. The following was decided:

– commissions on foreign securities should no longer be fixed;[246]
– the remaining fixed commissions should be abolished in one 'Big Bang' on 27 October 1986;[247]
– single capacity would end and be replaced by a system under which all Exchange firms would become broker-dealers, with some acting as market-makers with an obligation to deal continuously in specifically named shares irrespective of the market situation;[248]
– the gilt-edged market would be reshaped, with a specific number of brokers-dealers gaining direct access to the Bank and the government broker being put out of business after 200 years;[249] and
– outside investors would be allowed to buy City firms (with stakes being restricted to 29.9 percent) and start their own enterprises.[250]

In the summer of 1985, the changes were completed when Goodison announced that the 29.9 percent limit would be abolished, and that member-

---

246   Augar 2000, p. 45.
247   Reid 1988, p. 55.
248   Reid 1988, p. 54.
249   Thomas 1986, p. 72; Reid 1988, p. 64.
250   Reid 1988, p. 55.

ship at the Exchange would be based on firms and no longer on individuals as primary units.[251] In sum, the restructuring triggered by the Parkinson-Goodison agreement transformed the Exchange from a restricted into an open securities market.

Liberalisation and Economic Order Politics

As a piece of economic order politics, liberalisation widened access to the Exchange and allowed outside investors to get involved in City firms. This triggered processes of centralisation and internationalisation, which reflected a drive for exploiting economies of scale. City firms started to look for new partners in order to become part of bigger conglomerates.[252] Conversely, outside institutional investors sought to enter the Exchange through acquiring City firms. Once the 29.9 percent limit was lifted, City firms ceased to exist in their traditional form:

> Altogether during the stock market's reshaping to its new form, over a hundred Stock Exchange firms were bought up in the biggest and swiftest take-over spree in the financial industry's history. Virtually all the large and medium-sized concerns lost their independence in the huge sell-out, which continued with a trickle of deals even after the Big Bang ... All told, in the giant buy-up movement, more than £1.5bn has been laid out on the purchases of Exchange firms which have given numerous banks entry to the City's deregulated stock market ... On top of this outlay ... the new owners have channelled in probably something like as much again to recapitalise their acquisitions and fit them for their role in the City's revamped stock trading forum.[253]

In a situation where actors in the financial markets across the globe were highly unequal in terms of their capitalisation, liberalisation favoured the 'giants', which were mostly US financial corporations.[254] These generally found investing in the UK appealing, as the political situation appeared similar to that in their home country. Moreover, US retail banks were attracted by the UK because they could get involved in investment banking – a business they were barred from under US financial regulations. Apart from that, US investment banks had

---

251 Hamilton 1986, p. 144.
252 Compare Thomas 1986, p. 1333.
253 Reid 1988, p. 66.
254 Reid 1988, p. 46.

institutional structures and a corporate culture that equipped them well to expand into foreign markets.[255]

In the period between 'Parkinson-Goodison' and the Big Bang, the foundation for the 'Wimbledonisation' of the City was laid, that is, a situation similar to the one at the most prestigious Tennis tournament in the world: 'held in Britain, staffed by locals, dominated by foreigners but still generating bags of prestige and money for the UK'.[256] If looked at against the backdrop of the breakdown of Bretton Woods, the restructuring of the NYSE and the removal of exchange controls, liberalisation of the Exchange was another important step in the transnationalisation of financial markets.[257] The Thatcher government closely followed the lead of the US on this front, thus reinforcing pressures on other countries to follow suit.[258]

The processes of centralisation and transnationalisation in the City reinforced the neo-Ricardian accumulation strategy. The Thatcherites saw it as a positive that 'free competition' led to an influx of capital, triggered centralisation and improved the capitalisation of British-based financial institutions. They took a similar line on transnationalisation: if it increased competitiveness, there was nothing wrong with it.[259] Alexander Fletcher, an under-secretary at Trade, stated in the Commons in 1983:

> We are asked whether the Government want more mergers of stock exchange firms. We want to see strong financial institutions in London that can compete for business worldwide and exploit new business opportunities as they arise. However, it is a matter for the commercial judgment of the City and not for the Government how the institutions can best organise themselves to meet the future. We should be concerned if mergers threatened competition or reduced services to customers, but in present circumstances it seems more likely that they will generate greater diversity. With regard to the Government's attitude to overseas bids for city firms, the fact that one or two of the most enterprising United States banks have taken maximum permitted holdings in London brokers is a clear sign of the continuing importance of the City as a financial centre and of the general expectation that London is the place where things will

---

255   Augar 2000, pp. 70–2.
256   Augar 2000, p. 3.
257   Compare Plender 1987, p. 47; Candeias 2004, pp. 111–17.
258   Compare Overbeek 1990, p. 183.
259   Compare Plender 1987, pp. 45–6.

happen in the securities market. We attach the greatest importance to the continuing role of the City as an international centre. One reason for our part in the present programme of reform is to promote the international status of London.[260]

The only state apparatus whose officials dominantly disagreed with this course was the Bank. Its strategy reflected its historical role as the 'ideal collective capitalist' of the existing City institutions. It tried to instigate mergers between City brokers and banks in order to create British investment banks able to compete with foreign institutional investors.[261] Yet these attempts proved futile. Transnationalisation and centralisation meant that, by the onset of the new century, there were hardly any British-based City firms left:

> Taking the top ten merchant banks in London in 1983, only two – Lazards and Rothschilds – were still independent at the beginning of the twenty-first century ... The top ten brokers of 1983 have been through so many changes of name, management and ownership that they are nearly unrecognizable today. None of the leading investment banks that took over from the UK's merchant banks and brokers is British-owned. There are five pure American firms, two international firms with strong American influences (Lazards and CFBS), and three Continental Europeans.[262]

Inter-Class and Intra-Class Divisions

Liberalisation also had a marked effect on class relations. It formed a piece of class politics insofar as it was intrinsically linked to the Thatcherite 'two nations' hegemonic project. Not only did it increase inequality between financial capitalists and their supporters in other classes on one side and the remainder of the population on the other. It also afforded the government with the opportunity to disarticulate deepening material inter-class divisions by discursively highlighting intra-class divisions, which it did so by taking on traditionalist elements in the City.[263] Liberalisation resulted in the reconfiguration of the power bloc and the marginalisation of the gentlemanly milieus in the City. In other words, for once a part of Central London underwent a process of 'de-gentrification' – if only in the literal sense.

---

260   Hansard HC, 49, 184–261.
261   Jessop and Stones 1992, p. 184.
262   Augar 2000, p. 309.
263   Compare Hobsbawm 1989, p. 17; Lawrence and Sutcliffe-Braithwaite 2012, p. 134.

Against this backdrop, liberalisation must be seen as an attempt to expand share-ownership and boost 'popular capitalism'. Tebbit, the Trade Secretary, uttered in 1983:

> I ... suspect that the likely changes in the security markets may lead to the establishment of far more extensive retail outlets, which would benefit the private client. This could do much to promote wider share ownership and to reverse the continuing distancing of the small investor from the share market, which was confirmed by the latest stock exchange survey of share ownership.[264]

Lawson reiterated this theme in his budget speech of 1986, in which he also announced that the Big Bang would be accompanied by a cut in stamp duty, a tax payable after share transactions, by 50 percent:

> This further halving of the stamp duty on equities should enable London to compete successfully in the worldwide securities market, and it will also provide a further fillip to wider share ownership in the United Kingdom. Just as we have made Britain a nation of home owners so it is the long-term ambition of this Government to make the British people a nation of share owners, too; to create a popular capitalism in which more and more men and women have a direct personal stake in British business and industry. Through the rapid growth of employee share schemes, and through the outstandingly successful privatisation programme, much progress has been made – but not enough. Nor, I fear, will we ever achieve our goal as long as the tax system continues to discriminate so heavily in favour of institutional investment rather than direct share ownership.[265]

In her speech at the banquet of the Lord Mayor of the City in 1986, Thatcher very clearly spelled out the class political implications of 'popular capitalism'. She concluded a passage on this very topic by saying: 'Our aim is to consign to the dustbin that most damaging of phrases "the two sides of industry". We want to see an end to the "them and us" attitude which has done so much harm to Britain'.[266]

---

264   Hansard HC, 49, 184–261.
265   Thatcher Archive, 109503.
266   Thatcher Archive, 106512.

The plan to cover up class antagonism by popularising share-ownership, however, was far from successful. Riddell quotes a study showing that the number of shareholders rose from 3m to 9m between 1979 and the beginning of 1989. However, a substantial number only possessed small stakes and soon sold them.[267] Moreover, the proportion of shares in personal sector-wealth rose from 5.9 percent in 1979 to only 7.6 percent.[268] This implies that the expansion of share-ownership was not reflected in the composition of assets people held. Thus it can be inferred that the value of the shares obtained remained negligible. In conclusion, the interpellations of popular capitalism in the area of shares might have had an effect at the level of discourse, but they were not underpinned by substantial material shifts – as had been the case in the housing market.

Nevertheless, liberalisation did have a lasting effect on class relations: it deepened the divide between the City and the remainder of the population in terms of wealth and provided the Thatcherites with an opportunity to disarticulate this divide by talking about 'popular capitalism'. Most importantly, it triggered an influx of capital into the City; the initial beneficiaries were the partners bought out. Around 1,500 people obtained a share of the 1.5bn invested in order to facilitate take-overs. Reid assumes that more than 500 of these people made more than £1m in the process; Augar puts the number at 750.[269]

At the same time, the £1.5bn invested led to the creation of a vast number of new jobs. Following Nigel Thrift and Andrew Leyshon, the annual growth rate of employment in the City was 7.5 percent.[270] This was accompanied by an increasing demand for skilled workers, which reflected the fact that there were few people available on the labour market with the skills to operate under the changed conditions.[271] This lack of supply, combined with the fact that US firms usually offered higher wages, led to a 'pay explosion'[272] that increased wage differentials between 'City dwellers' and the rest of the population: Whereas

---

[267] Riddell 1991, pp. 118–19.
[268] Johnson 1991, p. 301.
[269] Reid 1988, pp. 68–9; Augar 2000, p. 81.
[270] Thrift and Leyshon 1992, p. 285. Correspondingly, employment in financial services in all of Britain rose by 57 percent between 1981 and 1989, compared with only 4.3 percent across the whole economy, and was 'very much a phenomenon of Britain's southern economy' (Leyshon and Thrift 1993, p. 231).
[271] Reid 1988, p. 71; Thrift and Leyshon 1992, pp. 285–6; Augar 2000, p. 92.
[272] Reid 1988, p. 71; compare Thrift and Leyshon 1992, p. 290.

gross average earnings were about three times higher in the City if 1979 and 1989 are compared, for the British population as a whole the number was 2.5 times.[273]

Looked at against the backdrop of the Thatcherites' persistent attack on organised labour and wage demands made by industrial workers, the push for liberalisation appears as a way of strengthening the City at the expense of the working class. The government made no attempts to impose a special levy on those who pocketed massive profits thanks to buy-outs or to increase taxation for those whose wages had exploded.[274] Rodney Bickerstaff, general secretary of the National Union Public Employees (NUPE), asked: 'Why is it necessary to pay the rich more – and the poor less – to get them to work?'[275]

In line with their 'two nations' hegemonic project, the Thatcherites rearticulated liberalisation in a way that covered up its class political dimension. They presented themselves as the guardians of small investors in particular and hardworking people in general, and claimed to take on the 'vested interests' in the City on their behalf. Along these lines, the 1987 general election manifesto of the Conservative Party stated:

> Like other sections of British industry ... the City was held back by restrictive practices until they were swept away in last year's 'big bang'. This has brought nearer the day when shares can be bought and sold over the counter in every high street.

This statement was part of the first general election campaign after the miners' strike and the Wapping dispute. If seen in this context, it is clear that the 'other sections of British industry' marred by 'restrictive practices' are those that had witnessed labour unrest and worker resistance to productivity drives. Considering this, the statement insinuates that there is a link between gentlemanly capitalists and militant labour. In so doing, it not only reiterates the distinction between the 'productive' and the 'parasitic' nation, but also links up purported elements of the latter across class lines. Besides, it also restates the idea of 'popular capitalism' ('in every high street') and attempts to justify liberalisation by invoking the alleged needs of ordinary shoppers.

---

273   Compare Thrift and Leyshon 1992, p. 289.
274   Reid 1988, pp. 80, 83.
275   Cited in Reid 1988, p. 72.

The Erosion of the Gentlemanly Code of Conduct

The intensification of competition and the dissolution of the oligopoly resulted in the 'death of gentlemanly capitalism', as the title of Augar's monograph has it.[276] The expansion of the City and the end of the partnership model rendered the traditional operational structure of the Exchange with its foundation in personal contact impractical. Augar quotes an employee of stockbroker James Capel as saying:

> Selling our firm changed our lives; we were no longer a partnership and the whole ethos changed ... The effect of the takeover and the sudden expansion of the firm were that there were enormous strains and tensions and the firm became rather divided and by 1987 it was a rather unhappy place. There was no longer the kind of commitment which prevailed under the partnership agreement.[277]

Patterns of interaction were also changed profoundly as liberalisation altered the physical-technological environment in which traders operated. The 'Big Bang' was accompanied by the computerisation of the Exchange. Market makers started to display their prices on screens, which made asking for them by walking around the floor redundant. Transactions could now be executed over the telephone. As a consequence, location no longer mattered, and 24-hour trading, at least in international securities, became a reality.[278] The fact that trading no longer involved face-to-face contact, which had been one of the foundations for the tight-knit social network that had existed among traders, triggered 'deep behavioural changes'.[279]

These changes were also driven by the strategy predominantly adopted by the financial services industry in the light of the skills shortage. According to Leyshon and Thrift, there was 'constant poaching by firms of people or teams of people with particular skills/contacts from other firms'.[280] In other words, headhunting became common, and the target was the so-called 'marzipan layer' ('below the icing but above the cake') of senior executives who had not become partners yet.[281]

---

276 Augar 2000.
277 Augar 2000, p. 106.
278 Thomas 1986, pp. 103–7.
279 Augar 2000, p. 120.
280 Leyshon and Thrift 1992, p. 290.
281 Augar 2000, pp. 74, 107.

The courting of competitors' employees was incompatible with the obligations of gentlemanliness. A member of one of the British 'stockbroking dynasties' described the difference between the old and the new ways:

> When I came into the Stock Exchange, my father wouldn't let me hire somebody from another firm without first ringing up to check that it was all right. But that kind of courtesy stopped ten to fifteen years ago. I think we've lost a lot of the nicer aspects of City relationships, ethics and so forth, and I think the rest will disappear in the aggro of competition.[282]

Increasing competition for staff dissolved the bonds between individuals and eroded their ties to a specific firm, on both of which the gentlemanly culture had thrived.[283]

This was reinforced by competitive pressures, which rendered the gentlemanly work ethic obsolete. Work hours and work intensity increased. Michael Spencer, founder of inter-dealer broker ICAP, says:

> Culturally, Big Bang changed everything. The City was a much more relaxed place. It's hard to believe that the gilt market didn't open until 10. The three-Martini lunch was alive and strong.

He adds: 'When I started in the city, I remember the excitement and camaraderie of walking around the Stock Exchange floor. That's gone'. And: 'The City has changed enormously in terms of the discipline and professionalism, and its multiculturalism as the big foreign firms came in'.[284]

Similarly, Andy Stewart, founder of City firms Collins Stewart and Cenkos Securities, utters: 'When I first started, there were toilets for partners and toilets for clerks'. He adds: 'Somebody would wear brown shoes to work and there would be an absolute riot'. Stewart confirms the importance of personal relationships in the pre-liberalisation era: 'You couldn't just phone up a potential client if you didn't already have a previous relationship or hadn't been to school with them. All commissions were fixed and the spreads were so wide, you could drive a truck through them'. In turn, he sees a great deal of change in the post-Big Bang era: 'There's massive competition between big and small firms, none of that ridiculous closed shop, and the ability to establish new firms'.[285]

---

282   Cited in Reid 1988, p. 85.
283   Compare Augar 2000, pp. 307–8.
284   Cited in Parkinson 2006.
285   Ibid.

In sum, although foreign firms entering the City appeared to display 'the same bias towards products of Oxfords, Cambridge and other top-rank universities like Bristol as their British counterparts',[286] and the new generation rushed to buy country-houses just as their predecessors,[287] the patterns of interaction within the firms no longer conformed to the gentlemanly code of conduct. Its romanticising tone notwithstanding, Augar's account of the changes appears to capture what was at stake:

> The exposure of stereotyped gentlemanly capitalists to a new work ethic was accompanied by a breaking down in the old relationships. Staff mobility soared. Money replaced honour and short-term reward long-term commitment.[288]

Effects on Regulation

The erosion of the gentlemanly code of conduct had a significant effect on the operational structure of the Exchange. The code had safeguarded the oligopoly by inhibiting competition and had served as a disincentive for fraudulent activities. City firms struggled to adapt to the new situation, because they had been deprived of the 'cultural resources' that had traditionally equipped them with a capacity for self-regulation:

> The old City was ordered and hierarchical. Every firm had a clearly defined set of relationships with its clients and with the other firms that provided services and competition. Firms were prevented from breaking out of these boundaries by rules and customs. Suddenly, most of these relationships were thrown up in the air by Big Bang and, when they landed again, were very different. The City's response to this new landscape was hindered by its lack of experience of institutional change. It needed either a period of protection while it adjusted or help in raising its standards.[289]

In other words, liberalisation disembedded the City from the cultural setting that had underpinned procedures of self-regulation, and this undermined its traditional firms.[290] The intimacy of the old City and the gentlemanly code of

---

286 Leyshon and Thrift 1992, p. 292; compare Augar 2000, p. 308.
287 Leyshon and Thrift 1992, p. 297.
288 Augar 2000, p. 115.
289 Augar 2000, p. 50.
290 Compare Moran 2006, p. 462.

conduct had streamlined behaviour and generated a self-imposed regime of social control – something which expansion and technical change rendered unworkable. Thus City firms struggled to implement procedures of risk control capable of dealing with the host of new trading practices, among them a range of derivatives, whose importance grew during the 1980s.[291] This, combined with the fact that single capacity was in the process of being abolished, implies that liberalisation created a regulatory vacuum.

The government reacted by implementing a new regulatory regime, which, however, remained weak compared to US standards.[292] It was still based on self-regulation, which was re-embedded by introducing flanking measures of state control. Essentially, the Secretary of Trade granted powers of oversight to the newly established Securities and Investment Board (SIB), a private corporation with the task of setting out 'model rules' for more specialised 'self-regulating organisations' (SROs), initiating prosecutions if offences occurred, licensing businesses, and authorising SROs.[293]

Accordingly, under the new regime, state apparatuses became more important, even if they operated at a distance from the Exchange. State intervention was now possible, as is shown by the fact that the government flanked the establishment of the SIB with tightening legislation against insider trading, thus moving from 'inefficient' to more 'determined enforcement' in this area.[294] Moran argues that this move can at least in part be seen as an importation of US regulatory practices introduced with a view to pleasing foreign investors.[295] One might add that there was political leverage for the government in campaigning against insider trading because it ran counter to the ideology of 'popular capitalism' and the Thatcherite claim to protect 'small investors' and stand up to vested interests.[296]

This stance had a material foundation in the fact that insider trading increased inefficiency in the market, with 'outsiders' obtaining unfavourable deals thanks to information asymmetries. This issue was aggravated under conditions of 'dual capacity', when firms could potentially protect or improve their

---

291   Compare Augar 2000, pp. 105–6.
292   Compare Augar 2000, p. 114.
293   Moran 1991, p. 59.
294   Moran 1991, p. 81. Insider trading can be defined as 'the practice of dealing for gain using non-public information acquired through privileged access to the details of an enterprise' (Moran 1991, p. 48).
295   Moran 1991, pp. 82–3.
296   Compare Moran 1991, pp. 84.

positions at the expense of their clients.[297] Accordingly, the new legislation was not just an attempt to please US firms entering the City or to assuage Conservative voters infuriated by scandals in the City,[298] but also a reaction to the regulatory vacuum created by liberalisation.

Nevertheless, the measures soon proved futile: First, insider trading legislation in Britain was 'light' in terms of enforcement and punishment if compared to its US equivalent – despite the fact that it led to prosecutions.[299] Second, thanks to the difficulty of proving that an insider transaction had been carried out, it was generally next to impossible to efficiently prosecute people resorting to such practices.[300] According to Adrian Hamilton, insider trading remained a common and accepted practice both at the LSE and the NYSE.[301]

Consequently, it is not so much noteworthy *what* British state apparatuses did in this area, but simply *that* they got involved. Given that the state appeared to play a more pronounced (if limited) role than before, Moran concludes that it does not make sense to refer to the changes at the Exchange with the term 'deregulation'.[302] Accordingly, I speak of 'liberalisation' and 'reregulation'.

In sum, the new regulatory remained inconsistent. It brought state control, but state control at arm's length:

> The regulatory structure was beset by three key deficiencies. Firstly its powers of supervision and enforcement were insufficient. The impression was that gentlemanly capitalism persisted despite the extension of state regulation. Secondly the regulatory structure remained fractured along sectoral lines while markets and institutions spanned those boundaries. Finally the City's regulators were trapped by the territoriality of their authority while markets continued to integrate across state boundaries.[303]

The weaknesses of the new regulatory arrangement reflected the priority the government gave to increasing the City's competitiveness, and, despite claims

---

297 Compare Thomas 1986, pp. 132–4.
298 Compare Moran 1991, pp. 83–4.
299 Moran 1991, pp. 81–2.
300 Moran 1991, pp. 48–9.
301 Hamilton 1986, p. 230.
302 Moran 1991, p. 82.
303 Woodward 2001, p. 5.

to the contrary, its disregard for protecting the 'small investor'.[304] Consequently, the new regime failed to address the vacuum left by the decline of gentlemanliness and the weakened capacity for self-regulation created by City expansion. Its inconsistency reflected a dilemma for the government rooted in the path-dependencies of capitalism in Britain: On the one hand, it was impossible to leave the path of self-regulation altogether – an earlier report calling for the SROs to be subsumed under a public body led to heavy protestations in the City.[305] On the other hand, it was not plausible to preserve the regulatory autonomy of the City. The result was an incoherent compromise of state control and self-regulation. Moran comments: 'It was a solution riddled with ambiguities and contradictions produced by a coalition of interests itself founded on contradiction and ambiguity'.[306]

Phase IV: The 1987 Crash

The liberalisation of financial markets and the consequent inflation of credit led to a global stock market boom. Werner Bonefeld et al. dub the practice of the US and the British governments to trigger economic booms via creating incentives for the expansion of debt 'Keynesianism of the New Right'.[307] The resultant discrepancy between the value symbols in circulation and the actual value generated in production found expression in a demand bubble, which was further inflated by the regulatory vacuum at the Exchange as well as the lack of know-how in the City regarding risk management in the changed environment. The consequence was a realignment that took on the form of a stock market crash and was triggered in October 1987 by a sudden rise in US interest rates.[308] It resulted in British shares losing a third of their aggregated market price.[309] In the fourth quarter of 1987, the losses accrued by the Exchange member firms amounted to £375m.[310]

The crash posed a serious class political problem for the government because it exposed the limits of 'popular capitalism'. It was revealed that share ownership was not a quick route to wealth for small investors, but an asset type that came with considerably risk. Credit inflation did not substantially alter the economic position of most. This meant that the Thatcherite strategy of man-

---

304 Compare Leyshon and Thrift 1993, p. 230.
305 Moran 1991, p. 72.
306 Moran 1991, p. 73.
307 Bonefeld et al. 1995, p. 66.
308 Augar 2000, pp. 4, 96–7, 121; Kannankulam 2008, p. 275.
309 Reid 1988, p. 96.
310 Augar 2000, p. 123.

aging the tendency to produce increasing inequality inherent in the CMP was under threat. There was a risk of intra-class divisions receding and the social basis of Thatcherism eroding.

At the level of public political discourse, the Thatcherites reacted by externalising the blame for the problems. This was helped by the fact that the crisis had first erupted in the US.[311] At the level of fiscal policy, they chose to reflate again, mostly through drastic tax cuts, which formed part of Lawson's 1988 budget. As a result, the realignment was confined to the stock market and remained short-lived. In other words, the crash took the form of a 'short sharp shock'.[312] The full effect of the crisis tendencies triggering it only played out two years later when Britain hit the next recession.[313]

In conclusion, the 'Big Bang' produced fissures in the hegemonic project of Thatcherism. These would turn into visible cracks under the Major government, when there were constant arguments over whether what I call the 'two nations' hegemonic project should be left behind or not.[314] In other words, the results of the crash foreshadowed the problems that would eventually lead to the erosion of Thatcherism.

Medium-Term Consequences: 'Compradores' Replace 'Gentlemen'

In the area of economic order politics, financial liberalisation brought hard-to-reverse changes, which were embodied in the integration of the Exchange into the emerging transnational financial markets. The Thatcherites used their positions within the state in order to destroy the gentlemanly oligopoly and further entrench their neo-Ricardian accumulation strategy. They found support in the international City, which broadly favoured restructuring. Moran comments:

> From the conclusion of the Goodison/Parkinson agreement of July 1983 the state was deeply and publicly involved in the reconstruction of financial markets, principally with the object of preserving London's leading position in a world marked by competitive struggles between rival centres ... The rise of the state was accelerated because, by the 1980s, it was clear that reforming coalitions within the City could not, unassisted, defeat the traditional interests who were doing well out of restrictive practices. It took state intervention to destroy the old guard.[315]

---

311 Compare Bonefeld et al. 1995, p. 66.
312 Augar 2000, p. 326.
313 Compare Kannankulam 2008, p. 275.
314 See below.
315 Moran 1991, p. 83.

Liberalisation triggered the expansion of the City, which led to an influx of foreign capital and laid the foundation for the restoration of its global dominance.[316] At the same time, however, the changes created a regulatory vacuum, which the government did not manage to fill: state control over the operations at the Exchange remained at arm's length.

If taken as a piece of class politics, the very same process led to the internal recomposition of the City as the dominant fraction in the power bloc, altered its ideology and changed its external relations. Financial capitalists heading institutions that operated on a transnational scale sidestepped the coterie of gentlemanly capitalists at the head of the Exchange. As a result, neoliberal ideology marginalised the gentlemanly code of conduct. At the managerial level, this played out as loyalty to the firm and the observation of existing hierarchies being replaced by a commitment to individual advancement and competition. At the level of investment strategies, the financial corporations now operating at the Exchange subscribed to short-termism and 'shareholder value', which reflected the competitive pressures that resulted from their status as listed companies. This in turn led to a quick succession of acquisitions, mergers and disposals, which created less stable and transparent relations of ownership than pre-Big Bang.[317]

Also, the influx of foreign investment, even if it strengthened the hold of the City over the British power bloc and sustained capitalist class domination, still heavily modified the latter's relations to financial fractions based elsewhere in the world. After World War I, the US had replaced Britain as the dominant capitalist power.[318] Nevertheless, the City had remained a 'national' fraction of capital in terms of its external relations,[319] that is, a fraction capable of formulating its strategies in consideration of, but at a distance from, US financial capital. This changed with liberalisation – at least for the firms represented at the Exchange.

By 2000, the leading investment banks in the City were no longer British-controlled.[320] Accordingly, the section of the City active at the Exchange had

---

316   Compare Candeias 2004, p. 132.
317   Compare Augar 2000, pp. 314–15.
318   Ingham 1984, p. 174; Eichengreen 1996, p. 45.
319   Poulantzas 1975, p. 71.
320   As Leys observes (2001, p. 63), this was part of a broader influx of foreign direct investment into Britain and a wave of mergers and acquisitions targeting British-based companies. Nevertheless, the case of the Exchange is specific. First, it was at the heart of the financial sector, which means it was the field of operation of the hegemonic fraction of the power

been reduced to 'comprador' status,[321] acting as an 'intermediary' of capital based in the US and, to a lesser degree, in continental Europe and Japan.[322] Its strategies were formulated against the backdrop of the conditions and needs of national economic zones other than Britain, with the City being no more than the physical place where they were executed. In other words, foreign investment banks were now most likely to be committed to and bound by strategies emerging out of power blocs outside Britain – at least in the last instance.[323] In sum, 'compradores' replaced the gentlemen. As a result, the City may have survived and even expanded and thrived as a global centre of the securities trade, but it did so 'only at the cost of its growing domination by foreign financial institutions'.[324]

Obviously, this does not apply to all of the financial sector in equal measure. The 'big four' of retail banking – Barclays, NatWest, the Royal Bank of Scotland and HSBC – remained institutions under British control.[325] After Big Bang, some of them made the attempt to branch out into investment banking. Yet their operational structures proved incompatible with those of the City firms they bought; and they were ill-prepared for their new environment. In contrast, US investment banks could draw on their long experience in securities trading, and presided over substantial revenues to reinvest thanks to the size of their domestic markets. Thus UK retail banks made considerable losses at the Exchange and had completely withdrawn from investment banking by 1997.[326]

In terms of their external relations, the British firms formed the 'internal' section of the City.[327] They formulated strategies in transnationalised, US-dominated financial markets, but much of their business was conducted under specifically British conditions. Hence they were neither national nor 'comprador' in character. Instead, their strategies reflected how transnational financial markets were interiorised in the British economy.

In sum, in the post-Big Bang era, internal and comprador elements co-existed with each other in the City, with the latter dominating the strategically

---

bloc. Second, there was a more or less complete takeover of firms at the Exchange by foreign investors, which was not the case in at least some of the other industries.

[321] Poulantzas 1975, p. 71.
[322] Leys 2001, p. 59.
[323] Burgi and Jessop 1991, p. 189.
[324] Needless to say, my description should not be taken as expressing sorrow over the loss of tradition. It is merely meant to capture change.
[325] Compare BankStats, 2009, p. T149.
[326] Augar 2000, pp. 109–11, 124–5, 255–72, 316.
[327] Poulantzas 1975, p. 72.

important space of the Exchange. This in turn implies that the British power bloc became at least partly internationalised, and, due to the dominance of US-based financial corporations, began to interiorise US-based capital. A material substratum emerged for the 'special relationship' between Britain and the US that went beyond US foreign direct investment in British industry. US interests now played a key role in the hegemonic fraction of the power bloc and thus had access to key positions in the British state.

This observation not only provides us with an explanation for the continuous opposition of the British power bloc to continental European productivist accumulation strategies.[328] It also reveals that from the 'Big Bang' onwards, capitalism in Britain was characterised by a scalar class configuration that was much to the detriment of the working class. The latter was, at best, organised at the national level, while it confronted a power bloc whose commanding heights formed part of transnational networks. As a result, the power bloc could easily out-manoeuvre opposition to neo-Ricardianism and neoliberalism by claiming that changes to the foundations of economic policy would result in capital flowing out of the City and plunging capitalism in Britain into crisis again.

∴

The Entrenchment of Neoliberalism

All in all, the third period of Thatcherism was marked by instability, which was caused by open class warfare and the active reshaping of financial markets. Since the Thatcherites prevailed, they managed to entrench the neoliberal regime of condensation. They weakened the opposition to their agenda profoundly and created institutional supports for their strategies. This was visible in the area of economic order politics as much as in that of class politics.

With the gentlemanly capitalists in the domestic City marginalised, the key stumbling block to the insertion of British financial markets in the emerging transnational trade networks had been removed. In turn, the 'transnationalised' City served as the main institutional support of the neo-Ricardian accumulation strategy. With the implementation of top-down chains of command and the streamlining of the Parliamentary Conservative Party, there was no longer a meaningful opposition to the authoritarian state strategy of the

---

[328] Compare Jessop 2002b, pp. 119–23.

Thatcherites. In other words, the implementation of the new economic-politic order reached the stage of completion.

Much the same can be said about the class political regime: With the smashing of militant trade unionism and the demise of the socialist current in the Labour Party, there was no forceful collective actor that could have reversed the changes in this field. The Labour leadership and the trade union right had subscribed to what they had dubbed 'new realism'[329] – an ideology mixing the accurate and realistic assessment that crucial struggles had been lost and the relations of forces had shifted with the unrealistic assumption that acquiescence would pay off in such a situation. Similarly, the leadership of the militant wing of the trade union movement had, at Wapping and Dover, decided to give in despite rank-and-file pressure. This reflected a realistic assessment of class relations of forces and of the cumulative effect of the different pieces of trade union legislation implemented over the years.

The retreat of organised labour is illuminated by medium-term developmental trends regarding industrial relations. Between 1979 and 1988, British trade union lost roughly 3m members and union representation within the overall workforce decreased from 57 to 46 percent. Looking at employment figures, Leys describes the underlying changes in the employment structure: 'Nearly all the new net employment of over a million jobs created during the Thatcher years down to 1987 were part-time, overwhelmingly low-skill jobs, and mainly filled by women, all of which features made them less easy to unionise'.[330] The resultant polarisation of qualifications within the labour market deepened divisions in the labour movement, with more high-skilled sections (for example, engineers) threatening to break away from the TUC or forming 'yellow' organisations like the UDM or the EEPTU.[331] Accordingly, the number of working days lost per 1,000 employees started to decrease markedly after the miners' strike. The UK annual average from 1969 to 1979 had been 544. This fell to 484 between 1980 and 1984, and then to 180 between 1985 and 1989.[332] All of this accounts for the success of Thatcherism in restoring capitalist class domination, or, more prosaically, the 'right to manage'.[333]

In sum, the Thatcherites' successful promotion of profound changes in industrial relations and financial markets in this period put them on course to entrenching the position achieved through their offensive. And yet, the Big

---

329 Compare Hain 1986, p. 296; Gamble 1988, pp. 220–1.
330 Leys 1989, p. 147.
331 Compare ibid.
332 Johnson 1991, p. 312.
333 Compare Leys 1990, p. 123.

Bang episode reveals that stabilisation carried within itself the seeds of decline. The 1987 crash brought to light the limits of the neo-Ricardian accumulation strategy and the 'two nations' hegemonic project, which over the medium term failed to unite the social basis of Thatcherism behind its political leaders and led to constant arguments over the party's course.

CHAPTER 8

Stabilisation: Entrenching the Advance (1988–92)

Stabilisation and Internal Conflict

Step IV of the Thatcherite offensive was marked by overall stabilisation. The neoliberal regime of condensation had become entrenched. As a result, class politics moved to the background again. Moreover, Thatcherite economic order politics had become normalised so that there was very little opposition to it anymore from the political mainstream. Andrew Gamble describes the dominant discourses at the time in the Labour Party as follows:

> There was widespread recognition that the new politics was not just a conservative politics, which could be reversed by the election of a Labour government, but reflected deep and irreversible changes in the organisation of the world economy and British society. Labour was forced to accept that the Thatcher years had permanently changed the agenda of British politics. Changes which looked irreversible included the sale of council houses and the spread of share ownership (notwithstanding the crash); the denationalisation of public sector industries; the abolition of exchange controls and the international integration of financial markets and production; the permanent contraction of manufacturing employment; and the reorganisation of work and industrial relations.[1]

---

1 Gamble 1988, p. 221. Since Gamble refrains from commenting further, it appears that he is broadly sympathetic to this view. In hindsight, there were alternatives to Labour's obeisance to the dominant orientations in economic order politics. As the economic dimension of the miners' strike demonstrates, there were substantial shortcomings in government economic policy on which the opposition could have tried to capitalise more than it did. Moreover, episodes like the strike and the early 1980s recession reveal that there were times when Thatcher governments were under serious threat. This implies that a U-turn was at least conceivable. Add to this that there were no neoliberal regime shifts in other Western European countries at the time, but at most policy adjustments, and it becomes clear that no one 'forced' Labour to accept the new status quo. Rather, the party leadership chose to do so. In sum, Gamble's assessment of the conjuncture, which mirrors the main line of the Labour Party and parts of the trade union movement, is as realistic as it is defeatist – realistic because a turning point had been reached, and defeatist because he portrayed political change as the product of developments unfolding with structural necessity rather than as the contingent (yet institutionally conditioned) result of open struggle.

In short, it was clear by 1988 that those opposed to neo-liberalism had abandoned any attempts at organising effective resistance – whether at the level of production or at the level of the political scene.

It appears a paradox that a crisis at the level of the political scene occurred at the point when the neoliberal regime of condensation had stabilised. Support for Thatcher (but not for Thatcherism) evaporated – not only within the ranks of the government and party, but also in the public at large. In the moment when Thatcherites triumphed politically, Thatcher was forced to resign and give way to Major.

Thatcher's resignation reflected a conflict over strategy and ideology in the Conservative Party that had lingered from the mid-1980s. After the ousting of the 'wets', there were broadly two currents within the Conservative leadership, who differed in terms of strategy as well as ideology: the 'radicals' and the 'consolidators'.[2]

With a hint of irony and following Rodney Lowe,[3] the 'radical' strategy can be described as 'Maoist' because just like Mao's concept of 'permanent revolution' it was based on the idea of constantly overhauling society in order to completely transform it. This can be taken further insofar as Thatcherite 'radicalism' aimed to trigger a 'cultural revolution' – even if it was a revolution in favour of the market. The 'consolidators', in contrast, advocated entrenching the achieved changes rather than continuing to push forward. The controversy between the two camps in the area of strategy was, in my terms, whether to instigate a new offensive of the power bloc or to consolidate the existing one.

Correspondingly, at the level of ideology, the 'radicals' were committed to 'pure' free market capitalism. In contrast, the 'consolidators' insisted that there was still a 'caring' element in conservatism, which was not wholly reducible to the idea that politics was about ensuring that people as individuals could pursue their ends in the marketplace.[4] Whereas the 'radicals' in principle advocated the extension of the market as a mode of social co-ordination to all areas of society, the 'consolidators' doubted that this was feasible and desirable.

The rifts reflect that the neo-Ricardian accumulation strategy and the 'two nations' hegemonic project had reached their limits. The rise of the Thatcher-

---

[2] The use of the term 'radical' is no doubt misleading, because all the Thatcherites were 'radicals' in that they wanted to destroy the institutional legacies of the post-war settlement. Hence, for 'consolidators' (a term sometimes used by the group in question) read 'flexible' or 'realistic radicals', and for 'radicals' read 'doctrinaire' or 'idealist radicals'. Despite these reservations, I adopt this distinction because it is widely known and instantly understandable.

[3] Lowe 2005, p. 359.

[4] Middlemas 1991, pp. 401–2.

ites occurred against the backdrop of the crisis of the post-war settlement. They advocated doing away with its institutional supports by smashing militant trade unionism, eradicating corporatist institutions, abolishing Keynesian deficit spending and going against state interventions in the economy. Their electoral successes were premised on uniting the City, the lower middle class and sections of the non-industrial working class behind this agenda. Yet once the rollback had been completed and the 1987 stock market crash had revealed the brittleness of promises of a quick route to wealth, it was doubtful whether the class alliance behind Thatcherite rule would hold. A majority of people still appeared to be against the establishment of a social order completely dominated by the market. Despite a decade of Thatcherite government, there remained widespread suspicion of individualist strategies of attaining wealth. The British Social Attitudes Survey of 1989 revealed that 80 percent of respondents stated that the 'gap' between 'high' and 'low' earners was too high, whilst 15 percent opted for it being 'about right'.[5] Polls also indicated that the provision of welfare services through state institutions enjoyed widespread support, and that people were willing to pay higher taxes if these were used to improve the welfare state.[6]

With benefit of hindsight, it appears that the rifts in the Thatcherite camp were caused by popular dissatisfaction with the 'two nations' character of the Thatcherite hegemonic project. The social base of Thatcherism had accepted the suspension of a hegemonic project based on 'inclusive' nationalism and its replacement by 'divisive' nationalism only temporarily, that is, as long as the government was engaged in an active struggle against organised labour. Once the Thatcherites had defeated militant trade unionism, acceptance of overtly divisive policies receded. This suggests that the Thatcherite hegemonic project was tied to a specific stage in the cycle of class struggle, namely the offensive of capital against labour.

The shifts in popular mood produced a strategic dilemma for the Thatcherites, which explained why they were divided into two camps: The public broadly favoured consolidating the welfare state and moving away from the 'divisive' nationalism of the 'two nations' hegemonic project. However, steadfastness, aggressiveness and an unwillingness to compromise were defining features of Thatcherism as a class political regime, reflecting its offensive character. Thus any fundamental change of course would have amounted to a rupture and would have threatened to transform Thatcher into the reincarnation

---

5 BSAS III, 2009.
6 Lowe 2005, p. 337.

of Heath in the public eye. The Thatcherites found themselves in a 'lose-lose' situation: The continuation of the 'two nations' hegemonic project ran the risk of undermining the social basis of Thatcherism; its discontinuation was likely to make the government appear weak and out of its depth, which would not go down well with the electorate either. In this situation, some Thatcherites advocated reinvigorating the social basis by seeking out new institutional targets for further attacks, whilst others believed popular support could only be stabilised by adopting a more conciliatory approach with a de-polarising effect. In other words, the rifts reflected the difficulty for the Thatcherites of managing the transition to a new stage in the cycle of class struggle once the initial offensive had stabilised. What followed was 'a combination of confusion, caution and contradiction',[7] which played out in two areas that became the primary political battlegrounds in the new conjuncture – the welfare state and Europe.

The principal outcome of the argument was an arrangement that did not resolve the strategic dilemma but bought time for the leading circles in the party: They decided to sacrifice Thatcher, who was aligned with the 'radical' ticket, and replace her with Major, who did not have a clear profile. The trigger for Thatcher's forced resignation was the poll tax – a piece of policy fully in line with new right ideology that was brought down by popular resistance. Against this backdrop, Major chose to fight the 1992 general elections on a 'consolidation' platform and won. But he never managed to completely ditch radicalism and make a full transition from an offensive to a consolidating step. This created a political vacuum, which would soon be occupied by New Labour.

Internal Divisions over the Welfare State

From the outset, the Thatcherites formed a radical movement in that they aimed not just to implement policy adjustments but also to engineer a regime shift. From the mid-1980s, 'consolidators' and 'radicals' quarrelled over whether change had gone far enough. Initially, their arguments mostly concerned the restructuring of the welfare state, which, with the exception of council housing, had hardly been touched by the government so far. As early as 1982, the Central Policy Review Staff, a think tank working for the Cabinet and entrusted with co-ordinating long-term strategy,[8] suggested moving to an insurance-based healthcare system and ending the public funding of higher education. These

---

7 Lowe 2005, p. 371.
8 Kavanagh 1990, p. 254; Ling 1998, p. 81.

suggestions were subsequently shelved,[9] which was in tune with the calculated caution of the first Thatcher government.

The mid-1980s brought a subterranean shift in favour of the 'radicals'.[10] This reflected the fact that the open attack on organised labour had brought unprecedented, quick advances, and that parts of the mainstream press, in particular *The Economist* and Murdoch's *Times*, joined forces with the 'radicals' by demanding that the government take things further.[11] The shift found expression in the 1987 general election manifesto. It committed a future government to 'radical Conservative reform' and announced that key sites of the welfare state would be restructured – above all, education, healthcare and unemployment benefits. The decisive victory at the corresponding elections appeared to show that the public supported this course. Yet the election result reflected quite specific conjunctural conditions. It turned out to be a Pyrrhic victory for the Thatcherite cause once the economy started to overheat. Middlemas notes:

> [T]he moment was now tied to prosperity and growth in a logic of economic management similar to that of 1962–64, so that it came to depend on fulfilling a tacit proposition that there should be few losers, no matter what the reform ... A cultural revolution can only occur in conditions of governing party unity ... On the evidence of most opinion polls, the party had not yet established its claim to represent the nation. Consequently, as a collective of MPs concerned with what their constituencies thought, it began to waver – and wavered more once the boom was exposed as unsustainable in 1988.[12]

The conflict between the 'consolidators', who, under conditions of profound public support for the welfare state, committed themselves to *Realpolitik*, and the idealist 'radicals' began to flare up again, continuing to haunt the Conservative Party until Blair took office in 1997 and after.

Despite the profound shift in the relations of class forces, perceived electoral pressures meant that the record of the last Thatcher government remained patchy in the area of welfare and public services. The only initiative that can be deemed successful in terms of fully implementing manifesto commitments was the 1988 Education Reform Bill, which instituted a national curriculum, increased schools' control over their budgets and appointments, gave them the

---

9   Lowe 2005, p. 325.
10 Jessop et al. 1988, p. 65.
11 Middlemas 1991, p. 401.
12 Middlemas 1991, pp. 403–4.

opportunity to opt out from control through local government and increased parents' 'choice'.[13]

This was still far from truly commodifying education, but it did introduce elements of a new system insofar as an internal market was created. In theory, parents could now 'shop around between local schools'[14] – a policy that tended to deepen inequality by favouring middle-class students whose parents were likely to believe in educational attainment. In practice, however, the implementation of the internal market soon hit institutional obstacles because popular schools could not easily increase their capacity. Moreover, take-up for the opt-out clause remained minuscule: by 1992, only 200 out of 24,000 schools made use of it – despite financial incentives and greater freedom for participating schools to select students.[15] The most contentious issue, however, was the national curriculum, which teachers rejected as an incursion into their autonomy and an extension of bureaucratic procedures. They even boycotted some of its provisions on tests, which led to a partial revision. Furthermore, some of the libertarians within the 'radical' camp, among them Joseph, dismissed the national curriculum on the grounds that it vastly expanded the government's capacities for central control.[16] Government Minister Rhodes Boyson spoke of 'the ultimate triumph of the comprehensive socialist philosophy, part of the command economy'.[17] Against this backdrop, Evans sees the act as an 'inconsistent ... mixture of free-market ideology and tighter state control'.[18] In contrast, I contend that this specific policy was no more inconsistent than the overall economic-political order with its marriage of neo-Ricardian economic liberalism and authoritarian state control. That said, the act had limited success in terms of restructuring the education sector on the grounds of new right ideology and did nothing to bridge the rift in the Thatcherite camp.

The changes in the area of benefits were less ambitious.[19] In 1988, child benefit underwent a freeze.[20] Moreover, the entitlement to benefits for 16 and 17 year-olds was made conditional on claimants taking part in a Youth Training

---

13   Lowe 2005, p. 361.
14   Lowe 2005, p. 363.
15   Ibid. The push for autonomous state schools is another instance of the onslaught on the local state and, more specifically, of positions of the working class within it.
16   Lowe 2005, pp. 361–2.
17   Cited in Lowe 2005, p. 362.
18   Evans 1997, pp. 71–2.
19   Compare Alcock 1999, p. 212.
20   Lowe 2005, p. 342.

Scheme.[21] Deemed 'training-fare',[22] the policy was an early version of 'welfare-to-work'. Its introduction amounted to a system change, albeit on a limited scale.[23] The systematic introduction of welfare-to-work measures did not occur until the Major government set up 'Jobseekers' Allowance'. The decision, in 1988, to transfer the provision of services from the Department of Employment to executive agencies was an outright rupture, because it removed them from direct government control and accountability, and once more revealed the authoritarian streak of Thatcherism. Moreover, it decisively weakened a state institution where the working class had been present for more than 80 years.[24]

One of the main lines of attack for Labour against the government in the 1987 electoral campaign was its handling of the NHS, which was virtually bankrupt in 1987.[25] In response, it became the welfare institution over which the fiercest arguments in the Thatcherite camp broke out. Part of the 'radical' advance was the appointment of John Moore to Secretary of Health and Social Security after the elections in 1987. Moore refused to speak of the NHS, referring instead to the 'healthcare industry'. Moreover, he advocated moving towards an insurance-based system, which was strongly opposed by Nigel Lawson, the chancellor, who argued that this would be less cost-effective than a tax-based one.[26]

Kenneth Clarke, Moore's successor, managed to formulate a plan for restructuring in 1990. However, this was opposed by the Prime Minister, whose protests were unsuccessful, indicating her loss of authority in the final phase of her premiership. The outcome of the new plan was the 1990 NHS and Community Care Act, which amounted to a compromise between supporters and opponents of the NHS. It did not introduce an insurance-based system, but instead, as had happened in education, it brought a system change within the existing framework – the introduction of an internal market. From now on, providers of healthcare within the NHS would compete with one another. District Health Authorities and so-called fund-holding GPs would purchase services for their patients from public or private hospitals. Moreover, the former were

---

21 Riddell 1991, p. 136.
22 Lindsay and Mailand 2004, p. 196.
23 Another piece of policy that foreshadowed welfare-to-work was the 1986 'Restart' programme, under which the government forced long-term unemployed people to attend interviews that were intended to make them sign up for training schemes (Aufheben 1998; Lowe 2005, p. 343).
24 Lowe 2005, pp. 344, 348.
25 Kerr 2001, p. 175; Lowe 2005, p. 354.
26 Compare Lowe 2005, pp. 340, 356.

allowed to become self-governing trusts.[27] The NHS now incorporated an element of privatised healthcare but still provided universal access and was funded through taxation. The Thatcherites had secured internal agreement on healthcare, but their measures were opposed by the British Medical Association and proved unpopular with the electorate.[28] Against this backdrop, it was no surprise that the rift running through the Thatcherite camp was to deepen further instead of being bridged.

The Poll Tax: A Strategic Blunder

The arguments over the welfare state exposed how deeply divided the Thatcherites were. The political project which transformed this crisis internal to the Conservative Party into an outright political crisis was the introduction of the Poll Tax, whose aim was to restructure the regime of location taxation on domestic properties. The Poll Tax was different from the old system, which was based on 'rates' reflecting the rental value of a property. It moved the tax base from the existence of a (possibly jointly occupied) property to the residency of individual adults, who had to pay a uniform rate that was set by local authorities.[29] Thus, it was a capitation tax, that is, a tax under which every individual was charged an identical amount regardless of their income or wealth.

The implications of the poll tax for social inequality were obvious: it had a 'negative redistributive effect'.[30] Under the poll tax system, an owner-occupier of a mansion who lived alone paid less tax than a large low-income family crammed into a small house. Michael Lavalette and Gerry Mooney comment:

> The poll tax was a clear piece of class legislation. By treating all adults over the age of 18 years as equals it attempted to reinforce the vast social and economic inequalities of wealth and power in society. The effect was to increase further the burden of paying for local welfare services on to the working class and to undermine any notion that tax should be related to income, wealth and ability to pay.[31]

---

27   Jones 1999, p. 173; Lowe 2005, p. 355.
28   Morgan 1990, p. 494.
29   Johnson 1991, pp. 135, 138.
30   Bonefeld et al. 1995, p. 157.
31   Lavalette and Mooney 2000, pp. 210–11.

Thatcher interpreted her 1987 general election victory as confirmation of the 'radical' course lined out in the manifesto. Otherwise, she would hardly have announced after the event that the 'Community Charge', as the Thatcherites euphemistically had named the Poll Tax, would be the 'flagship' of her new government.[32] There were two reasons why the Thatcherites wanted this new tax:

(1) In 1985, the conflict between institutions of the national and the local state or between the government and 'municipal socialism' reached new heights when local authorities chose to boycott the setting of rates.
(2) An earlier revaluation in Scotland had increased domestic rates and caused widespread discontent among the regional Tory constituency.[33]

In line with her 'two nations' approach, Thatcher deemed a capitation tax the adequate response. As stated in the manifesto, the expectation was that it would increase the accountability of local authorities by making taxation more transparent. It was assumed that it would be clear how many people were paying the tax, and, since tax increases affected everyone, how much local authorities were spending.[34]

Although Thatcher appeared to have won a mandate for introducing the Poll Tax through her election victory, the plan was still dividing the government along the usual lines. Lawson rejected it both on the grounds of strategy and feasibility. The Chancellor argued that it would prove both 'politically unsustainable'[35] – he expected that the population would reject it – and unworkable because local authorities would use the system in order to increase levies. He proposed to reform the 'rating' system instead.

Nevertheless, Thatcher insisted on proceeding with the measure. The Poll Tax was implemented in Scotland in the tax year 1989–90; England and Wales were to follow a year later. In hindsight, it was a political blunder. Lawson's critique was proven right. A popular movement formed against the tax; it would play a key role in Thatcher's downfall in 1990 and would force Major to abolish the new system in 1993.[36] The fact that the Poll Tax had been spelled out clearly in the election manifesto and did not appear to dent the Tories' electoral appeal reveals that the popular mood had started to swing against them towards the

---

32   Smith 1991, p. 421; compare Johnson 1991, p. 134.
33   Smith 1991, p. 421; Lavalette and Mooney 2000, p. 210; Kerr 2001, p. 177.
34   Johnson 1991, p. 138.
35   Cited in Johnson 1991, p. 137.
36   Compare Smith 1991, p. 422.

end of the 1980s. Furthermore, soon after the introduction of the Poll Tax, it emerged that local authorities did indeed increase expenditure, and that there were massive local variations in rates.[37]

Unsurprisingly, popular resistance started in Scotland, where the Poll Tax was initiated. For the average household, local taxation rose by 20–50 percent. The government reacted to local councils' use of the new tax to increase revenues by capping rates. True to its anti-democratic and authoritarian spirit, it ensured that, in the first year after the system change, this measure only affected Labour-controlled local authorities.[38]

The affected councils responded by cutting public services, which meant that a tax increase coincided with deteriorating public services.[39] This was a development that caused public consternation: After all, people were largely accepting of higher taxes as long as public services improved. The most important vehicle of popular mobilisation against the levy was the formation of anti-Poll Tax unions, which campaigned for mass non-payment. They were established all over Scotland, often with the backing of trade unionists and members of the radical left, and formed around community meetings. Apart from committing people to the non-payment of the tax, the unions gave legal advice and tried to prevent the execution of warrant sales of the properties of non-payers through direct action.[40]

The campaign was highly successful. According to estimates quoted by Mooney and Lavalette, between 800,000 and 1m people refused to pay the tax in the year after its introduction, which amounted to around a fifth of the population concerned. As the day approached when the tax was to be introduced in England and Wales, the movement spread quickly in all parts of Britain: 1,500 unions were set up across the country; eventually, 17m people refused to pay. The highpoint of popular resistance was a demonstration attended by 200,000 people in central London on 31 March 1990. It led to the 'Battle of Trafalgar' – a riot triggered when the policed attacked the crowd, which resulted in 450 arrests. According to polls, the public mostly blamed Thatcher for the violence, which reveals the degree of popular defiance caused by the tax.[41]

Thatcher's downfall was partly due to the unpopularity of the tax,[42] which once again exposed the rift running through the Thatcherite camp and the

---

37   Johnson 1991, pp. 139–40.
38   Lavalette and Mooney 2000, pp. 211–12.
39   Lavalette and Mooney 2000, p. 212.
40   Lavalette and Mooney 2000, pp. 218–19.
41   Lavalette and Mooney 2000, pp. 219–24.
42   Smith 1991, p. 422; Bonefeld et al. 1995, p. 157.

wavering of the Thatcherites between ideology and popular sentiment: Howe, Lawson and Michael Heseltine all attacked the tax publicly, whereas Major initially defended it. Once he had become Prime Minister, he changed his mind, which reflected the difficulties attached to administering the tax and the fact that the Tories lost a by-election at Ribble Valley in March 1991.[43] In the end, the Poll Tax was replaced by the Council Tax,[44] which was similar in design to the 'rates' system and was based on the value of the property occupied.

For the first time, a mass movement had managed to derail a key policy formulated by a Thatcher government. This reflected how the Thatcherite 'two nations' hegemonic project was increasingly at odds with the public mood: The episode demonstrates that the majority of people in Britain did not favour a further deepening of social inequality, which was consistent with public support for the welfare state. In turn, Thatcher's resignation and Major's wavering reflected the rift over strategy in the Thatcherite camp. Major's indecisiveness also suggests that he wanted to buy time by avoiding the fundamental decision of whether to commit the party to the 'radical' or the 'consolidating' course. This allowed him to cover up the rift and shift it into the background for a while.

At a more general level, the Poll Tax episode also reveals the stability of the neoliberal regime of condensation. Popular protest remained confined to a very specific issue regarding taxation; it did not extend to other issues, for example, industrial relations. Moreover, while it contributed to a change of leadership in the governing party, it did not challenge the latter's overall ideological orientation. As the result of the 1992 general election demonstrates, it did not even substantially strengthen the parliamentary opposition. In light of this, I contend that Thatcher's resignation actually reinforced the regime of condensation. By stepping down at this point, she confirmed the public perception that she had simply gone too far – which in turn implied that her earlier moves were acceptable.

Further proof of the normalisation of the neoliberal regime of condensation lies in the wavering of the parliamentary opposition over the poll tax. In the 1987 general election campaign of the Labour Party, the issue only figured heavily in Scotland. After Labour had won 50 seats there, some Scottish MPs felt confident enough to attack the policy explicitly. However, the party leadership under Kinnock did not pursue this further. From 1987, the Scottish Labour Party and the Scottish TUC ran a campaign named 'Stop It', which called for people to slow the implementation process of the tax by returning registration

---

43   Lavalette and Moone 2000, p. 224.
44   Riddell 1991, p. 235; Bonefeld et al. 1995, pp. 156–7.

forms with a series of questions. Yet Labour-controlled councils refrained from obstructing the collection of the new tax; in fact, they prepared for it meticulously.[45] Lavalette and Mooney comment:

> [A]t the heart of the Labour Party's campaign was a contradiction. On the one hand, the main argument by the Stop It campaign was that the tax was unworkable. On the other hand, the Party's commitment to working within the law and operating as a recognised, responsible and legitimate political opposition, at both national and regional government levels, meant that Labour councils actively sought to facilitate the smooth introduction of the tax.[46]

Once again, the Labour Party leadership resisted orchestrating the opposition to Thatcherism, fearing that it would not break into the latter's social base if it was perceived as being aligned with a militant social movement. And again, acquiescence did not pay off: Kinnock lost the 1992 election even though the Conservatives had had to change their leader and had made a major political blunder.

In conclusion, Thatcher's political weakness can easily distract from the stability of the newly established regime of condensation. Indeed, the latter was further consolidated through the very critique mounted against her: It targeted a limited area where concessions could be made without reversing the central tenets of neoliberalism.

Arguments over Europe

The poll tax was probably the most divisive policy of 'late' Thatcherism in terms of popular dissent. But the policy issue most corrosive to the unity of Conservative governments between 1987 and 1997 was European monetary integration. Given the defeats inflicted on organised labour, it was no surprise that class politics had moved back into the background and economic order politics had come to dominate debates in the Conservative leadership once more.

The arguments were over how to respond to European political leaders pushing for closer economic and political integration, and how to preserve

---

45   Lavalette and Mooney 2000, pp. 213–15.
46   Lavalette and Mooney 2000, p. 215.

British state institutions and the dominant economic policy. None of the leading Conservative politicians subscribed to the vision of Jacques Delors, the then president of the EC commission, of a United States of Europe, which was premised on the creation of a European federal entity.[47] They argued over how to preserve the status quo. Whereas the pro-Europeans believed that British interests could only be served if Britain played a strong role in the EC, the Euro-sceptics claimed that closer European integration would erode British sovereignty.

Importantly, the disagreements over how to ensure continuity in the field of economic order politics were not all there was to this debate. Conflicts over the future of Thatcherite class politics lurked behind them. The bickering over Europe exposed, once more, the rift running through the Conservative leadership as regards its mode of leadership and domination. The Euro-sceptics feared that closer integration would eventually force Britain into adopting a more conciliatory approach, which might have meant abandoning the 'two nations' hegemonic project. In turn, this was a scenario welcomed by the pro-Europeans, who were trying to formulate a response to popular discontent with the divisive effect of Thatcherite policies.

The arguments between both sides mainly played out in the area of monetary policy. There were two questions over which fierce battles emerged in the Conservative leadership:

(1) Should Britain join the European Exchange Rate Mechanism (ERM), which had been introduced in 1979?
(2) Should Britain become part of the European monetary union, which European leaders wanted to install on the foundation of the ERM?

The aim of the ERM was to re-stabilise exchange rates between European currencies after the Bretton Woods arrangement had been abandoned, and after a first intra-European arrangement, the 'Snake', had proved unworkable.[48] Re-stabilisation was to be achieved by fixing the exchange rate of the participating currencies in the Deutsche Mark (DM). The system was similar to Bretton Woods in that it aimed at establishing 'managed flexibility', which was to be achieved by allowing participating currencies to fluctuate by 2.5 percent from their respective prescribed exchange rate. The countries involved were allowed to retain capital controls to give them room for manoeuvre, but these were

---

47 Stephens 1996, pp. 108, 313.
48 Eichengreen 1996, pp. 152–60.

to be relaxed gradually.[49] The aim was to export the German Bundesbank's anti-inflationary credentials to the other participating countries and increase overall monetary stability.[50]

Callaghan decided to keep sterling outside the ERM because he feared that aligning the pound with the mark would produce deflationary pressures and weaken the competitiveness of British industry.[51] This course was continued by the Thatcher government, which was unsurprising given that it was in line with the fundamental opposition of monetarism to pegging currencies and the 'benign neglect' of the exchange rate under the MTFS. Nevertheless, the issue kept returning to the agenda. Given sterling volatility and the quiet retreat from the MTFS, leading Conservative politicians toyed with the idea of joining the ERM. However, this was rejected by Thatcher, lest it reduce Britain's room for manoeuvre under conditions of a substantial difference between German and British rates of inflation.[52]

At first sight, the disagreement seems to have been over economic order politics and how to create stable conditions of accumulation. The key issues at stake were controlling inflation and promoting British economic interests at the transnational level. A closer look reveals that the argument also concerned class politics. Leading Thatcherites like Howe and Lawson were for entering the ERM. They argued that ERM membership would force capital and labour to act 'prudently' in terms of keeping costs and wage demands to a minimum because neither side could rely on the government stepping in and responding to the declining competitiveness of the UK with a devaluation of the pound.[53] Moreover, ERM membership promised to be a means of undercutting contestations to the dominant course in economic policy:

> By confining the future direction of economic policy-making and by effectively placing it under the control of an externally defined system, membership of the ERM would also enable the government to remove key economic policy decisions from the realm of democratic control and accountability, and so thereby displace pressure over these issues away from the state.[54]

---

49 Eichengreen 1996, p. 163.
50 Kettell 2004, p. 120.
51 Stephens 1996, pp. 5, 15, 25.
52 Ironically, Thatcher, as opposition leader, criticised Callaghan's decision and complained that it would prevent Britain from exercising leadership in Europe (Stephens 1996, p. 6).
53 Kettell 2004, p. 126.
54 Kettell 2004, p. 131.

Should high interest rates during an economic downturn generate bankruptcy and unemployment on a large scale, the government could deflect the blame and hold the unions responsible for undermining economic competitiveness through wage demands. The adherents of the ERM assumed that it was an effective external means of disciplining the working class.[55] Thatcher, in contrast, stressed that ERM membership would amount to an admission that the government had failed to improve competitiveness, and that it would be unrealistic to assume that either capital or labour would bow to pressures imposed on them from the European level.[56]

Nevertheless, ERM membership enjoyed broad support across class lines: the leaderships of the City, of industry and of organised labour were all broadly in favour. The City saw it as a way to strengthen London's role as a global financial centre, and industry and the TUC – the latter now guided by 'new realist' assumptions – hoped for an industrial revival. Since ERM membership ruled out boosting exports through devaluation, the leadership of the trade union movement assumed that it created incentives for a new settlement based on trading wage discipline for investment and training.[57] Such a settlement, however, would have amounted to a retreat from the repressive extraction strategy and the 'two nations' hegemonic project, which explains why Thatcher remained hostile to ERM membership.

In this constellation of forces, the 'consolidators', some of them with one nation leanings, sensed that they had a chance to alter the course of the government. Their most important representative was Michael Heseltine. After his resignation as defence secretary in 1986, he had begun to lay out a new one nation approach to Conservative politics, calling for a revival of British industry on the grounds of German- and Japanese-style neo-corporatist 'partnerships' and Britain's full integration into the European project.[58] This suggests that behind the demand for ERM membership lurked the threat of a strategic U-turn in class politics, which, for Thatcher, a 'conviction politician', remained out of the question. Her suspicions were probably heightened by the fact that Delors, architect of the monetary union and a member of François Mitterrand's Socialist Party, intervened in the debate at this exact point. He chose the 1988 TUC to spell out his vision of a united and more socially 'inclusive' Europe – a decision which Thatcher can only have interpreted as a 'declaration of war'.[59]

---

55 Compare Bonefeld et al. 1995, p. 8.
56 Kettell 2004, p. 127.
57 Kettell 2004, pp. 126, 131.
58 Compare Stephens 1996, p. 124.
59 Stephens 1996, p. 108; compare Middlemas 1991, p. 338. In her autobiography, Thatcher

Thatcher's hostility to the idea of joining the ERM was aggravated further because it threatened to detach the government from the social basis of Thatcherism and derail the attempt to 'popularise' capitalism. Since inflation was higher in Britain than in Germany, aligning the pound to the mark would have put pressure on the government to maintain high interest rates.[60] This would have made mortgages more expensive and would have threatened the expansion and consolidation of home ownership among subaltern groups. In light of this, it is not surprising that Thatcher was prepared to go as far as threatening resignation when the proponents of membership pressed the issue in 1985.[61]

A Crisis Contained in the Political Scene

The rifts within the Conservative leadership deepened further thanks to Lawson's 1988 budget. It was presented as a 'hat trick' that consisted of 'a budget surplus, increased public spending and sizeable reductions in income tax rates'.[62] At the same time, interest rates were at the lowest level since Thatcher took office.[63] Lawson's reflationary fiscal policies stoked a consumer boom that soon proved unsustainable.[64] It became apparent that the economy was overheating:[65] There was rapid growth, a sizeable and increasing current account deficit, a significant expansion of credit in general, a considerable increase in personal debt, and a housing market bubble.[66]

Obviously, the 'Lawson boom' increased inflationary pressures – inflation reached its highest level for seven years in 1989. As the pound started to depreci-

---

refers to this event in a fairly neutral tone (1993, p. 742). But at other points in the text, her hostility comes out clearly. Commenting on a statement of Delors before the European Assembly in Strasbourg in December 1986, she says: 'M. Delors – quite a new M. Delors whom I had never seen or met before – began to speak. It was Euro-demagogy, designed to play to the prejudices of the audience, to belittle the British presidency and to ask for more money' (Thatcher 1993, p. 558).

60   Compare Kettell 2004, p. 126.
61   Compare Stephens 1996, pp. 41, 51.
62   Stephens 1996, p. 88. The reduction especially favoured people with high incomes: the number of tax bands was reduced to two, one of 40 percent and one of 25 percent. This amounted to the top rate being cut by 20 points (Stephens 1996, pp. 90–1).
63   Compare Stephens 1996, p. 86.
64   Morgan 1990, p. 496.
65   Compare Jessop undated; Middlemas 1991, pp. 272–5; Kerr 2001, p. 177.
66   Stephens 1996, pp. 89–91.

ate again, the Chancellor decided to raise interest rates.[67] Furthermore, he now tried to talk Thatcher into granting the Bank of England independence and giving it the responsibility for interest rates, which, he assumed, would depoliticise the setting of rates. Thatcher refused repeatedly on the grounds that this would amount to a government admission that it had failed to rein in inflation.[68]

Given the lack of support from Thatcher, Lawson forged an alliance with Howe at the Foreign Office aimed at once more putting pressure on the Prime Minister to accept ERM membership. They threatened to resign if she did not comply with their demand. Thatcher responded in June 1989 by announcing that Britain would join, but only on two conditions: there had to be a European Single Market without exchange controls, and UK inflation had to fall to the average of all ERM member states.[69]

This attempt to buy time failed to resolve the underlying tension, which was a reflection of diverging approaches among the Thatcherites in the area of the mode of leadership and domination. The arguments between leading Tories weakened the party and began to produce a political crisis. By 1989, the public mood seemed to turn against the Conservatives and its leader.[70] Polls predicted a clear Labour victory in a general election; the party defeated the Conservatives decisively at the European elections and also won the by-elections in the Vale of Glamorgan, Glasgow Central and Vauxhall.[71] Soon, it appeared that the erosion of support for the Tories was more than just a flash in the pan. In March 1990, opinion polls predicted a landslide victory for Labour with a lead of 23–28 points.[72] Moreover, the Tories lost three more by-elections – in Eastbourne, Bradford North and Bootle.[73]

Discontent with the Tories was surely linked to the Poll Tax episode, but fundamental economic factors were also important. By 1989, wages were increasing above the rate of inflation, and price rises in the UK exceeded those in almost all the major industrialised countries.[74] In October 1990, according

---

67 Stephens 1996, pp. 105, 121.
68 Kettell 2004, p. 128.
69 Ibid.
70 In an Observer Harris poll conducted on the occasion of 10 years in office for Thatcher in April 1989, 40 percent of respondents stated that Thatcher's anniversary was 'something to mourn' as opposed to 35 percent who said it was 'something to celebrate' (*Observer*, 30 April 1989).
71 Morgan 1990, p. 502.
72 Lavalette and Mooney 2000, p. 222.
73 Humphrey 1991, p. vi.
74 Johnson 1991, p. 281; Bonefeld et al. 1995, p. 77.

to the RPI, inflation stood at 10.9 percent, which was 0.3 points higher than in May 1979 when Thatcher took office.[75] This undermined one of the key Thatcherite claims to success in economic policy: Thatcher and her associates tended to pride themselves with having brought inflation under control.[76]

Rising public discontent reinforced disputes in the Thatcherite camp. The most visible sign of an impending political crisis was that during Thatcher's last government, she fell out with most of her key allies, among them Howe, Tebbit and John Biffen, who had been Leader of the House.[77] A statement by Biffen revealed that the arguments reflected a fundamental conflict over the 'two nations' hegemonic project. In a newspaper article in April 1989, he announced that it was time for 'change', and that the Conservatives had to be 'explicit about the virtues of a publicly financed social policy'.[78]

In July 1989, Thatcher reacted to the blackmail by Howe and Lawson. She forced Howe to resign from the post of Foreign Secretary and become Leader of the House.[79] By autumn, Heseltine raised the stakes of the infighting by attacking Lawson's monetary and fiscal policy, pressing for ERM membership, and demanding government aid for industry. A little later, Lawson finally resigned. In his resignation letter, Lawson made it clear that he stepped down over disagreements with Thatcher; and in his resignation speech, he once more advocated ERM membership.[80] In July 1990, even Ridley, one of the chief strategists of the war against organised labour and Thatcher's 'last real ally around the cabinet table', was forced to resign after making derogatory comments about the German re-unification.[81]

It was Major who took over from Lawson as Chancellor. Although he had never publicly voiced doubts about the course of the Prime Minister, once in office he proved more independent-minded than she would have assumed. Just like his predecessor, he came to adopt the view that ERM membership was the appropriate response to inflation – all the more since increasing interest rates had not decisively reined it in. Douglas Hurd, the new Foreign Secretary, was also sympathetic to Britain's closer integration into the European project. As a

---

75   Johnson 1991, pp. 74–5.
76   Compare Conservative Party 1987.
77   Gamble 1988, p. 210; Morgan 1990, pp. 494–5.
78   Cited in Morgan 1990, p. 503.
79   Stephens 1996, p. 127.
80   Stephens 1996, p. 136.
81   Stephens 1996, p. 167.

consequence, Thatcher once more had to deal with the fact that the Chancellor and the Foreign Secretary co-operated in order to achieve their aim of entry to the ERM. Her cabinet re-shuffle had not got ERM membership off the agenda – especially as there was still strong support for it among all the key social and political forces in Britain, that is, Cabinet, the Treasury, the Bank of England, the City, the CBI and the TUC.[82]

In the summer of 1990, Thatcher finally conceded defeat. By now the mood within the Tory Party had swung behind stronger participation in Europe. In the eyes of a majority of the rank-and-file, the fundamental geopolitical shifts in Europe at the time necessitated British involvement. Phillip Stephens describes the dominant attitude with the phrase 'We may not like it but we have to be part of it'.[83] In this situation, the Treasury leaked to the press a report of a meeting with Number 10, which indicated that Britain would enter come autumn. This led to a sharp appreciation of sterling, which removed Thatcher's leeway for countervailing action. Going against the Chancellor now would have meant risking a sterling crisis. In light of this, she finally agreed to Britain entering the ERM.

Thatcher's U-turn was not a change of heart. Rather, she realised that her opponents were supported by a coalition too strong to be ignored any longer. In other words, she had to concede ground to prevent them from turning against her premiership. Accordingly, she connected the British membership to quite specific conditions. She insisted on a rather high rate of entry at 2.95 or 2.96 DM, and declared this rate non-negotiable. Moreover, she secured a 6 percent margin of fluctuation for sterling, which was considerably wider than the 2.25 percent margin that all other currencies enjoyed (with the exception of the Spanish peseta). Most importantly, she remained hostile to Delors's plan for a monetary and political union, and was prepared to air her views in public. This left her isolated at a European summit in October 1990. Her abrasiveness once more turned members of the Conservative establishment against her: Hurd, Major and Howe favoured an approach premised on slowing down monetary integration and opting out if necessary, but at the same time ensuring that Britain was seen as a partner of continental Europe by adopting a diplomatic style of negotiation.[84]

Thatcher's uncompromising stance at this point was the trigger for an open political crisis. As a consequence of her diatribes against Europe, as well as

---

82   Stephens 1996, pp. 140–1, 146, 149, 163; Kettell 2004, pp. 131–2.
83   Stephens 1996, p. 154.
84   Stephens 1996, pp. 163, 168, 171–2, 177, 179, 181–2.

further by-election defeats at Mid-Staffordshire and Eastbourne, Howe stood down as Deputy Prime Minister. In his resignation speech, he attacked Thatcher openly:

> The tragedy is – and it is for me, personally, for my party, for our whole people and for the Prime Minister herself, a very real tragedy – that the Prime Minister's perceived attitude towards Europe is running increasingly serious risks for the future of this nation. It risks minimising our influence and maximising our chances of being once again shut out.[85]

The rifts over Europe had finally torn apart the leading circles in the Conservative Party. As a reaction to Howe's speech, Heseltine announced that he would stand in the annual ballot over the Party leadership.

In this ballot, Thatcher won a majority (204 to 152). However, under the statute of the Conservative Party, the result was insufficient for her to be declared the winner – a second round was required. This outcome badly damaged Thatcher's authority as a leader. Nonetheless, she vowed to fight on and declared her candidacy for the second round. At this point, *The Sun*, the flagship tabloid of the Murdoch press, turned against her, and several Cabinet members told her that she stood no chance of winning.[86] In light of this, Thatcher decided to step down, which prompted both Major and Hurd to announce their candidacies. Major prevailed in the second round with 185 votes (as to Heseltine's 131 and Hurd's 56) and became the party leader.

The political significance of the leadership challenge lies in revealing that Thatcher was no longer capable of managing the rift running through the cabinet. Importantly, it was still far from clear what would happen to the 'two nations' hegemonic project at this point. The agendas of the second-round candidates were ambiguous. Despite his credentials as a pro-European and a one nation Tory, Heseltine styled himself as a 'radical reformer' who claimed to carry the Thatcherite project further.[87] Hurd, in contrast, simply stated 'I'm a reformer', but he also used the attribute 'radical' approvingly. Nevertheless, he pledged support for state-run education and healthcare.[88] The wavering was

---

85   Howe 1990.
86   Kavanagh 1990.
87   Hastings 1990a; Owen 1990.
88   Hastings 1990b.

even clearer in Major's case. When asked in an interview whether he was a Thatcherite, his response was:

> What does that mean? And why are you people so keen to put labels on one? If you mean, am I a very strong admirer of Mrs Thatcher, do I believe that Mrs Thatcher has been an unmitigated good in terms of British politics, then yes I do. And yes, I want to build upon that.[89]

Despite this refusal to disown Thatcher, Major still tried to sell his politics as breaking with the Thatcherite hegemonic project:

> John Major yesterday pressed his claims to be the heir to the conciliatory traditions of 'one-nation' Toryism when he stressed the importance of education and the welfare state which had 'saved my life when I was a baby and saved my leg when I was in my twenties. I am a very strong supporter of the National Health Service'.[90]

The fact that the new Prime Minister wanted to be both a supporter of the welfare state and a Thatcherite indicated that, even for the protagonists, the future direction of the party was unclear.

The wavering made it unlikely that there would be a full retreat from Thatcherism. After all, none of the candidates dared advocate a clean break with Thatcher's policies. Moreover, as the winner of the ballot, Major was the candidate who had the backing of Thatcher and the 'radicals'.[91] Consequently, the 1990 crisis in the political scene remained a crisis *in* rather than *of* Thatcherism. It was not articulated with the impending economic crisis, and there was no hegemonic crisis threatening to undermine the neoliberal regime of condensation.

This analysis is vindicated by the fact that Major managed to consolidate support for the Conservatives in the following months. As the candidate of the right who was at the same time pragmatic about Europe, he alleviated tensions by taking contradictory positions. His cabinet included 'radicals', 'consolidators' and 'one nation' Tories.[92] The fact that Heseltine was asked to become a member despite his role in facilitating Thatcher's downfall amounted to a

---

89   Hastings 1990c.
90   White 1990.
91   Compare Stephens 1996, p. 187. White 1990.
92   Ibid.

revival of one nation Toryism at the top of the Conservative Party and reflected public opposition to the Thatcherite hegemonic project.

Obviously, Major's attempt to base his government on a broad coalition did not resolve the tensions, but it did buy him some time and defused some of the conflicts. The Tory leadership returned to a more diplomatic style of negotiation in European policy, which centred on securing an 'opt-in' mechanism for the monetary union, allowing Britain to join at a time of the government's choosing, as well as an 'opt-out' mechanism concerning Delors's plan for a 'social' Europe.[93]

The ERM membership mitigated inflationary pressures. Due to a fall in the Deutsche Mark, the government was able to make a series of interest rate cuts.[94] However, it was not all good news for the government. Around the same time, it had also become clear that the economy was in recession: Housing prices and manufacturing output plummeted.[95]

Against this backdrop, the government decided to agree to the Maastricht treaty, which was signed in December 1991.[96] The treaty contained provisions aimed at driving the member states towards convergence, most importantly a three-stage transition to a full monetary union. Stage (I) required the participating governments to remove capital controls; stage (II) obliged them to meet macro-economic 'convergence criteria' and established the European Monetary Institute, a body charged with co-ordinating the economic policies and the process of transition; and stage (III) was the implementation of a full monetary union under the auspices of the European Central Bank.[97]

In line with the government's premises of European policy, Major secured an 'opt-out' mechanism from the third stage and Britain's permanent exclusion from the social chapter.[98] The latter arrangement revealed that the government was intent on protecting the repressive extraction strategy instituted under Thatcher. It prevented the introduction of regulations in the areas of health and safety at work, minimum wages and equality of opportunity.[99]

Major had managed to stabilise the Thatcherite project by making several concessions to the project of European integration. These were traded for more fundamental safeguards that prevented institutional changes likely to

---

93   Stephens 1996, p. 188.
94   Kettell 2004, p. 133.
95   Stephens 1996, p. 189.
96   Stephens 1996, p. 199.
97   Eichengreen 1996, pp. 170–1.
98   Stephens 1996, p. 203; Kettell 2004, p. 135.
99   Bonefeld et al. 1995, p. 94.

threaten the neoliberal regime of condensation. As a result, the issue of Europe temporarily receded into the background. It hardly figured in the 1992 General Election campaign.[100]

The election result showed that, despite Thatcher's resignation and constant bickering within the Conservative leadership, Thatcherism was still alive. Major secured a fourth term for his party on a platform that did not advocate a rupture with the past. The entry into the ERM and the transition of the leadership offered, for sure, only temporary respite and did not bridge the rift running through the party. And yet, it averted the sudden abandonment of the 'two nations' hegemonic project, which for a time had been a real possibility – as was evidenced by the resurgence of 'one nation' Toryism under Heseltine at the end of 1980s.

Steven Kettell indicates that the ERM episode worked in favour of the Thatcherites because it delivered 'real benefits for governing authorities'.[101] In my view, this goes too far. After all, the government had to abandon the ERM only two years after its implementation, which amounted to a devastating blow to its political standing and paved the way into government for New Labour. And yet, the Thatcherites temporarily managed to contain the crisis caused by incompatibility between (a) their mode of leadership and domination, and (b) the conjunctural shift from a catastrophic equilibrium to the successful completion of an offensive against labour. Government continuity in terms of successfully fending off challenges to neoliberalism implies that 1988–92 was, all in all, a period of stabilisation. Two countervailing trends were at work: A crisis in the political scene coincided with the entrenchment of the regime of condensation.

Exit from the ERM: The Point of No Return

Against the backdrop of the recession, the pegging of the pound to the Deutsche Mark eventually proved unsustainable. The fundamental problem was that, thanks to the transition of East Germany from an authoritarian socialist command economy to capitalism, there was a boom in recently reunified Germany that diverged from the conjuncture in other ERM countries. Budget deficits, capital imports and surges in state spending created inflationary pressures in

---

100   Kettell 2004, p. 137.
101   Kettell 2004, p. 142.

Germany while the remainder of Western Europe found itself in a recession.[102]

Within a year of reunification, the Bundesbank had increased interest rates by 2.75 points in order to alleviate the pressures.[103] Other ERM member states had to follow suit in order to stay within the fluctuation margin – even though this threatened to have a pro-cyclical effect.[104] The tensions were reinforced by a series of interest cuts in the US, which were aimed at averting a recession. These caused investors to move capital from the dollar into the Deutsche Mark.[105] The resultant weakness of the dollar harmed export-oriented industries from ERM member states.[106]

The Major government initially responded by maintaining high interest rates – despite Britain being in recession. Yet in December 1991, this changed. After another Bundesbank rate increase, the government did not follow suit, which was unsurprising given the impending general election in spring 1992. This caused a wave of speculation against sterling, which pushed it down to 2.85 DM – 10 pfennigs below the rate at which Britain had entered.[107]

The pound temporarily stabilised at this lower level, but the underlying tensions soon heightened. In light of the recession, Norman Lamont, the new Chancellor, chose to introduce a 20p band of income tax, which amounted to a substantial tax cut for certain parts of the population. This decision, of course, reflected not just economic but political circumstances, namely, the impending general election.[108] Be that as it may, it failed to instigate a recovery. Tax cuts and the rising costs for benefits caused by increasing unemployment led to a substantial increase in the budget deficit, whilst wages were still rising faster than inflation.[109] Under these conditions, it became increasingly clear to those familiar with monetary policy that the Treasury and the Bundesbank were on a collision course.[110]

Further pressure on the ERM came from the political processes connected to European integration. Most importantly, the ratification of the Maastricht treaty soon ran into difficulties. In a referendum in June 1992, the Danes voted against the treaty. Since there was to be another referendum in September

---

102   Eichengreen 1996, p. 172; Kettell 2004, p. 136.
103   Kettell 2004, p. 136.
104   Compare Bonefeld et al. 1995, p. 88; Stephens 1996, p. 192.
105   Kettell 2004, p. 136.
106   Compare Stephens 1996, p. 196.
107   Stephens 1996, p. 192.
108   Compare Stephens 1996, p. 196; Kettell 2004, p. 136.
109   Kettell 2004, p. 136.
110   Stephens 1996, p. 196.

1992, this time in France, it seemed possible that the ratification would be halted altogether. This could have derailed the project of a monetary union, so that some people doubted whether it was still worthwhile for participating countries to keep their currencies within the ERM bands.[111]

In this situation, conflict re-erupted within the Conservative Party. The Euro-sceptics, now led by Thatcher, called for a halt to the ratification process. When Major refused to take up this demand, they argued that there should be a referendum over Maastricht, which he also rejected. The cabinet was soon in disarray again, with 'radicals' like Michael Howard, Michael Portillo and Peter Lilley demanding that the Treaty be abandoned.[112] This confirms my earlier claim that the transition to the Major premiership may have bought time for the Conservative Party, but did not bridge the rift dividing its leading circles.

In August, sterling weakened again, and the government chose once more to hold interest rates. It was no longer possible to disguise the contradiction between the exigencies of ERM membership and the exigencies of containing the effects of the recession. At this point, the inner circle around Major realised that they were caught in a trap, with few ways of escaping without being critically injured. The Bundesbank consistently refused to cut interest rates, arguing that as the Deutsche Mark acted as anchor of the ERM, its task was to uphold an anti-inflationary course. The French government refused to accept a realignment of currencies within the ERM, because it feared that a devaluation of the Franc would undermine its prospect of winning the September referendum. A unilateral devaluation by the Bank might have been interpreted as a sign of weakness by traders, which would have increased pressure. Raising interest rates in a recession would have highlighted the contradiction at the heart of the governments' policy and may have invited further speculation against the pound. Abandoning the ERM would have threatened to restore the inflationary pressures Britain had faced before joining, and would have been a massive political defeat for the Prime Minister and his supporters. It would have reinvigorated the Euro-sceptics and would have amounted to a public volte-face – all the more since a few weeks earlier Lamont had showered praise on the ERM in a public speech.[113]

The last open avenue for the government appeared to be the intervention in the foreign exchange markets. The Treasury raised a 10bn ECU (European

---

111   Eichengreen 1996, p. 172.
112   Stephens 1996, pp. 204–5.
113   Stephens 1996, pp. 210–23.

Currency Unit)[114] credit on the international capital markets and secured the approval of the Bundesbank for denominating half of it in Deutsche Mark. The Bank drew up a defensive strategy aimed at containing a major speculative attack against sterling, which comprised three steps. The first was to purchase pounds secretly, the second was to intervene openly, and the third – the last resort – was to increase interest rates.[115]

By the end of August, the pound had reached its ERM floor, and the Italian Lira had fallen through its floor. This triggered massive interventions by the Bundesbank to stabilise the system.[116] In early September, the reserves of the Bank of England began to dwindle because it had intervened to stabilise the pound.[117] Lamont reacted by announcing the credit negotiated with the Bundesbank, which appeared to calm the situation. A meeting of central bank governors and European finance ministers was called but achieved nothing; the devaluation of the Lira a couple of days later and a small cut in German interest rates proved equally ineffectual.[118] On 15 September, sterling again came under considerable pressure, and it was agreed that the government would react in line with the emergency plan. 16 September became known as Black Wednesday, because sterling was forced out of the ERM. After massive interventions on the capital markets, and with two interest rate rises within a day having failed to alleviate the pressure on sterling, the government announced that it would withdraw from the mechanism.[119]

The botched stabilisation procedure, which was the largest intervention in the currency market in the Bank's history, cost it $30bn in reserves. For the Treasury, it created a debt of 33bn DM at the European Monetary Fund, plus the 10bn ECU borrowed on the international capital markets. Stephens estimates the loss to the taxpayer at £3bn to £4bn. Consequently, he sees Black Wednesday as a 'failure of government'.[120]

It is beyond the scope of this text to discuss which micro-level decisions of high-ranking members of government may have been 'tactical errors' or to speculate over counterfactuals.[121] What is evident is that Black Wednes-

---

114 The ECU was a transnational currency which only existed on paper and reflected a weighted average of all currencies within the EC and, later, EU (Kettell 2004, p. 120).
115 Stephens 1996, pp. 221–2, 229.
116 Eichengreen 1996, p. 172.
117 Kettell 2004, p. 139.
118 Stephens 1996, pp. 229–35; Kettell 2004, p. 140.
119 Stephens 1996, p. 245, 250–3.
120 Stephens 1996, pp. 255–7.
121 Stephens 1996, p. 260; Kettell 2004, p. 143.

day finally undermined the Conservatives' credibility in the area of economic policy. Moreover, it led to the re-eruption of internal strife, which exploded after the event, and to the re-emergence of a crisis in the political scene.[122] As a result, the significance of Black Wednesday lies in it being the point of no return in the erosion of Thatcherism as class political regime:[123] It was obvious now that there would be no return to the Thatcherite status quo ante, and that a new stage had started in the cycle of class struggle.

Although the Conservatives would be in government for another five years, they had already blown their chances of re-election. This was because they looked incompetent and incapable of reuniting behind a common project.[124] In the words of Lamont's resignation speech in June 1993, they were 'in office, but not in power'.[125] The leadership transition may have averted the immediate abandonment of Thatcherism, but this was to the detriment of the Conservative hold over the political scene. It meant that Tory class politics remained out of sync with the cycle of class struggle: the infighting continued; it would paralyse the government over the remainder of Major's term. This in turn paved the way for New Labour gaining control of the political scene and keeping it for more than a decade.

---

122 Compare Gamble 1996, pp. 5, 21.
123 Compare Jessop undated.
124 Compare Kerr 2001, p. 182.
125 Cited in Stephens 1996, p. 287.

CHAPTER 9

Erosion: Losing Control (1992–9)

Strategic Contradictions

After the ERM crisis, the key interventions of Major's government lay in the areas of welfare and state policy. Whereas some interventions foreshadowed key planks of the Blairite agenda, others aimed at deepening the Thatcherite class political regime. Major continued to waver between starting a new offensive against organised labour and consolidating the economic and political gains made by preventing further deterioration in the living conditions of those who had lost out under Thatcher. It follows that he failed to undo the damage caused by the ERM exit, and that he created policies riddled with contradictions. Jessop gives an apt description of the conjuncture:

> [Thatcherism became] Thatcherism with a grey face ... a new government under the premiership of John Major sought to distance itself from some of the more disastrous economic and political consequences of radical Thatcherism whilst asserting its continuing commitment to the overall neo-liberal strategy – but succeeded only in magnifying the internal disputes which brought Thatcher down, in becoming identified with massive economic incompetence, and in disclosing the limits of neo-liberalism.[1]

Overall, Major administered the decline of Thatcherism by muddling through under conditions of eroding support. Unsurprisingly, he lost the general elections in 1997 to Blair. However, the change of the governing party did not mark an end to Thatcherism. It amounted to a rupture at the level of the political scene, but the incoming Labour government chose not to touch Conservative fiscal policy for another two years. Only in 1999 did Blair and the other main representative of New Labour, Gordon Brown, trigger political changes that amounted to a comprehensive break with Thatcherism. As a consequence, I argue that Thatcherism as a class political regime did not cease to exist before 1999.

---

1 Jessop undated; compare Kerr 2001, pp. 179–80.

The Erosion of the 'Two Nations' Hegemonic Project

In the area of economic order politics, the Major government pressed ahead with fortifying the regime inherited from Thatcher. The ERM exit had led to a drastic depreciation of the pound;[2] the question was now what the government's new strategy in monetary policy would be. Lamont advocated granting the Bank independence – a move that Major rejected for the fear that the public would hold the government responsible for the level of interest rates, which the government no longer controlled. In the end, the Cabinet settled for a formal target area for inflation, which was located between a 1 and a 4 percent rate.[3] It aimed to achieve this through pragmatically using instruments of monetary and fiscal policy.[4]

All in all, post-ERM monetary policy amounted to a return to the status quo ante. There was no longer a target exchange rate around which the pound would gravitate. The 1993–4 budget brought drastic cuts in interest rates and business taxes, while the income tax rose.[5] On the whole, the strategic aims of the accumulation strategy initiated by Thatcher were left untouched. The commitment of the government to low inflation plus low taxation again revealed a neo-Ricardian approach to competitiveness on the grounds of cost advantages.

At the level of the state project, the Major government deepened managerialism. The growing financial deficit caused by the recession in the early 1990s led to a re-think about how to finance public services. Lamont's autumn statement of 1992 announced the introduction of the Private Finance Initiative (PFI). The latter was based on the assumption that the funding and management of certain public services could be outsourced to the private sector if the government retained overall control. This was supposed to lead to a 'win-win' scenario: capitalists would see extra opportunities for profitable investments, the public would gain extended and improved services, and state institutions would spend less and divert fewer resources to running the services in question.[6]

Predictably, the reality turned out to be different. Matthew Flinders describes it as a 'Faustian bargain' that delivered 'short-term gains' in terms of attracting private sector investment whilst producing 'great costs' over the

---

2 Stephens 1996, pp. 274, 361.
3 Kettell 2004, p. 141.
4 Stephens 1996, pp. 268–9.
5 Stephens 1996, pp. 277, 284–5, 292–3.
6 Kerr 1998, pp. 17–18.

medium term.[7] For one, the record of PFIs in terms of efficiency gains remained patchy. Moreover, private investors could pass on the risk of investment to the state wherever projects could not be allowed to fail for political reasons. Finally, PFIs made it more difficult for state institutions to exercise control and raised issues of accountability.[8]

In sum, the exit from the ERM was followed by a phase of stabilisation in the field of economic order politics. This was facilitated by the improvement of economic fundamentals: driven by an expansion in exports, output started to pick up, while inflation stabilised at the comparably low level set by the target area.[9]

This was different in the area of class politics. The Major government chose to preserve the Thatcherite extraction strategy,[10] and the redistributive effects of the changes in taxation in the 1993–4 budget were fully in line with the 'two nations' hegemonic project. Nevertheless, with the resurgence of one nation Toryism, a force existed in the inner circle of government that toyed with building a 'productivist' agenda around which a new hegemonic project could have emerged.[11]

In October 1992, the very last chapter in the struggle against the NUM was opened, when, of all people, Heseltine, now Secretary of Trade and Industry, announced the closure of 31 of the remaining 50 pits, which meant that 30,000 miners would lose their jobs.[12] The fact that the former champion of a British industrial renewal and staunch anti-'Maoist' now proposed to finish off coal-mining in Britain and toll the death knell for the NUM shows that the Major government fully subscribed to the Thatcherite extraction strategy.

In this situation, it was significant that a broad movement against the closure formed, which not only built on a more united working class, but also won wide public support. The fact that the NUM could capitalise on popular anti-Tory sentiment demonstrates a profound shift in the public mood.[13] This was further proof that the Thatcherite offensive and its class political regime were eroding.

The movement did not alter the fact that changed legislation and the brittle organisational structures of the working class had entrenched the shift in class relations of forces triggered by the offensive of the power bloc. The protest

---

7   Flinders 2005, p. 234.
8   Flinders 2005, pp. 225–31.
9   Stephens 1996, p. 293.
10 Compare Kerr 2001, p. 185.
11 Compare Heseltine 1994; 2000, pp. 493–4.
12 Milne 1995, p. 14.
13 Compare Stephens 1996, p. 275; Cohen 2006, p. 119.

slowed down pit closures, but could not halt them. In December 1994, British Coal was privatised, with only 8,000 miners still in their jobs.[14] The defining industrial conflict of the Thatcherite era had finally come to a close; and even if it had resulted in a complete victory for the power bloc, its last chapter demonstrates that the 'Maoist' line risked uniting the working class and even causing other class groups to build alliances with it.

Similarly, the 1993 Trade Union Reform and Employment Rights Act was the latest in the series of amendments of trade union and employment laws that began in 1980 and aimed at undermining militant trade unionism. The new act abolished wages councils, introduced a range of restrictions on strike ballots, and made ballots for check-off arrangements compulsory.[15] In addition, the opt-out from the social chapter of Maastricht averted the introduction of regulations that would have strengthened the individual rights of workers.[16]

Importantly, the 1993 act was the last piece of legislation in this area in the Thatcherite era. There were few subsequent government initiatives to further weaken trade unions. This is unsurprising given that strike activity had stabilised at record lows. Then, in 1996, a major industrial dispute broke out for the first time in more than ten years in which organised labour adopted a militant strategy and won. Through a series of short stoppages, postal workers managed to fend off a management initiative aimed at restructuring the labour process and extending teamwork.[17] The industrial action, taken together with the shift of public opinion evidenced by the protests over pit closures, suggests that the shift in class relations of forces in favour of capital, which had begun in 1978, had ground to a (temporary) halt.

The continuity at the level of the extraction strategy contrasted with constant wavering over the hegemonic project. Initially, Major portrayed himself as a champion of the welfare state in general and the NHS in particular. He stressed that he aimed to create a 'classless society', and that the welfare state was an 'integral part of the British instinct'.[18] Yet his foreword to the 1997 Conservative general election manifesto struck a different chord. Here, Major presented himself as a 'two nations' Conservative in the Thatcherite mould, insinuating that people relying on welfare transfers lacked self-respect:

---

14   Cohen 2006, p. 121.
15   Shackleton 1998, p. 586; Kerr 2001, p. 185.
16   Cohen 2006, pp. 106–7.
17   Ibid.
18   Cited in Lowe 2005, p. 327.

> *We have strengthened choice and personal ownership for families, and rolled back the state from areas where it was interfering unnecessarily in our lives*. But we now have the opportunity to achieve a massive expansion in wealth and ownership so that more families can enjoy the self-respect and independence that comes with being self-sufficient from the state.

All these pronouncements were of course rhetorical interventions guided by strategic and tactical assessments reflecting the specificities of the conjuncture. From the start of his premiership, Major embarked on a pragmatic course aiming to bridge the divides within his party.[19] His cabinet contained 'Maoists' like Portillo and Lilley, as well as proto-Blairite one nation Tories like Heseltine and Kenneth Clarke, who had become Chancellor after Lamont's resignation in 1993.[20] The fact that their attitude toward the welfare state roughly coincided with their stance on the EU again demonstrates that the rift over Britain's role in Europe had a class political dimension.

The strategic centrepiece of the second Major government was the Citizen's Charter. It consisted of a programme of public service restructuring, which was set out in a White Paper in 1991 and was extended throughout the term. The charter's aim was to improve the quality of public service provision. This was supposed to be achieved by creating and publishing standards and targets; by offering redress when these were not met; by introducing complaints procedures; by carrying out inspections; and by producing league tables.[21]

The charter was neoliberal in that it aimed to restructure the state along managerial lines modelled on the private sector – for example, by defining public service users as 'customers' and by establishing internal markets.[22] Moreover, it replicated neoliberal authoritarianism by disarticulating the societal dimension of public service provision. It connected services to individual needs rather than the needs of groups or of society as a whole, thus foreclosing collective debate and democratic decision-making on the issues at stake.[23] If the focus of, say, education policy was satisfying the 'consumer demands' voiced by students and parents, then education was no longer discussed as a political issue concerning society as a whole, but instead became a technical-organisational problem only relevant to those people with direct links to the

---

19   Compare Stephens 1996, p. 187.
20   Compare Lowe 2005, p. 328.
21   Osborne and Plastrik 1998, p. 35.
22   Compare ibid.
23   Compare Bonefeld et al. 1995, p. 121; Ling 1998, p. 150.

education sectors. In other words, it was removed from the remit of general public debate and thus depoliticised.

This aspect of the charter also had a specifically Thatcherite tinge directly concerning class politics. The focus on 'consumers' covered up the question of how efficient public services were at bridging social divisions or even redressing inequality. Since the efficiency and quality of public services were measured on the grounds of 'customer'-oriented criteria, this precluded any discussion of the broader social impact of a service. Accordingly, what was passed off as an assessment of the quality of public services with a universal field of validity was in fact a highly particular assessment from a managerial standpoint derived from the private sector.[24]

An apt illustration of this process is the implementation of targets under the Charter at the Benefits Agency. These targets measured the speed and accuracy of payments, but not the rate of take-up by those entitled to them – with estimates at the time stating that £2bn in benefits per year remained unclaimed.[25] This suggests that the agency was inefficient in providing people in need with financial help, and hence in delivering the public good of alleviating poverty – but this figured nowhere in the evaluations.

In light of this, the charter might appear a 'Maoist' project. However, its introduction also amounted to a departure from certain assumptions about the welfare state that had guided Thatcher. On the one hand, it was informed by the arch-Thatcherite belief that people in the first instance were 'consumers' and not members of a society, which was at odds with one nation Toryism and its concern with 'social exclusion'.[26] On the other hand, it was also based on the belief that people were entitled to use certain public services, and that the quality of these services was a matter of concern to the government. This amounted to a break, at least at the level of rhetoric, with the Thatcherite hostility towards the public sector, which was embodied in the 'radical' agenda of welfare state restructuring after 1987.[27] In sum, the Citizen's Charter is a good example of the continued existence of a rift within government that led to inconsistent policies.

The fact that the Cabinet presided over a recession deepened the divide. The government was faced with soaring unemployment, a slump in the housing market and substantial increases in social expenditure. In 1991–2, the latter rose by 8.9 percent – a level to which budgets under Thatcher never came

---

24 Compare Bellamy and Greenaway 1995, p. 478.
25 Bellamy and Greenaway 1995, p. 484.
26 Compare Bellamy and Greenaway 1995, p. 476.
27 Compare Lowe 2005, p. 327.

close. Against this backdrop, Portillo and Lilley instigated a review of the government's welfare policy, which toyed with the idea of substantially restricting the existing commitments. Portillo introduced the Jobseeker's Allowance, which replaced the unemployment benefit. This extended the welfare-to-work approach already tested under Thatcher. Claimants now received contributory benefit for only six months, and no longer twelve, and had to prove that they were actively seeking work.[28] In 1993, Major publicly put forward the notion of 'workfare' as organising idea for the restructuring of the welfare state.[29]

This was not an attempt to inch towards a 'one nation' hegemonic project, but rather was an effort to sustain the divisive character of the Thatcherite hegemonic project by resorting to repression against those deemed unproductive. The new programme exhibited 'all the goads and few of the incentives then being deployed in parallel "welfare-to-work" measures abroad'.[30]

Unsurprisingly, the Cabinet's one nation wing remained suspicious. Clarke chose to counter the repressive and individualist stance of the programme by granting subsidies to employers who re-employed people on benefits. This foreshadowed the move to a 'one nation' hegemonic project under New Labour, which involved a broad array of 'workfare' measures that were flanked by redistribution and incentives for businesses to create jobs for unemployed people.[31]

In short, the Major government did not steer a clear course in the area of welfare provision. This is unsurprising. Polls signalled that the population favoured inclusive welfare policies, which implied that the 'two nations' hegemonic project no longer enjoyed broad popular support. Yet it was not abandoned by Major, because this threatened to alienate the 'Maoists' and split the party.

The disagreements over Europe were similar to the disagreements over welfare[32] – both in terms of their intensity and in terms of the location of dividing lines within the party, which indicates that the European question had far-reaching consequences for class politics. The Euro-sceptics – reinvigorated by the ERM crisis, the Danish rejection of the Maastricht treaty in a referendum and the French approval in another by the tiniest of margins – continued to oppose closer European integration.[33] Major only managed to have the treaty ratified in the Commons by threatening to resign over the issue. The price of the

---

28   Compare Lowe 2005, pp. 328, 334, 348.
29   Jessop undated.
30   Ibid.
31   Compare Cressey 2001, p. 177.
32   Lowe 2005, p. 328; compare Kerr 2001, 183.
33   Compare Stephens 1996, pp. 300–1.

quarrels was that the Parliamentary Conservative Party started to decompose. Stephens details the extent of disunity among its ranks:

> Between December 1992 and July 1993 the debate on the European Communities (Amendment) Bill absorbed more than 170 hours of parliamentary time spread over twenty-five days as the government battled to secure ratification of Maastricht. When earlier debates were included, the treaty consumed more than 200 hours of parliamentary time ... Each hour of the Maastricht debate sapped the authority of John Major's administration. Between twenty-five and thirty Conservative MPs consistently voted against the treaty, and another twenty to twenty-five regularly abstained. Up to forty only supported the government reluctantly and under great pressure. The rebels, with their own organization and whips, broke with all past precedent by colluding openly with the Labour Party to maximize the chances of defeating the government. With by-election defeats beginning to erode his parliamentary majority of twenty-one, Major relied on the European commitment of the Liberal Democrats to deflect more than 600 amendments.[34]

Even though Major managed to get the treaty ratified, the issue did not go away. It continued to cripple the government's efforts to retain its control over the political scene.

Major chose to continue with muddling through by now pandering to the Euro-sceptics. He did so over matters that posed a threat to the Thatcherite class political regime. In 1994, the government successfully vetoed the implementation of the EU's working time directive, under which the working week would have been limited to 48 hours.[35] Two years later, the government even considered ignoring a decision of the European Court of Justice on this matter, which would have amounted to breaking European and British law. In the end, however, it backtracked and opted to defer the issue.[36] The vigour of the government on this front demonstrates that, all in all, the Prime Minister was not prepared to really depart from the course of his predecessor.

Once again, Major's wavering did not pay off. In the ensuing years, he resorted to threatening resignation over a Commons vote once again, stood in a leadership contest against the Euro-sceptic 'radical' John Redwood and reshuffled

---

34   Stephens 1996, p. 305.
35   Compare Bonefeld et al. 1995, p. 134.
36   Compare Stephens 1996, p. 348.

his Cabinet.[37] But the underlying tension between the Thatcherite mode of leadership and domination and the cycle of class struggle persisted.

The inability of the Conservative leadership to move beyond the 'two nations' hegemonic project started to turn the public against the government. People began to warm to Labour under Blair, who shared his opponents' assumptions in the area of economic order politics, but openly embraced a one nation approach to the welfare state. This indicates that the Thatcherite class political regime was now undergoing a process of erosion while the economic-political order remained intact. The power bloc was about to make a consolidating step after its offensive had been completed.

The End Game: New Labour in Government

In the 1997 general election, support for the Conservatives evaporated. This was a result of their inability to make the transition to the next stage in the cycle of class struggle, as evidenced by the incompetent handling of the ERM crisis and the constant bickering over Europe. The Labour Party under Blair won in a landslide and gained a majority of 177.[38] Thatcherism, however, was not finished just yet. There may have been a marked rupture at the level of discourse, as is expressed in this passage of a Blair speech: 'The third way seeks to combine enterprise with fairness. To make Britain more competitive, better at generating wealth, but do it on a basis that serves the needs of the whole nation. *One nation*'.[39] And yet, the rhetorical commitment to 'one nation' did not translate into material changes during the new government's first two years. Blair and Brown left the Conservative budget plans untouched, surely in order to pander to fears in the City and the power bloc over potential U-turns in monetary, fiscal and economic policy. This meant that there was no visible effort to start building a new hegemonic project by redirecting funds to improve the living condition of disadvantaged groups. In other words, the Labour victory transformed the political scene, but it did not, as yet, extend to a transformation of the Thatcherite class political regime.

Correspondingly, many key political initiatives at the time remained mostly symbolic, for example, the incorporation of the European Conventions of Human Rights into British Law and the commitment to an 'ethical' foreign

---

37 Stephens 1996, pp. 320, 328.
38 Compare Kaiser 2005, p. 185.
39 Blair 1998, emphasis added.

policy (in hindsight one of the most misleading or at least misguided announcements by New Labour). Some other targeted areas had not been key political battlegrounds under Thatcher and Major, for example, devolution and the question of peace in Northern Ireland. That said, there was also at least one initiative that was fully in line with new right ideology. One of Brown's first decisions as Chancellor was to grant the Bank full independence – a move that had been mulled over by the Tories at various points throughout their eighteen-year reign. Considering all this, Jessop once more provides an accurate description of the conjuncture:

> What this suggests is that New Labour has assumed the task of administering the legacy of Thatcherism. This involves more than the brute necessity of New Labour's having to govern 'in circumstances not of its own choosing' (since one cannot turn the clock back economically, politically, or culturally). It means that New Labour is seeking to consolidate many of the accomplishments of Thatcherism in the neo-liberal modernization of Britain. This is nowhere more evident than in the acceptance of the Conservatives' budget plans for the next two years. This commitment might have been justified as an electoral tactic in a period when New Labour was still worried about its high tax, high spend image and its prospects of electoral victory were still uncertain. What is surprising (at least to me) is that, despite the explicit recommendations of key business and financial institutions as well as independent thinktanks, the incoming Labour Government did not declare that the economic situation was far worse than the Major Government had suggested and that, reluctantly, taxes would need to be raised. If this seems too cynical, remember that the Conservatives themselves were willing to raise taxes when necessary despite their earlier promises; and they would certainly have been willing to break their promises again, had they won the election. In failing to create space for a reforming government, New Labour has locked itself into administering the legacy of Thatcherism.[40]

The only substantial institutional change foreshadowing a departure from Thatcherism was the fact that the Blair government signed up to the social chapter immediately, with both its provisions on employee representation and parental leave.[41] This, however, happened against the backdrop of a tacit under-

---

40   Jessop undated.
41   Coates 2000, p. 130.

standing between Blair and the CBI that he would block further European initiatives for a directive making provisions for the introduction of works councils.[42] Accordingly, the impact of signing up on class politics remained limited.

In conclusion, the Blair government, in the years 1997–9, on the whole preserved Thatcherism, while sowing some seeds for an amended extraction strategy and a new 'one nation' hegemonic project. These seeds, so far, consisted in mostly symbolic interventions. The new government did not resolve the tensions that had torn the Tories apart, and it did not bring its politics in line with the cycle of class struggle as yet, but it did lay the groundwork for doing so in subsequent years. With the 1999–2000 budget, New Labour instigated more far-reaching changes and won some public support for them. The budget contained provisions for a limited redistribution of wealth to disadvantaged groups and substantial spending increases on healthcare and education.[43] It follows that at this point the force now dominating the political scene had indeed moved towards orchestrating a consolidating step of the power bloc. In other words, Thatcherism had ceased to exist as a class political regime.

---

42 Taylor 2001, p. 263.
43 Jessop undated; compare Stephens 2001, p. 197.

PART 3

The Aftermath

CHAPTER 10

The Consequences of Thatcherism

In my view, Thatcherism was a class political regime, which emerged in correspondence with a free-market authoritarian economic-political order. The Thatcher and Major governments presided over both by instigating and co-ordinating an offensive of the power bloc. This offensive was reflected in consistently implementing policies that favoured capital and disadvantaged organised labour. The Thatcherites marginalised militant fractions of the working class and implemented a repressive form of industrial relations law that exploited divisions within the trade union movement and the Labour Party, and between both. They thus re-established the 'right to manage', which amounted to the reassertion of capitalist class domination. In other words, the 1970s impasse between capital and labour was transformed into the entrenched dominance of capital. This suggests that the offensive reached a point of stabilisation – something unprecedented in the post-war era, where earlier offensives of the power bloc had been aborted.

This might sound as if the Thatcherites were highly successful, but such an assessment is too simplistic. Any meaningful evaluation of their record requires clarifying the perspective and criteria used in the process. From my angle, it makes sense to look at the successes and failures of the Thatcherites in the areas of class politics and economic order politics. This translates into two straightforward questions:

(1) Did the Thatcherites manage to preserve the dominance of capital over labour and secure capitalist class domination?
(2) Did they ensure that the accumulation of capital was stable?

In the context of my book, asking these questions is useful in two senses. First, it corresponds to my intention of reconciling the two camps in the Thatcherism debate. After all, Hall et al. mainly judged Thatcherism on the grounds of question (1), while the gang of four primarily responded to question (2). Second, an evaluation of these criteria is not conducted from a standpoint external to Conservative politics in the 1980s and 90s. In other words, they are not foreign to the stated aims of Thatcher and her associates. Correspondingly, the 1979 general election manifesto of the Conservative Party announced that a Thatcher government would seek to reverse the tilting of the 'balance of power in bargaining throughout industry away from responsible management and towards unions'. This can be read as a commitment to pursuing an effective strategy in class politics. Furthermore, the manifesto also announced that a Thatcher government would encourage 'economic growth' – in my terms a pledge to embark on a successful course in economic order politics.

It is obvious from what I have described throughout the book that Thatcher and her entourage were successful in designing and implementing policies conducive to the establishment and reproduction of class domination. They actively shifted class relations of forces by entering confrontations with militant trade unionists, changing trade union law, increasing house-ownership, and boosting the financial sector. Their interventions moved Britain from an impasse between capital and labour that had characterised the late 1970s to a situation in the 1990s in which the dominance of capital was largely uncontested.

At the same time, the Thatcherites failed to create conditions for a stable accumulation of capital over the medium term. The stock market crashed in 1987; the Lawson boom turned out to be a bubble; and there were two recessions within ten years. Besides, the course pursued by the Thatcher and Major governments in monetary policy plunged Britain into a currency crisis, which resulted in the exit of the pound from the ERM. Most importantly, they locked Britain into a finance-driven accumulation strategy, which created several serious crises culminating in the Great Recession post-2007.

The flipside of the increasing dependence on finance is the shrinking of industry in Thatcherite era: Employment in manufacturing fell by 36 percent between 1979 and 1992. At the same time, the neo-Ricardian strategy of Thatcherism fostered competition via low wages and work intensification. Indeed, by 1986, Britain had lower labour costs than any other of the highly industrialised countries. This prevented the investment needed for an industrial revival. In fact, there was a serious decline in new investment in the 1980s, which concerned the physical structure of production, research and development, and education and training.[1]

In sum, to return to the debate between Hall et al. and the gang of four, the former were right to stress successes in the area of class politics, and the latter were right to highlight failures in the area of economic order politics. This, again, suggests that the positions of the two sides are not mutually exclusive.

Obviously, one can also judge the Thatcherites against stated aims that go beyond my conceptual framework. Their 1979 manifesto announced that the primary goal of a future Conservative government was to 'restore the health of

---

[1] Nolan 1989, pp. 83, 85; 1992, pp. 4–5, 16.

our economic and social life, by controlling inflation and striking a fair balance between the rights and duties of the trade union movement'. The emphasis on inflation, of course, corresponds to the monetarist assumption that sustained growth follows on from monetary stability. Overall, the Thatcher and Major governments managed to reduce inflation and, considering the record rates in the mid-1970s, their performance in this area was not bad. Nevertheless, the data are not entirely consistent. According to the RPI, inflation fell from 13.4 percent in 1979 to 4.6 percent in 1983; with the Lawson boom, it shot up again to 9.5 percent in 1990, and was at 3.1 percent in 1997 when Major left office.[2] And yet, the question remains as to how far the reduction of inflation was due to Thatcherite policies, and how far it was the result of trends at the global level.[3] In any case, it is questionable whether inflation is a good indicator of the overall 'health' of capitalism in Britain. After all, there were still two deep recessions during the Thatcherite era and the increasing reliance on the financial sector.

As for the notion of 'fair balance', the Thatcherites did not specify what this meant for them. Thatcher et al. curtailed the rights of unions and imposed obligations on the latter which seriously dented their capacity to act – hardly an act of 'balancing'. It appears that this term was a coded way of saying that they intended to marginalise militant trade unionism. In this, they succeeded.

Yet I contend that the implicit justification for taking on the unions – that they were to blame for the 1970s crisis – was just as flawed as the belief that weakening trade unions would improve British 'social and economic life'. It is not surprising that significant numbers of trade unionists embraced militancy, given that wage restraint under the various wages policies implemented by post-war governments (a) led to stagnating or – in the case of the Social Contract – decreasing standards of living for workers, and (b) did not substantially improve the overall performance of the British national economy. The widespread union militancy reflected the inability of the industrial fraction of the power bloc to prevail over the City and enforce a productivist strategy, as well as the weakness of the institutions that could have underpinned such a move. As the unions were not the problem, attacking them was not the solution.

In sum, even if the Thatcherites managed to reduce inflation and curtail the trade unions' capacity to intervene, it does not follow that they improved

---

2 Jackson and Saunders 2012, p. 271.
3 See chapter 6.

the economic and social 'health' of British society. On the contrary, their push for the liberalisation of financial markets and their crusade against industry created the preconditions for a crisis which makes the British economy today look no less 'ill' than it did in the 1970s. A few years ago, even David Cameron called Britain a 'broken society'.[4]

Obviously, Cameron's proclamation was an act of political point-scoring that was directed against the Brown government. Yet it would be bizarre to attribute the purported deepening of 'social problems' exclusively to the New Labour governments. Richard Wilkinson and Kate Pickett mobilise statistical data to show that key 'social problems' of highly developed capitalist societies – such as mortality, obesity, teenage birth rates, homicide, low trust, weak associations between people, conflict, racism, poor educational performance among children, the proportion of people in prison, deaths due to drug overdoses, and low social mobility – are correlated with social inequality.[5] It appears that a reliable index of the 'health' of a social formation is its degree of inequality.

Accordingly, we can judge how the Thatcher and Major governments fared in terms of achieving one of their stated aims, 'restoring the social health of Britain', by measuring the medium-term development of income inequality. The statistical instrument of choice for this purpose is the 'Gini coefficient'. It consists of a value between 0 and 1, and reflects the degree of income inequality in a social setting, with 0 expressing total equality and 1 total inequality (one person earning all the money available and everyone else earning nothing).[6]

According to data compiled by the World Institute for Development Economics Research at the United Nations University, between 1961 and 1979, the Gini coefficient for the UK was relatively stable: it moved between 0.233 and 0.264. From 1979 to 1992, it shot up and reached 0.338. After that, it stabilised again at the new higher level. When Blair took government in 1997, it was at 0.336.[7] In sum, it rose substantially under Thatcher and was consolidated under Major. As a consequence, there is good reason to assume that the Thatcherites substantially worsened the 'social health' of Britain rather than improving it.

In conclusion, judged against economic and 'social' criteria, the record of the Thatcher and Major governments is poor. They installed an accumulation strategy fundamentally different from but just as flawed as the Keynesian one that had dominated the country from the late 1940s until the late 1960s. In so

---

4 BPS Archive 2008.
5 Wilkinson and Pickett 2007, p. 1965; compare Wilkinson and Pickett 2009.
6 Wilkinson and Pickett 2009, pp. 17–18.
7 WIID, 2009.

doing, they contributed to 'breaking' British society by implementing policies that drove up inequality. Overall, they did not cure the 'British disease' of 'boom and bust', a weak industrial sector, a volatile currency and entrenched inequality; far from it. They administered a medicine which might have alleviated some of its symptoms for a while, but worsened the health of the patient over the medium term.

CHAPTER 11

New Labour and the Thatcherite Legacy

According to Conservative politician Conor Burns, Thatcher once remarked that 'Tony Blair and New Labour' were her greatest achievements.[1] Her statement indicates that despite the change of the government in 1997, she believed that her policies had, on the whole, proved irreversible. This raises the question of how New Labour dealt with the Thatcherite heritage, and whether Thatcher is right to claim Blair as one of her heirs.

Against this backdrop, I argue that 'New Labour' normalised the neoliberal regime of condensation: Blair, Brown et al. preserved the existing economic-political order while establishing a new class political regime.[2] In my terms, the Blairites managed to facilitate the transition from an offensive to a consolidating step of the power bloc. They created new institutional arrangements designed to extend popular consent to the status quo. In a nutshell, Blairism replaced Thatcherism, but free-market authoritarianism remained intact.

Blair, Brown et al. triggered these shifts by exploiting popular discontent over the divisiveness of Thatcherism and building a new political platform. Their brand of neoliberalism attracted 'Middle England', that is, petty capitalists and private sector-employees with median qualifications, but it was more inclusive than the neoliberalism of the new right and won wider support from traditional Labour-supporting class fractions, that is, unionised workers and public-sector employees.[3]

At the level of the extraction strategy, the Blairites' key strategic decision was to make small concessions to organised labour while preserving the repressive trade union legislation introduced under Thatcher and Major. Their approach was to keep avenues of collective organisation for workers more or less closed while improving their rights as individuals.[4] Besides, they opened new chan-

---

[1] Burns 2008. This assertion fits with earlier pronouncements from Thatcher et al. that Britain would benefit from the absence of a big social democratic party (see above).
[2] In my view, while significant differences between the Blairite and Brownite camp may have existed concerning class politics and economic order politics, they do not warrant differentiation at my chosen level of abstraction. In the short period between Brown becoming Prime Minister and the financial crisis hitting Britain, he did not perform a U-turn away from Blair's course. This is unsurprising given that Brown was Chancellor in all three Blair governments.
[3] Compare Jessop 2004, p. 498; 2007b, p. 285.
[4] Compare Howell 2004, p. 15; Nash 2006, p. 412; Waddington 2003, p. 336.

nels of communication between unions and government. In 2004, the party leadership and the leadership of the Labour-affiliated unions negotiated the 'Warwick Agreement'. Under it, the party representatives made some minor concessions in order to safeguard union members' support in the 2005 general election.[5] In short, there was a shift from a purely repressive to a repressive-consultative approach, which brought limited improvements for working people.

One of the centrepieces of employment legislation under New Labour was the introduction of a statutory minimum wage in 1999. Richard Dickens and Alan Manning argue that its impact was 'modest' because only about 25 percent of households with at least one person working in the two lowest income deciles benefited from it.[6] In other words, its level, initially £3.60 an hour, was set so low that only a small band of people were directly affected by its implementation. The minimum wage may have alleviated downward pressure on already low wages, but its redistributive effect was small.

On the whole, legislation in the areas of employment and industrial relations law did not amount to a U-turn away from the Thatcherite status quo. The 1999 Employment Relations Act addressed the individual rights of workers more than trade unions as collective bodies.[7] Importantly, it did not annul any of the key elements of Thatcherite trade union law. It brought some improvements for workers, which, however, did not go against the spirit of the existing laws: rights to parental leave were expanded; part-time workers gained the same rights as full-time workers; work hours were limited to 48 per week; the qualifying period for coverage by unfair dismissal legislation was halved to one year; employers were barred from laying off workers because they were involved in collective bargaining, union recognition procedures, or legal strikes that lasted no longer than eight weeks; and a statutory union recognition procedure was introduced.[8] Like the 1999 Act, the 2002 Employment Act and the 2004 Employment Relations Act did not reverse Thatcherite trade union legislation. The former improved the rights of working parents; the latter extended the 'protected period' during 'lawful' industrial action from eight to twelve weeks.[9] All in all, the impact of the changes amounted to normalising the repressive arrangements installed by the Thatcherites by partially moderating them.

---

5 Compare Bewley 2006.
6 Dickens and Manning 2003, pp. 201, 210.
7 Compare Clark 2000, pp. 107–8.
8 Taylor 2001, pp. 267–9.
9 Waddington 2003, p. 340; Morton and Smith 2006, p. 409.

The 'moderating' course of the government is also reflected in its decision to partially adopt the EU working time directive, which prescribed the maximum of a 48-hour working week. This prescription was honoured by the 1999 Act, but the government was granted an exemption by the EU, allowing workers to opt out.[10] The fact that the new government created a loophole allowing employers to continue competing over work hours underscores that it did not depart from the neo-Ricardian accumulation strategy pursued by its predecessors.

Regarding the mode of leadership and domination, the Blairites instigated the transition from a 'two nations' to a 'one nation' hegemonic project. They retained the liberal approach of their predecessors to consumer credit and mortgages, thus ensuring that people could increase their living standards by going into debt. But they flanked this with several measures aimed at widening 'social inclusion', which they mostly understood as expanding 'labour market participation'. In 1997, the government launched the 'New Deal', a 'welfare-to-work' programme. Its showpiece was the 'New Deal for Young People', under which 18 to 24 year olds who had been getting the jobseekers' allowance for more than six months had to take up work or training if they wanted to retain the full benefit.[11] This went further than Thatcherite experimentation with 'workfare' because it combined coercion with serious efforts to improve qualifications. It was also more 'inclusive' insofar as it sought to address material factors behind poverty like education, and not just attitudinal factors such as the alleged unwillingness to work. Nevertheless, it preserved the focus on the individual and the authoritarian idea that people had to be forced into wage labour for their own good. Thus it amounted to the 'expanded reproduction' of a Conservative policy, not a break with it.

Two years later, there was a clear if limited rupture with the legacy of Thatcher and Major. New Labour finally dispensed with the budget plans of the outgoing Major government and raised the social wage. The 1999 budget increased spending in health and education, and expanded 'top-down' redistribution through the tax system.[12]

This occurred through replacing the family credit, a tax credit aimed at families with parents in employment, with the working families' tax credit. Under the new scheme, payments were expanded; the aim was to enable parents to start work by subsidising their expenses for childcare. This shift still did not benefit poor families in general, but poor families with working

---

10   Compare Nash 2006, p. 405.
11   Jessop 2003, pp. 139, 146; 2007b, p. 284.
12   Compare Glennerster 2001, p. 386.

parents, which followed Thatcherite ideology. Nevertheless, it improved the living conditions of beneficiaries and extended the redistribution of wealth from better-off taxpayers to the working poor – especially as income support for children was also increased by more than 70 percent.[13]

This suggests that the Blairites adopted a form of negative income tax as their chosen vehicle of redistribution: The Department of Inland Revenue paid tax credits by topping up wages.[14] This approach had a tactical advantage over using designated benefits: the transfers were hidden, reducing the likelihood of public opposition. Thus Jessop speaks of 'fisco-financial redistribution by stealth'.[15]

The fact that the new government was committed to expanding 'top-down' redistribution shows that there was a shift from the 'two nations' to a 'one nation' hegemonic project. Yet it also preserved many aspects of the Thatcherite approach to welfare and the neoliberal assumptions informing it. A good illustration of the two-pronged nature of Blairism is the approach taken by the New Labour governments to healthcare and education. On the one hand, they poured money into these areas. If inflation is factored in, government spending on healthcare during Blair's first two terms increased on average by 6.1 percent a year, and spending on education increased by 4.8 percent,[16] creating huge numbers of new public sector jobs, which strengthened the economies of the former industrial regions.[17] At the same time, the government introduced legally independent foundation hospitals within the NHS, promoted academy schools that remained formally within the state sector but were sponsored and controlled by representatives of the private sector, and raised fees for higher education.[18]

Against this backdrop, it would be a mistake to see the redistributive measures as instances of 'socialism by stealth'. On the whole, New Labour did not act decisively on economic inequality. This is reflected in the low level of the minimum wage, the restrictions on eligibility for tax credits, and the refusal to revoke Thatcherite trade union legislation, which limited unions' ability to force wages up. Further proof is provided by the Blairites' consistent refusal to limit top earnings, whether by incomes policies, moral suasion, or higher taxes.[19] Peter Mandelson, one of the architects of New Labour and Secretary

---

13   Dilnot and McCrae 2000, p. 72 and Glennerster 2001, p. 296.
14   Stephens 2001, p. 197.
15   Jessop 2003, p. 151; compare Glennerster 2001, p. 396.
16   Goodman and Sibieta 2006, p. 11.
17   Tomlinson 2012b, pp. 205, 214.
18   Walshe 2004, p. 108; Ryan 2005, pp. 94–7; Coles 2006, p. 16.
19   Jessop 2007b, p. 284.

of Trade and Industry in the first Blair government, stated: 'We are intensely relaxed about people getting filthy rich as long as they are paying their taxes'.[20] In line with this, redistribution under New Labour only had an effect insofar as they prevented a further rise in the high income differentials that had developed under Thatcher.[21] In other words, the Blairites were battling poverty, not inequality. And even this concern was not all-encompassing: The restructured welfare system was highly selective because it was mainly aimed at the 'working poor'.

The Blairite ignorance of inequality was consistent with the rhetoric of 'inclusion'. The term invokes an image of society as a level playing field that is, regrettably, inaccessible to some. Accordingly, it is associated with a 'flat' topography of the social world quite different from that suggested by 'class'. The language of 'class' refers to a specific social division of labour and group – rather than individual – differentials in access to economic resources and political institutions. In contrast to 'inclusion', it is often associated with 'class struggle', which ascribes collective agency to those in a subordinate position. Against this backdrop, Robert Taylor argues that 'Blair's repudiation of the politics of class, with which many Trade Unions were still identified, was fundamental to his ideological outlook'.[22]

In sum, there was a shift in the class political regime. The Blairites increased the redistribution of money to the working poor and granted some concessions to the organised working class (which, however, cost capital little). Herein lies the key difference between Thatcherism and Blairism. While the Thatcherites only ever made concessions out of tactical reasons and dismissed top-down redistribution, New Labour built a new class alliance that included the unionised working class. The lack of effective opposition from the power bloc to this shift underscores that the New Labour governments were orchestrating a consolidation step.

These changes coincided with continuity in the area of economic order politics. The neo-Ricardian accumulation strategy remained intact;[23] the new class political regime was compatible with it because it did not question the hegemony of the City over the power bloc. In fact, Blair, Brown et al. were keen on establishing close relations with the City and had already done so when they were still in opposition. Once in government, they did not abandon the 'liberal' approach to financial markets taken by the Thatcherites. They created

---

20   Mandelson 2008.
21   WIID, 2009.
22   Taylor 2001, p. 249.
23   Compare Jessop 2007b, p. 283.

a new regulatory instance, the Financial Services Authority, but committed it to 'light touch regulation'. As a result, the City managed to consolidate its dominant position in the global financial markets; the inflation of the entire financial sector continued and contributed to creating the conditions for the global financial crisis.

In the area of monetary policy, the first key decision of the incoming government was to implement a Tory policy proposal: the Bank became independent, which removed decision-making over interest rates from government control and from parliamentary scrutiny. Concerning fiscal policy, Brown, as Chancellor, announced a 'golden rule' that permitted public sector borrowing to rise over an economic cycle only for investment purposes but not for funding current expenditure, thus ruling out a demand-oriented approach. In line with this anti-interventionist stance, the New Labour governments pressed ahead with privatising the remaining publicly owned companies – most notably the air traffic control system – and consistently ignored calls for the re-nationalisation of the railways.[24] At the same time, there were no serious attempts to spark a revival of British industry; in fact, the industrial decline continued uninterrupted during the Blair and Brown years.

The only creative element in New Labour's accumulation strategy was the call to transform Britain into a knowledge-based economy. But even this idea had not originated in the Blairite camp. It had its roots in the 'competitiveness' agenda formulated by Heseltine during his stint at the DTI.[25] In any case, the 'knowledge-based economy' remained little more than rhetoric. The Blairites not only decided to water down the EU working time directive, but also resisted drives to make continental-style works councils obligatory under EU law.[26] In other words, they preserved the weakness of institutions inhibiting competition via 'easy' factors like wages and work hours,[27] thus avoiding the need to put pressure on businesses to improve 'competitiveness' via innovation and re-skilling.[28] This was out of step with Blair's pronouncement that 'our success depends on how well we exploit our most valuable assets: our knowledge, skills and creativity'.[29]

---

24 Jessop undated; Stephens 2001, p. 191; Glyn and Wood 2000, p. 21.
25 Compare Heseltine 1994.
26 Glyn and Wood 2000, pp. 19–20.
27 The minimum wage was an exception and covered a restricted section of the labour market.
28 Jessop 2008a, p. 32.
29 Blair 1998.

At the level of the state strategy, continuity also prevailed: Blair, Brown et al. continued with reorganising the state along managerial lines. This is evidenced not only by the extension of market mechanisms in education and healthcare. The New Labour governments also promoted PFIS and restructured the civil service.[30] Apart from that, they maintained Thatcher's and Major's authoritarian course. Both Blair and Brown chose a presidential style of government and used manipulative measures to 'spin' the public's perception of their activities.[31] In addition, they significantly extended the capacities of the repressive state apparatuses. The most important piece of legislation in this area was the 2000 Terrorism Act, which permitted the detention without trial of suspected terrorists for seven days.[32] Besides, the police were granted the right to define areas in which stops and searches could be conducted in order to prevent 'terrorist' acts. Police forces subsequently used this power in order to harass political protesters.[33] At the level of foreign policy, Blair made a capital misjudgement by sending troops to Iraq. Britain's participation in the 'War on Terror' led to mass demonstrations and dented Blair's reputation permanently.

In sum, the New Labour governments shared the main assumptions of the Thatcherites in the area of economic order politics. Blair, Brown et al. consolidated and normalised neoliberalism by preserving the framework of state institutions within which markets operated, while restructuring the way in which popular consent to government policies was achieved. In other words, they adapted neoliberalism to the popular mood swing that had occurred in the late 1980s. In so doing, they preserved the Thatcherite legacy – and, in all likelihood, did so more efficiently than a 'two nations' Conservative government could have done at this point. Thus Thatcher was right to assume that Blair was one of her heirs.

The erosion of Blairism is closely connected to the global financial crisis. Shortly after Brown had succeeded Blair as Prime Minister in 2007, the crisis hit Britain badly: The turning point was the run on the mortgage bank Northern Rock in September 2007. The crisis destroyed the economic configuration on which Blairism had thrived: a political economy built around a booming financial sector, which, thanks to PFIS, tax receipts and a strong demand for British government bonds, made it comparably easy for the government to expand the public sector.[34]

---

30 Rhodes 2001, p. 108; Jessop 2007b, p. 285.
31 Grice 2004; *The Economist* 2 April 2009; Fairclough 2000, pp. 129–32.
32 This was extended to 14 days in 2003 and to 28 days in 2006 (Jones et al. 2006, pp. 61–2).
33 Monbiot 2005.
34 Compare Coates 2009, p. 425.

Triggered by the 'subprime mortgage crisis' in the US, interbank lending had started to dry up in 2007. As a result, Northern Rock experienced liquidity problems, which in turn caused the bank run. The Brown government reacted at first by guaranteeing the deposits of Northern Rock's customers, and in the end by nationalising the bank. Once the US investment bank Lehman Brothers had collapsed in September 2008, interbank lending threatened to freeze up altogether, which posed an existential threat to banking systems across the globe. In this situation, the Brown government opted for defending the British banks at any cost. It offered to inject fresh capital into the banks and to provide short-term liquidity, as well as providing credit guarantees for interbank loans. At the same time, the Bank of England opted for expanding the money supply by buying up bonds ('quantitative easing').[35]

The most far-reaching measure was the nationalisation of banks, which concerned a substantial part of the British banking sector, including big names such as Lloyds and the Royal Bank of Scotland.[36] This was not a return to a state interventionist course in economic order politics: The government did not use the newly established body tasked with managing the state-owned banks, UK Financial Investments (UKFI), to influence their business models. The people on the UKFI board were, in large part, recruited from the City.[37] UKFI disavowed any intention to direct banks' activities.[38] In a nutshell, the Brown government saved the banks with the help of public funds, but without taking control over them.

The government's decision to embrace nationalisation represented a crisis-induced, ad-hoc measure aimed at counteracting a freeze in interbank lending. It was a form of temporary crisis management to be reversed once the British economy would start to stabilise. The result of the interventions was that public debt exploded: from 43.7 percent in 2007 to 78.4 percent in 2010.[39] This suggests that the 'contagion' had spread from banking sector to the state. Against this backdrop, the 2009 budget announced a number of tax increases, but the planned expenditure over subsequent years was only possible with serious spending cuts.[40] In other words, the government departed, in the name of crisis management, from the expansion of the public sector that had underpinned Blairism. The fate of the Blairite class political project was finally sealed

---

35 BBC News 2013; Grossmann and Woll 2014, pp. 590–1.
36 Grossmann and Woll 2014, p. 591.
37 Engelen et al. 2011, p. 194.
38 UKFI 2009, pp. 9–10.
39 Eurostat II 2014.
40 Seager and Wintour 2009.

when Brown lost the general elections in May 2010. The formation of the coalition government, and its quick adoption of an agenda aimed at shrinking the public sector to a minimum, meant that the consolidating step orchestrated by New Labour had ended.

Conclusion

The neo-Poulantzasian approach differs from other approaches to political analysis because it focuses on the class dimension. Accordingly, my account of the British political economy from the 1970s to the 1990s reveals that the 'differentia specifica' of Thatcherism lies in the fact that the Thatcher and Major governments orchestrated an offensive step of the power bloc. Furthermore, the neo-Poulantzasian approach allows for reconciling the two camps in the debate on Thatcherism: it considers both the political-economic and the ideological plane, and demonstrates that both the analysis of Hall et al. and Jessop et al. produce important insights.

My short account of New Labour shows that there is value-added in adopting the neo-Poulantzasian approach for still another reason: It allows for establishing the continuities and discontinuities of neoliberalism in Britain. I argue that Blairism is neither just another version of Thatcherism nor completely unrelated. Rather, we are dealing with two different class political regimes accompanying the same economic-political order at different stages of the cycle of class struggle, and they form part of one and the same regime of condensation. In other words, British neoliberalism is marked by continuity in the field of economic order politics and discontinuity in the field of class politics (see Table 4).

This pattern appears to be specific to Britain, which indicates that my analysis is not easily transferable into other settings. What about countries such as France and Germany, where neoliberalism was adopted in a more protracted and step-by-step manner? All this merits further investigation. Indeed, reflecting on the cycle of class struggle and its reflection in government policies in different countries leads to an interesting research agenda: a history of neoliberalism based on a comparison of the trajectory of class struggle and its impact on state institutions in advanced capitalist economies. This would not just produce genuine insights into the physiognomy of contemporary capitalism in different national settings, but would also reveal the diverse conditions of struggle for the working classes.

Certainly my account of the Thatcherite era also reveals some limits of my approach, and it would be intellectually dishonest not to name them. There are several ways in which it is selective in focus and explanatory strategy. This reflects the fact that I have chosen to adopt a particular entry point in approaching my object. In my view, providing a limited yet theoretically grounded account of a real-concrete object is preferable to labouring under the misapprehension that giving an exhaustive account is possible.

TABLE 4   The continuities and discontinuities of neoliberalism in Britain

Years	Cycle of class struggle	Class political regime	Economic-political order	Regime of condensation
1977–99	Offensive Step	Thatcherism	Free-market authoritarianism	Neoliberalism
1999–2010	Consolidating Step	Blairism		

As I have discussed in Part 1, my entry point, in line with Poulantzas's problematic, has been the question of class. I have focused on the state's role in safeguarding the production and reproduction of capitalist class domination, rather than addressing the multiplicity of relations of domination in capitalism. Of course, there are analyses highlighting the gender dimension of Thatcherism,[1] and others that focus on race.[2] And obviously, these analyses broaden our understanding of Thatcherism. Furthermore, different relations of domination in capitalism do not exist in isolation; they may reinforce or counteract each other. Indeed, Poulantzas was right to insist that the state is present not only in the constitution of class relations, but also in the constitution of race and gender relations.[3] However, he has never explored systematically the implications of this remark. Likewise, Marx's account of the CMP does not include systematic reflections on non-class relations of domination. As a result, introducing them into my analysis would have created a gap in its theoretical grounding whose closing would have merited a monograph in its own right. For reasons of consistency and feasibility, I have instead chosen to abstract from non-class domination and opt for epistemological modesty. As the term 'entry point' implies, my approach is open to the future integration of additional fields of analysis.

In conclusion, I contend that my analysis, despite its limitations, has generated important insights that have been missed by other accounts – and these have their blind spots too. To conduct research on a real-concrete topic like Thatcherism from a variety of perspectives is unavoidable, and it is hard to imagine that there is a master approach providing a coherent and complete analysis. In light of this, I hope that my observations will find their place alongside the existing materialist accounts of the Thatcherite era.

---

1 Segal 1983; Campbell 1987; Wilson 1987; Franklin et al. 1991; McNeill 1991; and Nunn 2002.
2 Murray 1986; Kundnani 2000.
3 Poulantzas 1978, p. 43.

References

Archival Material, Speeches and Parliamentary Debates

Archive of the Margaret Thatcher Foundation (Reference format: Thatcher Archive, #DOCUMENT ID#), available at: http://www.margaretthatcher.org/archive/default.asp

Blair, Anthony 1998: 'A Vision of Britain', 27 May, speech at the CBI annual dinner, available at: http://britaininusa.com, accessed 9 January 2006.

CAB130/1228: Official Committee on Coal, 1983 (MISC 57, minutes), available at: http://09b37156ee7ea2a93a5e-6db7349bced3b64202e14ff100a12173.r35.cf1.rackcdn.com/PREM19/1984/CAB130-1228.pdf, accessed 9 September 2014.

CAB130/1260: Official Committee on Coal, 1984 (MISC 57, minutes), available at: http://09b37156ee7ea2a93a5e-6db7349bced3b64202e14ff100a12173.r35.cf1.rackcdn.com/PREM19/1984/CAB130-1260.pdf, accessed 9 September 2014.

CAB130/1268: Cabinet Committee on Coal Dispute, 1984 (MISC 101, minutes), available at: http://09b37156ee7ea2a93a5e-6db7349bced3b64202e14ff100a12173.r35.cf1.rackcdn.com/PREM19/1984/CAB130-1268.pdf, accessed 9 September 2014.

British Political Speech Archive (Reference format: BPS Archive, #DD-MM-YYYY#), available at: http://www.britishpoliticalspeech.org/speech-archive.htm

The Hansard (House of Commons) (Reference format: Hansard HC, #VOL#, #COLUMN#), available at: http://hansard.millbanksystems.com/index.html

Journalism and Blog Entries

Allen, Vic 1982, 'The Miners on the Move', *Marxism Today*, February, available at: http://www.amielandmelburn.org.uk/collections/mt/pdf/82_02_17.pdf, accessed 30 September 2014.

BBC News 2013, 'What is quantitative easing?', 7 March, available at: http://www.bbc.com/news/business-15198789, accessed 5 August 2014.

Burns, Conor 2008, 'Margaret Thatcher's greatest achievement: New Labour', *Conservative Home*, 11 April, available at: http://conservativehome.blogs.com/centreright/2008/04/making-history.html, accessed 1 September 2014.

Cadwalladr, Carole 2008, 'It's the clever way to power – part one', *The Guardian*, 16 March, available at: http://www.theguardian.com/education/2008/mar/16/highereducation.news, accessed 28 August 2014.

Clark, Tom 2013, 'Thatcher's flagship policies draw mixed support at her death, poll shows', *The Guardian*, 9 April, available at: http://www.theguardian.com/politics/2013/apr/09/thatcher-flagship-policies-guardian-icm-poll, accessed 27 August 2014.

The Economist 1978, 'Appomattox or Civil War?', 27 May.

——— 2009, 'Who runs Britain?', 2 April, available at: http://www.economist.com/node/13403920, accessed 30 September 2014.

Feickert, Dave 2004, 'Arthur was right by instinct', *The Guardian*, 11 February, available at: http://www.theguardian.com/politics/2004/feb/11/tradeunions.uk, accessed 27 August 2014.

Giles, Chris and Cathy Newman 2005a, 'Painful medicine proved financial cure', *Financial Times*, 10 December, available at: http://www.ft.com/intl/cms/s/0/e6825c2a-6920-11da-b30-0000779e2340.html#axzz3BuWUkdIv, accessed 27 August 2014.

——— 2005b, 'Revealed: Truth of Sterling Crisis', *Financial Times*, 10 December, available at: http://www.ft.com/intl/cms/s/0/f886ddbe-6921-11da-bd30-0000779e2340.html#axzz3BuWUkdIv, accessed 27 August 2014.

Grice, Andrew 2004, 'MPs demand Blair ends his presidential style and gives cabinet ministers more say', *The Independent*, 16 July, available at: http://news.independent.co.uk/uk/politics/story.jsp?story=541513, accessed 20 September 2008.

Harrison, John 1982, 'Thatcherism: Is it working?', *Marxism Today*, July, available at: http://www.amielandmelburn.org.uk/collections/mt/pdf/82_07_19.pdf, accessed 30 August 2014.

Hastings, Max 1990a, '"I could win assent for the policies they are pursuing", Interview with Michael Heseltine', *Daily Telegraph*, 26 November.

——— 1990b, '"We've got to push on, and in ways which are persuasive", Interview with Douglas Hurd', *Daily Telegraph*, 26 November.

——— 1990c, '"I have a very clear instinct for what the people feel", Interview with John Major', *Daily Telegraph*, 26 November.

Haviland, Julian 1984, 'Thatcher makes Falklands links: attack on "enemy within"', *The Times*, 20 July, available at: http://www.margaretthatcher.org/document/105563, accessed 2 September 2014.

Howe, Geoffrey 1990, 'Conflict of Loyalty I fought for so long', *Daily Mail*, 14 November.

Jones, Nicholas 2013, 'Cabinet records reveal how news media was misled over power cut threat in 1984–5 miners strike', 6 August, available at: http://www.nicholasjones.org.uk/articles/40-trade-union-reporting/260-cabinet-records-reveal-how-news-media-was-misled-over-power-cut-threat-in-1984-5-miners-strike, accessed 5 September 2014.

——— 2014, 'Thatcher cover-up: MacGregor's secret hit list for pit closures', 3 January, available at: http://www.nicholasjones.org.uk/articles/40-trade-union-reporting/279-thatcher-cover-up-macgregor-s-secret-hit-list-for-pit-closures, accessed 5 September 2014.

Joseph, Keith 1975, 'Is Beckerman among the Sociologists?', *New Statesman*, 18 April.

Kavanagh, Trevor 1990, 'Maggie, you can't win', *The Sun*, 22 November.

Leigh, David and Rob Evans 2006, '"National Interest" halts arms corruption enquiry',

The Guardian, 15 December, available at: http://www.theguardian.com/uk/2006/dec/15/saudiarabia.armstrade, accessed 27 August 2014.

——— 2007, 'Blair called for BAE inquiry to be halted', *The Guardian*, 22 December, available at: http://www.theguardian.com/baefiles/story/0,,2231496,00.html, accessed 27 August 2014.

Mandelson, Peter 2008, 'Letter to the editor', *The Guardian*, 12 January, available at: http://www.theguardian.com/politics/2008/jan/12/tonyblair.labour, accessed 27 August 2014.

Metcalf, Mark 2006, '1988–1989: P&O seafarers' strike', 10 September, available at: http://libcom.org/history/articles/seafarers-strike-1988-89, accessed 27 August 2014.

Monbiot, George 2005: 'Protest is criminalised and the huffers and puffers say nothing', *The Guardian*, 4 October, available at: http://www.theguardian.com/politics/2005/oct/04/ukcrime.humanrights, accessed 30 September 2014.

Morris, Nigel 2013, '"We are all Thatcherites Now": David Cameron leads tributes to Margaret Thatcher and defends funeral costs', *The Independent*, 17 April, available at: http://www.independent.co.uk/news/uk/politics/we-are-all-thatcherites-now-david-cameron-leads-tributes-to-margaret-thatcher-and-defends-funeral-costs-8576206.html, accessed 27 August 2014.

The Observer 1989, '10 Years at Number 10', 30 April.

Owen, Geoffrey 1990, 'Heseltine's Caring Conservatism', *Financial Times*, 26 November.

Parkinson, Gary 2006, 'What deregulation did for the City's leading players', *The Independent*, 20 June.

Priscott, Dave, 1981, 'Interview with Arthur Scargill', *Marxism Today*, April, available at: http://www.amielandmelburn.org.uk/collections/mt/pdf/81_04_05.pdf, accessed 30 September 2014.

Powell, Enoch 2007 [1968], 'Enoch Powell's "Rivers of Blood" speech', *The Telegraph*, 6 November [20 April 1968], available at: http://www.telegraph.co.uk/comment/3643823/Enoch-Powells-Rivers-of-Blood-speech.html, accessed 27 August 2014.

Rentoul, John 2013, 'Thatcher divisive, half-right and "not the greatest"', *The Independent*, 13 April, available at: http://blogs.independent.co.uk/2013/04/13/thatcher-divisive-half-right-and-not-the-greatest/, accessed 27 August 2014.

Scargill, Arthur 2009, 'We could surrender – or stand and fight', *The Guardian*, 7 March, available at: http://www.theguardian.com/politics/2009/mar/07/arthur-scargill-miners-strike, accessed 27 August 2014.

Seager, Ashley and Patrick Wintour 2009, 'Deepest budget cuts since 70s to fill "£45bn hole"', *The Guardian*, 24 April, available at: http://www.theguardian.com/uk/2009/apr/24/budget-spending-cuts-alistair-darling, accessed 5 September 2009.

The Telegraph 2010, 'John Gouriet', 13 September, available at: http://www.telegraph.co.uk/news/obituaries/politics-obituaries/8000573/John-Gouriet.html, accessed 27 August 2014.

Tempest, Matthew 2002, 'Mandelson: we are all Thatcherites now', *The Guardian*, 10 June, available at: http://www.theguardian.com/politics/2002/jun/10/labour.uk1, accessed 27 August 2014.

Tendler, Stewart 1985, 'How Scargill could move the police along', *The Times*, 5 February.

Toynbee, Polly 2012, 'David Cameron's men go where Margaret Thatcher's men never dared', *The Guardian*, 17 September, available at: http://www.theguardian.com/commentisfree/2012/sep/17/cameron-goes-where-thatcher-never-dared, accessed 27 August 2014.

White, Michael 1990, 'Momentum grows for one-nation heir', *The Guardian*, 26 November.

Statistics and Surveys

BankStats, 2009: Bank of England, 'Monetary and Financial Statistics', London, January.

BSAS I, 2009: British Social Attitudes System, (x)TU power by (Y)Year, available at: http://www.britsocat.com/BodySecure.aspx?control=BritsocatMarginals&var=TUPOWER&surveyid=223, accessed 14 February 2009.

BSAS II, 2009: British Social Attitudes System, (x)NOTRUDS2 by (Y)Year, available at: http://www.britsocat.com/BodySecure.aspx?control=BritsocatMarginals&var=NOTRUDS2&surveyid=231, accessed 14 February 2009.

BSAS III, 2009, 'British Social Attitudes System, (x)INCOMGAP by (Y)Year', available at: http://www.britsocat.com/BodySecure.aspx?control=BritsocatMarginals&var=INCOMGAP&surveyid=227, accessed 16 April 2009.

Eurostat I, 2014: 'Real GDP growth rate – volume', available at: http://epp.eurostat.ec.europa.eu/tgm/table.do?tab=table&init=1&plugin=1&language=en&pcode=tec00115, accessed 31 August 2014.

Eurostat II, 2014: 'General government gross debt – annual data', available at: http://epp.eurostat.ec.europa.eu/tgm/table.do?tab=table&language=en&pcode=teina225, accessed 31 August 2014.

NatStats I, 2009, 'Office for National Statistics, BBFW/Ims21', available at: http://www.statistics.gov.uk/STATBASE/tsdataset.asp?vlnk=538&More=Y, accessed 14 February 2009.

NatStats II, 2009, 'Office for National Statistics, CZBH', available at: http://www.statistics.gov.uk/StatBase/tsdataset.asp?vlnk=7172&More=N&All=Y, accessed 16 April 2009.

WIID, 2009, 'United Nations University, World Institute for Development Economics Research, Gini', available at http://www.widerunu.edu/research/Database/en_GB/database/, accessed 16 April 2009.

Other References

Adeney, Martin and John Lloyd 1986, *The Miners' Strike, 1984–5: Loss Without Limit*, London: Routledge & Kegan Paul.

Aglietta, Michel 2000 [1976], *A Theory of Capitalist Regulation: The US Experience*, London: Verso.

Alcock, Peter 1999, 'Poverty and Social Security', in *British Social Welfare in the Twentieth Century*, edited by Robert M. Page and Richard Silburn, Basingstoke: Palgrave.

Althusser, Louis and Étienne Balibar 1970 [1968], *Reading Capital*, London: New Left Books.

Apeldoorn, Bastiaan van and Henk Overbeek 2012, 'Introduction: The Life-Course of the Neoliberal Project and the Global Crisis', in *Neoliberalism in Crisis*, edited by Bastiaan van Apeldoorn and Henk Overbeek, Basingstoke: Palgrave.

Aufheben 1998, 'Dole Autonomy versus the Re-imposition of work: Analysis of the current tendency to workfare in the UK', available at: http://libcom.org/library/dole-autonomy-aufheben, accessed 30 May 2009.

Augar, Philip 2000, *The Death of Gentlemanly Capitalism: The Rise and Fall of London's Investment banks*, London: Penguin.

Backhouse, Roger E. 2002, 'The Macroeconomics of Margaret Thatcher', *Journal of the History of Economic Thought*, 24(3): 313–34.

Badie, Bertrand and Pierre Birnbaum 1983 [1979], *The Sociology of the State*, Chicago: University of Chicago Press.

Batstone, Eric 1988, *The Reform of Workplace Industrial Relations: Theory, Myth and Evidence*, Oxford: Clarendon Press.

Beale, David 2005, 'Shoulder to Shoulder: An analysis of a miners' support group during the 1984–85 strike and the significance of social identity, geography and political leadership', *Capital & Class*, 29(87): 125–50.

Beckett, Francis and David Hencke 2009, *Marching to the Fault Line: The Miners' Strike and the Battle for Industrial Britain*, London: Constable.

Bellamy, Richard and John Greenaway 1995, 'The New Right Conception of Citizenship and the Citizen's Charter', *Government and Opposition*, 30(4): 469–91.

Benn, Tony, 1981 [1980], 'An Interview with Eric Hobsbawm', in *The Forward March of Labour Halted?*, edited by Martin Jacques and Francis Mulhern, London: NLB.

Bevir, Mark and Rod A.W. Rhodes, 1998, 'Narratives of "Thatcherism"', *West European Politics*, 21(1): 97–119.

Bewley, Helen 2006, 'Raising the Standard? The Regulation of Employment, and Public Sector Employment Policy', *British Journal of Industrial Relations*, 44(2): 351–72.

Blackwell, Trevor and Jeremy Seabrook 1985, *A World Still to Win: The Reconstruction of the Post-War Working Class*, London: Faber and Faber.

Blair, Anthony 1998, 'Foreword', in *Our Competitive Future: Building the Knowledge-*

Driven Economy, available at: http://www.planotecnologico.pt/document/competitiveness_white_paper_executive_summary.pdf, accessed 27 April 2009.

Blake, Nick 1985, 'Picketing, Justice and the Law', in *Policing the Miners' Strike*, edited by Bob Fine and Robert Millar, London: Lawrence & Wishart.

Bleaney, Michael 1983, 'Conservative Economic Strategy', in *The Politics of Thatcherism*, edited by Stuart Hall and Martin Jacques, London: Lawrence & Wishart.

Boin, Arjen, Paul 't Hart and Allan McConnell 2008, 'Conclusions: the politics of crisis exploitation', in *Governing after Crisis: The Politics of Investigation, Accountability and Learning*, edited by Arjen Boin, Paul 't Hart and Allan McConnell, Cambridge: Cambridge University Press.

Bonefeld, Werner 1993, *The Recomposition of the British State during the 1980s*, Aldershot: Dartmouth.

——— 1995, 'Monetarism and the Global Crisis', in *Global Capital, National State and the Politics of Money*, edited by Werner Bonefeld and John Holloway, London: Macmillan.

Bonefeld, Werner, Alice Brown and Peter Burnham 1995, *A Major Crisis? The Politics of Economic Policy in Britain in the 1990s*, Aldershot: Dartmouth.

Bretthauer, Lars 2011, 'Materiality and Condensation in the Work of Nicos Poulantzas', in *Reading Poulantzas*, edited by Alexander Gallas, Lars Bretthauer, John Kannankulam and Ingo Stützle, London: Merlin.

Brittan, Samuel 1985, '… and the same old problems: Thatcherism and beyond', *Encounter*, 4: 51–61.

Brown, William, Simon Deakin and Paul Ryan 1997, 'The Effects of British Industrial Relations Legislation 1979–97', *National Institute Economic Review*, 161(1): 69–83.

Browning, Peter 1986, *The Treasury & Economic Policy, 1964–1985*, London: Longman.

Bruff, Ian 2008, 'The Continued Relevance of Nicos Poulantzas' State, Power, Socialism', British International Studies Association conference, University of Exeter, available at: http://www.bisa.ac.uk/2008/pps/Bruff.pdf, accessed 10 March 2009.

Buller, Jim 1999, 'A Critical Appraisal of the Statecraft Interpretation', *Public Administration*, 77(4): 691–712.

——— 2000, 'Understanding Contemporary Conservative Euro-Scepticism: Statecraft and the Problem of Governing Authority', *The Political Quarterly*, 71(3): 319–27.

Bulpitt, Jim 1985, 'The Discipline of the New Democracy: Mrs. Thatcher's Domestic Statecraft', *Political Studies*, 34(1): 19–39.

Bunyan, Tony 1985, 'From Satley To Orgreave via Brixton', *Journal of Law and Society*, 12(3): 293–303.

Burgi, Noelle and Bob Jessop 1991, 'Flexibilization and State Strategies: Coal and the City', in *The Politics of Flexibility: Restructuring State and Industry in Britain, Germany and Scandinavia*, edited by Bob Jessop, Hans Kastendiek, Klaus Nielsen and Ove K. Pedersen, Cheltenham: Edward Elgar.

Busch, Andreas 2006, 'Großbritannien in der Weltwirtschaft', in *Länderbericht Großbritannien*, edited by Hans Kastendiek and Roland Sturm, Bonn: Bundeszentrale für politische Bildung.

Cain, Peter J. and Antony G. Hopkins 2002, *British Imperialism, 1688–2000*, Harlow: Longman.

Campbell, Beatrix 1987, *The Iron Ladies: Why Do Women Vote Tory?*, London: Virago.

Candeias, Mario 2004, *Neoliberalismus – Hochtechnologie – Hegemonie: Grundrisse einer transnationalen kapitalistischen Produktions- und Lebensweise – Eine Kritik*, Hamburg: Argument.

Christian, Louise 1985, 'Restriction Without Conviction: The role of the courts in legitimising police control in Nottinghamshire', in *Policing the Miners' Strike*, edited by Bob Fine and Robert Millar, London: Lawrence & Wishart.

Clark, Ian 2000, *Governance, the State, Regulation and Industrial Relations*, London: Routledge.

Clarke, Simon 1988, *Keynesianism, Monetarism, and the Crisis of the State*, Aldershot: Edward Elgar.

Coates, David 1984, *The Context of British Politics*, London: Hutchinson.

——— 1989, *The Crisis of Labour: Industrial Relations and the State in Contemporary Britain*, Oxford: Philip Allan.

——— 2000, 'New Labour's Industrial and Employment Policy', in *New Labour in Power*, edited by David Coates and Peter Lawler, Manchester: Manchester University Press.

——— 2009, 'Chickens Coming Home to Roost? New Labour at the Eleventh Hour', *British Politics*, 4(4): 421–33.

Cohen, Sheila 2006, *Ramparts of Resistance: Why Workers Lost Their Power and How to Get It Back*, London: Pluto.

Coles, Jane 2006, 'Fault Lines in New Labour's Education Project: Points for Intervention and Resistance', *Forum*, 48(1): 13–22.

Conservative Party 1970, *A Better Tomorrow*, General Election Manifesto, available at: http://www.conservative-party.net/manifestos/1970/1970-conservative-manifesto.shtml, accessed 30 August 2014.

——— 1979, General Election Manifesto, available at: http://www.conservative-party.net/manifestos/1979/1979-conservative-manifesto.shtml, accessed 30 August 2014.

——— 1987, *The Next Moves Forward*, General Election Manifesto, available at: http://www.conservative-party.net/manifestos/1987/1987-conservative-manifesto.shtml, accessed 30 August 2014.

Cressey, Peter 2001, 'New Labour and Employment, Training and Employee Relations', in *New Labour, New Welfare State?*, edited by Martin Powell, Bristol: Policy.

Crewe, Ivor 1988, 'Has the Electorate become Thatcherite?', in *Thatcherism*, edited by Robert Skidelsky, London: Chatto & Windus.

Crewe, Ivor and Donald D. Searing 1988, 'Ideological Change in the British Conservative Party', *American Political Science Review*, 82(2): 361–84.

Crouch, Colin 1977, *Class Struggle and the Industrial Relations Crisis: Compromise and Corporatism in the Policies of the British State*, London: Humanities.

Danford, Andy 1997, 'The "New Industrial Relations" and Class Struggle in the 1990s', *Capital & Class*, 21(61): 107–41.

Darlington, Ralph 2005, 'There is no alternative: Exploring the options in the 1984–5 miners' strike', *Capital & Class*, 29(87): 71–96.

Darlington, Ralph and Dave Lyddon 2001, *Glorious Summer: Class Struggle in Britain 1972*, London: Bookmarks.

Dickens, Richard and Alan Manning 2003, 'Minimum Wage, Minimum Impact', in *The Labour Market under New Labour*, edited by Richard Dickens, Paul Gregg and Jonathan Wadsworth, Basingstoke: Palgrave.

Dilnot, Andrew and Julian McCrae 2000, 'The Family Tax Credit System and the Working Families Tax Credit in the UK', *OECD Economic Studies*, 18(31): 69–84.

Disraeli, Benjamin 1845, *Sybil, or the Two Nations*, Leipzig: Bernhard Tauchnitz Junior.

Dorey, Peter 1993, 'One Step at a Time: The Conservative government's approach to the reform of industrial relations since 1979', *Political Quarterly*, 64(1): 24–36.

—————— 2009, 'Conciliation or Confrontation with the Trade Unions: The Conservative Party's "Authority of Government Group", 1975–1978', *Historical Studies in Industrial Relations*, 27/28: 135–51.

—————— 2013a, '"It Was Just Like Arming to Face the Threat of Hitler in the Late 1930s": The Ridley Report and the Conservative Party's Preparations for the 1984–85 Miners' Strike', *Historical Studies in Industrial Relations*, 34: 173–214.

—————— 2013b, 'The Secrets to Margaret Thatcher's Success', *History News Network*, available at: http://hnn.us/article/151496.

Douglass, David J. 1993, *Pit Sense versus the State: A History of Militant Miners in the Doncaster Area*, London: Phoenix Press.

Eichengreen, Barry 1996, *Globalizing Capital: A History of the International Monetary System*, Princeton, NJ: University Press.

Engelen, Ewald, Ismail Ertürk, Julie Froud, Sukhdev Johal, Adam Leaver, Michael Moran, Adriana Nilsson and Karel Williams 2011, *After the Great Complacence: Financial Crisis and the Politics of Reform*, Oxford: Oxford University Press.

Engels, Friedrich 1957 [1845], *Die Lage der arbeitenden Klasse in England*, in *Marx Engels Werke*, vol. 2, Berlin, GDR: Dietz.

Evans, Eric J. 1997, *Thatcher and Thatcherism*, London: Routledge.

Evans, Steve, Keith Ewing and Peter Nolan 1992, 'Industrial Relations and the British Economy in the 1990s: Mrs Thatcher's Legacy', *Journal of Management Studies*, 29(5): 571–89.

Fairclough, Norman 2000, *New Labour, New Language?*, London: Routledge.

Ferner, Anthony 1989, *Ten Years of Thatcherism: Changing Industrial Relations in British Public Enterprises*, Coventry: University of Warwick.
Flinders, Matthew 2005, 'The Politics of Public-Private Partnerships', *British Journal of Politics and International Relations*, 7(2): 215–39.
Forbes, Andy 1978, 'In the Wake of Grundwick', *Marxism Today*, December: 386–91.
Franklin, Sarah, Cella Lury and Jackie Stacey 1991, 'Feminism, Marxism and Thatcherism', in *Off-centre: Feminism and Cultural Studies*, edited by Sarah Franklin, Cella Lury and Jackie Stacey, London: Routledge.
Freedman, Lawrence 1988, *Britain and the Falklands War*, Oxford: Basil Blackwell.
Fry, Geoffrey 2008, *The Politics of the Thatcher Revolution*, London: Routledge.
———— 2010, '"A bottomless pit of political surprise"?: The Political Mystery of the Thatcher Era', *Twentieth Century British History*, 21(4): 540–57.
Gallas, Alexander 2008, 'Kapitalismus ohne Bourgeoisie: Die "Gentlemanly Association" und der englische Block an der Macht', in *Philosophieren unter anderen: Beiträge zum Palaver der Menschheit – Frieder Otto Wolf zum 65. Geburtstag*, edited by Urs Lindner, Jörg Nowak and Pia Paust-Lassen, Münster: Westfälisches Dampfboot.
———— 2011, 'Reading "Capital" with Poulantzas: "Form" and "Struggle" in the Critique of Political Economy', in *Reading Poulantzas*, edited by Alexander Gallas, Lars Bretthauer, John Kannankulam and Ingo Stützle, London: Merlin.
———— 2014, 'The Silent Treatment of Class Domination: "Critical" Comparative Capitalisms Scholarship and the British State', *Capital & Class*, 38(1): 225–37.
Gamble, Andrew 1988, *The Free Economy and the Strong State: The Politics of Thatcherism*, London: Macmillan.
Gentle, Christopher and Daniel Dorling 1994, 'Negative Equity and British Housing in the 1990s: Cause and Effect', *Urban Studies*, 31(2): 181–99.
Gibbon, Peter 1988, 'Analysing the British Miners' Strike 1984-5', *Economy & Society*, 17(2): 139–94.
Glennerster, Howard 2001, 'Social Policy', in *The Blair Effect: The Blair Government 1997–2001*, edited by Anthony Seldon, London: Little, Brown & Co.
Glyn, Andrew and Stewart Wood 2000, 'New Labour's Economic Policy', *Economics Series Working Papers*, 49, Oxford: University of Oxford.
Goodman, Alissa and Luke Sibieta 2006, 'Public Spending on Education in the UK', *IFS Briefing Note No. 71*, London: Institute for Fiscal Studies.
Goodman, Geoffrey 1985, *The Miners' Strike*, London: Pluto Press.
Gramsci, Antonio 1971, *Selections from the Prison Notebooks of Antonio Gramsci*, London: Lawrence & Wishart.
Gray, Robert 1983, 'The Falklands Factor', in *The Politics of Thatcherism*, edited by Stuart Hall and Martin Jacques, London: Lawrence & Wishart.

Green, Ewen 1999, 'Thatcherism: An Historical Perspective', *Transactions of the Royal Historical Society*, 6(9): 17–42.

Grossmann, Emiliano and Cornelia Woll 2014, 'Saving the Banks: The Political Economy of Bail-Outs', *Comparative Political Studies*, 47(4): 574–600.

Hain, Peter 1986, *Political Strikes: The State and Trade Unionism in Britain*, London: Penguin.

Hall, Stuart 1983a, 'The Great Moving Right Show', in *The Politics of Thatcherism*, edited by Stuart Hall and Martin Jacques, London: Lawrence & Wishart.

―――― 1983b, 'The Little Caesars of Social Democracy', in *The Politics of Thatcherism*, edited by Stuart Hall and Martin Jacques, London: Lawrence & Wishart.

―――― 1988a, 'Authoritarian Populism', in *Thatcherism: A Tale of Two Nations*, edited by Bob Jessop, Kevin Bonnett, Simon Bromley and Tom Ling, Cambridge: Polity.

―――― 1988b, *The Hard Road to Renewal: Thatcherism and the Crisis of the Left*, London: Verso.

―――― 2004, 'New Labours doppelte Kehrtwende', *Das Argument*, 46(3/4): 483–93.

―――― 2005, 'New Labour's Double Shuffle', *The Review of Education, Pedagogy, and Cultural Studies*, 27(4): 319–35.

Hall, Stuart, Chas Critcher, Tony Jefferson, John Clarke and Brian Roberts 1978, *Policing the Crisis: Mugging, the State, and Law and Order*, Houndmills: Macmillan.

Hall, Stuart and Martin Jacques 1983, 'Introduction', in *The Politics of Thatcherism*, edited by Stuart Hall and Martin Jacques, London: Lawrence & Wishart.

Hamilton, Adrian 1986, *The Financial Revolution: The Big Bang Worldwide*, Harmondsworth: Viking.

Harvey, David 2011, 'Roepke Lecture in Economic Sociology: Crises, Geographic Disruptions and the Uneven Development of Political Responses', *Economic Geography*, 87(1): 1–22.

Hay, Colin 1992, 'Housing Policy in Transition: From the Post-War Settlement to a "Thatcherite" hegemony', *Capital & Class*, 16(46): 25–64.

―――― 1996a, 'Narrating Crisis: The Discursive Construction of the "Winter of Discontent"', *Sociology*, 30(2): 253–77.

―――― 1996b, *Re-Stating Social and Political Change*, Buckingham: Open University Press.

―――― 2007, 'Whatever Happened to Thatcherism?', *Political Studies Review*, 5(2): 183–201.

Hay, Colin and Stephen Farrall 2011, 'Establishing the Ontological Status of Thatcherism by Gauging Its "Periodisability": Towards a "Cascade Theory" of Public Policy Radicalism', *British Journal of Politics and International Relations*, 13(4): 439–58.

Heseltine, Michael 1994, 'Competitiveness: What, why and how?', *European Business Journal*, 6(3): 8–15.

―――― 2000, *Life in the Jungle: My Autobiography*, London: Hodder & Stoughton.

REFERENCES 301

Hill, Christopher 1952, 'Puritans and the Poor', *Past & Present*, 1(2): 32–50.

Hirsch, Joachim 1998, *Vom Sicherheits- zum nationalen Wettbewerbsstaat*, Berlin: ID-Verlag.

Hobsbawm, Eric J. 1968, *Industry and Empire*, Harmondsworth: Penguin.

——— 1981 [1978], 'The Forward March of Labour Halted?', in *The Forward March of Labour Halted?*, edited by Martin Jacques and Francis Mulhern, London: NLB.

——— 1983, 'Falklands Fallout', in *The Politics of Thatcherism*, edited by Stuart Hall and Martin Jacques, London: Lawrence & Wishart.

——— 1989, 'Another Forward March Halted', *Marxism Today*, October: 14–19.

Howell, Chris 2004, 'Is there a Third Way for Industrial Relations?', *British Journal of Industrial Relations*, 42(1): 1–22.

——— 2005, *Trade Unions and the State: The Construction of Industrial Relations Institutions in Britain, 1890–2000*, Princeton, NJ: Princeton University Press.

Howell, David 2012, 'Defiant Dominoes: Working Miners and the 1984–5 Strike', in *Making Thatcher's Britain*, edited by Ben Jackson and Robert Saunders, Cambridge: Cambridge University Press.

Humphrey, Richard 1991, 'A Very British Coup?', in *The Downfall of Thatcher – the End of Thatcherism?* edited by Anette Brinkmann, Richard Humphrey, Hans Kastendiek, Jeanette Nörling and Michael Schickerling, Giessen: Anglistik-Institut der Justus-Liebig-Universität.

Hunter, Bill 1994, *They Knew Why They Fought: Unofficial Struggles and Leadership on the Docks 1945–1989*, London: Index.

Hyman, Richard 1985, 'Reflections on the Mining Strike', *Socialist Register*, 22: 330–54.

——— 1987a, 'Unemployment and Trade Unions in Britain: The Politics of Industrial Relations in the Crisis', in *Unemployment: Theory, Policy and Structure*, edited by Peder J. Pedersen and Reinhard Lund, Berlin: Walter De Gruyter.

——— 1987b, 'Trade Unions and the Law: Papering Over the Cracks?', *Capital & Class*, 11(1): 93–113.

——— 2001, *Understanding European Trade Unionism: Between Market, Class and Society*, London: Sage.

Ingham, Geoffrey 1984, *Capitalism Divided? The City and Industry in British Social Development*, Basingstoke: Macmillan.

——— 2002, 'Shock Therapy in the City', *New Left Review* II/3(14): 152–8.

Jackson, Ben and Robert Saunders (eds.) 2012, *Making Thatcher's Britain*, Cambridge: Cambridge University Press.

Jacques, Martin 1983, 'Thatcherism: Breaking Out of the Impasse', in *The Politics of Thatcherism*, edited by Stuart Hall and Martin Jacques, London: Lawrence & Wishart.

Jacques, Martin and Francis Mulhern (eds.) 1981, *The Forward March of Labour Halted?*, London: New Left Books.

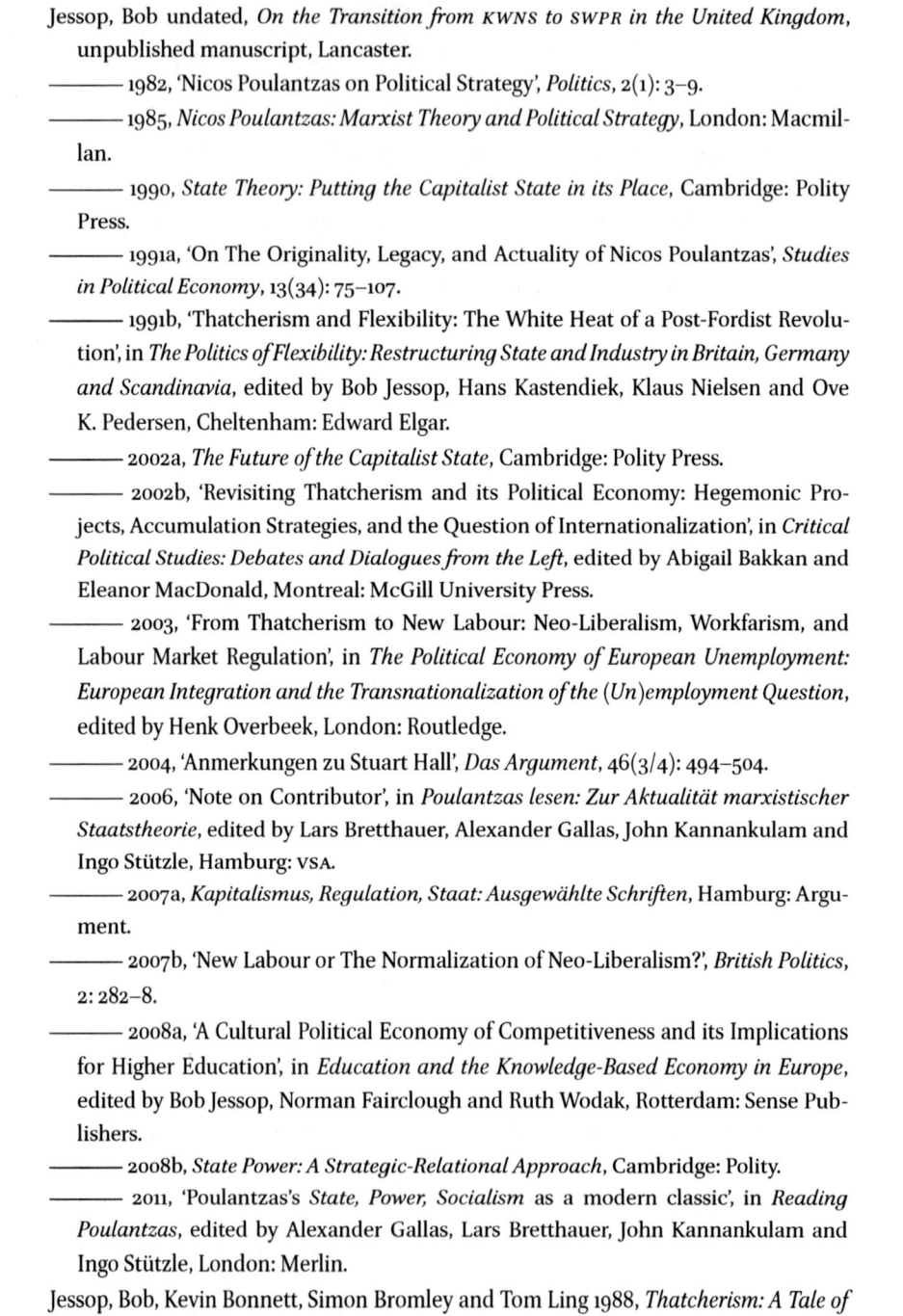

Jessop, Bob undated, *On the Transition from KWNS to SWPR in the United Kingdom*, unpublished manuscript, Lancaster.

―――― 1982, 'Nicos Poulantzas on Political Strategy', *Politics*, 2(1): 3–9.

―――― 1985, *Nicos Poulantzas: Marxist Theory and Political Strategy*, London: Macmillan.

―――― 1990, *State Theory: Putting the Capitalist State in its Place*, Cambridge: Polity Press.

―――― 1991a, 'On The Originality, Legacy, and Actuality of Nicos Poulantzas', *Studies in Political Economy*, 13(34): 75–107.

―――― 1991b, 'Thatcherism and Flexibility: The White Heat of a Post-Fordist Revolution', in *The Politics of Flexibility: Restructuring State and Industry in Britain, Germany and Scandinavia*, edited by Bob Jessop, Hans Kastendiek, Klaus Nielsen and Ove K. Pedersen, Cheltenham: Edward Elgar.

―――― 2002a, *The Future of the Capitalist State*, Cambridge: Polity Press.

―――― 2002b, 'Revisiting Thatcherism and its Political Economy: Hegemonic Projects, Accumulation Strategies, and the Question of Internationalization', in *Critical Political Studies: Debates and Dialogues from the Left*, edited by Abigail Bakkan and Eleanor MacDonald, Montreal: McGill University Press.

―――― 2003, 'From Thatcherism to New Labour: Neo-Liberalism, Workfarism, and Labour Market Regulation', in *The Political Economy of European Unemployment: European Integration and the Transnationalization of the (Un)employment Question*, edited by Henk Overbeek, London: Routledge.

―――― 2004, 'Anmerkungen zu Stuart Hall', *Das Argument*, 46(3/4): 494–504.

―――― 2006, 'Note on Contributor', in *Poulantzas lesen: Zur Aktualität marxistischer Staatstheorie*, edited by Lars Bretthauer, Alexander Gallas, John Kannankulam and Ingo Stützle, Hamburg: VSA.

―――― 2007a, *Kapitalismus, Regulation, Staat: Ausgewählte Schriften*, Hamburg: Argument.

―――― 2007b, 'New Labour or The Normalization of Neo-Liberalism?', *British Politics*, 2: 282–8.

―――― 2008a, 'A Cultural Political Economy of Competitiveness and its Implications for Higher Education', in *Education and the Knowledge-Based Economy in Europe*, edited by Bob Jessop, Norman Fairclough and Ruth Wodak, Rotterdam: Sense Publishers.

―――― 2008b, *State Power: A Strategic-Relational Approach*, Cambridge: Polity.

―――― 2011, 'Poulantzas's *State, Power, Socialism* as a modern classic', in *Reading Poulantzas*, edited by Alexander Gallas, Lars Bretthauer, John Kannankulam and Ingo Stützle, London: Merlin.

Jessop, Bob, Kevin Bonnett, Simon Bromley and Tom Ling 1988, *Thatcherism: A Tale of Two Nations*, Cambridge: Polity.

Jessop, Bob, Kevin Bonnett and Simon Bromley 1990, 'Farewell to Thatcherism? Neo-Liberalism and "New Times"', *New Left Review* I/31(179): 81–101.

Jessop, Bob and Rob Stones 1992, 'Old City and New Times: Economic and Political Aspects of Deregulation', in *Global Finance and Urban Living: A Study of Metropolitan Change*, edited by Leslie Budd and Sam Ehimster, London: Routledge.

Johnson, Christopher 1991, *The Economy Under Mrs Thatcher, 1979–1990*, Harmondsworth: Penguin.

Jones, Alun, Rupert Bowers and Hugo D. Lodge 2006, *The Blackstone Guide to the Terrorism Act 2006*, Oxford: Oxford University Press.

Jones, Helen 1999, 'Health', in *British Social Welfare in the Twentieth Century*, edited by Robert M. Page and Richard Silburn, Basingstoke: Palgrave.

Kaiser, André 2006, 'Parteien und Wahlen', in *Länderbericht Großbritannien*, edited by Hans Kastendiek and Roland Sturm, Bonn: Bundeszentrale für politische Bildung.

Kannankulam, John 2008, *Autoritärer Etatismus im Neoliberalismus: Zur Staatstheorie von Nicos Poulantzas*, Hamburg: VSA.

Kavanagh, Dennis 1990, *Thatcherism and British Politics: The End of Consensus?* Oxford: Oxford University Press.

Kelly, John 1990, 'British Trade Unionism 1979–89: Change, Continuity and Contradictions', *Work Employment & Society*, 4(5): 29–65.

Kerr, Derek 1998, 'The PFI Miracle', *Capital & Class*, 22(64): 17–25.

Kerr, Peter 2001, *Postwar British Politics: From Conflict to Consensus*, London: Routledge.

Kettell, Steven 2004, *The Political Economy of Exchange Rate Policy-Making: From the Gold Standard to the Euro*, Basingstoke: Palgrave.

Kettle, Martin 1985, 'The National Reporting Centre and the 1984 Miners' Strike', in *Policing the Miners' Strike*, edited by Bob Fine and Robert Millar, London: Lawrence & Wishart.

Khabaz, David V. 2006, *Manufactured Schema: Thatcher, the Miners and the Culture Industry*, Leicester: Matador.

King, Anthony 1988, 'Margaret Thatcher as a Political Leader', in *Thatcherism*, edited by Robert Skidelsky. London: Chatto & Windus.

Konzelman, Suzanne, Marc Fovargue-Davies and Frank Wilkinson 2013, 'Thatcherism: "A heavy hand and a light touch"', in *Banking Systems in the Crisis: The Faces of Liberal Capitalism*, edited by Suzanne Konzelman and Marc Fovargue-Davies, London: Routledge.

Kundnani, Arun 2000, '"Stumbling On": Race, Class and England', *Race & Class*, 41(4): 1–18.

Kurzer, Paulette 1990, 'A Decade of Thatcherism: The Debate on the Left', *Comparative Political Studies*, 23(2): 257–77.

Labour Party 1974a, *Let us work together: Labour's way out of the crisis*, General Election

Manifesto (February), available at: http://www.labour-party.org.uk/manifestos/1974/Feb/1974-feb-labour-manifesto.shtml, accessed 30 August 2014.

―――― 1974b, *Britain will win with Labour*, General Election Manifesto (October), available at: http://www.labour-party.org.uk/manifestos/1974/Oct/1974-oct-labour-manifesto.shtml, accessed 29 August 2014.

Lane, Tony 1983, 'The Tories and the Trade Unions: Rhetoric and Reality', in *The Politics of Thatcherism*, edited by Stuart Hall and Martin Jacques, London: Lawrence & Wishart.

Lavalette, Michael and Gerry Mooney 2000, '"No Poll Tax Here!": The Tories, Social Policy and the Great Poll Tax Rebellion', in *Class Struggle and Social Welfare*, edited by Michael Lavalette and Gerry Mooney, London: Routledge.

Lawrence, Jon and Florence Sutcliffe-Braithwaite 2012, 'Margaret Thatcher and the Decline of Class Politics', in *Making Thatcher's Britain*, edited by Ben Jackson and Robert Saunders, Cambridge: Cambridge University Press.

Lenin, Vladimir I. 1977 [1917], *The State and Revolution: The Marxist Theory of the State and the Task of the Proletariat in the Revolution*, Moscow: Progress.

Leys, Colin 1985, 'Thatcherism and British Manufacturing', *New Left Review* 1/26(151): 5–25.

―――― 1989, *Politics in Britain: From Labourism to Thatcherism*, London: Verso.

―――― 1990, 'Still a Question of Hegemony', *New Left Review* 1/31(181): 119–28.

―――― 2001, *Market-Driven Politics: Neoliberal Democracy and the Public Interest*, London: Verso.

Leyshon, Andrew and Nigel Thrift 1993, 'The Restructuring of the UK Financial Services Industry in the 1990s: A Reversal of Fortune?', *Journal of Rural Studies*, 9(3): 223–41.

Lindsay, Colin and Mikkel Mailand 2004, 'Different Routes, Common Directions? Activation Policies for Young People in Denmark and the UK', *International Journal of Social Welfare*, 13(3): 195–207.

Ling, Tom 1998, *The British State Since 1945: An Introduction*, Cambridge: Polity.

Lipietz, Alain 1987, *Mirages and Miracles: The Crises of Fordism*, London: Verso.

―――― 1998, *Nach dem Ende des 'Goldenen Zeitalters': Regulation und Transformation kapitalistischer Gesellschaften – ausgewählte Schriften*, Hamburg: Argument.

Lloyd, Cathie 1985, 'A National Riot Police: Britain's Third Force?', in *Policing the Miners' Strike*, edited by Bob Fine and Robert Millar, London: Lawrence & Wishart.

Lowe, Rodney 2005, *The Welfare State in Britain since 1945*, Basingstoke: Palgrave.

Lütz, Susanne 2004, 'Convergence Within National Diversity: The Regulatory State in Finance', *Journal of Public Policy*, 24(2): 169–97.

MacInnes, John 1987, *Thatcherism at Work: Industrial Relations and Economic Change*, Milton Keynes: Open University Press.

Marsh, David 1992, *The New Politics of British Trade Unionism: Union Power and the Thatcher Legacy*, London: Macmillan.

——— 1995, 'Explaining "Thatcherite" Policies: Beyond Uni-dimensional Explanations', *Political Studies*, 43(4): 595–613.

Marsh, David and Rod A.W. Rhodes, 1992, 'Implementing Thatcherism: Policy Change in the 1980s', *Parliamentary Affairs*, 45(1): 33–50.

Marshall, J. Neill, Richard Willis and Ranald Richardson 2003, 'Demutualisation, Strategic Choice, and Social Responsibility', *Environment and Planning c: Government and Policy*, 21(5): 735–60.

Marx, Karl 1960 [1852], 'Der 18. Brumaire des Louis Bonaparte', in *Marx Engels Werke*, vol. 8, Berlin, GDR: Dietz.

——— 1962a [1867/1872], *Das Kapital: Kritik der Politischen Ökonomie, Erster Band, Buch I: Der Produktionsprozess des Kapitals*, in *Marx Engels Werke*, vol. 23, Berlin, GDR: Dietz.

——— 1962b [1871], *Der Bürgerkrieg in Frankreich*, in *Marx Engels Werke*, vol. 17, Berlin, GDR: Dietz.

——— 1969 [1859], *Zur Kritik der politischen Ökonomie*, in *Marx Engels Werke*, vol. 13, Berlin, GDR: Dietz.

——— 1973 [1850], 'Die Klassenkämpfe in Frankreich', in *Marx Engels Werke*, vol. 7, Berlin, GDR: Dietz.

Marx, Karl and Friedrich Engels 1952 [1848], *Manifest der kommunistischen Partei*, in *Marx Engels Werke*, vol. 4, Berlin, GDR: Dietz.

Maynard, Geoffrey 1988, *The Economy Under Mrs Thatcher*, Oxford: Basil Blackwell.

McIlroy, John 1988, *Trade Unions in Britain Today*, Manchester: Manchester University Press.

McMullen, Jeremy 1985, 'Legal Strategy and the Unions', in *Policing the Miners' Strike*, edited by Bob Fine and Robert Millar, London: Lawrence & Wishart.

McNeill, Maureen 1991, 'Making and Not Making the Difference: The Gender Politics of Thatcherism', in *Off-Centre: Feminism and Cultural Studies*, edited by Sarah Franklin, Cella Lury and Jackie Stacey, London: Routledge.

Middlemas, Keith 1990, *Power, Competition and the State: Volume 2: Threats to the Postwar Settlement, Britain, 1961–74*, Houndmills: Macmillan.

——— 1991, *Power, Competition and the State: Volume 3: The End of the Postwar Era: Britain since 1974*, Houndmills: Macmillan.

Milne, Seumas 1995 [1994], *The Enemy Within: The Secret War Against the Miners*, London: Pan.

Moore, Stanley W. 1957, *The Critique of Capitalist Democracy: An Introduction to the Theory of the State in Marx, Engels, and Lenin*, New York: Payne-Whitman.

Moran, Michael 1991, *The Politics of the Financial Services Revolution: The USA, UK and Japan*, Basingstoke: Macmillan.

——— 2006, 'The Company of Strangers: Defending the Power of Businesses in Britain, 1975–2005', *New Political Economy*, 11(4): 453–73.

Morgan, Kenneth O. 1990, *The People's Peace: British History 1945–1989*, Oxford: Oxford University Press.

Morton, Gary and Paul Smith 2006, 'Nine Years of New Labour: Neoliberalism and Workers' Rights', *British Journal of Industrial Relations*, 44(3): 401–20.

Muellbauer, John 2002, 'Mortgage Credit Conditions in the UK', *Economic Outlook*, 26(3): 11–18.

Murray, Nancy 1986, 'Anti-Racists and Other Demons: The Press and Ideology in Thatcher's Britain', *Race & Class*, 27(3): 1–19.

Nash, David 2006, 'Recent Industrial Relations Development in the United Kingdom: Continuity and Change under New Labour 1997–2005', *Journal of Industrial Relations*, 48(3): 401–14.

Nolan, Peter 1989, 'Walking on Water? Performance and Industrial Relations under Thatcher', *Industrial Relations Journal*, 20(2): 81–92.

―――― 1992, 'Trade Unions and Productivity: Issues, Evidence and Prospects', *Employee Relations*, 14(6): 3–19.

Nowak, Jörg 2011, 'Poulantzas, Gender Relations and Feminist State Theory', in *Reading Poulantzas*, edited by Alexander Gallas, Lars Bretthauer, John Kannankulam and Ingo Stützle, London: Merlin.

Nunn, Heather 2002, *Thatcher, Politics and Fantasy: The Political Culture of Gender and Nation*, London: Lawrence & Wishart.

Osborne, David and Peter Plastrik 1998, 'Banishing Bureaucracy', *Policy Options*, 2(3): 33–8.

Overbeek, Henk 1990, *Global Capitalism and National Decline: The Thatcher Decade in Perspective*, London: Unwin Hyman.

Panitch, Leo 1976, *Social Democracy and Industrial Militancy: The Labour Party, the Trade Unions and Incomes Policy, 1945–1974*, Cambridge: Cambridge University Press.

Pashukanis, Evgeny B. 1978 [1929], *Law and Marxism: A General Theory*, London: Ink Links.

Pelling, Henry 1971 [1963], *A History of British Trade Unionism*, Harmondsworth: Penguin.

Plender, John 1987, 'London's Big Bang in International Context', *International Affairs*, 63(1): 39–48.

Poulantzas, Nicos 1973 [1968], *Political Power and Social Classes*, London: NLB.

―――― 1974 [1970], *Fascism and Dictatorship: The Third International and the Problem of Fascism*, London: NLB.

―――― 1975 [1974], *Classes in Contemporary Capitalism*, London: NLB.

―――― 1978, *State, Power, Socialism*, London: NLB.

Reid, Alastair J. 2004, *United We Stand: A History of Britain's Trade Unions*, London: Penguin.

Reid, Margaret 1988, *All-Change in the City: The Revolution in Britain's Financial Sector*, Basingstoke: Macmillan.

Rhodes, Rod 2001, 'The Civil Service', in *The Blair Effect: The Blair Government 1997–2001*, edited by Anthony Seldon, London: Little, Brown & Co.

Riddell, Peter 1991, *The Thatcher Era and Its Legacy*, Oxford: Blackwell.

Ridley, Nicolas 1991, *'My Style of Government': The Thatcher Years*, London: Hutchinson.

Ryan, Alan 2005, 'New Labour and Higher Education', *Oxford Review of Education*, 31(1): 87–100.

Saunders, Robert 2012, '"Crisis, What Crisis?": Thatcherism and the Seventies', in *Making Thatcher's Britain*, edited by Ben Jackson and Robert Saunders, Cambridge: Cambridge University Press.

Saville, John 1985, 'An Open Conspiracy: Conservative Politics and the Miner's Strike 1984–5', *Socialist Register*, 22: 295–329.

Sayer, Derek 1979, *Marx's Method*, Brighton: The Harvester Press.

Schofield, Camilla 2012, 'A Nation or No Nation? Enoch Powell and Thatcherism', in *Making Thatcher's Britain*, edited by Ben Jackson and Robert Saunders, Cambridge: Cambridge University Press.

Schwarz, Bill 1987, 'The Thatcher Years', *Socialist Register*, 23: 116–52.

Segal, Lynne 1983, 'The Heat in the Kitchen', in *The Politics of Thatcherism*, edited by Stuart Hall and Martin Jacques, London: Lawrence & Wishart.

Shackleton, John R. 1998, 'Industrial Relations Reform in Britain since 1979', *Journal of Labor Research*, 19(3): 581–605.

Sivanandan, Ambalavaner 1977, 'Grunwick: Report on the West Indian Community', *Race & Class*, 19(1): 69–75.

Smith, Peter 1991, 'Lessons from the British Poll Tax Disaster', *National Tax Journal*, 44(4.2): 421–36.

Stephens, Philip 1996, *Politics and the Pound: The Tories, the Economy and Europe*, London: Macmillan.

——— 2001, 'The Treasury Under Labour', in *The Blair Effect: The Blair Government 1997–2001*, edited by Anthony Seldon, London: Little, Brown & Co.

Stevens, Christopher 2002, 'Thatcherism, Majorism and the Collapse of Tory Statecraft', *Contemporary British History*, 16(1): 119–50.

Stewart, Michael 1977, *The Jekyll & Hyde Years: Politics and Economic Policy since 1964*, London: Dent.

Stützle, Ingo 2011, 'The Order of Knowledge: The State as a Knowledge Apparatus', in *Reading Poulantzas*, edited by Alexander Gallas, Lars Bretthauer, John Kannankulam and Ingo Stützle, London: Merlin.

Suddick, Anne 2005, 'Preface: "The past we inherit, the future we build"', *Capital & Class*, 29(87): 3–16.

Taylor, Robert 2001, 'Employment Relation Policy', in *The Blair Effect: The Blair Government 1997–2001*, edited by Anthony Seldon, London: Little, Brown & Co.

Thatcher, Margaret 1993, *The Downing Street Years*, London: HarperCollins.

―――― 1995, *The Path to Power*, London: HarperCollins.

―――― 2002, *Statecraft: Strategies for a Changing World*, London: HarperCollins.

Thomas, William A. 1986, *The Big Bang*, Oxford: Philip Allan.

Tickell, Adam and Jamie Peck 2003, 'Making Global Rules: Globalization or Neoliberalization?', in *Remaking the Global Economy: Economic-Geographical Perspectives*, edited by Jamie Peck and Henry Wai-chung Yeung, London: Sage.

Tomlinson, Jim 2012a, 'Thatcher, Monetarism and the Politics of Inflation', in *Making Thatcher's Britain*, edited by Ben Jackson and Robert Saunders, Cambridge: Cambridge University Press.

―――― 2012b, 'From "Distribution of Industry" to "Local Keynesianism": The Growth of Public Sector Employment in Britain', *British Politics*, 7(3): 204–23.

UKFI (UK Financial Investments) 2009, 'An Introduction: Who we are, what we do, and the framework document which governs the relationship between UKFI and HM Treasury', available at: http://www.ukfi.gov.uk/downloadfile.php?ArticleID=18, accessed 13 May 2009.

Vanberg, Viktor J. 2004, 'The Freiburg School: Walter Eucken and Ordoliberalism', *Freiburger Diskussionspapiere zur Ordnungsökonomik*: 11, Freiburg: Walter Eucken Institut.

Vinen, Richard 2010 [2009], *Thatcher's Britain: The Politics and Social Upheaval of the Thatcher Era*, London: Pocket Books.

Waddington, Jeremy 2003, 'Heightening Tensions in Relations between Trade Unions and the Labour Government in 2002', *British Journal of Industrial Relations*, 41(2): 335–58.

Walshe, Kieran 2003, 'Foundation Hospitals: A New Direction for NHS Reform?', *Journal of the Royal Society of Medicine*, 96: 106–10.

Weber, Max 2005 [1922], *Wirtschaft und Gesellschaft: Grundriss der verstehenden Soziologie*, Frankfurt/Main: Zweitausendeins.

Western, Bruce 1997, *Between Class and Market: Postwar Unionization in the Capitalist Democracies*, Princeton, NJ: University Press.

Wiles, Peter 1985, 'The Policing of Industrial Relations', in *Industrial Relations and the Law in the 1980s: Issues and Future Trends*, edited by Patricia Fosh and Craig R. Littler, Aldershot: Gower.

Wilkinson, Richard G. and Kate E. Pickett 2007, 'The Problems of Relative Deprivation: Why Some Societies Do Better Than Others', *Social Science & Medicine*, 65(9): 1965–78.

―――― 2009, *The Spirit Level: Why More Equal Societies Almost Always Do Better*, London: Allen Lane.

Wilson, Elizabeth 1987, 'Thatcherism and Women: After Seven Years', *Socalist Register*, 24: 199–235.

Woodward, Richard 2001, '"Slaughtering" the British State? Transgovernmental Networks and the Governance of Financial Markets in the City of London', paper delivered at the *Global Studies Association Conference*, Manchester Metropolitan University.

Young, Hugo 1989, *One of Us: Life of Margaret Thatcher*, London: Macmillan.

Index

Accumulation strategy   16–19, 29–30, 48–9,
    53, 63–4, 76, 104–8, 113–14, 117, 125–6,
    135–6, 142, 148, 157, 160–1, 165, 200, 209,
    215, 218, 229, 232–6, 263, 276–8, 282–5
Adamson, Campbell   100
Advisory Conciliation and Arbitration Service
    (ACAS)   154, 188
Aglietta, Michel   36n2
Alderson, John   182
Allen, Vic   150
Armstrong, Robert   180–1
Army   100, 158–9, 173, 187, 286
Association of Chief Police Officers (ACPO)
    179–80
Association of Professional, Executive,
    Clerical, and Computer Staffs (APEX)   96
Associated Society of Locomotive Engineers
    and Firemen (ASLEF)   153, 155, 177
Augar, Philip   204–5, 205n2, 221, 223, 225
Authoritarianism   62, 82–3, 122, 137, 142,
    160–1, 266, 280, 290
    Authoritarian populism   12, 15–16, 83
    Authoritarian statism   38n3, 44

Balance of payments   76–9, 126
Balloting   85, 89, 91, 144, 153, 169–74, 177,
    192–4, 197–9, 254–5, 265
Bank of England   42n3, 42n5, 129, 251–3, 260,
    287
Banks   129, 203n4, 207, 209, 211–12, 214–19,
    230–1, 248, 256, 258–60, 263, 271, 285–7
Battle of Orgreave   183–4, 192
Battle of Saltley Gates   55, 104n3, 167, 179, 183
Beckett, Francis   6n2, 149n7, 171, 180
Benefits   17, 54, 63–5, 91, 94, 106, 144, 146n5,
    149, 165, 184, 195, 239–40, 258, 267–8,
    283
Benn, Tony   67, 78, 119–20
Bickerstaff, Rodney   222
Biffen, John   252
'Big Bang'   96n3, 202–4, 207, 216, 222–3, 229,
    232–4
Blairism   7, 59–60, 62, 66, 262, 266, 280,
    280n2, 282–90
Blair, Tony   1n1, 2, 4, 43n2, 61, 63n1, 66, 239,
    262, 270–2, 278, 280, 280n2, 283–6

Blake, Nick   194
Bleaney, Michael   21, 156
Blunkett, David   195n3
Bonaparte, Louis   11, 33
Bonefeld, Werner   5–6, 6n2, 61n2, 132n2, 228
Bonnett, Kevin   11
Boom   76, 136, 162, 203n4, 215, 228, 239, 250,
    257, 276–7, 279, 286
Boyson, Rhodes   240
Bretton Woods system   79, 207, 211, 218, 247
British Coal   265
British constitution   83, 87
British Gas   106
British National Oil Company (BNOC)
    105–7, 134
British Rail   153
British state   3n4, 6n2, 15, 42n3, 46, 60, 63, 75,
    102, 137, 142, 195, 202, 211, 227, 232, 247
British Steel Corporation (BSC)   151–2, 166,
    168, 183
British Telecom (BT)   106, 134
Brittan, Leon   176, 181
Bromley, Simon   11
Brown, Gordon   262, 270–1, 280, 280n2,
    284–6, 288
Brown government   278, 287
Burns, Conor   280
By-election   158, 245, 251, 254, 269

Cabinet   78, 81–93, 101, 106, 110, 114, 132, 137–9,
    142–3, 148, 157–9, 168, 175, 181, 187, 238,
    252–5, 259, 263, 266–70
Callaghan, James   2, 6, 61, 78, 102, 117, 122, 157,
    248, 248n4
Callaghan government   59, 65, 68, 80, 97, 107,
    126
Cameron, David   1–2, 1n1, 1n2, 102n3, 278
Capital   2, 5, 6n2, 31, 34–6, 36n2, 40–3, 48–9,
    53, 56n1, 59, 65, 75, 77, 79, 81, 102n3, 103,
    122, 124, 126, 132n2, 133, 139, 147, 159–60,
    162, 188, 194, 200–1, 207–9, 214, 218, 221,
    230, 232, 237, 247–9, 256–8, 260, 265,
    275–6, 284, 287
    Comprador capital   229, 231
    Financial capital   78, 201, 211, 230
    Industrial capital   14, 35, 60, 86, 139, 165

INDEX 311

Internal capital 231
National capital 21, 100, 230–1
Capitalism in Britain 2, 5, 22, 59–60, 75, 77, 80, 84, 114, 120–1, 135, 202, 228, 232, 277
Capitalist class 3, 7, 15, 35, 49, 52, 53, 53n1, 201
Capitalist mode of production (CMP) 2, 29n3, 31, 34–6, 44–8, 50–5, 56n1, 59, 59n1, 125, 229, 290
Carrington, Peter 93, 98, 107
Carrington Report 91n7, 99–101, 104, 107–8
Centre for Policy Studies (CPS) 89, 109
Citizen's Charter 266–7
Citizenship 40
City of London 23, 42n3, 54, 66, 74, 76, 120, 129, 135, 135n2, 140, 142, 165, 200–4, 203n4, 207n3, 208–13, 216–32, 237, 249, 253, 270, 277, 284–5, 287
Civil service 42n5, 103, 138, 140–1, 286
Civil society 12, 79
Clarke, Kenneth 121n1, 241, 266
Clarke, Simon 5
Class antagonism 2, 34, 39–41, 49, 59, 146, 165, 221
Class domination 2–3, 5, 7, 15, 21–3, 29–31, 34–6, 38–43, 42n5, 43n4, 45–50, 52, 56, 62, 69, 75, 155n3, 161, 165, 192, 200–1, 230, 233, 275–6, 290
Class political arrangement/regime 7, 49, 60–8, 63n1, 73, 75, 95–6, 101–2, 104, 107, 124, 147, 156, 160, 215, 233, 237, 261–4, 269–72, 275, 280, 284, 289–90
Class political project 66, 68, 287
Class politics 6–7, 21–31, 32–3, 36, 46–51, 50n1, 56–7, 59–62, 63n1, 65, 68–9, 73, 77, 85, 91, 95, 98, 101, 107–8, 111–12, 125, 132n2, 142–3, 147–8, 153, 155, 161, 163–4, 196, 200, 216, 219, 230, 232, 235, 246–9, 261, 264, 267–8, 272, 275–6, 280n2, 289
Class power 45, 61n2, 143
Class struggle 7–8, 30, 32–5, 41–3, 43n4, 46, 50–62, 68, 73–5, 164, 237–8, 261, 270, 272, 284, 289–90
Class relations of forces 3, 39–40, 48–9, 65, 77–8, 101, 145–7, 160, 188, 194, 199, 201, 233, 264–5, 276
Closed shop 109, 154–5, 196–7, 224

Coates, David 5, 5n5, 61n2
Cohen, Sheila 103, 118–19, 143, 145, 156, 175, 189n2
Collective bargaining 109, 156, 281
Collective bargaining coverage 4, 67
Confederation of British Industry (CBI) 86, 100, 139, 253, 272
Conjuncture 2, 11, 23n1, 31, 57–8, 75, 78, 117, 148, 157, 159, 178, 186, 189, 194, 199, 211, 235n1, 238, 257, 262, 266, 271
Consensus 1–2, 14, 16, 80, 82, 140, 142, 159n3
Consent 5, 11–12, 16–17, 19–21, 25n2, 27–8, 42, 49, 53, 55, 85, 91, 105, 158, 201, 280, 286
Conservatism 4n1, 13, 20n1, 81, 84, 88, 139, 236
One nation conservatism 80–1, 88–90, 93–4, 96, 98, 100, 132, 139
Conservative Party 6, 19n7, 64, 75, 80–5, 88–95, 88n1, 96, 107, 109–13, 121, 137–8, 140–1, 157, 166, 222, 232, 236, 239, 242–5, 251, 254–6, 259, 266, 269, 271–2, 275
Consolidators vs. radicals 236, 236n1, 238–9, 243, 249, 254–5, 259, 267, 269
Consumer credit 162, 282
Corporatism 16, 75, 80–1, 87, 93, 116, 119–20, 137, 140, 157
Crewe, Ivor 26n1
Crisis 12–13, 23n1, 29–30, 34, 38n3, 51, 57, 59n1, 65, 67, 79–80, 87, 93–4, 110, 116–17, 120–2, 127, 142, 216, 229, 232, 237, 253, 257, 277–8
1976 sterling crisis 68, 76, 78, 115, 123
Crisis of corporatism 16, 79, 81, 137
Crisis of labour 5, 193
Crisis of representation 79–80, 137, 142, 157
Economic crisis 75–6, 79, 87, 93, 117, 122, 126, 255
Economic and Financial Crisis (2007–) 2, 24, 69, 135, 276, 280n2, 285–7
ERM crisis 262, 268, 270
Ideological crisis 75, 79–81, 84, 88
Oil crisis 79
Organic crisis 5, 12, 80, 83, 121
Political crisis 75, 79, 111, 236, 242, 251–3, 255, 257, 261
State crisis 15, 18, 79, 87, 137
Critique of Political Economy 33, 36n3

INDEX

Danford, Andy   146n3
Davies, John   113
Davies, Nick   180
Delors, Jacques   247, 249, 250n1, 253, 256
Democracy   25n2, 37–8, 78, 97, 145, 147, 173–4, 176n4, 215
Department of Trade and Industry (DTI)   138, 285
Deutsche Mark (DM)   247, 253, 256–60
Disraeli, Benjamin   19n7
Dickens, Richard   281
Division of labour   40–1, 44, 51, 118, 205, 284
Domestic labour   45
Douglass, David John   175, 189n2, 192

Economic growth   7, 16–17, 22, 76, 126, 276
Economic order politics   7, 21–4, 22n4, 30–3, 46–51, 56–62, 61n1, 63n1, 65, 69, 73–7, 85, 90, 95, 98, 101, 104, 108, 110, 112, 124–6, 142, 148, 161–4, 200, 208, 210, 215, 217, 229, 232, 235, 235n1, 246–8, 263–4, 270, 275–6, 280n2, 284–9
  Economic-political order   7, 49, 60–3, 68–9, 76, 95, 101–2, 124, 142, 160, 240, 270, 275, 289–90
Economic policy   2, 7, 21, 22n4, 23, 25n2, 49, 84, 88, 95, 98, 108–9, 122, 123n1, 126–8, 132, 137, 142, 161, 232, 235n1, 247–8, 252, 261, 270
Education   40, 64, 78, 147n1, 178, 203, 238–41, 254–5, 266–7, 272, 276, 278, 282–3, 286
Electoral system   21, 25n2
Electronic, Electrical, Telecommunications and Plumbing Union (EETPU)   165, 197
Engels, Friedrich   19n7
England   33, 83, 136, 180, 203, 243–4, 280
Euro-currency markets   207, 207n3
European Central Bank (ECB)   256
European Community (EC)   247, 260n1
European Economic Community (EEC)   83
European Exchange Rate Mechanism (ERM)   247
European monetary union   246–9, 256, 259
European Union (EU)   260n1, 266, 269, 282, 285
Exchange rate   79, 129, 131, 207, 247–8, 263
Exchange controls   82, 131, 135, 207n3, 209, 213–14, 218, 235, 251

Extraction strategy   49, 60, 61n1, 63, 74, 86–7, 104–7, 111–14, 124–5, 145, 147, 161, 164, 191, 195, 196n5, 201, 249, 256, 264–5, 272, 280

Falklands War   158–9, 173
Farrall, Stephen   4n1, 67–8
Ferner, Anthony   143
Financial markets   23, 60, 63, 123n1, 135–6, 165, 187, 200–2, 208, 213, 217–18, 228–35, 278, 284–5
  Financial market regulation   66
Financial liberalisation   63, 74, 133, 165, 200–2, 229
Fletcher, Alexander   218
France   33, 76, 171, 259, 289
Fiscal policy   63, 108, 129–32, 130n7, 135, 148, 156, 208, 229, 252, 262–3, 285
Flinders, Mathew   263
Foot, Michael   157
Foreign policy   270, 286
Foreign trade   36n3, 124
Form analysis   37n3, 38n3, 47, 155
Fractions of capital   14, 42, 53, 63, 122, 277
Free market economics   7, 62–3, 67, 82, 84–5, 88, 90, 95–6, 102, 107–8, 112, 130–2, 135–6, 142, 236, 240, 275, 280, 290
Friedman, Milton   1n1, 124n1, 130n7

Gamble, Andrew   235, 235n1
Gender Relations   44–5, 184, 290
General Election   21n2, 29, 56n3, 251
  1970   80, 84–5
  1974 (February)   65, 77–8, 80–1, 83, 88–9, 115
  1974 (October)   65, 77, 78n1, 80, 83, 88–9, 126
  1979   65, 88n1, 110, 116, 121n1, 123, 125, 138, 209
  1983   155, 158–9, 164, 168, 177, 193
  1987   158, 194, 222, 239, 241, 243, 245
  1992   238, 245–6, 257–8
  1997   4, 239, 262, 265, 270, 280
  2005   281
  2007   286
  2010   288
  General election manifesto   64n1, 77, 78n1, 84, 88n1, 121, 126, 128, 133n6, 137, 145, 222, 239, 243, 265, 275–6

INDEX

Gentlemanliness 42n5, 74, 96, 96n3, 139–40, 147n1, 165, 201–4, 206, 208, 210, 219, 222–5, 227–30, 232
Germany 11n2, 24, 76, 109, 101, 135–6, 171, 248–50, 252, 257–8, 289
Goodison, Nicholas 210, 212, 216–18, 229
Goodman, Geoffrey 188, 190n1
Gormley, Joe 169
Gorst, John 97
Gramsci, Antonio 19–20, 75
Gray, Robert 180n3
Greater London Council (GLC) 173, 195, 195n3
Green, Ewen 84

Hain, Peter 119, 186
Hall, David 180
Hall, Stuart 5, 11–25, 11n2, 11n6, 15n2, 25n2, 26, 29, 32, 46, 46n1, 50, 61n2, 69, 75, 78, 80, 122, 275–6, 289
Hamilton, Adrian 227
Harrison, John 150
Hart, David 176, 185, 190
Hatton, Derek 195n3
Havers, Michael 181, 186
Hayes, George 171
Healey, Denis 78, 102, 122, 123n1, 157
Healthcare 64, 78, 102n3, 238–9, 241–2, 254, 272, 282–3, 286
Health insurance 238, 241
Heath, Ted 77, 80–9, 92, 104, 107, 109, 125, 142, 148, 150, 238
Heath government 62n1, 64, 77, 81–8, 167
Hegemony 11, 19–24, 25n2, 27–8, 28n2, 32, 42, 47, 50, 79, 284
Hegemonic project 11, 15, 17, 19–20, 25n2, 26–8, 28n2, 48, 58n4, 63, 86, 104, 114, 229, 237, 255–6, 264–5, 268, 270
  'One nation' hegemonic project 20n1, 28–9, 48, 77, 80–1, 83–4, 88–94, 96, 98, 100, 208, 268, 272, 282–3
  'Two nations' hegemonic project 19, 19n7, 20n1, 28–9, 63, 74, 86, 94–5, 105, 107, 111, 124–5, 147, 160–1, 165, 192, 200–1, 210, 215, 219, 222, 229, 234, 236–8, 245, 247, 249, 252, 254, 257, 264, 268, 270, 282–3
Hencke, David 6n2, 149n7, 171, 180

Heseltine, Michael 245, 249, 252, 254–5, 257, 264, 266, 285
Hobsbawm, Eric 62n1, 67, 159
Hogg, Quintin 92–3
Hoskyns, John 98, 109–14
House of Commons 198, 218, 268–9
House of Lords 97
Housing 18, 128, 145–6, 162, 195, 201, 221, 250, 256, 267
  Council housing 63, 165, 195, 215, 238
Howard, Michael 259
Howe, Geoffrey 92, 107, 128, 131, 245, 248, 251–4
Howell, David 149
Hurd, Douglas 252–4
Hyman, Richard 6n2, 172

Ideology 1, 4n1, 12–17, 21, 23, 25n2, 66–7, 75, 80–4, 88–90, 93–6, 101, 122–3, 128–30, 135, 195, 206, 226, 230, 233, 236, 238, 240, 245, 271, 283
Immigration 13, 82–3, 85
Industrial policy 63, 98, 101n2, 135, 138
Industry 4, 15, 18, 23, 31, 61n2, 65, 74, 78–9, 86, 98, 103, 105, 116, 118, 132–3, 135, 139, 149, 151, 154–5, 163–4, 166, 168–71, 176–8, 176n4, 181, 187–9, 189n2, 191, 193–4, 199, 202, 211, 217, 220, 222–3, 232, 248–9, 252, 275–6, 278, 285
Inequality 135, 162, 219, 229, 240, 242, 245, 267, 278–9, 283–4
Inflation 13, 76, 79, 82, 84, 90, 108, 115, 124n1, 126–30, 132–3, 160–2, 228, 248–52, 256–9, 263–4, 277, 283, 285
Institutions 3, 5, 15–21, 29–32, 36, 40, 42n5, 48, 55, 60, 64, 75–6, 79–80, 83, 89, 108, 116, 120, 127n2, 129, 138–40, 142, 145, 156, 180, 184, 196, 203, 207, 209, 213, 216, 218–19, 227, 230–1, 237, 243, 247, 263–4, 271, 277, 284–6, 289
  Institutional vs. ideational 12, 12n5, 14–15, 25–6, 25n2
International Monetary Fund (IMF) 65, 78, 115, 122
Iron and Steel Trades Confederation (ISTC) 151–2
Isolation effect 40–1

Jacques, Martin   11–15, 15n2, 61n2
Jenkins, Roy   158
Jessop, Bob   11–25, 11n2, 11n6, 15n2, 20n1, 22n3, 25n2, 26–30, 32, 36, 45–50, 53, 59, 61n2, 64n1, 76, 79, 137, 162, 210, 262, 271, 283, 289
Johnson, Christopher   128
Joseph, Keith   4, 81, 88–94, 97–8, 107, 109, 113, 126–8, 127n2, 141, 149, 149n7, 210, 240

Kettell, Steven   257
Keynesianism   1n1, 2, 4n1, 23n1, 60, 76, 88, 123, 127, 132, 228, 237, 278
Khabaz, D.V.   178
King, Anthony   3n2
King, Tom   169–70, 181
Kinnock, Neil   26, 154n3, 178, 190n1, 196, 245–6

Labour Party   2, 14–15, 21, 23, 26, 39n6, 56n3, 60, 66, 77–8, 78n1, 80, 83, 89, 105, 111, 118, 122–3, 137, 140, 142, 149, 157–60, 177–8, 192–3, 195, 233, 235, 235n1, 241, 245–6, 251, 269–70, 275
Labour relations   4–7, 65, 77, 85, 87, 91n7, 92, 100, 106, 108–12, 143
Lamont, Norman   258–63, 266
Lavalette, Michael   195, 242, 244, 246
Lawson, Nigel   128, 145, 169–70, 181, 213, 220, 229, 241, 243, 245, 248, 250–2, 276–7
Leigh-Pemberton, Robin   212
Lenin, Vladimir Illich   38
Leys, Colin   5, 11, 14–15, 21, 27, 32, 100, 148, 195, 230n5, 233
Leyshon, Andrew   221, 223
Liberal collectivism   60, 77
Liberal Party   80, 158
Liberal Democratic Party (LibDems)   269
Liberalism   67, 81–3, 85, 88, 108, 108n5, 126, 129, 240
Lilley, Peter   259, 266, 268
Ling, Tom   11
Lipietz, Alain   36n2
Little Englandism   83
Liverpool   195n3, 196
Livingstone, Ken   195n3
London   23, 83, 96, 117, 165, 196, 201, 208, 213, 218–20, 229, 244, 249

London Stock Exchange (LSE)   201–4, 208, 210, 227
Lord Poole   203n4
Lowe, Rodney   236

Maastricht treaty   256, 258–9, 265, 268–9
MacGregor, Ian   152, 166, 169–71, 177–8, 188, 190
MacInnes, John   3n4, 61n2
Macmillan, Harold   64, 81
Major, John   21n2, 236, 238, 243, 245, 252–7, 259, 261–6, 268–9, 271, 277–8, 280, 282, 286
Major government   1n2, 2, 4, 63, 63n1, 66–8, 92, 114, 229, 241, 258, 262–4, 266, 268, 271, 275–8, 282, 289
Managerialism   63–4, 138, 263, 266–7, 286
Manchester   83, 154
Mandelson, Peter   1n1, 283
Manning, Alan   281
Marshall, Walter   168
Marsh, David   66
Maxwell, Robert   178–9
Marxism   11, 11n2, 30, 48, 52, 56
Marx, Karl   2, 11, 30, 33–6, 35n5, 36n3, 41, 48, 55, 55n4, 59n1, 290
Materiality   40
Maude, Angus   92, 109
Maudlin, Reginald   92
McGahey, Mick   61n2, 172
Media   65, 67, 73, 84, 101, 117, 122, 154, 159n3, 165–6, 169, 174, 178–9, 181, 183–4, 186, 189–90, 194, 239, 253–4
Medium-Term Financial Strategy (MTFS)   131, 132n2, 214, 248
Method   32, 32n4, 111
    Method of Periodisation   32, 59–61
    Method of Presentation   73–4
Middlemas, Keith   138, 148, 156, 162, 170, 239
Militant Tendency   195n3, 196
Milne, Seumas   172
Minimum wage   281, 283, 285n4
MISC 57   168, 181
MISC 101   175, 181, 183, 186–7
Mitterrand, François   249
Mode of leadership and domination   27–8, 49, 61n1, 63, 80, 105, 113, 195, 247, 251, 257, 270, 282
Mode of presentation   60n2

INDEX   315

Money   6, 51, 56n1, 59n1, 102, 124, 124n1,
    126–31, 133, 153, 185, 190, 203n4,
    205, 207n3, 214, 218, 225, 250n1, 278,
    283–4
  Money supply   82, 90, 108, 123n1, 124,
    128–9, 130n7, 131, 287
Monetarism   15n2, 66, 107–8, 122, 123n1, 124,
    124n1, 128–32, 248
Monetary policy   4–6, 6n2, 60, 65, 68, 102,
    108, 124n1, 126, 128–33, 139, 247, 258, 263,
    276, 285
Monopoly of violence   37, 41
Mooney, Gerry   195, 242, 244, 246
Moore, John   241
Moore, Stanley W.   37
Moran, Michael   210, 226–9
Mortgages   74, 146n3, 250, 282
Mulhern, Francis   61n2
Murdoch, Rupert   165, 178–9, 196–8, 196n5,
    239, 254
Murray, Len   117, 153–4

National Association for Freedom (NAFF)
    97–8
National Association of Colliery Overmen,
    Deputies and Shotfirers (NACODS)
    188–90, 189n2, 190n1
National Association of Securities Dealers
    Automated Quotations (NASDAQ)   208n3
National Coal Board (NCB)   65, 81, 149, 166,
    168–72, 176, 176n4, 179, 183, 188–90,
    189n2
National Graphical Association (NGA)
    154–5, 197–8
National Health Service (NHS)   102n3, 241–2,
    255, 265, 283
National Industrial Relations Court (NIRC)
    85, 87
National Reporting Centre (NRC)   179–81
National Union of Mineworkers (NUM)
    4, 4n5, 61n2, 63–5, 74, 88n1, 99, 107,
    149–50, 164–74, 176–9, 176n4, 183–94,
    195n1, 189n2, 264
National Union of Seamen (NUS)   165, 177,
    199–200
National Union Public Employees (NUPE)
    222
Nationalisation   6, 82–4, 88, 98, 101–7, 133,
    146n5, 149, 164, 202, 285, 287

Nationalism   19n7, 20n1, 54, 80, 157–60, 200,
    210, 237
Neoliberalism   2, 6n1, 7, 13, 18, 19n1, 23,
    23n1, 46, 62–4, 68, 75, 88, 102, 114,
    122–3, 141, 157, 161, 164, 179, 192,
    208, 230, 232, 235–6, 235n1, 245–6,
    255–7, 262, 266, 280, 283, 286, 289–
    90
Neo-Ricardianism   63, 64n1, 125, 132–6,
    142, 161, 165, 200, 209–10, 213, 215, 218,
    229, 232, 234, 236, 240, 263, 276, 282,
    284
Neo-Poulantzasianism   46, 48, 50, 289
New Labour   7, 11n2, 23n1, 63n1, 68, 238, 257,
    261–2, 268, 271–2, 278, 280–9
'New Realism'   155, 177, 233
New right   26n1, 64, 73, 81, 89–90, 101, 113,
    120, 122–3, 138, 141, 167, 195, 210, 228, 238,
    240, 271, 280
New York Stock Exchange (NYSE)   208, 211,
    218, 227
North of England   136
Northern Ireland   86, 141, 143, 271
North/South divide   136, 160, 221n4
Nixon, Richard   1n1
Nolan, Peter   61n2
Nott, John   210

Office of Fair Trading (OFT)   207, 212–13
Ordoliberalism   22n4
Organised labour   4, 6, 6n2, 15, 23–4, 26n1,
    29–30, 50n1, 54, 60, 61n2, 62–7, 77–8, 81,
    86–8, 87n1, 97, 101, 104, 107, 109, 113–14,
    116–23, 125, 127, 131, 137, 140, 143–6, 148,
    150–3, 155–7, 160, 164–5, 167, 193, 196,
    199, 222, 233, 237, 239, 246, 249, 252, 262,
    265, 275, 280
Organization of Petrol Exporting Countries
    (OPEC)   79
Overbeek, Henk   58n4, 61n2

Panitch, Leo   87n1
Parkinson, Cecil   212, 216–18, 224, 229
Parliamentary Conservative Party   157, 232,
    269
Party duopoly   80, 137, 140
Passive revolution   20, 28–9
Path dependency   59–60, 131, 202
Peirce, Gareth   183

Periodisation   59–61, 64, 66n1, 68, 73
Pentonville Five   87
Pickett, Kate   278
Policing   106, 168, 180, 182, 184, 204
Policy adjustment vs. regime shift   88, 235n1, 238
Political analysis   2, 5, 11, 16, 23, 25n1, 32n4, 33, 46, 48, 50, 56, 289
Political scene   2, 29, 39, 56, 65, 117–18, 132, 138, 141–2, 156–7, 160, 164, 192, 203, 209, 236, 255, 257, 261, 262, 269–72
Ponting, Clive   159
'Popular capitalism'   74, 107, 145, 147, 215, 220–2, 226, 228
Portillo, Michael   259, 266, 268
Post-war settlement   2, 18, 77, 79, 81, 83–4, 88–9, 94, 102, 108, 116, 123, 142, 160, 236n1, 237
Poulantzas, Nicos   2, 7, 32–4, 33n3, 33n4, 36–51, 36n2, 37n3, 53n1, 57–9, 57n1, 290
Pound sterling   68, 76, 79, 82, 84, 87, 112, 126–7, 132, 187, 207n3, 248, 250, 253, 257–60, 263, 276
Powell, Enoch   64, 81–8, 101
Power bloc   1n2, 42, 49, 52–3, 56–9
    British power bloc   42n3, 59, 61–3, 65–8, 73–80, 86, 94, 96–101, 96n3, 104, 107, 111, 115, 120–1, 128–30, 132, 135, 135n2, 139–40, 142–3, 147–50, 156–7, 160, 164–5, 179, 187, 193, 200–11, 219, 230, 232, 236, 264–5, 270, 272, 275, 277, 280, 284, 289
Price controls   78, 128
Prior, James   92, 98, 107, 114, 125, 139, 143
Private Finance Initiative (PFI)   263
Privatisation   18, 63, 64n1, 65, 101–2, 102n3, 105–7, 133–4, 142, 152, 161, 165–7, 176n4, 195, 215, 220, 265, 285
Public choice   108
Public expenditure   76, 82, 84, 90, 115, 128, 131, 134, 141, 149, 250, 257, 267, 272, 282–3, 287
Public sector   5, 90, 101–4, 107, 112, 116, 118–20, 125, 130, 151, 160, 170, 235, 267, 280, 283, 285–8
Public Sector Borrowing Requirement (PSBR)   130–1, 134
Pym, Francis   92, 113

Racism   83, 96
Recession   5, 12, 18, 60, 65, 69, 126, 132–6, 139, 149, 157–8, 161–2, 215, 229, 235n1, 256–9, 263, 267, 276–7
Redwood, John   269
Regime of condensation   49, 59, 62–3, 75–9, 101, 114, 137, 161, 164, 232, 235–6, 245–6, 255, 257, 280, 289
Regulation approach   36n2
Reid, Alastair J.   221
Reidy, Michael   183
Relations of production   2, 30, 34–8, 37n3, 40–2, 44–7, 155n3
Repression   7, 13, 18, 29, 49, 63, 65, 81, 86–8, 91, 95, 104, 107–8, 111, 124–5, 141–2, 145, 147, 152, 156, 160–1, 164, 166, 174, 179–86, 190–2, 198–201, 249, 256, 268, 275, 280–1, 286
Retail Price Index (RPI)   127, 252, 277
Riddell, Peter   106
Ridley, Nicholas   6, 98, 101–7, 101n2, 102n3, 134, 162, 167, 181, 252
Ridley Plan/Report   6, 67, 101–2, 104, 106–9, 111, 113–14, 125, 133, 143–4, 147, 149, 152, 156, 164, 167–8, 179
Ricardo, David   64n1, 124
Riots   141, 183, 224, 244

Saville, John   189n2, 191
Scargill, Arthur   150, 166–73, 185, 189n2
Securities and Investment Board (SIB)   226
Self-Regulating organisation (SRO)   226, 228
Scotland   136, 160, 169, 172, 174, 177, 231, 243–5, 287
Schools   40, 42n5, 108n5, 119, 140, 239–40, 240n3, 283
Shah, Eddie   154, 154n3
Sherman, Alfred   89, 109
Siddall, Norman   168
Simey, Margaret   180
Social Democracy   13–14, 18, 80, 93, 111, 119
Social Contract   65, 78, 80, 93, 108–9, 115, 119, 126, 137, 143, 277
Social Democratic Party (SDP)   140, 157–8, 193, 280n1
Social formation   33–5, 41, 44–50, 57, 60, 79, 278

INDEX

Socialism   6, 57, 78, 85, 93–4, 111–12, 119–20, 122, 140, 157, 195, 243, 283
   Authoritarian Socialism   116
Society of Graphical and Allied Trade (SOGAT)   197–8
Southeast of England   140, 151, 182, 212, 225
Special Patrol Group (SPG)   151
Spencer, George   174n3, 176n4
Spencer, Michael   224
Sraffa, Pierro   64n1
State apparatuses   3, 13, 17, 37–43, 47, 53, 53n1, 60, 64, 79–81, 125, 128–9, 132, 134, 137, 139–41, 164, 174, 219, 226–7, 286
State bureaucracy   94, 113, 138
State-owned industries   6, 63, 65, 87, 98, 101–3, 106, 133–4, 146n5, 164, 202
State strategy   16, 18–19, 29, 48–9, 60, 63–4, 76, 125, 141–2, 161, 212, 232, 286
Stephens, Phillip   253
Sterling, Jeffrey   199
Stevens, David   178
Stewart, Andy   176n4, 224
Stones, Rob   210
Strategic selectivity   47, 52–4, 57
Strategy   14–15, 18, 21, 24, 48–9, 52–9, 61n2, 68, 79, 90, 96, 101, 106–14, 117, 125, 132, 148, 151–2, 155–6, 164, 167, 169, 177–85, 191, 193, 195, 211, 219, 223, 228, 236, 238, 243–5, 260, 262–3, 265, 276–7
Strauss, Norman   98, 109–14
Strikes   3n4, 4–5, 4n4, 42n6, 62n1, 67, 75, 85–7, 91, 96–7, 99–100, 102n3, 103–6, 108, 116, 121, 141, 144, 149–55, 174n3, 265
   Grunwick dispute   96–9
   Miners' strike (1972)   64, 77, 81, 167
   Miners' strike (1974)   64, 77, 99
   Miners' strike (1984–5)   4–6, 43n3, 61n2, 62, 65, 74, 101n2, 106, 144, 164, 167, 233, 235n1
   P&O dispute   62, 66, 165, 199–200
   Steel strike (1980)   141, 151
   Stockport Messenger dispute   153–4, 196
   Wapping dispute   62, 165, 196–9, 222, 233
   Winter of Discontent   65, 115–26, 138, 147, 154, 156, 164, 193
Supply-side economics   93, 108, 128–32

Targets   128–33, 149, 214, 263–7
Taxation   52, 84, 115, 130, 196, 208, 222, 242–5, 263–4
   Poll Tax   238, 242–6, 251
Taylor, Robert   284
Tebbit, Norman   148, 156, 181, 187, 190, 220, 252
Territory   41, 159
Think Tanks   89, 238, 271
Thrift, Nigel   221, 223
Trade union law   4, 6n2, 66, 125, 143, 143n5, 148, 150, 153, 156, 160, 162, 165, 181, 184, 194, 198–200, 233, 276, 280–3
   1971 Industrial Relations Act   77, 85–7, 115n5
   1980 Employment Act   143–5, 152
   1982 Employment Act   143, 144, 153
   1984 Trade Union Act   143–4, 194, 195n1
   1986 Wages Act   194
   1988 Employment Act   194
   1993 Trade Union Reform and Employment Rights Act   265
   1999 Employment Relations Act   281–2
   2002 Employment Act   281
   2004 Employment Relations Act   281
Trade unions   3n4, 4, 6, 12, 23, 26, 26n1, 41, 55, 61n2, 63, 65–7, 74, 77–8, 81, 91–2, 96–9, 107–119, 121n1, 125–6, 140, 143, 146n5, 147–50, 153, 156, 158, 163–7, 175, 179, 188–96, 198n2, 202, 233, 235n1, 237, 244, 249, 265, 275–7, 281, 284
   Trade union density   3n4, 4, 62n1, 67, 199
Thatcherism   1–8, 1n2, 2, 4n1, 6n1, 11–15, 18, 20–2, 20n1, 24, 25n2, 26–7, 26n1, 27n1, 28n2, 29–32, 32n4, 46, 48, 59, 61n2, 62–8, 66n1, 73, 75, 82, 86, 95, 97, 107, 115, 120–2, 125–6, 139–42, 147, 155, 159–60, 166, 186, 192, 229, 232–8, 241, 246, 250, 255, 257, 261–2, 270–2, 275–7, 280, 284, 289–90
Thorneycroft, Peter   113
Trades Union Congress (TUC)   86–8, 92, 117, 148, 150–5, 177–8, 233, 245, 249, 253
Transport and General Workers' Union (TGWU)   86, 179, 187–90
Treasury   42n3, 42n5, 64, 82, 101n2, 123n1, 128–32, 137–8, 149, 210–12, 253, 258–60
Turnbull, Andrew   183

Unemployment   31, 65, 67, 79, 84, 105, 122, 126–7, 133, 135–6, 147–50, 162, 215, 239, 249, 258, 267–8
Union of Democratic Mineworkers (UDM)   176n4, 233
United States   207n3, 208, 208n3, 210–11, 217–18, 221, 226–32, 247, 258, 287
Universal suffrage   37, 39, 53, 203
US Dollar   79, 207n3, 258

Villiers, Charles   151–2
Vinen, Richard   11, 215
Violence   37, 41, 154, 192, 244

Wages   5, 13, 26n1, 55, 65, 76–7, 80, 103, 105, 115–16, 119, 126–7, 135–6, 141, 147–8, 161, 194, 221–2, 251, 258, 265, 276–7, 281–5
  Wage drift   127n2
  Social wage   115, 282
Wales   136, 146n3, 169, 177, 180, 243–4
Walker, David   211
Walker, Peter   169–71, 181, 190n1
Ward, George   96–7

War of Manoeuvre/War of Position   28, 125, 156, 164, 174
Warwick Agreement   281
Welfare State   1n2, 2, 54, 75, 80, 146, 149, 156, 237–42, 245, 255, 265–70
'Wets'   132, 138–42, 157, 236
Whitelaw, Willie   109, 112
Wilkinson, Richard   278
Wilson, Harold   78, 84, 116
Wilson government   77–9, 207
Windsor, Roger   185
Working Class   4, 31, 35, 39, 43, 49–59, 289
  British working class   2, 5–7, 6n2, 12, 19–22, 19n7, 32, 56n3, 60, 61n2, 62, 66, 74, 77–9, 86–7, 94, 105–6, 111, 115, 118–20, 130, 132n2, 146–50, 146n5, 156–62, 165, 167, 174, 179, 184, 191–6, 199–201, 215, 222, 232, 237, 240n3, 241–2, 249, 264–5, 275, 284
Workfare   66, 268, 282
World War I   31, 230

Yorkshire   167, 169–75, 183
Young, Hugo   98, 110